Bending

God

a memoir

Bending God

a memoir

Written by
Eric Robison

Edited by
Christopher Robison

Higher Balance Publishing
Portland, Oregon

Higher Balance Publishing
515 NW Saltzman Road #726
Portland, Oregon 97229

www.higherbalance.com
publishing@higherbalance.com
1-503-646-4000

Current Titles from Higher Balance Publishing:
- The Handbook of the Navigator by Eric Pepin

Library of Congress Control Number: 2006932368

Bending God: A Memoir / Eric Robison
ISBN 0-9759080-4-9

Printed in the United States of America.

IN DEDICATION

To you, whom I give it all for. May I truly say at the end of
this life, I used everything you gave to me and gave
everything I had.

To my teacher, who's giving and grace knows no bounds.
Never a soul has walked this Earth and devoted so much,
asking so little.

To my parents, whose open minds and giving hearts
gave me an infinite sky in which to fly.

To you the seeker, may you find your way home.

May you find your way home.

Alisonè.

TABLE OF CONTENTS

INTRODUCTION

PREFACE: To You, My Dearest Reader   11

I: The Messenger   13

II: Your Time Will Come   27

III: The Paragon Anomaly   43

IV: Flickers of Light   83

V: The Softest Steps   105

VI: A Higher Perspective   129

VII: The Instinct to Nurture   143

VIII: Hunt for Reason   175

IX: Social Security   187

X: Glimpse of the Future   205

Chapter XI: Surface Features   219

Chapter XII: Listen to God   231

XIII: The Secret Art of Scanning   253

XIV: The Force of Change   265

XV: So You Want To Be a Meditator?   275

XVI: Super-Hero Separation   295

XVII: Break Expectations   309

XVIII: Enter the Arena   325

XIX: Do or Do Not   *353*

XX: Find Your Way   **365**

XXI: Invisible Invader   *383*

XXII: Secrets of the Psychic   **401**

XXIII: Pyramid Power   *431*

XXIV: The Extraordinary Tales of Evil Richard   **439**

XXV: Eternity Sings   *473*

XXVI: The Discovery of God   **489**

XXVII: Enough to Know   *503*

XXVIII: The Step Beyond   **527**

THIS IS A TRUE STORY

Everything in this book happened. Many of the events that took place had several witnesses all of whom can testify to their accuracy. It is important that you remember this because, as you read this book, you may doubt that this is true.

I have made no exaggerations or distortions. Everything is exactly as it happened except in the case of conversations, which I had to reconstruct from memory, notes and journal entries.

As to the unusual or, 'paranormal', events which took place, every detail is exactly as it occurred.

BEFORE READING

To you, my reader, I give this warning as it was given to me.
It is not because I believe that this book will match the power
and presence of a personal journey; I do not.

I give it to you because I know there is truth in this warning.
There is a conscious acknowledgment.

Whether you choose to continue reading or not,
you have made the decision.

You have chosen your path.

THE WARNING

You cannot unlearn what you learn. You cannot un-know,
what you know.

This knowledge will change you.

Perhaps subtly, perhaps utterly, much of that depends on
you. Once the seed is planted, the flower will grow.
You may find that you will not be able to relate to things
or people the same. You may find you cannot
relate to yourself the same.

You may find everything that you have been searching for,
or... perhaps it will find you.

This is my wish for you.

To You,

My dearest reader. I do not know when you find yourself reading these words. What I do know is this; for you, it is the right time.

If it is not the right time, you will know, as you will never see this book to its end. Every obstacle and reason in the world will arise and distract you from reading it.

You see, this story, this true story... has a special purpose, which for now, I must keep from you. There is a mystery here. Within these pages, a trail of clues.

The events I have recorded are not supposed to be possible. Yet, by everything that I am... they are.

They defy reason and scientific explanation. Of this time. Moments that push too far beyond the scope of my life. Our shared flickering moment.

Who are you? The question is an identity. A few years ago, through Eric Pepin, I became aware of a certain group of people. Quietly, through the years, I have observed them slip in and out of the world around me. Their presence has left me with much to wonder.

This is my conscious acknowledgment of the reason. It is my invitation... and my permission.

You who have walked with Eric Pepin will have opportunities others will not. Your reasons will be very different. For yours is the time of 'the moment.'

Beyond 'the moment' will be those trying to piece together the why and the how.

In part, this is what I am trying to give. I'm trying to help you understand the 'why' and the 'how'.

The permission I give is to come. Understand these 'paranormal' and 'metaphysical' experiences. Take them inside yourself. Science will eventually unravel many of the in's and out's of it all.

But, the human mastery of it... the navigation of the mind to the final frontier and the mystery of who Eric Pepin is and how he is able to do the things he does... well, these are the ripples of my time.

It is for the future, to dissect and make use of the waves ringing out from now.

It is true that Eric Pepin often says the future is not pre-written, it is only predictable. With too much at stake I offer you this account to learn what you can and make of it what you will.

Come along with me. You are a visitor here – I know. Let me be your guide as I share all that I have been witness to. Let me try and help you on our way.

I owe you a great deal, for, I would not have done this without you.

~ Eric Robison, January 1st 2005

The Messenger

chapter one

"A floating head?"

"Yeah man, I know, crazy right? A disembodied floating head."
Justin tells me. His peaceful, small blue eyes quietly contrasting the
madness coming from his mouth.

Sitting on a single bed used for a couch, I lean back against the living
room wall for a moment. Crazy isn't exactly the word I would choose.
Mentally detached from the fine, upstanding and highly reputable
state of insanity, is a bit more like it.

Rubbing my rough, perma-stubbled face I sit up and stare into my
cereal. Man, how did I get into this? I turn my head ever-so-slightly
to peek at Justin out of the corner of my eye. I slyly survey his pale
face contrasted against his light, almost bright, reddish-orange hair,
scouring it for some answer. Not that you ever see his hair. One of
his favorite things to wear is a round-brimmed Gilligan type hat. He
pulls it down and flips it up, depending on his mood. A small flavor-
savor patch of hair under his lip is the only facial hair he ever seems
to have.

Ahh Justin, what's your game? He's a struggling actor, like my
younger brother Matthew who lives with me. They met on a movie
set about eight months ago.

Justin's young, Matthew's age, about 22, but he doesn't ever really act
it. Seems older except for the raver clothes he wears. Huge flaring
pants. His voice is deep, rich, mature and he's always calm, in

control. Never does any drugs. Intelligent, even sincere, now that I think about it.

He's a regular at our apartment. There's a reason my apartment is nicknamed, 'The Hostel'. On any given night 3 to 4 other people crash here. It keeps things interesting but there's a downside to living this way. Enter downside; soggy cereal. My cereal has turned into mush.

My dear brother Matthew, 'The Shepard of Lost Souls', brings them all in. Matthew's to blame for this. My soggy cereal. Justin and the freakshow of a morning I'm having. Yes, his fault. Because of him I can't enjoy my cereal in peace.

Quietly, I sigh as I take another look at Justin. Maybe he needs someone to perform for? One man show, 'The Night Justin Sucked Hallucinogenic Toad'. Hrmm. Doesn't make sense. Of all the people who stay at 'The Hostel' Justin's the most grounded. Unlike most people in L.A. he seems like he has his act together.

He has his act together? A clear voice in my head asks softly.

Great, The Council weighs in. When I was young I created different voices, characters, in my head. At first they were to play with. People to imagine and act things out, create stories. I've always loved to daydream. As I grew older they'd argue. Propose possibilities. At some point, who knows when, they became distinct voices. I call them The Council because when they start arguing it's like a great Roman senate debate. The last few years they never seem to shut up.

Well, I tell the voice, he did have his act together. Before this floating head story.

What happened to the routine? It's been the same for so long. Soggy cereal isn't the routine. I go to work, watching movies for THX Lucasfilm. It's my turn to serve time on the newbie Hell shift. It starts at ten or twelve at night until about eight in the morning. I recoil as the feeling of staying up all night hopped up on coffee mixed with energy drinks makes my stomach lurch.

It's the perfect job – on paper. Watch movies all night long. Get to say I work for George Lucas, the creator of Star Wars. All for the great Lucas. Of course, the little details are all left out. Like, I watch the same movie, on repeat, all night long. I live in L.A., a place of constant, brilliant sunshine, that I only see on my way to bed. If he hadn't done Star Wars I'd never subject myself to this.

Not that anyone in The Hostel cares. Gives them a reason to stay up late. Not that they really know staying up late. They don't know waking up at five in the evening to eat your cereal. They don't know the highlight of your day is sitting quietly, watching The Simpsons, before you fill your gut with liquid crack and your brain with the same fifteen minutes of film footage for eight hours.

The TV hasn't even been turned on. Where did I go wrong? The events of my morning flash back through my mind...

I wake up and wobble into the kitchen, my green blanket wrapped around me dragging along the floor. Like always, the whole kitchen is a catastrophe of dirty dishes and fast food wrappers. It takes a skilled eye to see beyond the wine bottles, old crusted plates and every other artifact left over from God knows when to find the least dirty bowl. My eagle eyes spot one. With a few quick swishes of water it's clean enough.

The kitchen is a little nook divided from the living room only by a shared counter. It's easy to look out from the kitchen into the living room. The Hostel has only one bedroom. I sleep there. Everyone else crashes on any open area they find. Normally when I come home in the morning the whole room is a mass of bodies lying in the darkened front room. The Hostel houses those Matthew finds out in the world that need a place to stay.

Matthew's king size bed is pushed against the wall closest to the balcony. Connected to that is a scavenged single bed that we also use as a couch. Directly in front of the counter is my old futon.
I pour some cereal for breakfast and notice Justin's the only one left in the apartment. Only, Justin's packing his things... getting ready to leave. Leave to where he actually lives.

This is not normal.

Normally, I leave people to their business but this strikes me as a little strange. The only people who think Justin lives somewhere else work at the Post Office. "Where you going?" I grunt out.

"Eh, I gotta go to a meeting." Justin says shrugging his shoulders.

"Oh.. " I say only half paying attention as I chomp cereal. Like a little gnome pulling at a string hanging from my shirt a thought nags at me.

Since when does Justin have anything to meet about? The clear voice whispers through my head.

I stop crunching for a second. Weird, you're right. His response was really vague. I suspiciously spy away from my cereal bowl to see what Justin's doing. He's stuffing his things into his backpack. In fact, I don't even think he looked up when he told me what he was doing...

Wait a second... he's trying to blow us off! A frantic voice cries out, panicked with excitement.

Yes, yes I think he is. My interest begins to peak. "A meeting huh? You could be more vague," I sarcastically goad him. I munch away on my cereal waiting to see what Justin will do. He pauses his hasty stuff job. A slight smirk forms on my face. Looks like I hit my mark. He must be considering whether or not to bother responding.

"Yeah man, you know, some weird things happened last weekend so we gotta meet." Justin drones practically in monotone.

It's so quiet now all I can hear is the sound of me chomping cereal. Chomp. Chomp. Crunch-crunch-crunch. I start to blank out on it. I'm exhausted and he brought up the whole 'meeting' thing again. My curiosity is in short supply these days. Going through a drought. Talking about meetings isn't the way to spend precious resources. His little speckle of certain conversation boredom is enough. I tune out.

Carrying my cereal bowl into the living room I sit on my futon and wonder which Simpsons will be on. Right on the verge of turning on the TV and forgetting the whole thing a thought kicks a vulnerable, squishy part of my brain.

He's hiding something! Secrets! Secreeeets! The frantic voice cries out, gleefully shaking the cobwebs from my dulled head.

What? My brain cranks back a few seconds. Justin's response was so casual and nonchalant I stop eating my cereal. Wait a second.... you're right! He's being completely vague and trying to make his 'meeting' sound as normal and boring as talking about traffic jams in L.A.

I can barely contain myself. A little bubble of joyful delight lurches up inside of me. It's been so long since someone's had a good secret! Inside I'm bouncing off the walls. On the outside... well, I may as well be watching paint dry. Mustn't let him know, or I will alarm the poor little creature, hiding his secret. Imagining Justin as a little fawn skipping through the forest I maintain a mask of total indifference.

Must crack the code, now, what did he just say to me? Something weird happened last weekend... something weird... weird, weird, weird. What the heck is that? What would Justin consider weird?

I don't know but repeating the word won't help you figure it out. My grating voice scolds at me.

Another chimes in, And we? We?? Who in the world is we and why would he leave it at that?!

It's too much. "Dude," I say flatly. "I hope you don't plan on leaving it at that. I mean, come on, a secret meeting because some 'weird' thing happened last weekend?" I give him my best look like, you gotta be kidding me. "You better cough it up." I say matter-of-factly.

Justin stops packing and shrugs his shoulders. He moves his hands forward and waves them around like he's getting ready to start rapping to me, "Hey man, it's not a big deal. You just normally don't give a shit so I wasn't gonna bother you with it." He finishes it off with a little laugh. Despite his animated movements his voice is steady and low.

Hrmm. That sucks. He has a point. I normally don't care.

My steady anchor of indifference pulls at me and I'm suddenly struggling with whether or not I should bother raising it. Maybe he's right. Maybe I should just leave it alone and enjoy what little peace and quiet I have. His statement worries me. How good can his secret really be? It's been so long since I encountered anything really interesting. I groan inwardly.

Just do it. I counsel myself.

"All right, just tell me what your deal is." I mutter, already half-regretting the decision to speak.

I have no idea what I was walking into.

Justin's demeanor immediately changes. Coming close he sits down on the futon across from me. The Gilligan-type hat he always wears is pulled down low on his head. With one hand he smoothly flips it up slightly so I can see more of his face and strands of his red hair.

Ah crap. Damnit. He just went into acting mode. I've trapped myself and now he's about to perform.

He clears his throat and lowers his voice to perfect pitch level. "So, last weekend... a buddy of mine, Jason, had this really weird thing happen."

He looks into my eyes to confirm he has my interest. I sit and stare forward saying nothing. I start to calculate in the back of my mind how long I have until The Simpson's begins.

Justin drives on, "See, he's sleeping and it's early in the morning when suddenly he wakes up. He tries to like, get up and stuff, when he realizes he can't move."

"He can't move huh?" I say with an edge of disappointed sarcasm. How lame is that?

Sleep paralysis. A voice grates through my mind informing me. As if it's all my fault the secret is so stupid.

Last time I think Justin has anything interesting to say. What a waste. I sigh quietly and turn my head to look at the TV. If Justin notices my sudden drop in interest he doesn't care. He's on a roll.

Justin confirms my question as if I were captivated. "Nah man. It's like his muscles are totally frozen. He can't budge!"

Every word he drags on makes me feel more tired. I scan the room searching for the remote control to the TV.

Justin doesn't stop or miss a beat. He scoots to the edge of his seat and pulls his hat down a little bit to add a more serious edge to his story. My eyes shift, nervously watching his body language. It's almost like he thinks he has me in the middle of a cliffhanger and he's about to deliver the climax.

Raising both hands, pointing to me for emphasis, Justin wails out in excitement, "Then, like this giant floating head comes through his freakin' wall and like, hovers over him!"

My brain, previously zoning out searching for the remote, is suddenly ripped into a bizarre reality. I picture a giant head floating over some guy with sleep paralysis. I shoot a quick look at Justin to examine his expression. What the hell? I don't get it, he actually looks serious! The sudden twist in his story doesn't make any sense!
I start to get frustrated and a little pissed off. If his secret sucks he needs to just get it over with so I can chill out, he doesn't need to fabricate stupid crap.

"What are you talking about?" I say, an edge in my voice, glaring slightly.

It throws me off and I'm momentarily confused. What is he really trying to say? Is he talking about a movie? A drug trip? What?

Justin rises off the futon a few inches and shakes his hands at me like he's not getting through. "A head! This ghost head comes like, floating through his wall!"

A ghost head?? My brain scrambles in total disbelief.

Justin starts getting really worked up. He jumps out of his seat completely and raises his voice, "It looks like a classic demon head right out of a movie. It's all red with glowing eyes and horns and like, a big beard! Yeah man!"

Justin's totally excited now. He starts acting out the evil eyes of his imaginary ghost head by flaring his own eyes and contorting his face. Then he moves his hands down his chin so I can picture just how long his demon beard is.

I sit there with my mouth a little open... waiting... hoping... *wanting* some kind of punch line.

A joke, this is some kind of joke. I shake my head in disbelief but he stops me, "No! It gets worse. Check this out! So, the head taunts him and says all this shit to him and stuff but he can't move! Then, the head like turns and floats through another wall into his girlfriend's room."

Suddenly, Justin pauses, leans in closer. In a hushed voice he says, "See they sleep in separate rooms for spiritual reasons." It's like he's giving me a little inside tip.

Inside, my brain pleads, *'What the hell is he talking about?!'* Considering the totally bizarre story this little fact makes it all seem even weirder. Why did he tell me that? Why is he saying all this stuff! My brow wrinkles as I try to figure out what he's really trying to do. I nod my head to keep him talking while I try to understand. Is he acting or being serious? Crap, I can't tell. Why can't I tell?

There's no way this is serious. Listen to what he's saying. He's insane if he believes it and you're an idiot for sitting here. The grating voice scolds me in disgust.

Man, all I want to do is go back to sleep.

Justin jumps on my nod and continues his tale of the bizarre. "Yeah, so then my friend says he hears his girlfriend just totally shriek. He says it's this completely, like, horror scream. And all this time he's trying to get up but his body is still totally locked up!"

I try to imagine all of it as real and it's too much. If Justin was telling me about an X-files episode I'd understand. If he was rehearsing some scene for a play or an audition, I'd get it. But to sit here listening to what he's saying and then place it in reality – I'm dumbfounded.

It all comes down to one thing: "A giant... disembodied... floating head?" I ask intentionally speaking very slowly emphasizing the whole thing so he can hear how ridiculous it all sounds.

He vigorously nods his head yes.

"A floating head?" I make sure to say every single letter of each word perfectly clear, heightened with an intense edge of complete and certain disbelief.

"Yeah man, I know, crazy right? A disembodied floating head."

Absently I poke at my poor, soggy cereal. My brain finishes rehearsing his story and it comes up blank. There's absolutely no sense in it. Who knew? I never even saw it coming...
Justin's restless. I've let my thoughts wander back too long. He brings me back to the unpleasant moment I've trapped myself in. He's eager to earn his stripes as the top local crazy.

"Yeah man. You don't even know. Listen to this last part. So the head floats back into my friend's room and hovers over him all like, laughing at him and stuff."

"Uh... huh." I say in a voice so monotone he has to know I'm beyond buying the freak show circus he's performing in his head. I picture the giant red demon-ghost-head floating over some guy with sleep paralysis after having *floated through a wall* to get to his girlfriend, only to laugh at the guy with sleep paralysis!

It's insane! My brain does the only reasonable thing a brain can do; it gives up and shuts down.

If Justin notices my reaction he doesn't seem to care. He's so wrapped up in his alternate reality he keeps going, "Then my friend is just like, screw this shit. So he pulls all his energy into like his chi center," Justin pauses and points to his belly button.

I stare at it for a second. What the... I have no idea why he did that but I'm not about to go down that road considering everything else. I slowly nod my head.

Justin, however, wants to explain the odd detail, "It's just something we're taught to do. He pulls all his energy into there," he points to his belly button again, "and then summons up all his courage..."

Moving his arms in a giant circle, ending pointing at his belly button, Justin takes a deep breath in as if he's preparing for the moment of truth.

"... and he licks the head right on its face!"

Justin sticks his tongue out and with his eyes closed licks along the air, acting the scene out for me. His friend, with all his strength, licks the giant, floating, demon ghost-head's face.
I feel this strange, internal torn reaction. Part of me wants to laugh, another wants to scream. Justin wants to end with dramatic flair. With a macho cheer and his hands out in front of him he suddenly makes a grand motion as if to say, poof!

"And then it suddenly... disappears!" he declares.

I remain still, quietly sitting in my spot, staring at him, my mouth slightly ajar. I wonder... what kind of reaction is he looking for? It's too much!

I am bewildered. I've never felt totally bewildered before. All I can grasp is the realization that I finally understand what utter confusion is. I've known what the words mean and I even thought I'd experienced it, but I was wrong. When something throws you for such a loop, and creates this bombardment of confusion to the point where you feel physically disoriented - that is bewildered. Justin has given me bewildered!

We sit for a minute or two staring at each other. Justin in his own little insane world and me in my new found state of bewilderment. I start to repeat what he's said to confirm I actually heard him say it. "He licked, with his..." I pause. Is it even worth saying? Justin has gone on long enough. I may as well see where he's going to end it, "...tongue..." I pause again.

What a joke. What a stupid idiotic joke. What are we even talking about? I try to acknowledge how ridiculous it is to even attempt to bring reason into such a thing. I shake my head so he understands, I find his story complete nonsense. More unbelievable... Justin is totally unfazed by my reaction.

"Umm," I continue, "yeah... so he licked the giant floating demon, uh, ghost head... with his tongue..."

I can't believe we're seriously having this conversation. I can't believe I'm even bothering to ask as if he's going to have some reasonable response. I could laugh at it for being a good joke but he's acting so normal and serious that I can tell he isn't joking.
"And that worked. It disappeared?" I give my best 'puzzled and concerned' look. Trying to mimic the kind of look you might give a friend just before you ask what kind of drugs they're on.

Justin raises his right hand like he's going to swear an oath. "I swear man. I swear to God that's what happened!"

"And..." Do I even want to continue? It's like feeding the absurdity of it. "And... you know this guy? Was he on drugs or what?"

Justin keeps his oath hand up and shakes his head no. "No way! I know this guy very well and he doesn't do drugs and so definitely wasn't on any. This wasn't about drugs and his girlfriend saw it and she swore to it too."

Well, there we go. I'm at a complete and total loss for words. Justin is dead serious and carrying on far too long for a joke. He's an actor so he may be milking the attention but he's always been pretty grounded. I've never seen him do anything like this just for attention. That's not it... that's not what this is about. There has to be some reasonable explanation.

Careful, you're starting to sound desperate. It's time to let this one go. Seriously, The Simpson's are almost on. The clear voice soothes me.

"Okay, and so, what's this whole meeting about?" I let out a big sigh. I'm grasping for some kind of normal conclusion to his story.

Justin's excitement pulls back. He seems calm again, rational. Maybe even a little disappointed at my lack of reaction. "Well, the millennium is coming up and more and more weird things are going to start happening so we're having a meeting to prepare."

So much for a normal conclusion.

You had to ask. Go ahead and ask more, just keep feeding it. The grating voice sarcastically criticizes.
He said the 'we' again without explaining it. Part of me wants to ask more. Another part thinks I've seen better things on X-files and the conversation has to have a more logical explanation. Dude, it's best to leave it alone and get on with your day. It doesn't seem like Justin is going to start making sense any time soon.

"All right," I say in a dull, I'm ready to stop talking voice. "Have fun." I turn away from him and lean back against the wall so he knows the conversation is over.

"You know it man. Have a good one Eric." Adjusting his hat into street traveling position he grabs his keys, throws on his backpack, shoots me the peace sign and takes off.

As soon as the door closes and I know he's gone I shake my head trying to get rid of the weird confused feeling.

"What in the world was that about?" I say to myself out loud looking for the remote. And just like that it's over. I make a mental note that I can't consider Justin 'normal'.

I know how it must sound to you, this floating head story. Keep in mind you picked up this book possibly without knowing me. A strange, uncertain reaction is a given. But for me, Justin is someone I knew. Sensible, intelligent, articulate... normal. It made the tale all the more confusing. Now, you may ask, what do I think of it now, seven years later knowing what I know?

Ever since I was young there comes a moment during winter when I am captured by a sight. It is something fresh, green and new shooting through the grey, cold waste. A single bud, sprouting from a tree or the leaves of a flower pushing up from the ground.

For days afterward it lingers in my thoughts.

Suddenly, everything inside of me begins to change. Quietly, I know even if another snow comes and blasts it all away, it has lost its grip. Spring, new life, is on its way and there is nothing that can stop it. It never comes suddenly in a flood of buds and sprouting life, this messenger. There is always the single moment first. A whisper of what's to come.

In my short life I have been fortunate enough to witness things beyond description. Moments so much larger than myself, I feel I have no right to have lived them. There is a way to bend reality. A method to alter the fabric of everything. Eric Pepin has shown this to me, many times, in many ways. If you read, and listen, you may begin to understand this way.

I once asked him about the way these moments and other experiences like them seem to flow. This is what he told me. 'When the Universe feels that you might be ready, it will peel back, part the veil and reveal itself to you. As soon as it does, it withdraws, closes the curtain and waits to see what you will do.'

It gives you a moment, a whisper of what's to come.

To this day, years later, the strange story told to me by Justin surfaces in my thoughts as my first memory of what it is to know Eric Pepin. Although I had not heard of him this was my first introduction to his world.

Stranger still, which is something I still laugh about, was my reaction to Justin. He knew what he was telling me was real having experienced similar things. He presented it with absolute belief.

Without any kind of reference for understanding the possibility of the experience, I had equal absolute disbelief. It never occurred to me to wonder why Justin believed. It was too far 'out there' and I'm amazed how my brain pushed it all away. In fact, within an hour after Justin left, I forgot the whole incident. It wasn't until much later that I was suddenly reminded of it out of the blue. But had I forgotten it? Or had I seen the first bud and despite my oblivious nature an inner spring was coming?

Perhaps, it was the Universe's strange sense of foreshadowing, its... invitation. Almost two months would pass before I learned the name Eric Pepin. These were strange, restless months. Although I didn't know it I had been given a moment. It was my whisper of what was to come...

the universe is never late, nor is it ever early. be steadfast and know this; at the moment of its choosing…

Your Time Will Come

chapter two

I roll fitfully on my bed, half asleep, in a dream I wish to wake up from...

My feet crunch in the snow as I walk alone through a barren forest.

The leaves on the trees have long fallen and blown away. Skeletal branches reach up into a pale, gray sky.

Each step vanishing into a foot of white powder. There's a thin crust of ice that snaps and crunches beneath each step. All I hear is the slow, exhausted exhale of my breath and the steady crunch of the snow I struggle through.

Winter has sealed the world for months, each new day the same as the last. Icy, snowy, savage and secretive. Its white cloak hides spring as the world has hidden answers from me... answers I know are there... that I'm trying to find.

My body shakes and my breath hangs in the air in a great cloud.

Something drives me forward. Strange desperate madness. Thoughts ravage . What am I doing? Why am I here? What do I hope to find? Why won't it stop... what am I looking for? Why, why, why...

I can see deep into the woods. No vegetation left to hide anything. I know this forest too well. It's near my home. I have lived here all my life. There's nothing here to hide from me anymore. There's nothing anywhere. What I want isn't a thing I can pick up. It isn't a thing I can see. Yet, I know there is something! Why won't it show itself? Fury and despair battle for my mind.

"Where are you?!" I yell, my voice echoes through the sleeping woods.

Plump, round flakes of snow pitter-patter on the trees. My echo fades. I stop and listen to the sound of my breath and then silence. No answer. There will never be an answer. The world never felt so dead and silent.

I fall to my knees and sink into a drift of powder up to my waist.

Inside I'm falling apart. What am I doing here? What am I looking for? Why can't I stop trying to find it? I want to cry but I can't. I want to be angry but it isn't there. There's only the drive, the deep calling desire, a gnawing sense that I have to find something… if only I knew where it was. If I only knew what it was.

I throw my head back and scream into the empty sky.

I jolt awake from the dream. My face and body are flush with heat and sweat.

"Not this again." I whisper out loud to myself. "I can't take this crap anymore."

I slide off the bed, which is nothing more than two mattresses on the floor pushed up against a wall. My whole body feels agitated and restless. It's the middle of the night. Work's been slow and I've switched back to a 'normal' schedule where I actually sleep at night with everyone else. Well, it would be normal if not for the constant, reoccurring dream.

Above the head of my bed is a window. I walk over to it and look out of our third floor apartment. It gives me a good view of the freeway and a small part of the city. I lean against the wall and look out into the night to watch the twinkling lights. There is never any real darkness here; always light from somewhere. I've been in this city three years. You'd think I'd get used to that.

I take a deep breath in and rub my forehead.

Always the same dream lately, always the same thing. For months now, several times a week. God, why won't it leave me alone? I just want to sleep.

Crazy is as crazy does. The clear voice mumbles.

"Shutup." I tell myself out loud.

That didn't make any sense. Another part ridicules.

"Well, I know, that's why I said shutup." I catch myself and stop. I'm tired and arguing with myself. If I don't stop them they'll argue for hours.

I grab my journal I leave sitting on the window sill and open the window. Switching my schedule screwed my ability to sleep so much I took the screen from the window out. I sit up inside the window and dangle my feet over the edge. There's a small balcony below me, big enough for plants, or to catch me if I fall.

The height calms me down and feels peaceful somehow. Even though I can see more of it, the city seems more distant from my window at night. Sitting with the cool night air on my skin I feel more alone. I feel like I have space to think.

Holding my journal in my lap, ready to write, I ask myself out loud, "Anything you want to talk about?"

It's long been a habit of mine to talk to myself out loud. I can't remember how it started. I talk to myself to help write and create other characters. When I was young I'd wander the yard reading plays out loud to practice speaking and use different voices so I could tell people apart. It also makes me feel like I'll listen to myself better that way because it's more like having a conversation with someone else.

I smile as I think of a redundant question but decide to ask it out loud anyway, "Something... oh, I don't know... on your mind?" I rest my head back against the window and look up at the night sky.

I can't go through this again. I can't go back there. We left it for a reason. We had to walk away. My thoughts drift back to the dream and to that cold, lonely day. Not purely a dream if it really happened, more of a memory. A haunting memory. How old was I then?

Seventeen, maybe eighteen. The clear voice answers. *Seems like so long ago.*

"Yeah, it does." I agree out loud. I've just turned twenty-four. I was so hopelessly naïve.

The only way we're going to get back to sleep is to start writing everything out. It tells me.

I know, I think back to it softly. Let's just sit for awhile okay?

I sit and stare at the city letting all of the old feelings drift off. The restlessness. The frustration. The desire... the old desire to search.

Don't you mean to serve?

I shut my eyes as old, buried emotions start to rise up inside of me.

Yes, that's it. The old desire to serve God. The desire to know God.

But I've put all of that behind me. It's what God wanted me to do. It's what I needed to do. There was nothing there anyway. No God, no answers. Only an endless circle. I quietly resent the part of me that won't let it go. It's going to drive me crazy again.

I spill my frustration out onto my journal. All the old stupid questions about the meaning of life, the nature of God and the reason for my being – they all need to go! Those old questions only make me frantic and moody.

I nearly drove myself crazy when I was younger looking for answers and it's stupid that it's back again! When I was 19 I made a choice. I turned away from God and any question of what God was.

At the time, deep in my heart, I felt that in some strange way, God wanted me to forget.

So why is it all coming back again? The last few weeks that's all there's been. Nagging, pointless questions and dreams. It's getting ridiculous!

Looking back I do not see random chaotic events and aimless sporadic choices. I see a design so absolute in its perfection to even sit and be aware that I am allowed to play a part humbles me to my knees. In my youth I almost drove myself crazy trying to understand and find God. Whatever that meant. I didn't know but every single ounce of my being felt it. When I was 12 I read a book on visualization meditation, runes, Magick, whatever I could get my hands on. At 14 I wrote to a Wiccan group and tried to attend classes. It was the only alternative religion available in Springfield, Missouri that I knew of. They told me I had to be 18. I searched and searched and searched. For hours, every day I prayed.

By the time I was 19 I had a collection of conflicting ideas. All of them seemed partially true. I see no coincidence that I chose to walk away. It was no mistake that my heart knew it was what 'God' wanted. The slate was wiped clean. In Martial Arts movies the teacher often tells the student, 'You must unlearn what you have learned before I can teach you.'

That is what I did for five years. I emptied the bucket of every notion I ever had. My longing to seek the answers to life and God also faded, though they made a few notable returns it was never long. Certainly it wasn't anything like the two months before I met Eric. It was almost unbearable. Every part of me that felt the desire to seek out spiritual truth came forward with a vengeance. An unforgiving restless nagging.

My need to end the restless nagging feeling brought me to take up what was, for me, excessive drinking.

At my prompting The Hostel created a designated 'wine night'. We bought large jugs of cheap red wine and got loopy. This was a nice even drunk you could sustain for hours so I didn't have to think. It was also the perfect condition to go to sleep and not wake up with haunting dreams of the past and some stupid inner voice that wanted to know things like, 'Why are we here?', 'Is there a God?', 'What is God?' and on and on until you wanted to pull it out of your head and shoot it.

This usually spun into at least another night of drinking, sometimes two.

I've never been much of a drinker, even through five years of college. So, for me, two to three nights a week was quite a lot.

Usually spaced between the wilder nights were slow ones. It was on one of these slow nights I found myself alone in the apartment with Justin and a girl who was about to 'officially' move in for the summer while she interned at a nearby studio.

I know now the Universe's sense of timing is a little different from our own. I was banging on its door 10 years before. In my mind it took 10 years to answer. As far as it was concerned... 10 years, 10 seconds, time means nothing. It was right on time. That's all that mattered.

Looking back... I don't disagree.

Walking into the living room I start scanning for the remote. It's always hidden somewhere stupid.

Peggy and Justin are here. No use asking them where it is, nobody ever knows. Justin's sitting on the futon putting clothes into his backpack. Peggy's standing around. She watches him. I wonder if everyone else knows they're getting it on? No one talks about it. I don't know if it is because it doesn't matter or if it's one of those things that is supposed to be secret, even though everybody knows.

Peggy's the youngest of our group, barely 18. She's a little short, with nice, dark curly hair and a cute, round pixie-like face. From the East Coast she's a freshman at a local college. A film was being shot on campus, that's how she met Matthew and Justin. She scored a film editing internship for the summer but she can't afford it unless she has a place to stay. Matthew and I both know how hard LA can be. It doesn't help that she's so young. We decided she could stay the summer for free. What's one more person? It's her attitude I really like and why I'm for helping her out and letting her move in. She's always positive, friendly but reserved, and easy-going.

Rather than pack his things and leave Justin hovers near me. Justin, for the most part, leaves me to myself. He seems to be in-synch with my moods and understands how I feel about the time I have alone in a small, crowded apartment.

Unfortunately it's been weeks since I've worked. My job watching movies at night is erratic and done on a per project basis. Once a project is done it's over until the next one comes along.

I'm about to ask him what his problem is when he asks me, "Hey, we're going to Tujunga, you wanna come?"

"Huh?" I ask, a little dumbfounded. In the time we've known Justin, a little over six months, I'd only heard about the place where he really lives. Nobody has actually been there except maybe Peggy and I'm not even sure she's been there.

This mythical home where Justin allegedly lives is in a suburb of L.A. called Tujunga. That's all I know. That's all anyone knows.

He's just being polite for Peggy. I play along with his game and scratch my head pretending I'm giving it thought. "No." I finally say.

"Ah, come on man, come up and get out of here for awhile. It's out of the city. I think you'll like it." Justin pleads slightly.

His response catches me off guard. If he's just being polite for Peggy's sake he should have taken my 'no' and bid me a good day. Now, he's pushing the idea. I don't know where he's coming from and don't want to dance around in a conversation trying to figure it out so I go straight to the point.

"Why would I want to go to Tujunga?" I say shortly.

He takes a second and shrugs, "You know, get out of the apartment, get out of the city. You can meet my roommate."

He acts real casual. He must be in a stupid talkative mood and wants to include me. I don't really want to be included in his mood. I'm not a mood accessory. I'm not in a sarcastic mood. I'm not feeling grumpy either. I'm in a dazed, mood-free zone. I have no interest in seeing Tujunga at all. Now the best thing he can come up with is, 'his roommate'? My comfortable dazed zone is a much better space.

"Nah," I say wrinkling my face hoping he'll get the hint and drop it.

Justin doesn't drop it.

"Dude, just come up. I gotta do some laundry and switch clothes out. You can see the place and talk to my roommate."

I can't believe it! He's actually being persistent and pushing the issue. Not only that but he plugged his roommate again. I'm not mean and I'm not a jerk. Only thing is, people want to push things on me and I don't like it, so then I come off as an irritable jerk. Nobody makes me do things I don't want to do. Justin knows me well enough to know I could care less about talking to most anyone. I decide to remind him of that well-known fact.

"Justin, why in the world would I want to drive up with you all the way to Tujunga, watch you do laundry, and... talk to your roommate?" I say the last part really sarcastically so he'll understand how excruciatingly boring and pointless it sounds in my mind.

Justin isn't deterred by my sharp fangs of sarcasm. "Man, he's really smart. He's a really smart guy. I think you'll get a lot out of it. He gives all kinds of lectures and stuff."

It isn't even worth groaning out loud so he gets how beyond boring it all sounds. The idea of being trapped in some outskirt burb of L.A., which as far as I know is in the Valley, a place that is also completely boring, is horrifying. What would I do? The only thing I could do for entertainment is either be stuck listening to some boring guy who thinks he's smart or sit and watch Justin do laundry.

Why is he even asking? It's like inviting someone to go watch grass grow. "No thanks. I'm just gonna chill out, here, where I am now, by myself." I say coldly, hoping he'll get the point so I don't have to act pissed off.

"Dude, Eric, why you wanna do that? You been sitting around for like, two weeks! Come on man, you need to get out." Justin tells me in his normal smooth, well-articulated, radio voice tone. Only he put special emphasis on 'need'.

Justin's pushing his luck. What's more, he's always been conscious enough of his actions to know this. Nice, reserved, easy-going Justin. But some strange clone has replaced that Justin with a persistent, nagging, almost whining Justin.

I need to get out? The only thing that needs to happen is you need to shutup! When he used the, I 'need' to get out, I felt myself getting a little pissed off. No acting this time.

I push back, leveling the reality of the situation to him, "Look, all I'm gonna do is go up, see your place, watch you do laundry and talk to your 'smart' roommate. Why would I even want to bother? I mean, hello? Jupiter to Justin because you're not even close to planet Earth. I could do something way more entertaining like, start building a cockroach circus." I laugh at the situation I presented. I can't believe he'd even push it to the point that I have to tell him this. "Now, why would I even need to get out again?"

Justin's still playing cool, almost like he doesn't even notice my growing irritation. "Look," he states, "my roommate is really, really cool. He's done a lot of cool shit. I think you'd really dig talking to him."

"Because..." I drone sarcastically throwing my hands out like I'm desperately searching for something to catch.

"Just come up Eric. Just get out with us," Peggy chimes in. I look over at her and she seems as exhausted with the conversation as I am. Her eyes have a slightly pleading look of, 'please make it stop'. Of course, she's going with Justin no matter what, so better to side with him. I forgive her for the error but make a mental note to give her crap for it later.

Justin rubs his white Gilligan hat as if he's really searching for a reason. Maybe he wants to argue, or annoy me, or both. I grate my teeth getting ready to tear into him and end it quick. Who knows what has gotten into him, we've never disagreed about anything before, he's so level-headed.

Justin raises his hand and blurts out, "Well, because man, he was rated like one of the top ten psychics in the country and – "

My attention shoots through the roof. In one second, with a single word, Justin has me.

'Psychic? Psychiiiic??' my brain asks. Though I don't think he realizes it he's suddenly sold me with that one word. I quickly cut Justin off. "He's a psychic?" I ask.

Justin suddenly perks up. He notices the sudden change in expression on my face and realizes the pulling of teeth is over.

"Yeah, he's psychic and stuff and talks about all these things..." Justin quickly starts rattling.

I smile, first to myself, and then outwardly. 'PSYYYCHIIIIC!' my brain harmoniously cheers to itself.

I clearly see two paths set before me.

One path involves me sitting on my butt in the apartment by myself doing the same thing I could do any night of the week. The second path involves me going to see the rumored home of Justin and meet his amazing, Miss Cleo-type roommate who will try to dazzle me with his psychic powers by reading tarot cards, maybe my palm, and if I'm really lucky, my aura!

I'm giddy with joy!

I don't have the slightest interest in any of these things. I don't think they have any rationale basis at all. However, the idea that there are people in the world who not only believe in them but believe they can do special tricks because they have 'psychic powers' and then make a profession out of it is so far out in left field they deserve to be visited with the same playful expectation one would have going to the circus. It's going to be such ridiculous fun!

Ahhh, Miss Cleo. Images of the large Jamaican woman who appears in all kinds of late-night infomercials for some kind of 'psychic network' dance through my head. She always wears these outrageously bright, gaudy, over-the-top clothes, like golden robes and turbans with astrological signs on them, and has a really fake accent. Meeting someone who thinks they're psychic and hopefully dresses like Miss Cleo will be a good bit of fun. It's going to be great. I can't believe Justin has hidden this sitcom life for so long.

I smile to myself imagining the kinds of scenarios Justin must encounter with the Tujunga psychic as his roommate. In my mind it's pure sitcom gold.

"Oh yeah," I say suddenly cheerful. "I'll definitely go."

We all pile into Justin's little red Subaru. His car is littered with dozens of two liter Coke bottles. I kick a few with my feet. Most aren't even empty. I imagine Justin getting into a car accident and all the Coke bottles suddenly foam from being shaken up and explode filling the car like a giant, spongy air bag. I laugh out loud to myself and Justin shoots me a wondering look.

"It's nothing." I say smiling as I quickly mumble, "Safety first..." fighting the bottles for floor space.

It doesn't take long before the main city lights are behind us. Justin rolls his windows down and I smell the change in the air. It smells fresher, greener, and more alive. I can smell life.

My thoughts drift back to summer in Missouri. I don't miss home often but the smell of fresh life and clean summer air always takes me back there. Sticking my hand out the window I let the wind blow through my fingers. We wind our way through dark hills and it isn't long before it really seems like we're out in the country. The reason we're traveling blows away on the wind.

After a long time driving through winding hills in the dark we come upon some city lights. "Are we in Tujunga?" I ask.

"Yeah, so listen, my roommate is really smart but like, he doesn't always get facts right. Like, he might say the Romans crucified Buddha but he would mean, you know, Jesus. So, he makes sense but his mind just works so fast it scrambles, but if you can overlook that then what he's really talking about is brilliant."

I nod more to myself than to Justin. His little fact catches my interest. Where have I heard that before? Einstein. His biography. A year before I read a book one of my roommates owned that was a bio of Einstein. It said he had to paint his door bright red so he could remember which house was his. That's genius, I think to myself smiling. So involved in your mind you don't even remember where you freaking live. Frowning I think back to my own school experiences. Text book robots. I've never respected people who absorbed knowledge only to spit it back out. It's all memorization, not true intelligence. Anyway, it doesn't matter whether or not we meet his roommate. Justin was right; it's good to be away from the city. Still, meeting his roommate will probably be good fun.

"I gotcha. No worries." I finally assure him.

We drive down a completely deserted street. It's empty. No cars or people. Compared to L.A. it's very surreal. Like a modern ghost town abandoned in the mountains.

Justin turns his signal on and points to a store on the corner of the street. "That's the bookstore. My roommate owns it."

I tilt my head down to get a better look at it. Disappointing. There aren't any bright neon signs declaring it is a mystical psychic abode. We park and Justin tries to get in but it's locked up and empty.

We start driving up to Justin's house. Pulling off the main street everything is suddenly black again. There are hardly any street lights at all. Night is actually night again and it's like being back home in Missouri where everything isn't blanketed in light.

Justin parks his car next to a large stone and wooden fence. I climb out but he signals for me to stay at the car. Peggy decides to stay with me.

We're all in the same quiet mood. The drive has made us more serene and nobody feels the need to chatter pointlessly.

The house is surrounded by a tall fence. More like a fortress. The first four feet of the wall is made of large round stones. A boarded fence sticks out of the stones extending it another five to six feet. Standing behind it, I can only see the roof of the house.

I look over at Peggy. "Have you ever been here?"

"Yeah." She pauses to think. "Once or twice."

It's strange Justin didn't want to bring me into the house. Being in a new place stirs my childish curiosity so I decide I need to have a look. If the bookstore isn't a mystical psychic abode maybe the house is where it all happens. Climbing up on the stones I'm able to grab the high wooden fence. Peggy giggles behind me and I freeze.

"What?" I ask her wanting to know the joke.

"They've got dogs." She says suspiciously.

"So?" The fence is so tall why would she tell me that? Then I stop again.

I jokingly narrow my eyes at her so she knows I suspect she isn't telling me something, "Wait a second... how big are they?"

She says, laughing, "One is pretty BIG!"

She's small. I wonder what she considers big? I'm almost up on the fence, may as well take a quick peek. Sticking my head over the fence I stare into the jaws of death! Flying back off the fence I hit the ground hard. Whatever kind of dog I'd seen the jaws of... it was at least five feet tall standing on its haunches.

The sound of loud barking and Peggy laughing echoes down the street. The gate shakes from the monster dog pushing at it. Looking up at Peggy, my eyes wide from the sudden surprise, I nod, "Pretty big." Justin yells for the dogs to get back as he opens the gate. He uses two names, Angus and Duncan. Jumping up I dust myself off.

We get in the car and I look calmly over at Justin. "So... you've got some dogs?"

"Nah, they're my roommates. They'll pretty much destroy anybody coming into the yard they don't know." He replies.

"Oh, cool." I say.

Peggy's laughing in the back seat. It puts me at ease and the contrast makes me realize I've been nervous. What am I nervous about? The bookstore looked different than I expected. The fairy tale fortress was different too. Before the jaws almost tore my face off I saw a large porch covered by vines. Two windows spilled glowing, orange light. Aside from certain death it looked cool. The anticipation of what's going on. I haven't thought this through. I don't really know what I'm getting myself into...

You're worrying over nothing. So what if Justin's not quirky or a space-cadet, his roommate has to be. Who's ever heard of a 'psychic' that isn't a bit goofy and weird?

it is at the most unexpected of moments, in the most unexpected places, you will find everything you've been searching for...

Paragon Anomaly

chapter three

Justin has the keys to the bookstore so we drive back and this time we're able to get in. We enter through the back, passing through a hallway. The hall is dark, empty. Justin disappears through a pink curtain and Peggy brushes past me. She heads down the hall, like she knows the way. I follow. Through the hall, past a few doors, we arrive in the main store area which faces the darkening street. Outside street lights glow through curtains spanning the glass windows of the storefront.

Justin flips a bunch of switches and suddenly everything is alive with light.

Standing frozen, for a moment, I forget where I am. Thoughts of making fun of the psychic I'm about to meet vanish.

Only in my dreams, or fantasy books, have I imagined such a place. It isn't a store, it's a library. No, not even a library; it's like the den of an ancient, magical wizard. It's a sanctuary without time or location; an alternate reality all its own.

Little lamps in the shapes of turtles and mushrooms glow orange as if warm candle flames breathe beneath multi-colored glass shades. Two huge soft brown couches sit in the middle of the room and three little cafe tables are tucked in a nook surrounded by shelves of books inviting hours of leisurely study.

The bookshelves are made of a light, tan wood and seem to grow out of the dark, earthy carpet. Friendly hanging plants dangle down from the top of the shelves making them feel like living trees holding books.. Artifacts are hidden among the books whispering confirmations of their mystical nature. It's out of a dream. Some kind of fable. They look like ancient relics and add to the fairy tale feel. The whole place is small, intimate and immediately inviting. I imagine sitting for hours, browsing through the books and hidden treasures.

I am captive, lost among the intricacy. My attention floats lightly among the hundreds of things competing, demanding more time. The details are overwhelming!

Justin enters, carrying two large thermoses, one holds hot water and the other coffee. He tells me the coffee is Kona and it is provided for visitors. I raise my eyebrows at the idea. I say nothing. I had Kona once before, in Hawaii. I loved its smooth taste but it's expensive coffee. How can they have full pots around just for people who browse the store? I turn and notice a small plastic cage sitting on a low shelf beside the big brown couch. Inside live the smallest, cutest hamsters I've ever seen.

They're so tiny, I could stand a quarter on edge and it would be about the size of these creatures.

Too busy watching the hamsters I don't notice the back door alarm beep as it opens. A loud voice bellows behind me, "So, where is he?" Turning around, a man stands next to Justin and Peggy. Justin looks lost for a moment, then raises his hand and points to me.

"Uh, right there." Justin says.

The man turns to look at me.

"Oh, right." He smirks and then smiles while I walk over.
"Hi," he says, "I'm Eric."

He extends his hand and I oblige by shaking it. I normally only shake hands with people trying to sell me something so it feels awkward.

"Oh..." I say, suddenly surprised. "I'm Eric too."

We have the same name and Justin never mentioned it? That's a bit strange. Maybe he doesn't think it's strange but I've only met one other Eric before.

"Well," he laughs with a broad smile, "that should make things easy."

He must still need to go put his Miss Cleo robes on. Part of me snickers at the thought. Taking him in I feel a bit disappointed. He's a little taller and larger than I am, with a husky build, like a football player in the off-season. A rich goatee surrounds his mouth and chin and he's mostly bald on top with short brown hair around his head. Despite his size and facial hair, which make him look older, his round face is strangely youthful. He could be barely older than I am, or could be my parents' age, it's difficult to know. His youthful glow, combined with his shining smile, make him seem like a very large, friendly cherub.

Lightly tinted eyeglasses rest on his nose and slightly conceal his eyes in the dim room. He wears a plain brown shirt with some khaki shorts and sandals. Where are the multi-colored robes? Where's the turban? He doesn't even seem like a New Age Malibu hippie-type. It's confusing. I struggle to adjust my expectations. His appearance doesn't fit someone that would believe in psychics. The store has made me feel good so I try to brush it off.

He walks over to the little hamsters I'd been looking at. Complaining, he tells me about how many times they've escaped and points out the ones that have nasty tempers and like to bite.

His manner surprises me. No strange voices. No weird clothes. He could be a camp director from Missouri or one of my college professors. He almost seems out of place among the rest of the store. It's so mystical and exotic and he's... well... he's kinda like me. Normal.

"So..." he says as if he's trying to think of something. "What was your name again?" He gives a big grin and laughs. "I'm sorry. These things just slip my mind."

I can't believe it. "Eric," I say in the nicest possible voice. I struggle with the idea that Justin said I would enjoy talking to him because he was smart. He can't even remember someone who has the exact same name as him!

He doesn't try to hide the awkward moment. "Well, that was stupid. That should have been a hard one to forget." I'm a bit taken back by his honesty. His admission makes me smile. No way I would have said that. I'd be too embarrassed to say anything and would've made up an excuse. Then I remember Justin telling me he can get simple things confused. Didn't think he meant that simple. He laughs it off and offers me a seat on the big brown couch which I happily take. It's surprisingly comfortable.

"Do you want the tape recorder?" Justin suddenly shouts out from behind the curtain.

"Well, I guess we probably should." He turns to me. "Do you mind?"

A tape recorder? The idea puzzles me but they are both so casual about it I shrug. "No. That's cool." I tell him. Let's see where they go with this. I kick back and watch as Justin brings in a large, old style tape recorder. He sets it up on the table in front of Eric and places a large microphone on a little stand beside him.

"I don't care for this thing," Eric assures me. "But they insist I not lose anything."

"Uh-huh." I say not really caring about the reason for it. This is definitely not the kind of prop I was expecting.
Justin kneels down by the table and grabs the microphone. With his hat and flaring pants I almost expect he's going to rap. Instead he

starts testing the recorder, "Test, test one, check, check, check... "
Eric motions to Justin. "So, what has Justin said about me? All good
things I hope."

Eric's eyes twinkle with impish delight as he puts me on the spot.
Justin doesn't say anything and leaves me helpless, right in the
crosshairs. "Well, umm." Suddenly embarrassed by all my psychic
jokes which now flicker through my mind. Don't laugh stupid.
Breathe in. Did Justin tell me anything I can't laugh at? Dumb sense
of humor, I make fun of everything. I clear my throat. "Uhh, not
much of anything... actually."

"Really? He didn't say anything at all? Boy, you're pretty brave or
he's got it in for you." He laughs looking over at Justin. "He didn't
even give you a warning huh?"

Justin looks up from fiddling with the tape recorder to protest,
"That's not true... I told him a few things."

Not wanting to make Justin seem rude I confess. "Well, that's true.
He did tell me, umm, that you were..." keep it together, "a psychic and
–" I quickly add, "that you lecture on stuff and you're really smart."

Eric smiles and slaps the table. "Wow! Lecture on stuff and I'm really
smart! Well, what else is there? Guess that pretty much sums it up
huh Justin?"

Eric turns his gaze to look down at Justin labeling the tape with a pen.
Justin's head is down and his wide brimmed Gilligan hat hides his
face. I get the sense there's something Justin didn't tell me.

Taking a deep breath in Eric turns his attention back to me as a
steady calm sweeps through the bookstore. "Okay, well, let me tell
you a little about myself then so you're more comfortable. I was
chosen as one of the top ten psychics in the US by a parapsychology
institute. I've found over 124 missing people. When I was 12 I
tracked submarines for the US navy, which is a long story I'll tell you
about some other time, but I was 98 percent accurate and I spent
most of my youth, ever since I can remember, doing psychic work,

which I was incredibly good at. Predicting the future, doing readings, that kind of stuff. I lecture on all kinds of topics from quantum physics to the biochemistry of the human brain and on and on and on, but you get the idea."

Shifting uncomfortably I feel bad he has to talk about himself. It seems like he's proud of everything he tells me but I don't have a clue what most of it is. Parapsychology institute? A 12 year old tracking submarines? Tracking submarines with what? Who the heck is going to let a kid around sensitive military equipment? And how does being a psychic mix with lecturing on biochemistry of the brain? Seems like any rational, intelligent person would dismiss anything he has to say as soon as he tells them he's a 'psychic'.

I politely nod and tell him it sounds cool. Justin hasn't finished setting up the recorder so Eric and I get a glass of water from a water cooler. Inside I laugh to myself that he openly admits to being psychic. Come on, where are the rest of the props? Bring forth splendid colorful robes of the seventh galactic order of psychics! I'll take a cheap crystal ball, anything.

We sit back down and Eric comes right out with a question, "So, Justin tells me you have a theory about angels."

Angels? The first question out of his mouth and I'm frozen like a squirrel in front of a riding lawn mower. I'm sure this should be easy but... I'm stumped. Scanning through my memory I try to remember ever talking to Justin about angels or why I would have any reason to. '...' is all my brain comes back with. I'm drawing a complete blank.

"Uhh, angels?" I ask. "I don't think I have a theory on angels."

Images of cheesy New Age-type angels float through my head. Floating lazily through the air tooting bugles, praising pyramids and stuff like that. Why would Justin say we've talked about something like that? I'm not sure, maybe it will lead Eric to talk directly to angels and channel dead people. I smirk at the thought.

"Yeah, we were out on the balcony one night and, I like, don't remember how, but you started talking about how you thought angels are made." Justin chimes in. He emerges from behind a curtain as if he's been part of our conversation the whole time.

Scrunching my forehead I try to remember what I told Justin. Maybe Matthew explained it to him. Man, I haven't talked about my angel theory in 4 or 5 years.

"I know what he's talking about but I don't remember talking about it specifically..." I mumble out.

Maybe you were drunk. The grating voice suggests, a trace of disdain directed toward the picture of me blathering like a drunken idiot and now I don't remember.

Eric isn't deterred by this little fact and goes on. "Well, doesn't matter. Just explain it anyway. What is your angel theory?"

I let out a sigh. It's been awhile since I've talked about this. How does it even go? I remember when it first came to me. I remember how excited I was. I was seventeen. I'd been thinking for weeks about the idea and when it came to me I told all of my friends about my 'amazing' realization. Now, it leaves a bitter feeling of a foolish youth. But I do remember it.

"Well, you see, I used to think that it didn't make any sense how someone would just like, die, and then suddenly poof!" Droning sarcastically, "They're an angel!"

Eric nods his head understandingly, "Sure, sure."

Now, how did it go exactly? I rub my finger against my chin as I try to remember the details.

"So, I started to think, well, what if angels are real? Because, before then I never really believed in them. It didn't make sense to me and seemed too much like, just a story. But I thought that if we had some kind of a soul, or something, like an eternal energy, then if we tried hard enough we could make a connection with our immediate personality and we could embed who we are now onto this energy, or soul or whatever, which would move on after we die. This would create like..."

Closing my eyes for a moment I try to picture how it went. Suddenly the structure and image of it becomes clear.

"It would create an image of our self but made of energy, so, we could move around like that and that would be what people think of as an angel. I even thought they would do this by praying really hard or something. Like if you prayed and prayed you could make a strong link to this energy and that would keep you who you are. It would, like, be a transfer from one form to another but it would take a strong link to pass on who you are."

Eric nods his head in a way that suggests he already knows all this. "I see and how old were you when you came up with this?" he asks casually.

"Uhh, 17 I guess, or 18." I strain to remember when it was actually.

Justin comes back into the room and interrupts. He asks if we're all set. Eric looks over at me and I nod. We both agree we are. Eric double-checks if I want to stay and talk and I say sure. I don't really know why we're talking about angels but maybe he needs to know where I'm coming from so when he makes up his predictions he can use some of what I tell him.

"So..." he says, "If you believe in angels you must believe in God, right?"

Well... it seems like a logical sequence for our conversation to follow. I'm not exactly sure what this has to do with a psychic reading, but I guess I've got nothing else to do.

"Yeah, I guess. Or, I believe in something, I'm not sure if you should call it God or not, but I guess you could."
"I see." He says nodding his head with certainty. "So, you don't believe in the typical religious God."

"Right, no old man up in the clouds wandering around throwing lightning bolts for kicks, judging people with a naughty and nice list." I grin.

"Yeah, I never understood that either. So what do you think God is?" Eric asks bluntly.

My brain skips. He's very straight forward. There's even a certain intensity in the way he asks. We've only begun to talk and the air almost feels like it is becoming thick. His attitude is casual but serious, not wacky at all. Glancing at his face I notice for the first time his eyes. They are hard to make out in the dim room behind his tinted glasses. They're bright crystal blue. Sharp. This guy's sharp. It's either intelligence or insanity. I've met some old hippies that have taken too much acid who have the same keen sparkle but they can't hold it together. It's all too scrambled. Which is he? I sit there for awhile thinking about his question. What do I think God is... I used to have an idea... what was it? I gave it up. Well, whatever, I gave up the whole thing years ago. What am I supposed to say? There isn't anything I truly believe.

"Well, I don't really know anymore. I mean, I used to think about it but I can't say I have any certain idea about it now." I confess.

"Well, just give me your best guess or anything you think might explain some of what you believe."

"Right." I say pausing for a few seconds to put my thoughts together. "Well, I guess I believe, or believed, God is more like an energy... or something. It's an energy that is everywhere and somehow 'in' everything or at least connects everything. I mean, I used to read these Wiccan books," he nods his head to tell me he knows what that is. He's probably read most of the books in this store. Still, it doesn't mean he can retain it all. He couldn't even remember my name.

I continue on, "And the Wicca books talked about the great web of life, which is like this web of energy that connects everything. I could see where they were coming from on the whole connection to everything, but I didn't think it was like a web."

"Well, what is it like?" Eric asks.

"Uh," I struggle to explain what I see in my head. I can picture it perfectly somehow, or not even picture it but I have this slippery sense of it, but I have trouble capturing the words.

"It's more like this giant ocean of energy and it's just everywhere and it's kind of aware and can feel, love, or something, but it's not like a man, it doesn't think like a man."

"Ok, what about anything else? How does it think? And what is its purpose? Where did God come from?" Eric rolls the questions out, digging for details I don't have.

Inwardly, I groan. I hope it isn't going to turn out to be another endless philosophical conversation on where God came from or some dream inside a dream theory where all life is just a dream of a greater being dreaming who is inside another being dreaming. I've heard too many of those back in the day when I cared and I don't see any point in running around in circles looking for answers that don't exist now that I don't care.

"Yeah," I shrug my shoulders. "I don't know. That's about as far as I ever got."

He nods his head like he knows and that my lack of understanding is somehow to be expected. It almost feels like a challenge. It's hard to imagine that someone who forgot my name was Eric, his own name, would try to get into an intellectual debate. Still, I feel a little foolish for not having a better explanation of what I think. My posture shifts. I'll be more critical of what he says, in case I can use it later.

"Well, still, that was very good." His tone seems to suggest, 'Nice try.' "You've given it more thought than most, it just seems like you haven't taken it very far."
I nod my head. It's a fair statement assuming he can take it farther. I silently commend myself for my view because the majority of it came from my own thinking and isn't something I'd exactly read and

recycled from a book somewhere. I wonder if he's going to start citing books or views from this person or that person or if he actually has something to say himself. If he starts citing authors and books the conversation's over. I half expect he will because if he isn't a Miss Cleo psychic he must be a bookworm.

"Do you want to know what I think God is?" Eric asks calmly, with a strange, silent seriousness.

Yes... but maybe no. Might as well see what all these books'll get you. He's not what I expected, so if I'm lucky he might say something mildly interesting. New Age encyclopedia, page 52, what is God? "Sure." I say trying not to smile at my own jibe.

"Are you sure? We can talk about something else if you want." Eric waves his hand as if he could give or take the subject and what we talk about doesn't really matter.

I smile. That's clever. He noticed my indifference and now he's baiting me and provoking my interest. It's like a teaser trailer for a movie. Damn but it works.

"No, no. I'd like to know what you think God is." I assure him trying to hide my smile with a crooked grin. He doesn't know me but I'm certain he's caught on to my sarcasm. I don't intend my response to be overt; it's for my amusement. An inner dialog more than anything else. I don't intend for anyone to notice. It's weird he picked up on it.

"Okay..." he says pausing to take a drink and clear his throat. "Oh," suddenly looking down at the tape recorder. "I guess I should turn this on." He hits record and adjusts the microphone slightly.

"Okay, I believe that the planet is a living organism floating in space. I believe that all the living creatures of the planet are part of the microorganisms to the Earth. I believe that the human race is the central nervous system of the planet."
He states all this in rapid succession. It's like he's reading it or has said it many times before.

"It's like to say to you, are 'you' the only thing of your body that thinks? Most people say. Yes I am the only thing that thinks. And I would say no, you're not. You are made out of trillions, I've used the word not millions not billions, trillions... probably more than that even, of living organisms in your body, all who think, individually, on their own, without any assistance on your part."

Nodding my head I try to picture, using my own body, what he's saying. He doesn't need any confirmation from me that I'm listening. He keeps talking right along. His voice is very active and there's something strangely captivating about it.

"For instance you have blood cells, red and white blood cells, okay. White cells for instance. White cells will find a virus, they will size up that virus to see if they can attack it, destroy it, whatever. If they decide they can't they summon, communicate to other white cells, to kind of get together. When they sense there is enough of them they will attempt an attack. Is that not rationalization, is that not a form of intelligence? In my opinion absolutely it is."

He has a point and it makes sense. Imagining little red and white blood cells moving through my body it's like feeling for the first time how independent they really are. He's speaking quickly but his words and sentences are clear. Remember, this could turn into some kind of debate and he's obviously more prepared. Pay attention! Listen more critically. Capture his argument. Memorize his facts and find the false ones.

He continues on while I collect my thoughts. "On your skin you have billions of arachnoid-like creatures, spider-like creatures, all choosing their mate, having children, knowing which children are theirs which aren't, knowing their territory, etc, etc, etc is that not intelligence?"

He rolls along, almost sounding bored, as if he could recite what he's telling me in his sleep. Still, it's nothing I've ever considered before so his question catches me off guard. Spiders? Do I have spiders on my skin? Crap, I've never heard of that. It's possible. But little spiders on my skin that mate? Damn, I can't say either way.

"Absolutely it is." He continues.

I smirk. He doesn't expect me to answer.

Looks like you get off easy. Don't even know your biology. Idiot. Guess, he's not going to figure out how stupid you are.

My cheeks burn. It's true. It's been so long since I've had to engage someone in an intelligent conversation I already feel like I'm falling behind.

"In your eye, you have millions of living organisms again, protozoan living organisms. All know which species is theirs, which isn't, which to attack, which to run from. Is that not intelligence? It absolutely is You are made out of trillions of living organisms. There isn't one inch of your body that isn't packed with millions and millions of living organisms. All of whom work for one being, you, one singular being. Yet they are all individual and independent in their thinking. Right or wrong?"

He sits there staring at me for a few seconds. Answer! He wants you to answer. Suddenly, I realize he expects to me respond.

"Right." I state. He's going into more detail than I've ever dug into before My mind teems with images of all the things crawling all over me and swimming through my eyes. I know the body is made up of all kinds of different cells and organisms. So, I'm sure he's telling the truth. I'm stuck on the idea of little creatures swimming through my eyes like it's a great ocean. What happens to them when I cry? End of the world I guess. What a way to go.

"If you become depressed, if you become psychologically distressed with yourself you can create cancerous tumors, ill-health, bad cellular structure, collapsing of your arteries, etc, etc. We know that as a scientific fact now. They've also found that when people have illnesses that if you think positively cells tend to regenerate. They tend to reciprocate somehow to you. They tend to know that there is a drive or a will saying that you need to do certain things, you need to create and you need to enliven the body. They believe also that this has to do with your consciousness communicating with this giant living organism of a body. Now, taking that into consideration... your body is roughly 75 percent water, 25 percent mass, do you know that? Ha! I quickly answer, "Yes". I've heard that fact before. I guess I know he has some ability to keep his facts straight.

"Do you also know that the planet is roughly 75 percent ocean and 25 percent mass? Which, I really, truly think that's a coincidence, but it's an amazing coincidence."

I nod. I never equated the composition of the planet with the human body though. It doesn't matter, as long as I nod when I know something, he'll know he isn't throwing anything at me I'm not already aware of.

"Your body regulates its temperature, 98.6 degree's. The Earth, which exists in space, which is sub-zero and below, maintains its own temperature. Very similar. Do you know that in uhh... World War II... or World War I... I can't quite remember anymore, that when we ran out of plasma do you know what we used for blood?"

Crap. He wants me to answer this one. He's waiting for an answer.

Busted. The grating voice provokes.

It's not fair. He has his ideas prepared and now he's pulling out something I don't know. I put my hands together and lean forward thinking. Guesses burn through my head. None of them are right! Eric shifts impatiently which causes his chair to creak.

Give up. You don't know.

"No." I finally say shaking my head in defeat.

He gives no indication that he's surprised like before. He continues talking which makes me feel a bit less on guard. "Basically purified ocean water. And the body accepted it. What gives you life is found in the ocean. It's found in the Earth, all the vitamins and minerals that make electrons in your body, one teaspoon, there's tons and tons of it. I mean think about where you get nutrition from, from the earth, plants, vegetables, meats, grass is eaten by cows, whatever! It's

still a transformation. It's a recycling of different forms of minerals. All of that food which gives you life is found in the Earth."
He finally stops. My eyes feel dry and I force myself to blink. Damn, he's been talking a long time and I got stuck staring at him. He takes a deep breath and clears his throat.

Listening to him speak is engrossing. While he seems at once very calm, part of him is always moving. In the Midwest people hold their bodies very still. Nobody uses much body language to speak. It's very reserved. When he speaks his whole body is speaking, not only his mouth. His hands speak with his eyes, and his face and it all compliments the subject he's covering. It's probably hard not to listen to him.

He proposes another question to me. "If you have micro-organisms living inside your body that give you life, and you think separately from them, and the Earth has all the species on the planet which are its micro-organisms, then how does the Earth think? How does the Earth think as a living organism?"

As an aside he quickly explains, "Micro is the very small and macro is very large." It's the only part of the whole exchange my reeling brain understands.

What do I say to that? A tumbleweed rolls through my head. Nodding my head slightly side to side I let him know I don't have a clue. I've never thought about it. How can I have an answer? I've heard ideas about the Earth being alive but this approach is very different. I'm still imagining millions of organisms swimming through my body and spider-like creatures crawling across my skin. It's like watching a movie that's slowly unraveling in my mind. A camera sweeps and zooms over my skin like a National Geographic video. Marching across the plains of my arm hair are little spider organisms, all finding mates and roaming looking for food. Then the camera passes through my skin into the swirling fluid of my arteries and follows all the micro cells and organisms. All going about their animal kingdom lives.

None consider me, their giant host, who should be the central aspect of their tiny existence. Then the camera blurs going through the layers of my body and flashes out far above me to show all the little people, animals, and cars traveling over the Earth's skin. All the little micro-organisms larger than my micro-organisms equally unaware and unconcerned about the larger organism upon which they live.

God, roll credits my brain won't stop. The whole human race is the macro equivalent of little spider organisms crawling on the skin of the Earth and we think like the spiders only completely differently?? How am I supposed to have an answer?

Eric seems to notice my confusion. With a raise of his hand he gestures for me to take is easy and slow down. He assures me it's very simple. "The brain uses a form of energy, electricity if you will. The problem is we've learned how to harness electricity but we don't actually know what it is."

Glancing around all the lights in the store I find the statement mind boggling. It's all over the freaking place, is he serious?

"There was some research done on the outside of the Philippine islands called the 100th monkey, have you ever heard of it?"

Still baffled about whether or not we actually know what electricity is I quickly give up on this one admitting with a shake of my head that it's nothing I've ever hard of.

"Well the 100th monkey-"

He stops suddenly as his whole body shakes with a loud, almost violent cough. It makes me jump a little but he takes a quick drink of water and keeps going as if nothing happened.

"Basically goes like this: there were uh, monkeys on an island being researched. There's a food shortage, a natural food shortage, and they started feeding what looked like sweet potatoes or yams to the monkeys. They would throw them out to them and they would fall into the dirt and the monkeys would pick them up, eat most of it, spit it out, and then only eat the inner core. What happened was after months and months of this observation, they observed a baby monkey who dropped his potato in water, thus learning how to wash his potato. The baby monkeys who played with that baby monkey obviously learned to wash their potato and the mothers who nursed the young learned to wash their potatoes and the males that mated with the females learned to wash their potatoes from the females. This took about a year and a half to get up to about a hundred monkeys. Okay? But they all learned to wash their potato on an isolated island. What took a year to a year and a half on an isolated island, what is most amazing now is that within, I believe within 60 days, about two months, there was observed that monkeys all over and in captivity in the United States and Asia, in mountains in zoo's, everywhere in the world began demonstrating one thing that was amazing, they started washing their food instinctually."

Running my finger along my chin I soak the story in and what it suggests. The idea is so interesting and intriguing but... argh... it's a little unbelievable. Forget the facts. I don't know right now what's true or not. I've got to focus on the meat of the concept he's trying to present. I've never cared about the detailed rules of dotting the I's and crossing the T's. I want the heart of the idea. If I'm going to argue something it will be about the very core of the logic of it and not in the outlying facts and figures. This is how I went through most of college and it frequently made things a little more difficult for me. My personality has always been to put aside my own beliefs and look solely at the other person's point of view. I smirk. It used to help me get along with others or make peace. Later it became a key to understanding people. If I wanted to truly know them I had to become them. I need to see his argument from his view. I won't understand what he's saying if I keep myself locked in my own personal view nitpicking how I think the world works.

"So the question is, how did they know? How did they learn this new behavior? It's called collective consciousness. In other words, I believe that the monkeys, their brain wavelength is a frequency, like 106.7 or 98.5. It's exclusive to each species. When their consciousness builds up momentum, instead of independently over a long, long time, it builds up and they're still kind of thinking this new conscious thought or effort. I believe it's like throwing a stone in water, it makes a ring that encompasses the planet. Each species that's on a similar wavelength, which is basically the same species of monkey per se, it builds up and encompasses the whole planet as a form of thought, as a form of consciousness." He stops talking and smirks slightly. "Am I boring you?"

It's a redundant question. He knows I'm far form bored. When was the last time I moved at all? I suddenly shift. I've been sitting perfectly still for a long time now, leaning slightly forward. My mind swirls putting all the pieces together.

I crack a smile. My old habit of trying to hide my smile. Never did a very good job of it. "No." I admit.

Eric knows it and keeps talking about the planet as a living organism. He tells me more about the collective consciousness of all the species in the world and how they all pool together to form one consciousness. That is the consciousness of the Earth. He raises his hands and shrugs his shoulders, "Just because the Earth doesn't have arms or legs why can't it be considered a conscious being? Why does it have to exist on a scale we understand? Why can't it be incredibly larger than us? It's only our capability of understanding that limits us."

Could something the size of the planet really think? Could it be aware and alive like... a giant elephant? Maybe it thinks more like an animal than a human but even then, could it really have thoughts of its own? It's hard to consider. I've always thought of it as a giant ball of... stuff. A giant floating space rock with life on it. Not alive in the sense that I'm alive.

Eric motions out with one hand towards the sky that I take as pointing towards space. "There's an energy field that goes around the whole planet from the deserts to the deepest ocean. As far as I'm concerned this is proof of a sense of being, a soul, whatever you want to call it. Your body is controlled by electrical thought, so is the planet. I find no reason it has to look like us to be alive and conscious."

He gives me an example of veins in my body. "Moving through your veins is blood. Billions of cells exchanging data, carrying nutrients, cargo all around your body doing different things. The Earth has highways, jetways, different things all carrying data, cargo like blood cells all doing different things. Different forms of communication."

Eric clears his throat. "All part of a living organism, it's just a different way of viewing it. You with me so far?"

"Yeah." It's a strange connection to make between the body's veins and the Earth. It also makes it interesting, if only as something to philosophize about and not really consider the possibility as a definite truth.

"Good." He says, somewhat satisfied. He pauses for a moment and takes a long drink. The store is perfectly quiet, my breathing sounds really loud. His ice clanks to the bottom of his, now empty, cup.

Eric starts again, painting a scene of going on a journey using a boat. We start on an island and can see all the teeming micro-life of ants and birds on the island. As soon as we roar out over the ocean we can't see any of the life inside because from far away the island looks like one thing. Same as if we were to zoom into my body and see all the little blood cells swarming around and then zoomed out. I wouldn't be able to see any of them. I look like one thing. The analogy makes me laugh.

Eric explains more, "If you want to understand something very large you should look at something very small. They mirror one another. Micro-macro and macro-micro. From a distance your body seems like one thing. When you zoom into it you can see it's millions of things. If we look at the Earth from a distance it looks like one thing. If we zoom into it it's millions of things! It's the same for solar system, the galaxy, and the universe. We know," he says slowing down, "that the universe started off with the Big Bang. If the Big Bang was an explosion then it's a big ball of stars, planets and universes. Billions upon billions upon quadrillions! It's still expanding. What," he asks me, "is it expanding in?"

He doesn't expect me to say anything and starts to answer it but I shrug my shoulders to show him I'm listening anyway.

"Absolute nothingness. Pure black, infinity, no planets, no stars, no meteorites, not even dust."

He is suddenly interrupted by the back door beeping. Eric tilts his head towards the curtain that hides the small back room but doesn't look directly at it. Someone sit down in a chair. It creaks and then a computer clicks on and it starts to boot up.

Eric pushes a button on the recorder. "Hang on."

He gets up and walks behind the curtain. A few moments later he comes back. He waves his hand as if to suggest it's nothing. He clicks record on the microphone and we keep going right along.

"From space the Earth looks like one thing. One being. The name of the ancient being that is Earth is Gaia. If there is a place where my body stops, it has a border, and I can say that is me... then Gaia also has a boundary. If we jump in a rocketship and fly past all the planets, solar systems, and galaxies to the edge of the universe..."

He says 'the edge' with his hands raised as he moves them over the air like he's presenting the idea for an amazing movie title.

"The edge," he says with the same intensity, "of the entire universe. And we get to the very edge and we shoot out, vooom!" His hand is flat to represent the spaceship and he zooms it around really fast. It's hysterical and interesting at the same time. He acts out little parts like it's a live play. He keeps going his voice rising and increasing in intensity,

"We push out into the infinite blackness the universe is expanding in and we would also see the universe has a boundary. If we looked back we would see one thing. One glowing, blobular thing. That thing is God. It's the body of God. And everything inside of it is the matter, like we are matter."

He stops and looks at me. My mind is buzzing with flashing images of galaxies, solar systems and enormous brilliant suns. Freaking crazy. I'm amped up like experiencing some strange adrenaline rush. The absolute enormity of it starts to slowly sink in. I can't think of any questions. I have none. This strange giddy joy bubbles up inside of me. I've never considered the scale of the universe this intensely before. I mean, I knew it was big but why haven't I stopped and thought about how big? How could I have never marveled at it before? Yet, here I am for the first time. In total wonder, my brain unraveling everything! He shifts, his chair creaks loudly, breaking me from my thoughts.

"That's it." He states plainly like a zoo tour guide telling me to exit the tram. He crunches on some ice.

I give no reaction. I have none. My brain wanders back to my previous thoughts.

He seems to think for a moment, "God's soul, prana, the Force, is the energy that intertwines it all. It's what interconnects it, it permeates all things, just like you are conscious of your body. Aware of everything but yet not aware of any one thing. Same thing. You are made in the image of God but in a much different way than you expected. Not with hands and feet, but as an inner-cosmos. Your liver, your kidney, all different organs, yet co-operating and working together to create a synchronicity of life to create one being. It's duplicated over and over and over from micro-verse to macro-verse."

He gets up to refill his water to give me a moment while it sinks in. When he returns he sits in his chair and stares at me. "What do you think?" He asks.

I let out a long exhale. It's interesting and fun to listen to but I immediately lock onto a conclusion. It's the same end. Regardless of how much he colors it up or how much fun it's been to listen to it has the same fault as every theory I've ever heard on the 'Big Questions' of life. It doesn't explain why. The real why. Why life is here and why God is here and where God even came from. Without providing that piece his ideas remain incomplete.

"I agree with what you're saying, and it makes a lot of sense but where..." I struggle to find a way to explain myself. I want to be nice and not offend him. He put a lot of energy into the presentation. "I guess my problem with God is... where did all of it really come from? It's just- "

He quickly cuts me off and pushes a question, "Do you think I have an answer for that?"

I think about my statement. I must have insulted him. Well, crap, I didn't mean to.

Smiling I try to let him know I only meant it to as a friendly discussion and not a combative debate. "It's just a question." I say as I hold my hands open somewhat apologetically.

He furrows his eyebrows together in an extreme point. It makes him suddenly appear quite serious and even a little angry. "What you're asking me is... basically the ultimate question."

He holds up his hands as if to ask, what do I expect? I nod my head. What do I expect? I know he can't answer that question. Nobody can. That's the point. There is no point because nobody knows. Might as well tell him he did a good job but that's the only thing that really matters. I open my mouth to let him know. Instead he puts up his hand so I know he's going to speak.

"The ultimate question is where did everything come from? No man can answer that." Eric tells me with an edge to his voice.

I'm surprised he comes out and says it. Well, that makes it easier. Now I don't have to worry about offending his sense of intellect by suggesting he's fallen short. "Oh." I say nodding my head as if it's common sense. It is common sense, which is why he shouldn't have been upset by my suggestion that he hadn't answered it.

His brow lifts and he cracks a knowing grin. His voice, which was pitched and agitated only moments before, is smooth and confident, "Except for this one." His eyes gleam with mischievous knowing.

My breathing lurches. Is he freaking serious? I open my mouth to ask if he's freaking serious but he continues, "Now if I can answer that, it would make me a pretty amazing person don't you think?" He raises his eyebrows playfully. He's playing overly cocky and enjoying it. I can't tell if he's truly serious about the answer.

Maybe he's wacky after all. I can't believe him. Who would even think to suggest they can answer that! It's hysterical! My opinion of him shifts again. I see his confidence and the way he smiles at the impossible. He's either the most arrogant guy I've ever met or the most ignorant for not knowing when to stop. There's also something suddenly exciting at someone facing such a challenge so boldly.

It's like watching a daredevil boast that they're about to perform an unbelievable feat, knowing in the back of your mind they are definitely going to crash and burn. It's only a matter of how splattered they will be.

"It would make you a very amazing person." I admit with a cheshire grin I can hardly contain.

"Are you sure? Would you like an answer? Would you like to know where God came from?" He's playing to the crowd; me. It's justifiable. He's making a large boast and is either going to soar or crash and burn. Either way it'll be a good ride.

I nod my head wanting to laugh. "Yes."

"I'm not sure you'll be able to follow it, but I'll try to keep it into such a..." His thoughts seem to trail as he glances down at the tape recorder. He motions to the recorder. "Plus we have this tape going, so I'll have to search for words to explain it."
He holds up his hands and takes a huge, drawn-out, deep inhale. He's getting ready to spit a lot of words out for a very long time.

Instead of talking at the fast pace he's been using he starts off very slow and calm. "A lot of it, because you're not a physicist, I'll use analogies, and hopefully my analogies will be correct so I hope that's noted on the tape." He gives a big, toothy grin and gestures towards the tape recorder. I split a smirk.

He begins on an almost Biblical sounding note. "In the beginning there was nothing…"

I snicker. Then he explodes. He tears into the very beginning of time. The moment of the very first reaction triggering levels and forms of energy which slowly grow and evolve through unfathomable lengths of time. The vacuum, the tension, enormous pressure.

I feel my brain stretch thin trying to fully conceive it. I can't get it. The movie in my head that marvels at the size and scope of the Universe is starting to hit its limits.

He covers everything he can which is more than I can imagine. How the Universe became aware, how it thinks, what it even looked like at the beginning of time. For a long time he continues taking me on an incredible journey through time and space. There are moments I slip away from the bookstore entirely. Instead I'm captured, wandering the Universe, the full scope of his vision unraveling all around me.

He pauses and takes a long, slow drink as I descend from the stars back to the comfy brown couch. I try to process everything he explained. Inside a strange giddy feeling grows.

He finishes his drink and continues weaving his view of the beginning of God. Patterns and variables and giant forms of self-aware energy that grow, learn, experience and become intelligent. This is God, or the Force. An intelligence so different from ours that it's hard to imagine.

He places his hand on his chest to accentuate that this is all his personal opinion. Looking around his store I wonder how much of what he's told me are his own views or things he's read in books. Even if they are from the books, at least I'm getting the best of it and don't have to read them all to get the good stuff.

I can't tell how much time has passed. Two hours, maybe three. My limitations break into my awareness. I'm not getting it. I sense it, know it. I don't fully understand what he's saying. At the same time I don't want to break his rhythm. It might all snap together in five minutes. Listen better. Think harder. It will come clear. Asking questions on the spot is lazy. I've thought that since I can remember. No reason to be sloppy now. I decide to keep quiet.

Eric's voice is sharp, clear. The room has a weight. Like a cloud has descended on all the dark corners of the store. Only within our bubble is there lightness. Strange, unusual feeling around us. "God became intelligent over billions of quadrillions of years as an energy, as a giant, giant form of prana, the Force, whatever, before anything existed. Well, I believe there are levels of energy. Energy can be denoted as levels of dimensions; 3rd dimension, 4th dimension. I believe there are thousands of dimensions, not just four or five dimensions. Thousands!"

He raises his hands out towards the ceiling and shakes them as he raises his voice and widens his eyes. With a willful passion he tries to drive the existence of them home! I'm laughing in my head. He's crazy! It's awesome! He suddenly strikes me as a spitfire, southern Baptist! He's going to start beating the table with his fist as he shouts out the vastness of the universe.

"Energy came to a point where it started to solidify and it became different kinds of gases which were incoherent with one another. When that happened the largest explosion of all time happened... beyond anything, beyond all the nuclear bombs we could create on this planet all exploding at the same time. It would be a fart out of a fleas ass in comparison with what happened."

My thoughts stop like a running dog who has reached the end of his leash. Internally I shake my head, trying to lose the image of a flea passing gas. I keep listening.

"What happened was when it got to that point, between the energy and the molecules condensing the way they did, it created a super fusion explosion. And what happened was as soon as this energy was released it was sucked out from the higher dimensions per se, the higher electrons, and it instantly glued together certain ones that were attracted like magnets to specific other ones which solidified and created matter. Matter solidified very quickly and there was an explosion which separated it all into a million infinitive directions."

Eric kicks one leg up against the other in a relaxed position. "And that was the creation of God." Pausing briefly. "In this dimension. It was the creation of matter. Do you understand?"

His follow up comment grabs my attention. It seems out of place. "Yeah, but you said in this dimension, why is that?"

"Why is that? Because I believe that God exists in multiple dimensions. I believe this is just one dimension. Well, ask yourself one thing okay, are you one dimensional or are you multi-dimensional? Let's think about it. When I say, say the alphabet, where do you say the alphabet? You hear it in your head."

"Right." I nod agreeing.

He drills me with questions about what I believe is me. "So where are you? Is your arm you? Is your flesh you?" He challenges me to point to, exactly, where I am. "Come on, where? Are you the voice in your head? Where is the voice located? Can you point to it?"

He doesn't need to ask anymore questions. I already know. I can't do it.

Eric explains that the reason is because we aren't flesh. Who we are, is energy beings. He points to me and tells me that everything I am, everything I experience, I do because those experiences are converted into electricity. I exist and operate in several places at once, multi-dimensionally. Not satisfied with an overview Eric digs into the details of what he means by this. My already overflowing brain begins to swell.

Eric abruptly stops talking. "Am I boring you?"

"No." I assure him, feeling glazed.

"Good. I hope you're as entertained as Justin guaranteed you would be." He smiles. His comment makes me laugh. Justin never made it seem it would be like this.

"Yes, more so." I admit. "This is my question. I have two problems with that, the first being nothingness is almost completely incomprehensible to me." His explanation about the beginning of time and this dimension talked so much about infinity and absolute nothingness I'm struck with how I can barely conceive it.

"I understand." Eric nods.

"The second is that... even with the vacuum and nothingness and tension there was still as you say... electrons or whatever slowly..." I can't talk. I can't explain what I see in my head. Where did it all come from anyway? I struggle to speak coherently. "I guess my whole... or no... my whole... or one problem... well, one problem with where I always thought God would be intelligent or whatever is it seems like creation is almost an act of will... because where did the electrons come from, where did... to have nothingness you have to have something... where did THAT come from? It seems like there had to be-"

Eric stops me from rambling. "The electrons came from the vacuum. Okay-"

"Where did the vacuum come fr-?" We start interjecting over each other.

Eric slows me down. My head feels like I went through 'finals week' in three hours. He speaks slowly trying to explain his idea in a different way. I try to calm my brain down. It makes me laugh. I look at my hands and everything returns to a normal pace as if time had gotten ahead of itself. Paying attention to my thoughts pinging through my head I notice a rising giddiness begins to overwhelm me. He sits looking at me. I marvel at everything unfolding in my mind. It's like I'm not even doing it. It's there, playing itself. All I'm doing is stepping aside and observing. Doesn't even act like my own imagination.

He strums his fingers on the table. "It will take time, if I teach you, and if you want to be taught. There will come a time when you'll see it in your mind. You'll know it as clearly as you can feel that cup in your hand, for sure. I can't really quite explain why, or I could explain why you'll know but it would take too much of a conversation. Let's just say that there are ways that mystical people, people of great spiritualness, Christ, Buddha, Krishna, enlightened people, they knew a knowledge far beyond themselves. Somehow, someway they just understand things. Much how I know things."

I can't respond. I can barely get the grin off my face. He turns his head sideways and looks at me. With no response from me he continues to explain how it's possible to know what he knows.

"Well, I told you before that all of the thoughts of the world, from every species, from every creature, from all of time is collectively energy. It's everywhere. So there is a collective database of information from the planet, it's just stored electrically. Remember when I said to you earlier, one of the reasons why I like computers so much is because I found out there was a truth between computers and spirituality? That's what I'm saying. If you think about memory in a computer, it floats, if you unplug the power it collapses and it's gone. The point is, this energy, this information, is flowing much like it would be in a memory chip. There is energy here from the sun so it constantly has an electrical field providing it. I believe and I teach that one can reach, what is called the mind of Gaia. In ancient words it was called the Akashic records. The totality of all knowledge. Well, I believe that you can harmonize, like a tuning fork, your mind, your consciousness to the vibration of the planet, you can pretty much know anything you want to know, it just comes to you. It just makes sense. It's... it's like you always knew it, you just didn't know how. Like remembering an old memory that was kind of stagnant and all of a sudden you start to remember it." Eric falls quiet and watches my expression. Why is he looking at me? I suddenly realize he must be looking for some kind of response. I open my mouth to talk and then laugh.

Eric isn't fazed by my reaction. He continues as if my random laughter is perfectly normal. "So the answers to things that I'm giving you came from this place. So when I say to you, someday if you learn, you'll understand what I mean. You'll see it. That's the only way I can describe it to you. And it'll just make sense."

His answer fits in perfectly with everything he's said.

He raises his glass to me and smirks. "I know you're bored to death and can't stand it huh?"

I smile and don't try to hide it. "Yeah, I've had a good time but I have brownies baking at home." That doesn't make any sense. I meant baking is more important.

Eric attempts to laugh at my joke. "So I think that's it for this tape, I hope..."

He shuts the recorder off. "Well, I hope it was informative." He clasps his hands together as if to suggest we're all finished.

I laugh. My whole body feels lighter. There's this strange bubbling sense of, happiness. So light. I feel so light! My whole heart feels happy, joyful. God! I lower my head and chuckle.

"What's so funny?" Eric asks a curious expression on his face.

I can't even go there. "Nothing." I say trying to wipe an enormous grin off my face. I can't stop smiling. My insides spin with insane energy. I feel like dancing! Almost by itself, my body starts laughing again. Everything feels so good, but in no way I've ever felt before, it's not physical like a drunk. I can't place it! "I.. uhh. – " Lowering my voice I try to compose myself. He's going to think I'm nuts. "I'm just in a good mood."

"Oh? Well, that's good." Eric says looking unconvinced. "So, you're a pretty happy person then?"

Sure. I'm happy. I'm upbeat.

Liar. You've been a moody grump for two months. The clear voice states simply.

Hey, I've been moody but I'm never sad or depressed. I do stay positive.

I feel like dancing? You might be happy but you don't giggle randomly and you don't sporadically dance out of the blue... Memories of me running through my apartment dancing by myself when I'm alone pop up in my brain.

Well... not very often then. And not like this... no, 'Sound of Music', twirling dancing.

It's true. I feel like skipping and twirling around like I'm stuck in a freaking musical. That's not normal. Damn it. What am I supposed to tell him? For no reason at all I want to burst out laughing and skip all over your store? I can't stop giggling and the one time in my life I smoked pot never felt anything like this either. My thinking is clear. It doesn't feel physical at all except my heart... feels so free, light... I can't say that.

I nod my head, straining to smirk so I don't sit there with a donkey grin plastered across my face. "Yeah, yeah, I'm a pretty happy person."

Eric nods his head with a little smirk. He doesn't believe me. "I see. So it's normal for you to sit there grinning and laughing to yourself. This is how you usually are?"

He doesn't believe a word I'm saying. Fine, he can not believe me all he wants. Doesn't mean I have to open my mouth and sound like a crazy. Better for him to suspect than know. "Uhh, yeah. You know, I'm always pretty happy. I'm out, having fun. I like your store." I try playing it cool but I can't wipe the smile off. I don't even know why it's there or why it won't go away.

"Uh-huh. Okay." Eric says in a slow monotone. He definitely doesn't believe me. I wouldn't either.

We sit for a few minutes. He takes a drink and I squirm trying to contain my exploding feelings of energy and happiness. As strange as the feeling is, there's something very familiar about it. There's something familiar about all of this. I can relate to this, this bizarre spin of emotion. Struggling I try to remember where I've felt like this before. Suddenly it hits me.

Christmas. Coming home for Christmas.

When I went away for college and spent my first Thanksgiving away from home that first Christmas I came back was unlike any other. It was familiar but new again. Safe, comforting like a reunion. All the cares of the world could melt away because I was wrapped in a place where there was no danger, no struggle, only love. A moment out of time where nothing else mattered and for a night, staring into the twinkling lights, I knew peace.

This feels like that time. Only, it makes no sense why.

Slowly, I get my face to resume its normal stoic expression but I know my eyes are bigger than they should be. Feels like they're beaming out.

A question pops out of my brain. "So, do you believe that God has developed its own consciousness?"

"Well, see, there you go, that's a question." He turns the recorder back on. "Can you repeat your question?"

"Sure, do you believe that God now has developed its own consciousness?" I ask.

"Does God have a consciousness? Well... it's a yes and no question. Okay? And I'll explain why. Yes it has a consciousness but no, for us to conceive how God's mind works is so... DIFFERENT, than our thinking."

I have no expectation of his answer or even if he has an answer. He dives into the question. Molds it, fans the flames of my mind and brings it to life. The answer that emerges makes perfect sense. I laugh at the idea of it. He tells me how God thinks. How God's thoughts influence the universe. Then he begins to talk about if God is aware of us, each person, individually.

"There is a level of awareness, but it's not the kind of awareness that we perceive. Are you aware of your liver right now working? Are you aware of your kidneys? But they're there. Yet, they're part of you. Yet they function for you. But there's no awareness unless you feel pain, unless you feel death. So in the same respect I believe that God is basically kind of not aware but is aware because we are a part of it."

"Right. I guess that's what I was trying to say earlier when I said I thought God was... primal." I slowly think out loud recalling when he first asked me what I thought God was. His explanation sounds like what I was trying to describe only I couldn't find the words or clarity.

"Uh-hrmm." He thinks I'm stretching.

You never said primal. Duh. The grating voice scolds me. Trying to make yourself sound smart huh?

My cheeks flush and I try to recover, "I mean, that it's... aware."

Eric slowly nods. "Riiight... and as I said I complemented you because there was a little truth there, you just really hadn't taken it on a long journey yet. So I believe that its energy, and its body, you could say that the planets and the stars are the flesh and the blood. The matter, okay? And God's soul, its consciousness, is intertwined like your mind is intertwined with your energy which is intertwined with your body, the mass. So electrically, you are the spirit, or the force to the micro-verse of your body."

Perfect. It's perfect. The energy, conscious, aware like my own consciousness. Everything I ever wanted to say but couldn't find the words. He's right, I never took it on so long a journey.

"I also believe that you can tap this energy and do amazing and powerful things, if you simply know how. Call it tapping the Force, the power of the Force, call it whatever you want, be a Jedi warrior! It doesn't matter, in truth, in the end... there is a way to tap the Force... there is a way to tap energy as a singular being. And you can consume this energy. You can change your tonal, your vibration like a tuning fork."

I can tap into God's consciousness? My mental spinning attempts to unravel the possibilities if things are as he suggests.

Eric explains the levels and frequencies of consciousness. How I can raise and lower my tonal. "You can conceive and become a vibration with God and that's called enlightenment and you simply act here in this dimension using that knowledge and that power."

There's a long pause. My whole body buzzes with the flood of information. Eric gets more water. He comes back and I'm still sitting with a smile on my face. I feel so good. Information, knowledge, a whole new world to discover. Like learning the rules to a whole new fantasy game. I want to know how his world works, why he thinks these things, all the intricacies. Like an elaborate puzzle. I can solve it.

"Well, we better talk about something. We got this long empty section in the tape now." Eric mutters eyeing the spinning tape recording our entire conversation.

I smile and shake my head, "Yeah, I don't really know where to go from there."

Eric does. He smiles. All he needed was a reason and he takes off again. "So, I believe that it is possible, to tap what I call a super-energy, a super-power, beyond all comprehension. And I believe it's absolutely possible. I believe it's a state of consciousness that does it. And it's refinement, through study, through practice and one can achieve amazing things. I believe that you consume this energy. Everything needs an exchange of energy. A car does not run without gasoline, a tree does not grow without water, fire does not burn without wood for fuel. Everything in our universe requires an exchange of energy. So when one learns to absorb prana, which is a technique I teach, way beyond what anyone else has done... I can show someone how to draw in this energy and when you consume mass quantities, beyond even what a martial artist would do for kung fu to absorb chi and use it to throw someone across a room. Imagine being able to absorb a hundred-million times that amount inside of you so you can do amazing psychic things. From heal the sick to see other dimensions to things that I wouldn't even want to put on tape. These are the things one can do once they learn to tap into that kind of power, into this kind of energy and it does exist."

Limitless power to do extraordinary things, what does he really mean? He can't be serious about healing the sick.

Eric doesn't leave me to my thoughts for long. He breaks the silence, "And the next question you haven't asked is, if God exists, is there evil? Is there an opposite power? And my answer to that is yes, there is."

Evil? Evil never even occurred to me. If he isn't serious he never suggests it. Eric relays to me his view of what evil really is. It's as complex as his view on God. He explains that true evil is a counter to the purpose of why life is here. The purpose of God. Evil is a reaction. For every action, an equal and opposite reaction. As God exploded and entered this dimension so did it create a counter-force that pushed against everything that was expanding. Using Star Wars as an analogy he calls it the 'Darkside'.

Smiling I can't believe he pulls it off. It should be cheesey. It works.

In the movie Star Wars there are two sides. There is the Force and the Darkside. He explains how when the Force pushed its energy into this space, creating our dimension, there was a natural reaction. A counter action. It's the laws of physics here. For every action there is an equal and opposite reaction. The action of the Force expanding in space created a reaction pushing against it to go away. That is the true evil. That is the Darkside. It is anti-matter. It is anti-life. The two are intermixed through all of reality. They are both present. He believes that God doesn't know everything. It is here to experience just as we are. The Darkside wants to destroy matter and remove life which will end the experience. The threat to the Darkside is the growth of life.

There is a Divine Plan. The Darkside has an interest in the Earth because it does not want it to spread life throughout the universe through humans. We will move into space taking the life from the Earth to other planets. The Darkside pushes against that action by reacting, which is to destroy it. He continues on unraveling the details of how humankind fits into the scheme of the Divine Plan. How the Darkside attempts to influence it. How everything plays out in the clash of these two universal forces.

My head swims and I don't even notice that he's stopped. Images flicker through my mind so quickly I can't even pick them out. No point. Not even sure how I'm taking everything in and where it's all coming from.

Eric shudders with a cough that jolts my head up to look at him.

"Falling asleep over there or you with me?" Eric asks.

"No." I snicker with a whispery laugh.

He hits pause on the tape again. "It will take time. You'll forget most of this. It'll slip away. Interesting stuff though?"

Laughing I nod my head. Can't even talk right. Words won't come out of my head. "Yes... umm, definitely. Interesting."

"So, what do you think? You want to learn more?"

"Umm," I grin, "yes... but, I don't know about now. My..." can't think of word. I point to my head. "Is so... bazzzt! I can't get a straight thought."

Eric throws his head back with a hearty laugh. "Yeah, I hear that a lot." He leans slightly forward on the chair. "Well, if you want to learn and be a student..." He looks at me as if he expects an answer.

Nodding my head, "Yes. Definitely."

He nods. "Then there's one test you need to pass. Everyone who comes to me that I truly teach, must pass it. You see, you can use what I teach you to do amazing things. Powerful things. I have to make sure I'm giving that power to the right people. People I can trust."

His tone hardens with intensity. Thick air, quiet but deep. My nod is barely noticeable. I'm afraid to move from my spot. "Okay." I whisper, my voice cracking.

To be truly faithful to this, my first meeting with Eric, I would have to fill an entire book.

You may ask, a whole book? We had a few hours of conversation.

Perhaps... you could look at it like that. It would be a very limited way of looking at it. When we were done it felt like we had been talking for weeks. Barely noticeable then... I have become aware over time of how Eric teaches on multiple levels. I don't mean that in some abstract, philosophical way. I mean it literally.

At the time all I noticed is that as he was speaking there were images flashing through my head, almost as if they were appearing on their own. What kept me so entranced was that I sat back on his couch and literally watched this movie unfold about the universe. I have always had an active imagination so it was easy to dismiss at the time as his choice of colorful words and descriptions, over a period of a few hours, and off I went.

However, given enough time and more chances for observation I can say with certainty that when Eric speaks images, emotions, and other things harder to define will appear. These things will either enter your mind before he's actually said anything, or have nothing to do with what is coming out of his mouth but relate, or are nothing you ever considered, imagined or had the resources to conceive on your own.

After knowing him for about four years he admitted that you could say inside his words are embedded codes of information. Little packets of knowledge that can't be explained by any vocabulary he knows but once they hit your mind expand, grow and burst like bubbles of thought. DNA fibers that carry a vast library of encoded data.

There's no way I could have known, believed or even imagined that this was possible when I first met him. It is interesting to me that, even then, I became aware of its effect. Only, there was no way for me to understand the source. What I also know is that sometimes these little packets are planted in your mind, like seeds, and won't fully expand and release their information until they've had time to grow.

That is why these few, short hours of conversation would take me years to unravel. Sifting for the gems he'd embedded, following the crumbs he carefully laid out, and simply realizing other levels to things he said that I believed I understood very clearly, until at last I would reach the end.

I did not reach the end because I discovered everything there. No. I'm no longer so naïve, though I once thought that way. It came to an end because the necessary details I needed washed away in the slow churn of time. The trail grew cold. It was lost to me despite memorizing every detail and constantly rehearsing it in my mind, again and again, for seven years.

Do not be idle. It is too easy, especially when you're young which is where I've stumbled, to be passive with your time, thinking a later date is as good as today. When the forge is hot throw yourself into it. Perform the great labor with all your heart and all the strength you can muster. The cooling comes all too quickly.

Not that I despair. I've had many, many such conversations with Eric. All of them their own mountain of knowledge with secret trails and hidden caverns. Each to be explored in their own time. I say this to point out something that took me a year to finally understand. That a conversation with Eric is never just the words you hear. There are levels, layers and the more you dig the more rewards you reap.

At the time I lacked the awareness, the basic understanding, the sensory to notice many things I now suspect were there. If I could go back I'd kick myself. Pay attention! Be more open minded! Don't be so sure of yourself like you know it all!

Eric was like nothing I expected. Everything he told me was overwhelming but in the back of my mind I formed assumptions. I assumed everything he was telling me he'd learned in a book and so wasn't his own. I also assumed if he'd read it in a book he wasn't much different than myself. His spark of intelligence was hard to miss. It was also difficult to gauge. I'd never met anyone like Eric. My mind sought a place to put him and once I put him at my level I removed possibilities that a more open, curious mind may have caught.

Go ahead and say it. Young and dumb. Maybe, to be nicer to my 24 year old self, we can say young and inexperienced. How was I supposed to know what I'd stumbled on? Most likely, you don't even know. How could you? Only, learn from my mistakes. Stop categorizing. Don't be so quick to make assumptions. Every assumption is a wall in your mind, that removes the possibility to travel to a place within yourself, that could be just the place you seek.

Don't make walls, break them down. Actively seek to break them down. If you don't know it, trust me, they are there. Part of you is very good at making them and hiding them from yourself.

Part of it, you may not be able to help. When Eric told me he'd found missing people, or tracked submarines, I had no way to understand what he was saying. Nobody had ever even told me it was possible to use the human mind to see across any distance, any person, or place. Terms that are more common today, like the CIA Remote Viewing program, I never heard of. With no groundwork for understanding I dismissed it, quickly.

How many times in history do we have to go through this? When it was suggested little invisible creatures lived in our food we cried witchcraft. Once upon a time I laughed thinking I would never be that ignorant. It's humbling when life shows you otherwise. It's also very freeing and I am fortunate to have had experiences to reveal boundaries inside myself I believed weren't there.

Go slow. Accept you don't know it all. Neither do I... but guess what? You're reading this book because chances are there's something you're searching for. Now there's something I must confess... after a year and a half with Eric my search was over. I found what I was searching for. I was 25 years old.

Don't let that make you defensive. Yes, I said a year and a half. I know you have probably been searching longer. Now, that's not to say my journey is over. Far from it. But it should tell you something at least. I know what you are searching for. I know you can find it too. It's true; I have had opportunities you may not have. Please, know this; I am trying to help you. I can only do that if you put everything aside and for the rest of this book... listen... openly, consider...

... every hole I have ever put Eric in he's defied. Every pedestal he's placed on he'll be the first to knock down. Every assumption I ever made has been wrong until at last... I realized... the only thing I can say for certain is he is the paragon anomaly.

However you may have expected it to happen, in whatever form you thought it would come... put it on a shelf for now. It will still be there. There is more you should know before part of you starts to pour the cement...

what happened to the moments, when we were young, when we could sit with the unknown, night slipping in, uncertain of what happens next and see for the first time...

Flickers of Light

chapter four

I sit staring at the floor on a thin sheet of tense silence. The strange giddiness I felt is sucked from my body and replaced with unexpected apprehension. It's a struggle to swallow. My throat seems to know more than I do. Why the sudden change? Without any idea about what kind of test he could possibly deliver I'm locked in a vice grip.

Eric peers through me. He hardly seems the same person.

In a steady voice, razor-like in it's delivery he explains the test to me. "Tell me one thing about you that you're afraid to tell most people. Tell me something maybe even your closest friends don't know. When you tell me, I'm going to check if you're lying. If you're lying, Justin will come and pick you up, you'll go home and we'll never speak again. This is one time in your life you do not want to lie. I stand by what I say and I do not tolerate dishonesty. Do you understand?"

My throat tightens further. Can't swallow. His gaze locks onto me. Too late to look down. Butterflies rattle and crash through my gut. If I pass the test, he will consider teaching me.

What do I really have to lose? I'm not even sure what he means by teach. Even so, I'm gripped with unreasonable fear. I know this is one test I do not want to fail.

What don't I tell people? God, I'm always making fun of myself. I say everything about my life.

You have to say something or he'll think we're lying!! Say anything! The frantic voice cries out.

No. We can't say anything, that's lying too. It isn't a secret if other people know. Each second puts me more on edge. Any moment... he could say enough and that's it. I've never had anyone ask me this before... crap. What do I say?!

Frantic, clammy hands, I desperately think of every horrible thing I've ever committed or endured.

Green leaves. Backyard of the old house. A white kitten sneaks along the fence. I've got a tennis ball in my hand. I'll throw it right by it to scare it off. Sling tennis ball. Flying through the air... everything slows down. Panic, fear and guilt. It's going to hit! Run kitten! The tennis ball nails him right in the side and he jumps three feet into the air. He hits the ground and bolts. Shame. Sorrow. I want to cry I feel so full of guilt. Had I actually tried to hit the kitten I would have missed. My aim is horrible. I never hurt anything before.

No good. Everyone knows about that.

Kitten smasher. That's a weak one.

Am I afraid to talk about my sex life? Not comfortable but not afraid. Nothing I wouldn't tell people. Girls I've been with, all normal. Ever been a jerk? I've had my moments, never anything bad, nothing to feel guilty about. My ex-girlfriend and I fought and ended things when I took her to Hawaii, does that count?

You told everyone you know about that. They laughed. That stuff always happens to you. The grating voice mocks.

Right. Nothing secret about that.

Eric sighs. "Well? Anything you want to say or should I call Justin?"

Agh! I hold up my hand signaling for him to wait, "No! I'm trying. I want to say something, only I can't think of anything."

A little smirk and he raises his eyebrows. "Can't think of anything? Come on. Everybody's got something. I need to know what you are willing to lie for. What do you struggle to keep secret? I also need to know what shape your life is in, to be perfectly honest. When I reach into somebody's life it affects mine and everyone around me. If you're honest with me, it's easier to help. If you're going to lie, your heart isn't ready. Here, I'll help you out. Are you on any drugs?" He chuckles. "Ever done any drugs?"

"Uh, I've tried pot before. Twice. Drink alcohol. Don't smoke, if you consider that a drug I guess, never even tried it."

"You've never even tried a cigarette? Well, that's a little weird but not really a problem, you know?"

Eric gives me an amused look like I'm a funny little bug he's never seen before. "Alcohol doesn't count. Smoking pot twice is hardly doing drugs." He rolls his eyes a little as if to say it's not even worth mentioning. "So, no secret drug addictions, ever done anything really hard? Heroin? Crack? Cocaine? Acid?"

Shaking my head I shrug my shoulders. "No. I mean pot was a big deal. I never had much interest in doing it. No acid, or anything like that. Most of my friends were stoners, they've done all that stuff, been with people when they were on a lot of that stuff, I just never wanted to. Never saw the point and I never do anything because everyone else is doing it. Not much of a follower. I don't even like taking drugs when I'm sick."

Eric nods. His face bunches, like he's thinking. His fingers strum randomly on the table. "Okaaay then. Borring. Um, how about physical or sexual stuff? Huh? Ever do anything really weird there? Hire a hooker? Are you violent? Get in a lot of fights? Ever really hurt anyone? Anything you couldn't ever tell anyone or if people knew you'd be really embarrassed about?"

Sweat starts to bead on my forehead. Haven't I done something I don't like telling people? Anything? Keep speaking, it'll come. Roll tongue, roll! "Uh, you know... crap. Um, I first had sex when I was 17. Kissed a girl when I was 17. Umm, I tell people that though. Pretty standard. Umm –"

He cuts me off. Rubbing his hand on his forehead he looks at me like I have to be kidding. I'm not kidding. "Seventeen? Geesh, what was wrong with you? A little late don't you think?" He chuckles and waves his hand so I know he's kidding with me. "You a shy kid?"

Nodding my head, "Yeah, late bloomer. Never really thought about girls..."

"Did you have some bad experience growing up?"

I laugh. "No. No bad early childhood trauma if that's what you mean. I was just a spacey, really shy day dreamer. Never got into girls until later. Oh wait! This is a little weird – "

"Finally." He says as if he were exhausted.

"I never like... masturbated until I was 21." I throw my hands up as if to say it's just one of those things. It doesn't seem like a big deal to me but maybe he'll think it is.

Eric chokes as he tries to hold back laughter. "What?! What do you mean?"

I chuckle. Okay, it's a little odd. "I mean I never like, did it like that, until I was 21. I mean, people know, and it's a little embarrassing."

Eric holds a hand up looking lost and confused. "Why didn't you do it until you were 21?"

Leaning over I laugh. It sounds so stupid. "It never occurred to me!

I didn't think about it and nobody ever told me! I mean, people talk about masturbation but I never thought about how it would work or why people would do it! I was at summer camp once as a camp counselor.... and all these kids, who were younger than me, were all joking about it. They were saying like all guys jerk off and anyone who says they don't is a liar. And I didn't believe it so I told them I never had. And one of the kids was laughing saying how I was so full of it that I never worked one off and he did, you know, he did the hand motion. And then I was like, huh. So when the camp was over.... I, uhh..." My whole face is burning red. "I was taking a shower and remembered his hand motion so I..." I start laughing.

Eric shakes his head looking at me like I'm a two-headed, talking dairy cow. "Unbelievable. So then you tried it out. Okay, well, that's something. That's not really what I'm looking for though."

"Okay..." I trail off. I have no idea what I can tell him. I'm sure there are things I'm afraid to say but I think to anyone else they wouldn't be a big deal at all. Only, I can't even think of what's a big deal to me!

Eric clears his throat and recomposes himself from laughing at me. "I don't want you to think I'm judging you, okay? I've seen a lot of things in my life and one thing I'll never do is judge another person like that. People live their lives the way they want, as long as they aren't hurting someone else or repressing them you'll get no argument from me. There's nothing you could tell me that would surprise me. I have heard it all. Through the years I've had a lot of students and as a psychic I was in everybody's business and knew their private lives and I have seen some serious shit and heard things that would send you into shock! I'm immune. So, if you're into hard drugs, or masochism, or God, I don't even know what would really get me anymore... been an arms dealer! Who knows?" he chuckles, "I mean whatever you've got, it's not really going to surprise me. I'm not going to judge you for the speck in your eye before I take the log out of mine. We all do things we later regret, that's life. But are you willing to be honest about it and what lengths are you willing to go to keep your secrets locked up? That's what I want to know."

Slowly nodding my head. I get where he's coming from.

"Umm, well, I guess there's two things. The first is I guess I'm a curious person, but it really never dawned on me to even wonder much about sex. I think maybe people are afraid to talk about that the most. It's just... really never even entered my mind. I mean, I'm open to people who are transvestites, or gay, or whatever, it's just not me. But I'm not like prejudice. I'm totally open to people who are gay, I've even had friends and old bosses who were gay. I think they're all cool people. But even when I knew them it never really hit me to think about stuff like that much less act on it. Now..." I hide my face and snicker. "I guess having said that there was this one party in college."

Eric leans back, his face turns a little serious, "Oh, here it comes, never thought about it but what happened?"

He must think my dark secret is finally coming out. I shake my head. "No, nothing like that. I went to college in Olympia, Washington and it's a really diverse campus. Lot's of alternative kind of open minds. One of my roommates, or a guy who was living with my roommate was gay. One night we were all drinking and started playing truth or dare. Somebody dared him to kiss me... and..." Bending over again I start laughing.

"Okay..." His voice sounds monotone. The mere mention of a game as stupid as 'Truth or Dare' probably alerted him to the fact this would be as boring as the rest.

"Well, he came over, and I was all squeamish and yelling, playing around you know. I was drunk but I knew him and he was a cool guy. But pushing him away and I didn't think he'd do it but everybody was yelling at me that I had too. I was the Midwest guy who didn't even know what soy milk was so I think they got a kick out of it. And he did plant one right on the side of my mouth. I pushed him away and laughed about it but it felt weird."

Eric drones out, his interest quickly fading. "It felt weird? How do you mean?"

"Well, this is prolly going to sound dumb but, I'm pretty scruffy, right? I never shave much and I used to have girls complain about it and I figured, whatever. But he hadn't shaved and when he pushed his face against mine all his stubble stabbed me and I suddenly felt like a girl, like damn, that's what they complain about. It sucks. Also, as a few years went by I felt bad about it."

"Why did you feel bad about it? You regretted doing it?" Eric shifts in his chair leaning forward. My reaction to it catching more of his interest than the thing itself.

"No, I felt like I made a big deal out of nothing. I felt bad that I was so weird about it that maybe I made him feel bad or rejected unnecessarily. I read this story about this really lonely guy who was living in San Francisco. He never had many friends and his life had been really hard. He was walking down the street one Saturday night, alone, feeling really down on himself. Suddenly these three people, a girl and two guys, who were drunk came up on him. They were out living life and he was going home to his apartment by himself. One of the guys ran up to him, gave him a giant hug and kissed him. This guy wasn't gay but he said that made his night. He said better to be kissed by another guy on a Saturday night than to be totally removed from life and the human race. I think that story actually made me cry. Looking back I feel like this guy probably thought I was good looking and I could have made his night by just laughing and being okay. Girl, guy it's just the human connection and I cut him off rather than making him feel like he had just as much right to feeling a part of things as anyone else."

Eric nods and waves one of his hands back and forth to say so-so. "Well, that one's okay but it's still not great. Don't you have anything? Anything at all? I mean, don't take this wrong, nobody's *that* boring!" He bursts out laughing. I laugh because he's laughing so much. He holds up his hands. "I'm kidding, I'm kidding. But really? Are you sure there's nothing?"

Struggling for a minute I can't think of anything at all. Shrugging my shoulders I shake my head no.

Eric nods and let's out a long sigh. We sit for a moment. The room falls to silence. The sound of my own breathing catches my attention as the only noise. Eric is still. His face emotionless.

Suddenly, I feel a tingling on the top of my head. Like a concentrated electrical current. Once, when I was young, a friend's family put in an electrical fence for their dog. We both gathered near the lines, daring one another to touch it. Knowing enough to understand it wouldn't kill us, even the thought of mild pain kept us from it. Reaching down I plucked a long blade of grass near the fence. It was soft, slightly moist with dew as I rubbed it between my fingers.

My breath shook. The slender grass blade quivered in my hand as it became an extension of my arm. I would feel its pain. The current, traveling through it, to me. Closer, the tip moved just above the bright, sleek wire laced with volts of electrical fire.

My wrist twists, as if I were to grace the wire with the gentle stroke of a paint brush. All judgment subsides. I have no idea what to expect. Curiosity overcomes fear.

The blade grazes the metal line.

Immediately my whole hand goes numb with shock! A million stinging points covers my fingers, runs up to my elbow until it slowly fades around my shoulder. Inside my hand cries out with a burning vibration. Like a fire sweeping through the muscle and bone while the sparks and embers dance on the surface. Gritting my teeth I hold the blade a moment longer. I can feel it travel through the grass. Sense its movement. The trembling weed held in my hand, into my fingers, my skin.

Finally, I release it and grasp my arm rubbing it until it returns to normal. It faded quickly. The sensation. The experience, was mine forever.

This strange buzzing, focused into a single point on my head feels like that. What is it?

The tingling starts to move from the top of my head, through the inside of my skull, vibrating my brain, my eyes, sinuses, parts I've never considered noticing. It slides down toward my neck! My breathing stops as I hold the air in my lungs. What is this? It feels like a perfect line. If someone took an x-ray laser that was a single line and ran my body through it, this is what it would feel like. The unexplainable buzz runs through my head, I can feel it like a perfect line from my forehead, all through my head, to the back of my skull. Even my teeth buzz with the sensation!

Frozen. All I can do is feel it moving through me. What is this? Eric. Is Eric doing this? How is that possible? What would that mean?

The buzz runs into my chest, expands and moves perfectly through each arm at the same time it moves through my chest as if it were a perfect line. It runs all the way down to my feet. I'm stuck, still, in total wonder. Then it starts running back up!

Caught in amazement I stare at the floor. Can't move, or blink. The sensation is so strong I sit and feel it. Eric says nothing. The whole store is frozen in time and silence.

The buzzing travels back up my whole body. I've never even thought I could feel, physically feel, my organs but it makes everything tingle and shake with a fizzing sensation. My stomach, my ribs, parts of me I don't even know what they are but I feel it slide through them!

It reaches the top of my head and stops, then fades.

Eric suddenly comes back to life, shifting in his chair which makes it creak. He breaks the silence. "Okay. We can meet again and I'll see where you go. You need to pursue it though. If you want to learn, you must tell me it's something you want."

Stuck. Wondering. How? What? Unconsciously I nod my head. I passed the test. Whole body feels strange. Altered.

"When do you want to get together next?" Eric asks me, his voice echoing slightly, as if it comes from a different place inside him.

Next. Get together. The universe is so vast... I never thought about it. What is this? What is going on? Oh wait! I suddenly remember life outside of the store. "Ahh, actually I, have a friend coming tomorrow.

She'll be here for two weeks. I'm kinda going to be entertaining so I won't be able to do anything until after that."

"Too bad. Bad timing. But I think you'll do well. You're a sharp guy. You're thinking is quick, pretty intelligent. You should be careful though, this knowledge can be very, very addicting."

I grin and nod my head. My mind spaces out saying thank you. It hardly seems to matter whether I'm smart or not.

"What do you do for work?" Eric asks in a change of direction.

Briefly I explain my fascinating career watching movies on repeat all night long and my other hope to do more creative work later on in the movie industry.

Eric gets a puzzled look on his face. "Really? Well, have you ever thought about working in computers?"

I'm wrenched out of my mental space and stick out my tongue. "No way! Are you kidding? That would be slow death. Nothing I'm interested in at all." My total distaste for office work in general makes my skin crawl. Working with computers is right up there with accounting. The death of the soul. So much structure, restriction, cutting off your life. If I ever end up stuck behind some desk crunching numbers and working with computers someone better shoot me. Every ounce of me fears such a pointless and lifeless task. There's no creativity. No chance to think or express yourself. Death is more fitting.

Eric starts to strain his voice, "Ehhh, I don't know. You might want to rethink that. If you ask me, I actually see you working in something computer related within the next 2 years. The way your mind works I think you'd catch on quickly and do quite well."

Forcibly shaking my head I protest passionately. "Death would be more fitting! That's how I imagine Hell... seriously. God, that's not even funny. I need to write, to be expressive and creative... ugh! It's hard to even think about doing work like that. Like a slow strangling demise. I'd never do anything like that. No interest at all."

Eric shrugs his shoulders and shoots me a knowing grin. "Okay, if you say so. Don't listen to me. I'm just the guy who used to make his living by telling the future."

I scoff. I could never do anything like that. He couldn't be more wrong. No wonder he opened a bookstore if that's how good he was. The back door beeps as someone walks in.

Eric turns his head slightly. "Justin's here to take you home."

Eric stands up and stretches. Feels like it should be morning. Been here all night. How did Justin know to come? Weird perfect timing. Everything feels in a daze.

"Something you should know, I did a deep level scan on you and I picked up on something possibly wrong. It's right about here..." Eric moves his hand over the right side of his stomach area. Just above his waist but below his ribs. "It could be with your intestines or something like that. Have you ever had any physical problems like that?"

Deep scan? What does he mean? Looking at where his hand is moving I think if I've ever had any problems or felt pain near there. Nothing comes to mind.

"I don't think so. Never felt any pain anyway." I say a little confused.

Eric shrugs. "Well, I wouldn't worry. Might want to just keep an eye out."

Slowly nodding I'm barely listening. The rest of me is drifting off somewhere else. Wandering the solar system.

"Well, do you want to see an aura before you go?"
A record skips and scratches to a halt inside my brain. Shaking my head I try to readjust and come back to reality. Did he just say what I think he said?

Well now, here's your chance. The clear voice tells me with a tone that seems to expect a reaction.

No, it doesn't have the same effect. Feels like a different person who would have laughed at that. It should be funny but...

But what?

I don't know what to expect now. "What do you mean?" I ask cautious and unsure. Is he making fun of me for making fun of him? I never said anything to him about making fun of his psychic, Miss Cleo, aura, Tarot, crystal ball reading ways.

"An aura. It's like your energy body spilling off of your physical body. You can actually see it. Most people think they're small, like five feet off your body but it actually extends about 32 feet away. Though most people can't see that much. Have you ever seen one?"

Absently I shake my head no. Seen one? Shouldn't he ask me if I think they even exist? Justin and Peggy are waiting in the hallway. They remain silent.

Eric leads me behind the curtain into the office. Justin and Peggy follow us in. Eric has me stand about five feet away from him. Justin and Peggy move to stand on my left against a counter. What do they think is going to happen?

Eric puts himself against a bare white wall, facing me. A tall black lamp is to his right. A big stationary printer is on his left. His figure is suddenly very large, filling up what little space exists among the office equipment.

"Now, most people tell you that an aura is this big glow around a person and has all these colors and each color means something but... forget all that. Most people don't know shit, okay? It's all fluffed up and they don't know what they're talking about."

My view of him begins to twist again and I start to feel disoriented. He began as the wacky Tujunga psychic, morphed into a spiritual philosophizer on the nature of the whole freaking universe, and now he's changing into this rough, blunt, realist aura-seeing psychic.

It seems contradictory to say auras are real, which is ludicrous, and then tell me most people who talk about them don't know anything about something that doesn't exist.

The, now psychic, Eric continues explaining how auras work. "When you first see an aura, really see it, it will be this soft white haze about two or three inches around the body, okay? Barely noticeable. Not to say you can't see color, you can, but it takes practice. And don't think any one color means something absolutely. There's no universal law that says one color means this and another means that. More crap."

I chuckle, more out of nervous uncertainty than it being funny. He's so serious about it.

"It's all in the frequency, how it relates to you and how it makes you feel. You might see green and you feel like green is sickness so that's what your brain fills in for you. Your brain puts green in because you relate green to sick."

Half of me is listening, half is completely baffled by what's going on. A few hours ago, I'd be laughing at this. Now, I don't know what the hell is going on but it's not funny.

"So, when you first see it, you'll look for a colorless or white glow. Like a haze. You ever walk out to the sidewalk in the summertime and you see those heat waves coming off the cement?" He moves his hand in a wavy motion a few inches over his shoulder to demonstrate.

Silently I nod my head yes.

"Good. It might look a little like that. Now, what you're going to do is, stand about five feet away, where you are now, and focus your attention right on my nose. Right here."
He points straight at his nose.

"And with your peripheral vision, by peripheral I mean, you know how you can look at something but out of the corner of your eye see something else?"

My head nods on its own. Finally I get the psychic trick I was looking forward to. For some reason I have no need to laugh or snicker. Everything else he's said makes so much sense. My mind is absorbing so much. So much to think about. Is this going to be the same?

"Like you can look at me, but out of the corner of your eye you can see Justin and Peggy. So, you can look right at my nose but with your peripheral vision you can observe my head and shoulders, right?" Eric turns his head sideways and holds his hand out toward me to demonstrate looking one direction but seeing something else out of the corner of his eye.

Trying to stare right at his nose I can also see his head and shoulders, the lamp, the printer. My vision blurs as I go cross-eyed. Squinting I rub my eyes. "Yeah." I confirm.

"Okay, what you're going to do is look at my nose until you see the thin haze or glow around my head and shoulders. Don't try to look at my whole body. Just the head and shoulders should be enough. Remember, it won't be big, about two or three inches. Tell me when you see it. And relax your vision, don't strain and make yourself cross-eyed."

Nodding my head I smile a little. He must have seen my eyes go different directions. Relaxing my vision I stare at his nose. My eyes wander to his tinted glasses that look darker when he stands next to the lamp. Pulling my attention back to his nose I slowly try and pay attention to his head and shoulder area while looking at his nose. Slowly it emerges, a barely visible hazy glow around his head and part of his right shoulder. Only, it looks like double vision. If I stare at the light of the lamp and then look away I see a double image of the lamp. Like looking into a bright light and then looking at a wall. The light is burned momentarily into your eyes and then fades. He's so close to the lamp, it could easily be his body forming a double-image from the light. I squint and look again. The hazy glow is gone. After a few seconds of staring it comes back.

Hrmm. He can say that's an aura all he wants. There's no way. It's a double image. Frowning I clear my throat.

"Well?" he asks.

"Yeah, I mean, I see something." I say dismissively.

"Is it about two or three inches off my head and shoulders?" Eric wonders.

Still looking I capture the fuzzy outline again and then turn my head to see if his image projects on the wall. It doesn't really carry over, but I have doubts anyway. He's about a foot and a half from the lamp. It's a long floor lamp that stands about as high as he is. The light is shooting above his head and not on to him directly but it's close enough it could be making him bright enough to have the effect.

"Yeah it is... but I mean... it could be like a sun spot.. or a double image from the light. I can't tell really." I inform him.

Rather than being offended at my skepticism he nods his head. "That's fine. That's good. You need to question. Question everything and don't jump to conclusions. You might be right. It could be a double image like you say."

I'd gotten defensive waiting for him to come back with some other argument. I didn't expect him to say I might be right.

"I'm very different than other spiritual teachers. I embrace science and I always tell my students. Always, always, always when you find something you don't understand think of three possibilities of what it might be. Never take my word for it or anyone else's. I don't like mindless drones. Always question. Right or wrong Justin?"

Justin's been standing quietly against the counter but quickly stands up straight and speaks up. "Right actually. He always tells us to question things and think of other possibilities."

"See, if it's for real it will stand up to scrutiny. Only fake illusions and magic tricks or people who are full of it are worried about people questioning them. So, let's run with your idea. If it's like you say, a double image, then it shouldn't really ever change right? I mean, if you look at a bright light and then look away the shape and size of that light is imprinted on your eye, right? And it slowly fades but that's about it."

Nodding my head I mumble out that he's right.

"Okay, so here's what we're going to do. You're going to look at it again and I'm going to make it change and you tell me if you see it. Okay? The brain's a funny thing though and I think it's really important for people to be able to see stuff like this. You see, I always got a kick out of, you know, religions saying that we were kicked out of Eden for doing something bad. Like we had paradise and then were exiled. Instead, I say, Heaven is not a place we were kicked out of. It is all around us. Heaven was simply removed from our sight."

As he says sight he waves his hand in front of his face, making a motion that some kind of layer was placed over our eyes and we lost the ability to see Heaven, which is all around us. It makes my body tingle and goose bumps stand up all over my skin.

"Now, before you look again, do this. Are you right handed or left handed?" He asks.

"Right." What does that have to do with anything?

"Okay, so take your left hand. Hold it out flat in front of you and then wave it in front of your eyes and say, 'See now with my true eyes', and then place them by your side."

Shifting uncomfortably, I feel foolish. It sounds like something I used to do when I was young and playing around with Wicca and magical rituals. Still, I do as he asks. Waving my left hand in front of my eyes I repeat what he said. Nothing feels any different. Hope that wasn't the big effect he was going for. It's all the same.

"Now, focus in like you did before and tell me when you see whatever it is you think you saw." He tells me, his voice lowering to a softer tone.

Sighing I focus my eyes in again. This could turn out bad. He's having me wave my hands around saying things like a magick ritual. What does he think is going to happen? It's going to be like before and I'm going to have to just tell him that.

My eyes start to make out the thin, clear outline around his head and shoulders. Double vision, caused by the light. I sigh in my head. Going to suck having to say it in front of Justin and Peggy who are silently watching this whole ordeal.

Trying to hide increasing irritation at being put on the spot and having to, once again, be forced to sound like a jerk I mumble out that I can see the outline.

"Okay. Tell me if it changes." Eric speaks softly, quietly. He lowers his eyes and at once seems incredibly peaceful. Serene. He takes a deep breath in.

Yeah, right. "Oka-" I start to drone out.

Eric breaths out. Everything slows down. His breathe leaves his lungs. Exhale, echoes through my ears.

WHAM! Brilliant, shining, golden light, flares out all around his head and shoulders like a sudden giant solar burst! It appears in such a flash a ripple of unexplainable energy, like a shockwave, slams through the room!

My body rocks backwards and I catch myself on my heel, regaining my footing. My breath catches. Somewhere in my mind, I feel my chest heave. The rest of my body... somewhere else. The reality I knew... so certain of... nowhere to be found.

The light is at least four feet in a perfect, brilliant, shining globe. It's fantastic in its radiance! It's unlike anything I've ever seen! The light is strange, metallic like chrome in the sun but golden! Brighter than looking directly at the light bulb inside the lamp. It floods over the lamp's beam of light. Unlike a lamp's light that slowly disperses it is contained, perfectly. It's not even coming from Eric's head. Almost like it's self-luminescent! Like it's always been there flickering and glowing only I never saw it. There's no noticeable source. It's contained so perfectly I could trace the edge with a pen about four feet all around his head and shoulders.

Nobody has moved. Justin and Peggy are still standing by the counter. No natural or artificial light could ever make so perfect an illumination. It doesn't shine on the rest of his body, or the printer, or the ceiling above. But it shines with incredible light! Only it's self contained. The color is golden, but clear, with a richness I've never seen. Not yellow like a sunbeam, or gold like jewelry. Never in my life have I witnessed a color to match.

Dazed I close my eyes and shake my head. Brief hallucination. Play of my eyes. Opening them back up it's still there. Eric, head bowed, eyes slightly closed, hands folded in front. No physical source to explain it.

Riveted I can't move. Can't speak. Slightly aware of my mouth hanging open I don't care to shut it.

"Well." Eric whispers solemnly. "Do you notice it's changed?"

What does he expect me to say? Nodding my head I signal yes. He can't see me nod my head. Speak. There are no words.

Say yes.

"Yes." I stumble out in total shock.

Immediately it vanishes. I could have blinked and missed only my eyes were pulled wide open in mystified awe. Eric raises his head and looks into my eyes. Smiling he nods his head as if he were acknowledging me for the first time.

Dumbfounded I nod my head. No words come out of my mouth. I don't tell him what I saw. I don't say I saw anything at all. Standing there, silent, no reaction. If my face shows any sign of what I've seen he gives no indication. He could have been showing me how to tie my shoe, for all he knows. But... it wasn't his shoe... he showed me...

How? What? Did I really see what I saw?

"Okay then." He says quietly. "Well, it's late, I know you guys have a drive back. Justin, I'll talk to you later. Bye Peggy." He comes up and shakes my hand. "Eric, nice to meet you."

Looking at him I simply nod and smile slightly. My whole brain is locked up. I'm in total shock.

"I'll see you soon then." He calls from the office as I wander, like a zombie, following Peggy and Justin to the car.

None of us speak a single word. I crawl into the back seat and we drive to LA.

Halfway back Justin breaks the silence. "Did you have a good time Eric? Was it interesting?"

My head rests against the cool glass window. Wind blowing my hair. Street lights flicker in a rhythm as we pass. Light, space, dark, light, space dark. I'm vaguely aware of Justin's question. Spinning through my head, vast universe, galaxies, infinite time, so hard to grasp. Justin said I'd be meeting a psychic. I don't know what that was, but one things for sure, it wasn't just some psychic.

He asked a question. It could have been a second ago, maybe he's been sitting for ten minutes waiting for an answer.

"Yeah." I say raising my voice to carry over the wind. Then softer, "It was interesting." How else can I describe it? I don't even know what it was.

The reality you live in is a fortressed box of your own design. Whether you are aware of it or not makes no difference. It is still there.

Your brain will viscously defend these fortress walls to the bitter end. Filtering experiences and only granting entrance to what you have programmed 'your box' to allow. Should something slip through, past this guarded gate, it will not be hailed as an amazing wonder, but an invader to be repelled.

Now you know why, should the day come you see something right before your eyes, far beyond what you believe possible, you will react in a totally unexpected manner.

I locked up. Frozen by the sight of a thing that did not exist in my world. Internally, I fought to block it out, repel in from my mind.

Perhaps you think you would have done otherwise. Screamed, shouted out, gasped in surprise. 'Wow!' or 'That's incredible!'

Such a reaction would only happen if you allowed for the possibility. I did not.

There was a time I thought that seeing is believing. If only I could see something. Proof that reality isn't what it seems, that God is real, that miraculous things truly can happen. If it happened, right before my eyes, why then I'd believe!

Let me trouble you with the sobering reality. By the time I woke up the next morning I never gave the incredible light I saw, right before my eyes, another thought. Gone. Evaporated from my mind like ethereal mist in the night. The intruding experience, banished from the castle of my thoughts.

I have seen things in the clear light of day, right before my eyes, that even movies would have a hard time making up. Am I being clear? I have witnessed the change of everything that you might consider solid reality. Literally, no ambiguity. I mean precisely what I say. No drugs, no hallucinations, no vagueness. No room for a single shred of doubt.

We are not living in the same reality. The life I have is full of more wonder than I ever imagined, dreamed or hoped could be possible.

Most of what I have seen I was not alone. On one of these occasions, 15 minutes after it happened, the others with me were right on their way to forgetting about it. Eroded from their minds. They will never completely forget but the full weight of it, like morning fog wisps away. The moment is elusive as the thing that wove it.

Memories are fragile things. The world will take from you that which is not supposed to be. Do not hold to the conviction that seeing will make you believe. And don't be too baffled by my reaction.

There was nothing to prepare me for what Eric showed me. I didn't believe in auras. I didn't believe in psychics or enlightenment or any of that. It's not that I didn't believe as much as I didn't understand what they were.

Without the proper knowledge, to conceive what I saw, to have a place for it in reality there was nowhere for it to fit. It didn't belong in my reality so my brain blocked it out. This is why knowledge is essential. Understanding is the greatest tool you have. What good are all the techniques to experience, see auras or anything if you don't have the basic founding principals of what they are or why they are?

I don't believe it was Eric's intention to have me understand what I saw. He wasn't expecting me to shout out or suddenly be won over. It was a wrench in the system. He gave me exactly what I needed. A seed of doubt. Something I couldn't explain. A small, little thing to loosen the structure of the very tight-knit reality I'd constructed.

Even when my brain blocked it out and I went into some strange state of shock at having seen something I didn't believe was possible, somewhere deep down, it was still there.

Given that I went into shock over seeing his aura change it also shouldn't surprise you how I reacted to him 'scanning' me. When we were sitting on the couch I felt the strange, electrical tingling move through my whole body. It was very noticeable and physical. There was nothing soft and subtle about it. I even remember wondering if he was doing it but I had nothing else to go on.

Afterwards he even said to me, point blank, I did a deep scan on you. He understood what that meant but I had no grasp of the concept so why would I react to the word? I wouldn't and I didn't. But months later, when I started to, I would remember. Then, with a greater understanding of what and why, it would be more clear.

Eric Pepin doesn't work in the same time line. His future sight is somehow woven into his waking mind. Proof of this would come three months later when I was hired by an internet web company, out of the blue with no involvement on his part. Two months after being hired I started learning programming. As he predicted, I was good at it. As for what I believed about it, well, I wasn't completely wrong.

These are the breadcrumbs he left for me. This is why you should forgive what you are about to read. That this poor 24 year-old me, would have such an opportunity dropped in his lap and then forget it all. Like it was something he did every single day.

If you ever find yourself there, whether by chance or persistence, heed my warning. Delight in the uncertain, embrace the unknown, seize your moment. Hold fast! You may only get to see for a second and then the flickering light is gone. As elusive as the thing that wove it.

we rarely see the approach of the things that impact us most.
so profound a change they bring, their entrance made with
quiet grace, borne upon...

The Softest Steps

chapter five

Two weeks fly by. My strange meeting with Eric slips away as if it never happened. Justin comes over but he never speaks of it.

Even my moody restlessness eases. It's replaced by a different kind of restlessness. A craving for something different. Anything. New. Change.

What to do. What to do?

Having my friend Rene visiting from Kansas helps. We met when we both worked at the Kansas City Renaissance Festival. She's an incredible artist with a quiet, giving nature. Rene has long, wavy red hair with porcelain skin that's the perfect contrast to L.A. and just what I need.

Sitting around the apartment I begin complaining about a need to change. It's been bugging me and I need to vent. Rene's open to 'helping' me and eventually we decide on just the thing. I chop my hair short so it's spiky and sticks out all over the place and then we bleach it bright blonde.

Mission complete! I changed. And I look really weird. After a few days I'm dissatisfied again. Even though I look different I don't feel different. Stupid shallow, exterior, a surface change.

Rene and I spend the rest of her visit touring L.A. and scribbling in coffee shops. Occasionally she looks at my hair and giggles impishly. We don't speak of it or try to change anything else.

Finally the day comes for her to leave. She's safely flying home and all is right with the world. It's Monday and nobody's home. I'm moody. What else can I do except enjoy the space and lounge out? The phone rings. Oh right. I can answer the phone. The device is almost completely useless. I never use it. It's never for me.

May as well get it then. The clear voice suggests.

Why the hell should I get it?

It's never for you so then all you need to do is take a message.

Great, now that I've reminded myself it's never for me I may as well take a message. It keeps ringing. The sound is grating. Irritation crawls through my body. "All right, all right," I groan out loud. I sigh and reach over to pick it so the ringing will stop.

"Hello?" I drone.

"Yes, is this Eric?" a man on the other end asks.

My body freezes. Caught! I'm on the phone with nowhere to run. Like one of those traps made from rope where you step in the loop and it flings you into the air. The phone line has me! I can't place the voice. Who is it? I search my memory to try and make it fit. Should I lie? It doesn't sound like a bill collector. The people for my school loans have been hounding me about my payments being overdue. Maybe them?

No. They always sound like they're reading from a script.

You're right. I think we've got a live one here.

"Um, yes." I say not sure what else to do.

"Hi Eric, this is Eric. Remember me?" He asks casually, as if we spoke every day.

Really caught, caught! My heart skips faster, anxiety crawls up my throat. What does he want? Why is he calling me?! Panic starts to set in. There is nothing I can do! He has me on the phone.

If he's calling me he wants something!! People only call when they want something!! What does he want? Whaaat?? The frantic voice cries out in desperation.

"Yeah, sure, I remember you. Justin's roommate." I say trying to act casual and calm myself down.

"Well, I hadn't heard from you in awhile. I thought we were going to get together again."

God! That was over two weeks ago and he still remembers! I can't believe he didn't let it go. My mind flashes back to two weeks earlier. Crap, crap, crap. Yes, I said we'd get together again. I said I wanted to. Why did I say that?

I didn't think he'd follow through did I? Is he following through? He owns his own store, why mess with me?

"Umm, yeah, I've, uhh, been with a friend, out of town. I mean I had a friend in town, from out of town, for a few weeks." I admit scrambling for a way to escape.

"Oh right. You told me that." Eric says.

That's right. His memory is horrible. Should I tell him she is still in town?

Justin will tell him the truth.

Crap! We have an inside informer. There's no way –

He interrupts my thoughts, "Well, do you want to get together?"

There's nothing I can say. Justin could show up any time and tell him the truth.

"Yeah, sure..." I say drawing out my words for time to think of a way out.

"When?" he immediately asks.

"Umm, well..." I stall.

"How about today?" He asks directly.

Today? Yes, today, I'm going to work. No, I have to take my friend to the airport. No there's Justin. I have a meeting, or, no! Matthew has the car today. Yes, the truth will work just fine.

"Um, actually, my brother has the car today, so –" He cuts me off.

"That's okay. Justin will come down and bring you up. Can you be ready in an hour?" He asks nonchalantly.

My heart sinks. I'm stuck. There's no way out of it. No lounging today. Going to have to go through with it.

"Yeah, I can be ready." I mumble out, trying to sound polite and cheerful.

"Great, I'll see you then." Eric confirms.

I slide down into the couch. Never answer the phone. Never answer the phone. Never answer the phone –

I don't know why you answered it. You screen everything else. Your own fault. Idiot. The grating voice chastises..

Yeah. Why did I answer it? I'm a professional call screener. That is really weird.

Forty-nine minutes later someone rings the buzzer at the apartment entrance. "Like clockwork." I mumble as I roll off the couch. "Lounge time over."

Justin drives me up to the bookstore. We don't speak. I'm brooding and he probably feels like a taxi service.

Inside the store two customers browse. Sunlight pours in through the windows revealing all the places that were shrouded in darkness when I first visited. Like the cash register. It seems less like a magical wizard's study and more like an actual business. Justin slides behind the curtain to get Eric. I hover over a large glass display case. The case is filled with crystals of every color and shape. Some are huge. They sparkle and dance in the bright sunlight. Wonder what these things go for? I glance at a few price tags. Oh, six hundred and ninety-nine dollars. Okay then. Crystals are, apparently, very valuable.

I slide away from the case and start looking at all the books. One catches my eye. Here we go, a book on reincarnation. It has a picture of a bug, metamorphosing into a fox and then into a man. Come on people, are you actually proposing we come from bugs? It's hard enough to believe in any kind of reincarnation. Reincarnating from bugs? Absurd. I can't help but smirk. Reincarnation is all about thinking you were someone great from the past. Everyone is Napoleon, or Cleopatra, or Marco Polo.

Eric pushes aside one of the curtains hiding the back office. "Hello again," he says extending his hand.

Here we go with the hand shaking thing again. Awkwardly, we shake hands and I smile a hello.

"Well, what do you think? It's easier to see everything during the day." He waves his hand around the store. I oblige by following his hand to look around at all the various books. They cover every topic you'd expect in a metaphysical bookstore. It's a small store but packed with books. I examine him again. He has large curious eyes with glasses. He's also a bit large. It's hard to tell if it's stockiness or not. He reminded me of an off-season football player before, but maybe he sits around a lot.

"I think you've read a lot." I say honestly.

He huffs and throws his hands up motioning to the towering shelves. "You try to read all these books, see what you get out of it. Go ahead, take your time. Read them all! You'll barely get anything because the people who write these books haven't experienced anything. They don't really know anything. Sounds arrogant, but that's my opinion! And I mean, *know it,* know it. You know what I'm saying?"

I nod my head yes. One thing to read something, play it in your head, and say you know it. It's another to have it, firsthand. He said something before like that. It fits perfectly with my feelings. I like that he feels that way but he might be saying that just to get on my good side and make friends. Maybe he knows I feel that way. Did I tell him that first?

He runs his hands along the shelf I was looking at. "You can reduce this whole bookstore to maybe a handful of good books. Now, I haven't read them all and I don't care to. It might sound funny coming from a guy who owns a bookstore but I almost never read. But rest assured, I can tell you without reading them, most of them are a waste of time. But, you know, be my guest, have a seat on the couch and start reading."

His manner is very matter-of-fact. I struggle to believe him but can't. He has too much time sitting in the store when it's slow. I know what he means. There is a difference between learning something from a book and experiencing it for yourself. But, that's where I'm feeling him out. Is he just a bookworm or does his experience reach beyond books?

He brings me out of my thoughts. "Interested in reincarnation?" He asks noticing I'd turned the book slightly.

"Nah. Just thought it was funny." I snicker.

"Oh? You don't believe in it or you thought that book was funny." His attention suddenly focuses right on me like a laser scope. God, I forgot how intense he was.

I shrug, trying to wave off the feeling that I'm under the microscope. "I don't really believe in it. Seems a bit hokey."

He nods his head and looks around at the other books. The pressure fades. "Yeah, they put a lot of fluff in it. I don't believe in it the way most people think it works. You know, I don't think if you do bad things you will come back, like as a dung beetle, or something like that per se. A lot of religions try to say, well, if you do this or that you'll be punished in your next life and, personally, it's a bunch of crap."

My eyes pop open and I glance at his face. He's laying it out flat. His manner is so open and blunt. He could be telling me why some new brand of car tires suck. It's surprising coming from a guy who *owns* a metaphysical bookstore.

If he notices my contorted, puzzled look he doesn't care. Must see it all the time. Eric keeps drilling ahead. "It's like, if the Universe wants you to learn and grow, why would you go and live as a tree, or a dog? You're not going to remember anything. But I don't think everyone has past lives anyway. So, there you go. I think a lot of what people remember is recorded in DNA."

"DNA huh?" I ask somewhat skeptical. That's the first time I've heard that.

"Well, sure! Like, there's so much information in our genes and DNA, they will be uncovering and decoding everything that's in there for years and years, probably decades! Who knows? The point is that I think your DNA can store information from your parents before they passed on their information or had you per se."

My head tilts forward, I scrunch my face in thought.

Eric touches both of his hands together and searches for an example. It only takes him a second. "Like, say, for instance, that a man was badly burned in a fire. I mean, let's say he almost dies, or something, to make it clear. So he almost dies in a fire, then he and his wife get married and have a kid. Then this kid grows up and is terrified of fire."

Nodding slowly I start to project in my head where I think he's going.

Eric steps away from the bookshelf so he can move his hands. I forgot he talks with his whole body. His voice fills up the entire store, it's not loud but it's so clear they could probably hear him in the parking lot. "The kid doesn't know why, can't explain it, he just has this unreasonable and irrational fear of fire and feels like he's been burned before and maybe has died. Now, he may think well, it's from a past life. I remember dying in a fire. I say, no dummy, it's because your father almost died in a fire and his cells remember what that felt like. So the cells instinctually transmit that information to your body which tries to preserve the whole by making you really afraid. So when the father impregnated the mother his genetic blueprint was frozen and passed on. It won't keep up to date with everything else that happens later in his life. Get it?"

"Yep." I say shortly. My hand finds its way up to my chin and I start rubbing. Hard to prove. Doubt he'll list any facts, but it's logical.

Eric's eyebrows draw together in an exaggerated slant. It's a really strong feature that makes him look angry but I know he's not. "It's passed on to the child at the moment of conception. Now, that would be a bit obvious because it's just one generation. But what if something happened 4 generations earlier? Long enough that nobody remembers that your great, great, great, great grandfather such and such was in this big accident just before his wife became pregnant or something like that. Just like we have dormant genes that might skip a generation or something. Certain memories or characteristics might not get passed to all the children but someone else might end up with that memory."

I rub my chin. Interesting. I've never heard or read anything that backs up what he's saying. He didn't give any proof. It seems really fringe and I doubt anybody would look into it, even if they could. But, I can see some information like that being stored. I like it a lot more than reincarnation. I'd believe his DNA idea way before the idea that someone remembers something as ridiculous as a past life.

"What do you think? Makes sense?" Eric asks after standing silent a few moments.

"Yeah," I nod. "Makes more sense than past lives or whatever."

"Yeah, most people who say they remember a past life..." he shakes his head and makes a face like he doesn't believe a word of it. "They don't. They just want to make a story or imagine something that makes them feel important. You know, that they were somebody when they feel like a nobody in this life. I mean, how many people say they were Cleopatra, or you know, Socrates, Julius Caesar or some amazing historical figure? Why doesn't anyone have a really boring past life? Like, hey, I was some dumb peasant and I had to eat rats and it sucked." He puts his hands up and makes a face like that's the only thing that really makes sense.

I snicker quietly. It's true. Had to be more rat snackers than royalty.

Eric shakes his head. "No, it's always some fabulous person and they did amazing things because they feel shorted in this life. Ninety-nine percent of it is crap and they don't really remember. Or, like I said, it's genetic recall. That's not to say I don't believe in reincarnation or that people can't remember past lives, they can."

"Really?" I interject with a little surprise. How can somebody believe in DNA storing memories on one hand and then on the other say they believe in something as stupid as past lives? It doesn't seem like the two should live together.

He shoots me a look like I've got to be kidding to rule it out completely. "Sure. It's just really, really rare for someone to be able to reach a level where they can remember it. I mean, if you think about everything you'll experience in this life and how it affects you emotionally and all the information, even just compared to where you are now... and then you had to deal with the memories of a whole other life with family and friends and lovers and all the attachments and pain and love... it would be totally overwhelming. You couldn't function. But all these people who say they remember their past lives talk about it as if they have just watched some great thing on TV. It's like give me a break."

"Yeah..." I agree, my voice trailing off in thought. I agree with the give me a break part.

A short kid comes out from behind the curtain and calls to Eric. Eric motions for me to come back behind the curtain into the office. The kid sits down at one of the computers and they begin talking while I look around. Eric introduces us after a second. His name is Justin.

I laugh to myself. Justin and Justin with Eric and Eric. How weird is that? Little Justin is a web prodigy. Only 16 years old but already building web sites and doing all this other web stuff. Eric tells Justin to pull up the website for the school. A black page loads up with dark blue swirls in the background that look like water.

"Auxien?" I ask. The name of the site is Auxien. The bookstore is also called Auxien but the site doesn't look like it's about the bookstore. They both use the same logo design. I recognize it from the sign on the store. It's a red circle with three white shapes swirling to the center. They kind of look like rabbits with all their heads facing the center of the circle and their paws outstretched touching in the middle.

Eric explains that he wants to make a school where people can come and learn what he teaches. He wants lessons and courses and regular lectures. They've been papering Tujunga and LA with fliers but it's slow. Justin clicks around on the site for awhile. There's so much black and red it reminds me of a heavy metal site. Lot's of strange pictures make it all seem very gothic.

Eric tells me I should read it. He asks if I have a computer and the internet. I do. I complain about how slow my computer is and he immediately offers to fix it up. He goes into great detail about how he's been a computer tech and worked on computers for years. I decline. I figure he's being polite and making one of those gestures people never expect you to take them up on.

The other Justin comes and tells Eric there's a customer with questions. Eric apologizes and tells Justin to give me 'The Papers'. He says I should read them and we can talk about them later but things are busier than he thought they'd be.

I shrug and say I'll read them. Justin digs around in a desk drawer until he finds what he's looking for, 'The Papers'. He hands me a thick stack of papers stapled together. The type is small, squished together like it was written on a manual typewriter. Great, some crazy manifesto. What did I agree to read? I smile and hold them flat in my palms like I'm feeling the weight of them.

"Got a little weight here. Must be all the solid black ink." Smiling I snicker to myself. I picture some giant, medieval typewriter dripping with thick, tar-like ink, and some poor soul hunkered down in a dark basement trying to purposely type the papers in such a way that they fit as many words as humanly possible onto a single page. Justin and Justin say nothing. Fine. Funny to me. Frowning I remind myself, nobody appreciates my humor.

How can they when you keep most of it to yourself? Makes you sound like a retard.

Takes too long to say.

Then don't say it.

Whatever.

Justin takes me home and we hang out for the rest of the night not saying much about the papers, Eric Pepin or the store.

I open my eyes and listen to the sounds of... silence? The apartment is quiet for once. I creep into the kitchen for some cereal. People are sprawled all over the living room. Matthew's bed is farthest back against the sliding glass door. Through the dim morning light, I see him sleeping face down, a girl next to him. I don't recognize her. Justin and Peggy are passed out on her single bed pushed against the wall.

Farrah is nearest me, on the futon. Her head is hidden, tucked under a blanket. Farrah moved in soon after Peggy. She was renting a room from an older lady who thought she was too young and loud. Rather than jumping into a place she didn't like we let her move in until she could get her bearings. She was dating our friend Kevin, who came out for acting but gave it up and went back to the Midwest. I've always felt close to Farrah. Once she brought Dunkin' Donuts back from Ohio for me. Flew them right on the plane because L.A. doesn't do real doughnuts. Too fattening for the culture. Ever since then, Farrah can do no wrong.

Never heard them come in last night. Must have been late.

My cereal and I go back to my room. With the door closed I pull up my chair and sit at the desk. I flip open 'The Papers' and begin to read. It's a pack of seven chapters. Everything Eric told me the first time we met swirls back. Yes, we talked about a lot of this. Gaia, the planet, is a living organism. What the soul is and how it's created. Our body is really a machine, an organic robot. The real us is the driver, the thing controlling it. We're energy beings. It also talks about the aura as the Fingerprint of God. It's unique to each of us. It's our energy, a specific energy frequency that can't be duplicated or repeated. Then there's the sleeper. We're sleepers when we haven't connected to our higher consciousness. We haven't awakened to what we fully are and we believe we're just the person living this one life. Eric would consider me a sleeper. Do I believe in awakening? To become enlightened. A dimensional consciousness. Reads more like fantasy than science.

The final chapter is the clincher. It talks about an epic battle between the Force and the Darkside. Those who feel the Force calling are like warriors, who must awaken and serve, if the Darkside is to be overcome. I don't know what to make of it. Is this the treatment for a script? This is Hollywood after all. It's like a comic book. I toss it on my desk and lean back, thinking, wondering. Spinning it back and forth, all the angles, possibilities. I let it soak in, digest. How does Eric Pepin believe the world works? This is it. His primer. What a weird way to look at life, so black and white. After awhile my head feels heavy so I go back to bed.

Laughter. I've been asleep for awhile. Why are they laughing so loud?

Do you really want to know?

Hmm. Good point. No, I don't.

Rolling over I try to go back to sleep. All I hear is the other room coming to life. They keep laughing and carrying on in loud voices. It grows louder and louder. I stare at my wall. Pay attention to your breath going in and out. I try to think about breathing.

"Woop woop!" someone calls out from the living room.

I sigh. "They're never going to shut up now." Once they get into it they call out like that and then they start talking about sex. That's the end. The point of no return.

"Everyone in this apartment is totally and completely sexually repressed." I say out loud.

God, why did you say that out loud? What if someone heard you saying that?? The grating voice wails in a rising panic.

Well, it's true! All the time, with any excuse, everything has some sexual innuendo. They'll get all riled up and nobody will go back to sleep. Groaning, I roll off my bed and sift through an enormous pile of clothes bulging out of my closet. I smell a few shirts before finding one that seems mostly clean. Walking to the kitchen, I smell pot.

"What are you guys doing?" I ask in a sleepy, grumpy tone.
"You know The Hostel man. The party never stops." Justin says somewhat sarcastically.

Justin doesn't really party. Even sarcastically I don't know why he encourages it.

"You know it." Matthew chimes in. I look over and see the source of the pot smell. Matthew is smoking pot. Again. A lot earlier than usual. What time is it? Eleven something.

You should say something. The clear voice suggests calmly.

Argh! No no no. What am I thinking? Wake up before you think about doing stuff like that. Don't do it. You go there once and that's it. He needs to figure this crap out on his own. You're his older brother not his parent.

He's never going to quit on his own.

You don't know that. If you weren't here what would he do? Stopping, I stare at the dirty dishes scatted along the counter and think about what he might do. Make his own decisions I guess. Exactly. If he's going to grow up he's got to make his own decisions. If you start being the parent you'll only prolong it. Taking a deep breath, I sigh to myself. Always the same struggle with Matthew. When do I step in? How much of an influence should I be?

His pot smoking goes in waves. Sometimes he barely does it at all. Other times, well, lately it's been those other times. I sit and watch him smoke pot and that's it, his day is gone. Total waste. It hurts. Why does he do it? God, why does anybody do it? He has everything going for him. He got all the good genes. He looks better. His body adapts better, if he ever exercised. He got all the good parts of our parents. He's outgoing, everyone loves him.

He's walking such a fine line. How can he not see it? We've seen so many people get sucked in. Play with fire, you get burned. He should've learned from them. I sigh again. What a way to start the day. I'd go run but we live in a crappy neighborhood. Who knows what people around here would do to a jogger. People don't run here.

Everyone has an excuse, huh? The grating voice mutters snidely.

Shut up. Not running is way different than smoking pot. It's not doing something positive versus doing something negative.

Whatever makes you feel better. Lazy is lazy.

Grating my teeth I slam the cabinet harder than I mean to. It's empty, no clean bowls in sight. Whatever! Such crap. I feel so helpless. Damned if I do. Damned if I don't. Keep him safe. That's the best I can do. The rest is up to him.

"Yeah, time to party! Woot, woop!" The girl sleeping next to Matthew rolls over from behind him. It's Suzie. Her voice grated out like she'd prefer to sleep for eight more hours. Suzie has her jeans still on and looks like she hasn't slept in a day or two. I like Suzie. Good hearted girl from Iowa. She has long, wheat-colored hair and sparkling blue eyes. Matthew and her flirt to no end but it never goes anywhere. I know Matthew wants more but he'll never act and I don't see Suzie making the first move. Well, she might. She's much manlier than Matthew. I snicker to myself. She'd be the one wearing the pants.

"You.. guys... need to shut up!" Farrah moans from under her covers. She pushes her head to the surface and peeks at me standing at the corner of the kitchen counter. I smile down at her and go sit by her head. I'm too irritated to eat cereal.

The rest of them grate on my nerves at times but Farrah works for me. She's closer to my age so I tell myself that's why it works. I'm attracted to her but it's too strange because we met her through Kevin. He left her as part of the group but even if he never comes back I can't do anything with her. It would feel weird. Still, it works.

She has naturally olive-tan skin with full, dark brown hair and big brown eyes. Blinking trying to clear the fog from her head she looks up. "So have you heard?" She croaks at me.

"Heard what?" I ask dumbly.

"You haven't heard what they're going to buy now?"

Matthew overhears her and cuts her off, "Aw, hey now. Come on, don't be all like that."

Matthew and Farrah start to jibe back and forth. You can't ever argue with Matthew because he never bothers to actually get mad. Farrah on the other hand, short fuse. She gets mad.

I roll my eyes. They could banter for the next twenty minutes. "What is it Farrah?" I cut in.

"They are, well, Peggy and Matthew, are going to get a brick of pot."
She spills out.

I blink, somewhat startled. "Whaaaat? Seriously? Are you kidding?"

"Uh-ohhh, The Hostel police gonna break up your party." Justin says
trying to play it down.

I stare at Matthew. What is he thinking? I point to his failed eighty-
dollar growing project in the closet. "Eighty dollars! Eighty dollars is
a lot of money." Some stupid hydroponics system. He grew a plant
about three inches and then it fried. I had hoped by buying it and
having it go nowhere he'd see what a waste it is. We can barely swing
rent but he's got a hundred bucks for pot. Stoners make no sense! No
go. It's still sitting in the closet and he's about to throw more money
away.

Matthew and Peggy begin trying to convince me how it makes sense.
Peggy has a friend who got a big score. If they buy it in bulk they'll
actually save money than if they buy it a little at a time. They're going
to smoke it anyway so why not buy it all at once? It's not like they're
going to smoke more just because they have more.

Oh, of course not.

They definitely aren't going to sell it they assure me. All I can do is
shake my head.

You can't live someone else's life.

I know. He's gotta do it alone. What can I do? I know he's being
stupid. I know it's a waste. I'd like to think it's a phase. He's young
and going through a phase like all young people do. Only problem is
he's trying to do something most people don't do. He needs every
advantage he can get. He could wake up from his phase and find he's
not young anymore. Most people would be fine with that but he
should demand more. People like to dream big dreams. But at the
end of the day, it's hard. Smoking pot is so much easier.

Be a better example. Don't judge, just show.

You know, that's easier to say than to do. People make me sick. We come from the same background. Grew up together. I don't understand him. But whatever. I know if I judge him he'll blame me. All I can do is try to be a better example. Still, I can't resist throwing a barb! "Do whatever you're gonna do. All I have to say is... Cousin Tom!"

Matthew groans out loud. "Whatever! Why you gotta say that? It's nothing like that, okay? I am nothing like that. You can't even-" he blows it off but I smile to myself. I know I got to him.

"Cousin Tom, Matt!" I say again as I walk to my room.

"What?! You're going to let them buy it? That's all you're going to say?!" Farrah calls out after me.

She doesn't understand that with 'Cousin Tom' we just had an entire conversation. Our Cousin Tom came to live with our family and to finish high school. He'd take frequent walks to go smoke pot away from the house. You'd hear him at all hours of the day and night hacking his lungs out. It was disturbing. Someone under 20 with the health of a 70 year old. His memory wasn't too far behind. He worshiped pot. It was his life. He even made a comic book about it. He struck me as the perfect anti-drug commercial. Don't let this happen to you. Somehow, Matthew didn't seem to get that. But it's a great thing about family, with two words we can have an entire conversation.

I'm not his parent. If he has to learn by being stupid, nothing I can do about it. Closing my door I sit on my bed. It's hard enough getting through my life. What, am I supposed to figure out his too? Flopping on my mattress I don't want to be awake. I decide to go to sleep.

I wake up a few times during the day and into the night. Never leaving my room I block out my hunger and don't eat. Nobody bothers me. Waking up I look at my window. Morning. I slept through yesterday. Looking around I find the apartment empty.

Everyone must've gone to work on a movie set. They always get up at the crack of dawn for that stuff.

I'm not awake long before the phone rings. It's Eric. He asks if I've read the papers he gave me. I tell him that I have. I don't tell him if I liked them or not. He suggests we go get coffee. He can pick me up if I don't have a car. I shrug even though he can't see it. Coffee works.

I sit in my window and enjoy the silence of the apartment. Losing track of time some hours later I hear a knock on the door. It's Eric. Huh, must've gotten in without being buzzed.

He walks in looking around the apartment. "So, this is Justin's second home. I see the appeal. Kind of a hangout place."

He wanders into the living room and looks around at all the beds. He nods his head slightly as his eyes look around unsure of what he's seeing. "Well, it's got kind of a funky energy." He throws both hands up like he's saying wait a second, "Not that I'm knocking it or being mean but, yeah, a little rundown and... uh... funky feeling." He looks doubtful as if something's going to jump out from the stacks of dishes or blankets. He must want to say more but he's being polite.

Of all the things he could say, he mentions energy? I can't tell if he's serious or not. You only hear people talk about 'feeling energy' in movies and only when they're shaking crystals and waving incense. "Uh, yeah, well, I gotta take a shower real quick." I motion behind me to the bathroom and my towel hanging on the door.

"I see. Had to wait until I got here to take a shower huh? Guess you thought I'd find that entertaining?" He tells me flatly.

"Uh... yeah." I blurt out, embarrassed because he sounds annoyed. Time snuck past me somehow. I'd be ticked if I drove down and the person wasn't even showered. Didn't mean to do it. Makes me feel like a jerk. He's probably mad. Well, he didn't actually say when he was showing up. I stop walking to the shower. Wait, did he mean that? Did he think I did it on purpose? I don't get him at all. Oh God, it's his tone. It was a joke. He meant it to be funny. Crap. His tone doesn't carry sarcasm like other people. Most people learn sarcasm through TV shows like Friends, Seinfeld or the Simpson's. Their voice always has a specific sound so you know they're kidding. His doesn't have that. I feel a sudden need to explain myself.

Spinning on my heels, I walk back out of the bathroom. He's sitting on Peggy's bed that's also a couch.

"Um, I'm sorry, I'm still trying to get your sense of humor. That didn't really make sense to me, what you said before. It's like I can't tell when you're kidding and when you're not. But look, I just spaced on the time and didn't mean to have you sit here on purpose."

He holds up his hand and nods his head. "Don't worry about it. Not a problem. I figured you'd catch on but you're a bit slow, ya' know? I got here early anyway so just do what you have to do."

I nod my head and turn back around. Did he just say I was slow? Why did he say that? Did I miss something? How weird is it that I told him that anyway? Who tells people things like that? I should've just realized it was a joke and kept going. Not like I needed to explain anything.

I argue with myself in the shower. Finally I make myself stop thinking about it. For some reason, it still bothers me. Should I have said something or not? Why did I say anything?

You're a freak. Do you need any more proof ? The grating voice jabs.

After I shower and dress I come back into the living room. Eric is standing, looking at a picture on the wall. It's Matthew and his ex-girlfriend Michelle. They're standing on top of a mountain only Matthew has long, wavy brown hair that falls to his shoulders and looks a bit more rugged. Even though he's on the top of a mountain he's wearing the sandals he always wears. He's got a thick, scruffy beard but you can make out his strong face. There's a reason he's trying to be an actor. Both my brothers got better genes.

"Who's this? Is this your brother?" he asks.

"Yep. That's him and his ex-girlfriend Michelle."

"He looks kinda like one of those 60's people, you know?" Eric struggles to find the word.

I laugh. I know exactly what he means. "Yeah, you mean a hippie."

"Yeah, exactly." He looks at a picture below it resting on the top of the TV. "Who are these guys?"

I look at it. It's all of our friends from Missouri. It's one of the only pictures with almost everyone in our core circle in it. We'd gone to Kansas City for New Year's Eve to visit our older brother and his wife and son. We took the picture in the downtown plaza. Other than Matthew and I there are seven other guys. "That's all of our friends from home."

"Home in... where is it? Montana or.." Eric draws his words out for me to fill in the blank.

"Missouri." I remind him.

He studies the picture for a few more seconds and then points to one of our friends, Chad. "And who is he, how well do you know him?"

"That's Chad Tillman. We've known him the longest out of all those guys. We basically grew up with him and his brothers. There are three Tillman's and three Robison's and we're all basically the same age. Chad is the youngest with Matt."

"I see. Hmm." He puts the picture back but lingers on it. I feel like there's more he's going to say. Waiting, he says nothing. He decides we're going back to Tujunga for coffee. It doesn't really matter to me where we go.

To this day Eric and I have not spoken about why he lingered over that picture as long as he did. Part of me doubts he would remember. I have never forgotten.

After my life flipped a few hundred degrees, things changed and happened so fast, I began to realize what Eric was really offering. I would recall Eric lingering over the picture and thought he must have recognized a spiritual craving in Chad. It was never something Chad and I spoke of but I am sure he was also a seeker.

The few times I returned home after meeting Eric I never brought the subject up with him. I always hesitated, unsure how to talk about what I'd seen. Afraid of what he'd say.

I can find no words to express this. I want to explain now, its impact. Because you would read over my description without giving it another thought, such a slight moment it would seem.

I never got the chance to have that conversation with Chad.

My fear of judgment, hesitation of being so different to someone who knew me so long. Too timid to speak openly about things I'd experienced. At who I'd become. The incredible new world I found myself living in. The arrogance, or ignorance, of believing I had all the time in the world. All these things held me back. Stopped me.

Such small, petty, insignificant things. All my fears. The value of things we place importance on, are rarely what truly has weight. It's sad, the events we require before we get out the scale and measure what really matters. It should be a common practice to look at our lives through the lens of eternity. See if those small things we spend our lives worrying about are really as important as they seem.

Three years after this moment, where Eric singled Chad out and asked about him in the picture, I attended his funeral. His death was a sudden, strange, unexpected accident. This nimble, embodiment of cat-like grace slipped from a tree and left this world.

While there, I went to his apartment and received the answer to my question. He was a seeker, like me. One that I had failed.

There's no use in telling you how I felt. Let me just say, that I'm grateful that Justin was a better friend than what I've been, to have introduced me to what he'd found. Had he not, I would be a much different person today. But, that was not the end. The deepest mystery, is rarely so clear. I like to think, Chad left me a gift. You see, when I returned home, the impact made me examine my life. Deeply examine it.

I weighed the value of it. My hopes, dreams, actions, my inactions. I placed myself in judgment as if I was sitting there on my final day. Every aspect went before the jury and the prosecutor held nothing back. What if it had been me instead? What would I regret? Would I do anything different? What would matter when I am gone?

Such bitter tears. Mournful, regretful, grateful tears.

I found my life was not in harmony with the precious fragile nature of life. I'd been treating it with casual ease, as if it were a road that had no end. Everything took new meaning. All I wanted was meaning.

My spirituality, what I'd done with it and been able to share, is all that would matter in the end.

Everything else fell away and my inner knowing, my Navigator, set the course. It was then I decided to finally give up L.A. and return to the Northwest. I'd spent time there during college and fell in love with it. Eric, the only thing that would have held me back, also felt a pull to go to the Northwest. So, within 4 months from the time of Chad's death Eric, Matthew and I moved there. Soon after Higher Balance Institute was created, Eric agreed to open it to the public, and now here we are. You and I.

There have been other times with Eric where moments barely mentioned have come calling later with unexpected force. Though none have let so great a mark as this.

A few months after we moved, one sunny day driving alone through the

Oregon countryside after reflecting on Chad a few days before, I received another answer. You see, there is a very tangible reality to my spirituality. I would not trade it for anything in the entire universe. The answer I received was totally unexpected and very real. It's not something I think I could ever pass on to those who knew him, though I wish I could. Perhaps later I will find the words.

I miss my friend. But the real light, the person I loved, is the being within. Though I can hear your steps no more, I know you travel still and I wish you well on your journey through the great adventure.

life grabs us with an iron grip. why is it so hard to step away...
let it go and see it from outside our own eyes...

A Higher Perspective

chapter six

On the drive out to get coffee Eric tells me that he used to live in the city and liked it a lot until a friend of his invited him up to Tujunga. Right away he remembered what it was like to live near nature. He grew up in the Northeast among trees and grass, things that are hard to find in LA.

I know what he means. Turning my head so he can't see my face I let my guard down and look out the window. Closing my eyes I breathe in the life-colored air. Living things. Running in a thunderstorm. Things I miss about Missouri and the Northwest. Eric must either sense my wandering thoughts or enjoy the peace himself. We ride in silence for a long time.

We see a house on the outskirts of Tujunga. Eric tells me soon after he visited the first time he bought a house and moved out of L.A. He asks if I notice a difference when we get out of the city. I admit that the first time I came up with Justin I could smell the difference in the air. It smells like life.

Eric agrees he notices that too and then adds, "Of course," he mentions, "you also know Tujunga is a UFO hot spot, right?"

"Huh?" I heard what he said but I don't believe it. Is he honestly talking about flying saucer UFO's?

"You know, UFO's, flying saucers, black planes, unidentified flying objects?"

"Oh yeah, yeah..." I nod my head. "I know what you mean. I guess I didn't know there was anything special about this place."

"Yeah, they see lots of things in the canyons. It's because they're barely inhabited and there's an Air Force base not far from here." Eric points to the mountains looming on the horizon. Tujunga is surrounded by them.

"Really..." A little disbelief in my voice. I've never heard about an Air Force base outside L.A.

"Well, not near here driving necessarily, but easy for a plane to fly. I think most of what people see are secret test planes flying though the canyons. They have to test them somewhere. The rest might legitimately be UFO's. Who knows... but they get reported a lot around here."

"Huh." I can see test planes being reported, but the idea of alien spaceships strikes me as a joke. Glancing at him I can't figure out how he works. He thinks most past life things are made up fluff, doesn't buy into most of the books in his own store, goes with a theory based on scientific DNA recall, but he thinks UFO's are real! The combination doesn't click.

We drive down Tujunga's main street and pass the bookstore. *Auxien: Metaphysical Bookstore*, reads the giant sign on top. He starts asking me questions about the papers and if I read them all.

"Yeah," I say briefly, "I read them all."

"Wow. That exciting huh? A lot of work went into those you know. You could put out a little more effort to explain what you thought. Someone takes the time to write something, and give it to you, the least you could do is give some feedback." He replies sarcastically.

His remark stings a little. I'm not sure what he expected but I don't know what to say about them. I understand what he's saying and, I feel bad about not saying more. He's more forward than most people I'm used to dealing with. I don't like being pushed and I want to push back. Now that he's made his comment I don't feel like talking about them at all.

Eric pauses for moment to let his comment sink in then starts talking about the papers. "Okay, well, if you read the papers then you know that every organism, right down to your cells, is an individual living thing. Right?" Eric asks as if we're about to have a quiz.

That's an easy one. We talked about it the first time I met him, all the little things that make up the body and then I read it all over again in his papers. Must think my memory is bad or something. "Yeah." I say brushing the question off as a little easy.

Eric doesn't seem satisfied with my brief response. He holds out his index finger while he's driving as if it were a pointer stick. "Are you one, single thing or are you many individual things?"

Fine. He wants to get specific, I can get specific. I start trying to adapt to his speed of talking and thinking. He's intense and rapid-fire but I'm confident I can keep up. "The body's made up of many individual things. Like the little spider packs that roam the arms or the things that swim in your eyes."

Eric nods, "Right, but also even smaller. Even individual cells act without your direction."

My head turns towards the window as I frown. Of course I knew that. He always goes into so much detail. "Right."

"Okay. So, your energy or soul that resides within your body is 'The Force' of your inner universe. Science has stated that Earth is covered in an electrical field whether it is in the desserts, jungles, mountains or even over the oceans. This electrical field encompasses the entire planet. Could this be a clue signaling a planetary soul?"

I start thinking out loud to talk faster. "Well, I guess if they can measure the electricity moving through our own body and use that to measure our thoughts or how our organs function then, sure. If they can actually show that there is an electrical field moving through the whole planet." I intentionally say the last part doubtfully. If they can measure electrical pulses moving through a brain they could easily measure larger pulses surrounding the planet. I've never heard of that so I'm doubtful.

Eric had to notice my tone but ignores it completely. "Right, well, your body functions on electricity, even though a better word for it would be energy. This energy makes your individual body parts move by tiny electrical shocks, creating movement with a precision that, of course, took quite some practice to perfect in your childhood, like walking, or driving like I'm doing now." He demonstrates his point by moving his hands all around the car. With one hand on the steering wheel he turns his radio volume, switches his headlights, and flicks his blinker all in rapid succession. His point is made. He's electrically controlling his body to perform tasks that would be difficult for a child.

"This energy also tells your heart to beat, tells your lungs to expand and collapse; every nerve of your body communicates with this energy. Even your very thoughts are electrons of energy moving from place to place within your brain. This energy that controls your body is your soul or your inner Force. Think about it for a moment!" Eric passionately grasps his free hand near his head so I know the idea should blow my mind.

It's not hitting me. He's telling me I should be shocked but I'm not. But, what he's telling me I've never thought of before. So how come I'm not shocked? I'm separate. I'm an electrical being controlling a physical one. I stare at the road in front of me. Thinking about it makes me feel strange only, I don't know why. It's just an idea. Not like I'm really an energy being, right?

"The cells of your body are receptive to energy. If you're depressed, your cells can be effected and create cancer, tumors, or they could just not fight against intruding viruses. If people have positive thoughts, it has been seen that cancer patients show a positive result of cells trying to heal or repair the body. Why? Because your soul is what I call The Force, within all of us. Your soul is the Force of this universe, your body!"

I nod my head as he continues talking. We turn down a road I've never been on before. The area looks newer and wealthier than Tujunga. I try linking the Forces he's talking about. I have an inner Force that's my consciousness, then the planet has an energy consciousness, and then the whole Universe has an energy consciousness that's the Force. Only, if the Force of the universe runs through everything, what separates it? What makes it any different? Trying to visualize all of them interacting makes my head scramble.

Eric's voice lowers to a smooth, rich tone. "What is the soul made of? It's made of energy. This energy, the soul, inhabits a vessel, the vessel being your body. The reason it exists within your body is because as energy, it cannot touch solid objects, it would simply pass through them." He grabs his steering wheel and runs a hand along the dashboard. "A soul cannot smell because it has no nasal glands." He takes a deep breath and motions to the outside air. I smell the city, trees, and hot air from the canyons. All through my body.

Eric holds his hand in front of his mouth and motions outward as if to carry sound out of his throat. "It cannot speak because it has no lungs to propel the sound. So by placing itself within a vessel it can explore this physical dimension of matter." He extends his hand in a grand arc to show me the city laid out before us. All the different shops, people, cars, foods, everything around us would be nothing without a body to experience it with. I get it. Thinking about it that way makes everything seem, weird, more real.

"Going back to talking about Gaia, consider the statement that the human race is the central nervous system of the planet. The planet, Earth, Gaia, whatever you want to call it, is a living organism in space! Everything on this planet, all things, whether they are stone, wood, or steel, are part of a living thing."

Right, Gaia. The Earth is a living organism floating in space. Right. Earth is called Gaia. Okay. Gaia has a consciousness, an electrical, energy soul, separate from the life inside of it. Like I have a consciousness separate from all my little micro-organisms. If I'm depressed it affects my body.

I wonder, how are moods reflected in Gaia? How do we feel them? How does it experience? I can walk around, touch things, talk... a floating spaceball can't do that. Questions come to my mind that weren't there before and I forget thinking I know it all. I know what he's going to say. Only now, as he tells me the planet is a living organism I look at it in a different way. It's interesting.

We park the car and walk down a street to an old diner. Rocky Cola's. It has an old 50's flair and would be right at home in the Midwest.

We both order coffee. He doesn't wait long with chit-chat and goes straight into a deeper conversation. He begins telling me about red and white blood cells. Our conversation from the car has put me in a really quiet mood, so the combination seems to work. It gives me a chance to examine his theories a bit more. His manner and actions are really engaging. If he were on TV I could watch him on mute and be totally entertained.

He approaches his ideas with a strong sense of conviction. It feels like he really believes them. Maybe that's why I'm listening. I don't care what his ideas are so much as why he believes them. Most people approach ideas so loosely, like they could toss them aside if they don't match what they're wearing, so many degree's of indifference. Any idea of 'winning' an intellectual battle starts to fade. This other Eric is really wrapped up in all his theories but I don't see any motive for him to be so. He's normal, rational, intelligent. He has his own bookstore and it's an awesome place. Why believe all this stuff? Why does he want to make a school out of it too?

Eric continues. Red cells are the non-spiritual people of the planet. People who don't feel a need to connect to something beyond themselves. Who aren't tapped into the Force. Red cells become White cells through reflection, devotion. This is how a soul is made. What he says makes sense but it feels so cold. It feels like it leaves too many people out.

So what, it's better to think you live forever and go up to Candy Land in the sky and are given a soul just for being born? Does that explain it better? The clear voice questions.

No. It doesn't. I don't like the fairy tale crap. I don't believe that. Never have. It's just... well, once you take the fairy tale away and hear a bit of what could be reality... I can see why there is the fairy tale. It's comforting. Ignorance is bliss.

But you've never wanted ignorance.

I know. I've always wanted the truth. Have to look at all sides to find it.

Is this the truth? The clear voice subtly prods.

Staring down into the creamy confines of my coffee cup I absently stir it and watch the fluid swirl around. Truth. Right. Like there is such a thing. Part of me twists away from the bitter thought. Conflicted now. Who knows? I don't know what this is.

But there is something here.

Yeah, maybe, but what?

I knew you were going to ask that. The clear voice says with an air as if it were smiling.

Of course, only, I don't know what's here. That's what I've got to figure out.

"You still with me?" Eric cracks into my mental wandering. My head shoots up from my coffee whirlpool to look at him. He's staring at me with an amused smirk.

"Yeah. Yeah, I'm with you. Just thinking about it." I take a sip of coffee and put the spoon off to the side.

Eric nods and gives me a knowing look. He knows I was spacing out.

"I see. Well, tell me about your friends and family."

My guard immediately goes up. Nobody cares about another person's friends or family. Who asks about that? Maybe it's because he's older that he talks about it. He doesn't seem much older than I am. Maybe he is. I look at his face. He sings of youthfulness. His eyes have such luminous curiosity in them. I read part of a book once for fun. It was from the thirties or something explaining to women how to recognize and find a good man for a husband. I wanted to see what women looked for. One part told women to find a man who constantly looks around. A man who is engaged in the world in which he lives. One who remains curious, remains alive, the book wrote, will never be a bore and will always be able to entertain her. I've always noticed how few people ever look around the world they live in. But this guy, his eyes tell me he's engaged in the world in a way I do not know. I've never met someone that I could see that, where I could look at their face and know they're looking at it with a radically different lens.

"That's weird. Why would you want to know about my family? Not much to them." I play it off like there's nothing to say when really I want to know why he'd ask in the first place.

"Well, I disagree." He tells me. "Your family is who you're going to be. It's the first example you have as a kid on how to act, how to live, what a human is. And, whether you are aware of it or not, it's the course you are most programmed, psychologically and genetically, to follow. If you really want to know someone find out about their parents and who raised them. That will tell you, with good accuracy, what that person is probably going to be like. You know, the apple doesn't fall far from the tree type stuff. You will become your parents. Nobody likes to think that but it's true. Unless you really push to change course and even then, you'll still end up a lot like them. They mold you for too long in too many ways. Make sense?"

"Yeah." I admit. I'm pretty private but I like his approach. I smile as my mind starts to wonder about the parents of everyone I know. He's made his point so I tell him about my family.

I briefly explain that my dad is in insurance but first went to school for accounting. When my older brother was born my dad left school and started working in insurance. He owned his own business for awhile but sold it. He's a good man. When I was young we'd go canoeing. We would always be one of the last canoes in the group because my dad would go all over the river picking up trash. If he saw a can sunk down in the bottom of the river he'd be on it. Leave the world a better place. It drove me crazy as a kid, but I see it now. I too, want to leave the world a better place. I smile to myself.

Even if it's picking up trash?

You do what you can I guess.

My mom was a stay at home mom for the most part. When my dad started his business she went to help him. We were old enough to fend for ourselves by then. I was 11 or 12. Plus we always had kids hanging out at our house. When we got older she went to school for child psychology but was working in a hospital to help people with sleep disorders. She's a dreamer. Always telling me I can do anything. If I told my mom I thought I could fly she'd probably tell me to go for it. They divorced when I was 17, big surprise there. Everyone's parents are divorced. They were both really active in the church youth group growing up. I shrug. Pretty normal I guess. He nods and asks about the church I was raised in.

Ugh. I know what he's going to say when I tell him. It's what everyone says. "The Reorganized Church of Jesus Christ of Latter Day Saints – not the Mormons!" I emphasize the last part.

"So…" Eric starts to ask looking a little unsure, "You were Mormon?"

Of course he has to say it anyway. Everyone does. "No." I state calmly and clearly. "It was the same movement originally until Joseph Smith, the church's founder, was killed by an angry mob. Then the Mormon's went west to Utah to become weird and marry multiple people and wear special underwear. The RLDS, my church, stayed in Missouri and became their own church. They both believe in the Book of Mormon but that's about it."

"So... " he said struggling with the separation. "Is your church real conservative, or, I mean are they just big Bible beaters or what?" He laughs because I can tell he couldn't find a better way to ask it. I grin. Probably wants to know if we were fundamentalist whacko's. The Midwest has its share that's for sure.

"Nah, they're actually really laid back. They're pretty liberal and seem to stay pretty focused on doing the right thing without damning people to Hell for kicks. I mean, they were the first church to allow women into the priesthood."

He seems surprised by that. I explain that our church never slammed anything down our throats and I always felt open to explore what I wanted. Both my parents are also very open so I've been lucky.

Eric nods, "What about your parents' nationality? What's their background?"

The question throws me off a bit but I tell him the best I know our background is English, Irish, Danish and some Icelandic. I'm not sure if that is completely accurate, but it's my best guess based on conversations I've had in the past.

Eric and I stay at the diner for a few hours talking off and on about different subjects. He tells me more about what I'd read in the papers. I listen with interest to see if there are things I hadn't thought of. Then we both get too shaky from coffee. He decides that's enough and says he'll drop me off at home.

Driving back down Foothill Blvd he pushes a tape into his radio. My head is spacing out buzzing from too much caffeine. The music that starts playing isn't quite like anything I've heard before. It's electronic, fast and rhythmic, with lots of sweeping dramatic surges. I laugh out loud.

"What is it?" he asks.

"This music." I say pointing at his tape deck as if he needs to know where it's coming from. "What is this stuff, like, techno?"

"Yeah, actually it is. Fuck, I've had this tape for so long. This is my favorite album. You should listen to it, I think you'll like it. It's trance music, like techno, but not so electronic keyboard stuff, you know?" He cranks up the volume so that it fills the car. I nod. The fact that it's electronic keyboard music is freaking funny. As I listen my mood starts to swing. It feels good. This stuff makes you feel good! It's strangely liberating. I stop caring that it comes from cheesy electronic keyboards, even though he says it doesn't. It's so energizing and uplifting.

We cruise down the freeway into L.A. listening to the music the whole way. The windows are down and the trance fits perfectly with the journey. Such good driving music. We start swinging around the bend heading into the heart of L.A. Immediately, the freeway starts to jam. Don't stop! The music doesn't want us to stop. It's flying music. The car should be able to fly the way the music blasts off.

Reality crashes in. The wind dies as we slow down. Look at all the cars in front of us. It's a long line. Bumper to bumper red break lights. Bumper to bumper and we're all packed in. Squeezing down this little tube of a freeway. I look ahead, little red dots as far as I can see. Relaxing my head back against the seat I start to consider how long we'll be stuck in traffic. My eyes glaze and the cars blur together, a mesh of multicolored steel. The red lights, because each car has two, seem to multiply and float until it looks as if the whole part of the highway is being flushed with floating red orbs.

Taking a deep breath I try to relax and listen to the music. Drift into that timeless state of not feeling like I have anywhere to be. Makes the waiting time go faster. My eyes shift to the other side of the freeway, white headlights of the other cars speed past. They turn on our same curve. Not enough to shine the light into the car but enough to make them blur from the speed. Only our side is moving at a crawl. I stare, almost zoning out, all the way down until the freeway curves under a bridge and out of view. The whole freeway is a long stream of floating red dots on one side and streaming white dots on the other.

My brain suddenly opens up. It takes its own direction. I imagine myself flying over the freeway. Zooming quickly away from Eric's red Thunderbird I flash high over the skyscrapers. Soon the cars blend into the pavement. A mash of colors marked only by the movement of the lights. The red and white colored dots. My field of view opens up as I stretch my arms out to embrace the open sky around me. So much room! I imagine the wind softly brushing against my cheek. A feeling of peace I felt when I'd gone skydiving once. Watching all the streets of Los Angeles down below. A mazelike network moving people and cars. Each street is filled with the same scenario. White lights and red lights. White dots moving in one stream. Red dots moving in another stream. Each squeezes and pushes their way through the narrow concrete corridors. The higher I go the less structured and separate they seem. Soon I can't tell that they are split. Red lights on one side and white on another. They are all mashed together, little units with their own purpose and agenda. Traveling on their own, individually, with no direction or awareness given by the larger organism, the Earth.

It's just like he said. It's like red cells and white cells in the human body. Little cells pushing their way through the veins in my body. All these cars carrying stuff, us, people, down concrete veins through this larger organism that is Los Angeles. It's amazing. My mouth opens and I try to catch my breath. Incredible. I know the cars aren't perfect representations but it's so close. Suddenly it's all there. The realness of it. The side by side comparison.

Suddenly, I'm in three places at once. Part of me is in the car, sitting and watching it unfold. Another is inside my body, feeling the cells moving through my veins. Still another is high above, watching it all unfold at a larger level. But they are all the same. Eric says the world is alive. It's a living organism and we're all micro cells like little cells moving through my body. Inside my body are veins and little, tiny cells are moving through my whole network of veins. They're pushing information, nutrients, oxygen. Here we're sitting on long freeways moving through a larger organism. Cars carrying people that serve functions for the city. Giant trucks carrying food, machinery, equipment.

I picture little cells moving through my veins and then shoot out to see cars moving through the streets all over the city and then shoot out to see trucks moving on freeways between cities and then shoot out to see jets and boats carrying stuff between countries. It's all there. So similar. Holy crap. My heart starts to race. My brain buzzes with amazement. It's always been here. My whole life. The comparison fits so well, I can't believe I've never saw it.

How can you not see how it's like a giant body? It makes perfect sense! My eyes widen as I watch the freeway with my normal sight, while also seeing it from above, in my mind, and at the same time imagine it all moving through my veins. How can I sit and watch all of this from my top window every night and see it from high above and not realize how it's all one giant thing? It's only from a different perspective! I can't believe I never noticed! I sit and wonder at the traffic. How many times? How many times have I passed through this completely unaware of how it looks on a different scale? I'm blind. I'm a blind idiot. It's so clear.

We finally reach my apartment. I'm still in a strange daze. I fumble opening the door. The music. I suddenly think enough to ask what the music is.

"Desert Skies." Eric tells me with a knowing smirk.

"Thanks for taking me up." I say as I close the door.

The window rolls down as I start to walk away. "Hey!" he yells out. I walk back and look inside. "You need to do something."

"What's that?" I ask, unsure of what I could do for him.

"You need to find someone else who is interested in talking about this. You need to find a friend. Don't you know anyone who might like talking about this?"

I'm buzzing from seeing the freeway in a whole new light. Everyone I know will laugh and make fun of this stuff. Just like I would have. Suddenly I think of someone. Someone who is actually open and believes in a lot of this stuff. Sarah. Don't commit until you talk to her.

"Maybe. Most people I know aren't really into this stuff but, I might be able to find someone." I tell him sounding doubtful.
Eric looks into my eyes for a moment and then nods as if I'd answered a question for him by staring back. "Have her read those papers I gave you then let's meet up."

He rolls the window back up and drives off. Right. Simple. Read the papers and then explain... did he say her? I didn't say she did I? Weird, good guess. God, how am I going to explain all of this and not sound nuts?

what bird would ever learn to fly if it never went out on a limb, free from the nest, away from its mother, away from...

The Instinct to Nurture

chapter seven

"Sarah, um... I met someone you might find, well, interesting." I struggle with exactly how to tell her. I pace my room, rehearsing the scene and getting my nerve up. Why is this so hard for me? Sarah's told me things I've found hard to believe.

Crazy things. The grating voice mutters.

Not crazy, more like, strange things.

They should get along great if they both believe everything they say.

Come on, Sarah is a total free spirit. Always up for anything with a completely open mind. She's the first person I've really connected with in L.A., outside of school.

Crazy likes company.

She's not going to think I'm crazy. I've never heard her judge anything. I'm not sure how we first began talking about spiritual or psychic stuff. She probably brought it up. I followed suit telling her about some of the books I read and what I thought. We met when I interned for the small production company she worked for. Not long after I started there the company broke up. Two of the agents, one

143

who represented actors and the other writers, kept me on. Sarah kept working as an assistant for Seth, who represented writers.

After the split things slowed down and there wasn't as much to file. I'd read scripts and Sarah and I found more time to talk about what I'd read and then drift into different topics. We always clicked. I enjoyed how much she openly embraced life.

Sarah's not much older than I am. Two years. How old is she now then? Well, our birthdays are like a few days apart. Right. She just turned 26. Doesn't seem like it. In terms of worldliness she's miles ahead. I'm a late bloomer. As I've come out of my own little world I have been adventurous and eager to experience life but cautious with what I have engaged in personally. Sarah seems like she's always been full throttle. Anything and everything. This outlook has led her to some strange things. She's told me about out of body experiences she's had and telepathy with friends.

Nobody else I know could get away with that. Anyone else I would have scoffed or made fun of them, but Sarah's an exception. For her, it makes sense. It works. I can't explain what she's experienced but I don't doubt what she has said.

Well, the 'what' and the 'how' is the trick, isn't it? The clear voice chimes in.

Yeah, doing acid since she was 12 might explain some of it. Flashbacks don't explain all of it. The mind is a powerful thing. You open things up so young, some doors you may not be able to close. Not my way but could be *a* way. I've always believed I can make my mind do anything I want, without drugs. Drugs are for the lazy. But, I also allow for the possibility that drugs can open things up. Things that might stay with you long after the initial experience. Sarah's been through all of that and I've never judged her for it. She won't judge me either. So, why is it so hard to tell her about this?

Sighing, I know there's no easy way. I have to bite the bullet and just do it.

The next day I'm over at Sarah's house in the Hollywood Hills. There's a space in the conversation so I jump in, head first and eyes closed.

"Sara-Ah —" my voice cracks. Christ, puberty's long gone but my voice still cracks for no reason at all. Clearing my throat I start again. "Sarah, I met someone I think you might find interesting."

"Oh really? Who is it?" She asks with her normal air of intense curiosity. Her bright youthful blue eyes, framed by her wavy red hair, are wide with anticipation.

"Well, I met this... psychic." I go for the word that had gotten me to meet him. Sarah will have a different reaction to it; a positive reaction.

"Reaaally? How cool! Did they do a reading for you? I have a psychic that I've called." She asks excitedly.

She's told me about her psychic before and how accurate she thought she was. I know she believes some people are like that. It feels strange to hear me say something like that.

"Nah, no reading or anything like that but supposedly he's found all these missing people and used to track submarines when he was like, 12 or something." I assume Sarah will understand the submarine tracking thing better than I do. After giving it more thought, it has something to do with being psychic I'm pretty sure. I doubt the Navy would have any other use for a young kid, but a child psychic prodigy, well, Sarah will understand.

"No waay! How cool is that? That's pretty crazy. Can I meet him?" She asks.

God, I love Sarah. She's down for anything. I hoped she'd ask something like that. Even though I feel like I can say anything I want to Sarah, it doesn't make me feel any less awkward talking about things I feel strange about. I can't believe I said psychic. Ugh, it's not like that at all, it's much more reasonable and interesting.

Keep telling yourself that. Whatever works.   The grating voice says sarcastically.

Oh shut up.

"Yeah, sure. You can meet him. I'm curious what you'll think of him. I don't really know myself."

I give Sarah the papers to read. She agrees to check them out and that we can meet Eric when she finishes. We quickly move away from the psychic topic before I have to say 'psychic' more than I already have. Sarah's life is busy and a little insane at times so she catches me up on everything that's been going on.

Over the next few days I meet with Eric here and there. Each time he goes over topics we've already talked about but finds something else to add or different ways to explain things. At the end of one of our meetings he asks me about meeting my friend that I mentioned. I tell him about Sarah reading the papers and how she's been out of her body and had other psychic-seeming experiences. He hesitates. I assure him she's not a whacked out California freak and she's pretty down to Earth, only she's had some experiences I can't explain. He nods, seemingly satisfied by the answer. If she's interested, he's happy to meet her. Then he asks if I think my brother Matthew might be interested.

It's a no-brainer. "I'm sure he would be. He's more open-minded about all this stuff than I am, always has been I think."

Eric smirks. "Justin said basically the same thing."

Trying to stop my lips from twitching I nod. I wonder what else Justin said? It's hard for me to understand Justin. He talks to me and I can tell he likes me but he definitely approaches me in a certain way. He adjusts himself somehow, maybe acts older when he talks to me. I feel like Matthew and the others know a younger, raver, dance-and-be-free Justin. Sometimes I see that Justin. I mean, I never even heard about Eric, or that he's a student or interested in any of this stuff. Until the day he took me up to meet Eric. He's more Matthew's friend than mine, so maybe they talk about it more.

"Yeah, I mean, I'm sure Matthew and Justin have talked about it. Matthew loved that book, umm, The Celestine Prophecy. He tried to get me to read it."

Eric nods, his eyes narrowing a bit like he's studying my face, "And did you read it?"

Sighing I shrug, "I tried. A lot of my friends raved about it. I couldn't do it. Just a little, I don't know, maybe boring." I can't tell if he's read it or not. Everyone I've ever met who was into this stuff has seemed to like it. He said he only likes a handful of books. It would suck if it that was one of them.

Whatever liar. You couldn't stand that book.

No, don't make me feel bad about that. I'm not lying. There's no reason to put down what other people like. Visions of me struggling to be interested in the book, day after day, Matthew asking me where I was in it, float through my mind.

Eric chuckles. "I find most of my students aren't big readers. I never read it either, so I can't really say. It's not something that sounds interesting to me."

With perfect non-expression I nod slightly. Inside I sigh in relief.

We try to meet Matthew several times. Each time something comes up. Matthew's schedule is always fairly busy, but whenever we try and arrange a meeting it gets insane. Matthew gets called into a job at the very last minute or something suddenly happens and he has to stay late. After nine or ten attempts I'm ready to give up. This is freaking ridiculous. Meeting someone shouldn't be so much work.

Finally, I get a call from Sarah. She's finished reading the papers and wants to meet with Eric. After trying to get Matthew to meet Eric I half expect Sarah's life to go nuts as soon as we set a date.

Surprisingly, she shows up right on time the first day we set. Sarah and I meet at my apartment and wait for Eric to show up. We start talking about the papers. She sits on Matthew's bed and looks around the living-dining-bedroom area. Something's weird. I look at her. Her long straight red hair catches the sun. Her posture seems casual and relaxed. She never comes to my apartment. I usually go over to her house, maybe that is what's weird.

I tell her the main thing I found interesting was the concept of the Earth as a living organism. Just like we're living organisms and animals. I like that it doesn't put man at the top of the food chain and how there are greater organisms above us. It makes everything seem so alive. I don't think the Earth is a floating giant dirt hill, put here solely for us to use. I don't believe that everything revolves around man. I like that the Earth and the whole universe, exist as something beyond our limited vision. Eric's vision makes it alive, its own being. Beings experiencing life on so many levels. Occupying every degree of space. That's intriguing.

Sarah blows off the idea as something she's read about many times.

I'm a little stunned. "Really? Are you sure Sarah?" I'm surprised. Can it be that it's nothing new? Is Eric only a bookworm after all? Everything he's told me, the details and angles, it all seems so close to him. His knowledge of it so intimate. Who do I believe now? I'm a little unsure if Sarah's really read it the way Eric describes it. "I mean, I've heard reference to Mother Earth, or the concept that the Earth is alive so we have to take care of it. Never in any of those Native American-type philosophies or enviro-religions do they give it such detail. They never make the comparison so rich and fleshed out. That's what it's all about, what makes it interesting."

"Oh yeah, yeah, totally." Sarah agrees and confirms she isn't talking about any of those ideas. She's really heard of almost the exact same concept before and has even thought of such a thing herself.

Damn, I'm so dumb. I start to withdraw internally to re-examine everything I previously thought. How come I've never heard or considered such a thing? No. I need to look into it more. I want to know where she's heard it.

"Are you sure, sure Sarah? Where did you hear it or read about it?" I ask feeling torn.

Sarah's eyes roll around as she strains to remember. "Uhhh, oh, I don't remember but it's out there! I mean, I've even thought things just like it!"

I try and press her more on it but I can't get anything solid out of her. She can't pin down where she's heard it, but it's enough to make me doubt that they're Eric's ideas.

Moving on she mentions how the last chapter about the Darkside seems like a movie script.

"No way!" I laugh. "I thought the exact same thing."

She laughs too and tells me we've got Hollywood in our brains like a drug. We both work around movies and we had to read a lot of script treatments at the production company she worked for. The last chapter is pretty much made from a comic book. It's probably true, we relate everything we see to Hollywood.

"So, what is, what is this guy like?" Her voice drops, quieter.

Is she nervous? I get the sense she's a little nervous to meet him. It's a weird concern. Never dawned on me to be nervous. I've never felt threatened or intimidated by him. His ideas are out there but they're interesting. I tell her about the first time I met him and his amazing, magical bookstore. She relaxes and becomes more comfortable, laughing at my excitement.

"Wait, wait a second." My head jolts away from looking at her. Staring at the floor I try to concentrate on the thought. A thought flashes through my mind, have to hold it, grasp it. There was something else. A light. Aura. Holy crap, I saw his aura. How could I forget about that?

Sarah looks at me, puzzled. "Is everything okay?" she asks.

Somehow it slipped my mind. Completely. Entirely. My memory is one of the few things I actually have going for me. It's always been sharp. It doesn't make sense that I would see something like that and then don't remember. I realize my strange silence isn't helping to calm her. Smiling again, I look back up at her. "He showed me his aura and I saw it. I mean, I don't even believe in them but I saw it bright, brilliant, right before my eyes. I forgot all about it."

This energizes her and she gets really amped up. "What do you mean you don't believe in them? Eric! How does that make any sense at all? I see aura's all the time! I mean, you don't believe in them??" She grabs her hair like I blew her mind. Classic Sarah. I love it. She starts laughing at me. I grin. She's practically wailing at me through her laughter, "I mean, that's like not believing in... in... I don't know! Coyotes or something!" She howls.

Shaking my head I can't believe it. She just compared it to coyotes. Hollywood Hills coyotes. "Sarah, it's not like that. I mean, come on, not everyone can see them. Now, really, I mean really, do you really see them?"

She throws her hands up in the air and leans forward, her mouth and eyes open in total surprise like she was watching a caveman unthaw.

"Are you kidding!? Of course I do! All the time! I've seen them ever since I was young!"

Sitting back on the futon I smirk. It's Sarah. It's a Sarah thing. Of course she's seen them since she was young. She's a weird exception to normal, logical universal laws. I don't doubt for a moment that Sarah can see them, only, that hardly makes a case for the rest of the world being able to do the same.

She explains that when she meets new people she even looks for their aura. Sometimes she even sees color.

Of course, I think, they're all supposed to be different colors and each color means something. I've heard it before, only I never had a reason to think there was any truth to it. Golden. Eric's aura was golden. Ohh, but why? I can picture it clearly in my mind. I've seen one! Why then is it such a stretch to believe people other than Sarah can see them too?

"Okay Sarah. Maybe you do see 'something' but why can't it be a play of the light or double images from your eyes?" I ask, almost pleading, with sincerity.

Sarah freezes for a moment looking at my honest expression. Then she bursts into laughter. She thinks it's hysterical. "Oh Eric! You've seen one and you don't believe your own eyes!" She laughs. "No really," she insists, "they are real. And it's really cool that you saw one."

I frown. But how can I be sure about what I saw? I ask her with my hands extended in a, please help me, kind of way. "Sarah, how can I be sure? How do I know what I really saw?"

Sarah looks at me again. She can tell I'm struggling. "Okay, okay. Explain it to me," she tells me, "what you saw. Tell me about it." She straightens her posture and looks at me seriously.

I lean closer to her, trying to recreate the moment clearly. "Now that I remember I can picture it perfectly in my mind. I can't believe I forgot. Eric was standing against a white wall. It's pretty bare except some office equipment to his left. A doorway to his right. I'm standing 5 or 6 feet away. Justin and Peggy are standing off to the side. Eric explains what I'm looking for. I see, well, what he calls the aura. It's some vaguely luminescent outline around him. It's white-ish but really mostly translucent. Kind of fuzzy looking."

Sarah nods her head with a smile.

I struggle on. "It seems really up in the air if I'm seeing it or not. He tells me to say when it changes. A second or two later this crazy, vibrant, crystal clear, golden glow surrounds his head and shoulders.

It went about four feet around him and ends, not like, dispersing or tapering off as a light would, but perfectly. I mean, Sarah, I could have drawn a line with a pen on the wall behind him exactly where the golden glow stopped. So, my thinking is, because the light was contained that rules out any lamps, flashlights, things like that. His face and body were not glowing and weren't changed by the glow at all. In other words his face and clothes, his body, weren't glowing golden so it's not like the light was bouncing off other objects which rules out any kind of spotlight."

Sarah laughs at all my created possibilities. "Eric, you're trying too hard to explain it. Look how hard you're trying to find some other explanation. Why couldn't it be what you saw?" She asks.

"Maybe I am trying too hard." I admit. "But... I don't know, the glow was so, soo... brilliant. It was so bright, I mean, bright, bright, bright. As bright as three lamps stuck together."

Sarah's eyes get a little bigger. Great, she's never seen anything like that either. Now I am alone.

"What did you do?" She asks, her voice quieter now.

"I stood there and told him something changed." I shrug.

She shakes her head confused. "You didn't freak out?"

Snickering to myself, "No, I feel like an idiot now. I didn't do anything. I didn't know what the hell I was looking at. What was I supposed to do?" I start to laugh because I see her point of view. It's really weird that I didn't do anything.

Sarah's quiet still demeanor is suddenly broken. She spills into laughing at me. "I don't know! Some kind of reaction! Scream, jump up and down. I would have been really happy it sounds so cool!"

Is it cool? It feels more scary than cool. What if there really is something to see? If there is, why can't I see it all the time? How come Sarah can see them but I can't? It doesn't make sense.

Eric arrives before long. Sarah decides she wants to drive since Eric drove from Tujunga. We roam around for awhile trying to decide where to go. We finally settle on the Bourgeoisie Pig for coffee.

Walking to the coffee shop Eric turns to Sarah and points to my hair. "So, what's your opinion on his new hair?" Eric asks her.

My gut tenses up. He never said anything before.

Why wait and say something now?? What are they going to say?? Anxious worry fills my head.

I'm suddenly insecure, nervous, unsure of what they think. It's the first time Eric has mentioned it. I almost wondered if he thought I always had blonde hair.

Sarah smiles. "It's cool! I like it, it's different for him."

Eric looks at my head again and looks like he doesn't completely agree. "It's not bad. I don't dislike it. I can't say I'm completely sold on it. But I get it. You were looking for a change."

Turning away I stare at the sidewalk. Relaxing my stomach I try to get rid of the tense feeling. He nailed it right on. So weird. I was looking for a change. Of course, you go from plain brown hair to bright bleached blonde maybe that's a given. Would I have thought about that though? It's strange. I don't really think about why people do what they do on a really deep level anymore. I always did when I was younger. Delving into everything about a person, always wondering. Why did I stop? Got bored of it I guess. Once I figured people out where was the mystery? Better to not know and let them surprise you. At least that way life is left with something unknown.

"The eyebrows though..." Eric chuckles, "They were a bit much."

I grin but he's walking slightly behind me, I don't think he can see. Nobody else noticed that I bleached my eyebrows too. They say you aren't supposed to but that's because they don't want some idiot to get bleach in their eyes and go blind. It always looks weird when people have really light hair but dark eyebrows. So I lightened them up. He doesn't miss much.

We sit at a long table near the entrance. I sit by Sarah, we face Eric, our backs are to the door. We sit, chatting idly, mostly small talk. Sarah decides she's done with small talk and asks Eric about seeing energy and auras.

Eric shrugs. "I don't know what there is to say, I see auras all the time. It's not like people normally think, with them just coming off the body a few inches or, crap, even a few feet. They go out about 32 feet. That's where I see them."

I look across the coffee shop. Thirty-two feet is more than the width of this place. Eric explains it's like thick smoke surrounding the body. Sarah, excited, shares that she can only see them up to 3 or 4 feet away.

Oh boy. Now I've done it. Can they both believe what they're saying?

It's interesting though. Isn't it? The clear voice whispers sounding curios.

Yeah, I guess it is. Like a riddle, something to figure out.

Eric goes on to explain. He can see a lot more than auras. About 5 or 6 years ago he started seeing energy shapes. Twitching I try not to choke on my coffee. Energy shapes? What is he saying? Sarah leans forward with a big smile. He's hooked her.

Sarah talks in a low voice, a childish grin on her face, "You mean all around us?"

Eric looks around and nods. "Yeah, I can see them moving through walls, zipping through the air, passing in and out of this dimension. When I first started to see them I wasn't sure what to do. They would come flying through a wall and I would be like, oh shit, and duck!" He quickly ducks to demonstrate. It's how I would react if something bizarre whizzed at my head. It's crazy. Totally crazy! His reaction seems real.

Eric continues, "All my friends thought I was insane. I mean, they knew me well enough to know... you know, I'd seen and done some weird shit but this was a new level. It was nuts. You can ask. Some of them still live here." His posture returns to casual and he rests his arm up on the top of the chair. "I'd be sitting there having this normal conversation and then all of a sudden they'd see me dive to the floor, or suddenly jump sideways. After awhile, you adjust. I see them all the time now. They're like giant amoebas, just like flying through this space. I've gotten used to them I guess." He sips his coffee as if this was completely normal.

Whoa, what the, how would that even?? I picture him sitting there, sipping his coffee, watching giant multi-colored video-game like asteroid creatures fly through the walls. Un-freaking-believable! He's so calm about! I don't get it. I look over at Sarah. She's fascinated. What the hell? She believes him! He's nuts. Completely crazy. God, that means she's nuts too. I just invited two crazy atoms together and now they're exploding with insanity! How would that even be possible? Drugs, gotta be drugs. He must be tripping on acid all the time.

Are you sure about that? The clear voice sounds uncertain. It doesn't ring true.

Right, that doesn't make sense either. He doesn't look like he's tripping. I look up from my coffee cup to study him. You're right. People on acid have weird pupils. He looks completely normal. A normal, smart, with it, together guy. So, he can't be some strange, whacked out hippie whose burnt-out his brain on too many drugs. Fine. Then, what's the other option? Well, he must be screwing with us. This is all fun for him. He tells people really weird stuff, to see if they believe it. He knows Sarah believes this stuff, so he's playing with her. Umm... I start to go back over everything I just thought.

That doesn't make any sense eith-

Oh shutup! I know. He's got too many friends, has his own business, there's no reason for him to do that. I start to become annoyed. Why would anyone lie about something like this? What's the point? For sure he has better things to do than see if he can make people believe stupid stuff.

So, moving on. What's the alternative?

I don't know. He actually isn't on drugs and believes he can see this stuff? Those answers aren't really satisfying. It doesn't make sense. What if he doesn't *think* he can see this stuff? What if he really can? I block the idea out.

Stupid! Only a gullible idiot would believe that. The grating voice insults.

Right, I mean, science would have detected them in some lab, some research experiment somewhere! We can split atoms, for sure we can see floating energy globs!

It has a strange logic to it though. Something about it feels right. The clear voice soothes.

Part of me isn't convinced. Something about it clicks. But to accept it...

Please! Nobody in the whole world would believe this crap! It would have been discovered by now! Are you gonna fall for this? The grating voice protests.

No, of course not. He's insane. But at least he's interesting. Sarah goes on with the energy shapes. "Okay, so if you can see those energy shape things, can you see ghosts?"

Eric grimaces and rolls his eyes slightly. "Welllll," he strains, "I don't really believe in ghosts per se."

Sarah looks disappointed. "Oh. Really?"

"Well, not like, not the way Hollywood," he makes quotes with his fingers as he says Hollywood, "would have you believe in them. I mean look at how they portray ghosts. There's always a person who screams out and the ghost answers them back in a strange, scary voice and it's like, wait a second, do ghosts have vocal cords? Do they have lungs to propel sound with? Do they have eardrums to hear with? Do they have bodies to make sounds with or eyes to see the way we do? No way. They're energy. They're made of energy so they aren't going to hear, see, smell or anything the way we do. Right?"

Sarah shakes her head a little bit and laughs. "Makes sense to me."

I smirk. Ghosts making sense. But if they were real, his way does make sense.

Eric nods and takes a drink of coffee. "Right, so, not only are ghosts inaccurately portrayed in movies and stuff. But, most of the things people think are ghosts really aren't. I'm not saying I don't think they exist, okay? They do. I mean, I remember when I was young lying in bed and getting ripped right off my mattress and thrown onto the floor. I mean, it took me off so fast my blanket was still on my bed. I've had an entity, which is like a ghost, throw a knife that was sitting on my kitchen table right into the back of my leg. That's the first time I ever had one move objects like that and when it happened I was shocked and scared but also like, no way! I have a scar I could show you. Ever since I can remember, they've been there. But they certainly aren't all 'ghosts' like 'dead people', okay? I don't believe everyone on the planet has a soul, so not every person who dies is going to be a ghost. I mean, if everybody had souls, I'll tell you right now, we'd have hauntings all over the fucking place." Eric leans in close to the table and holds his hands out like, get ready, and then looks around at all the people crowded into the coffee shop.

With Sarah sitting next to me I notice his language for the first time. Everyone around me swears constantly so it's not something that phases me. Eric uses it like everyone else for the most part, as added color. A few times he's reminded me of a standup comedian using his cussing to drive a point or make something stand out. For the first time I wonder if it's something a spiritual psychic is really supposed to do. Sarah doesn't react to it at all. She smiles and looks as entertained as ever so I brush it off.

Eric opens his eyes and points all around the coffee shop. "We'd see ghosts everywhere we went! Just the sheer number of people who have died in even the last 5 years... there's like, 50 million people dying every year. Multiply that by 5, then by 20... it's a huge fucking amount of people! Well, if you went back the last thousand years that's billions of spirits and entities. Wherever the fuck they're going, they're going to move through this place like an interstellar highway. But they don't. Hauntings are very, very rare, and that's because not every person who dies has a soul. Of those who have developed souls only a small percentage of those get stuck."

Looking around the coffee shop I imagine if even a fraction of the people who died came back as ghosts. The whole place would be like a giant Ghostbusters movie. We'd be getting slimed right now. Because, ghosts would have to live forever. So their population would grow and grow.

Sarah puts her hand on her chin and then looks at her coffee cup.

Eric notices. "What? I can tell you want to say something."

Sarah's never been shy so she takes the invitation. "Well, it's just... I don't get it. I mean, okay you don't believe everyone has a soul. I read that in your paper. But, I mean, ghosts do exist right? You do believe that, right? Because I've seen some things that I definitely believe and know that. So –"

Eric nods his head and cuts in, "Oh yeah. Yes, definitely. Like I said, I've been attacked by entities since I was young. When I got older I began investigating haunted places and I can tell you, one out of, maybe... maybe a hundred actually has something to it. Even then most are barely worth mentioning. And the rest- "

Sarah nods her head and interrupts him, "Okay, so what are they? I mean, if most aren't 'ghosts' or they are... what are they?"

Eric smiles as Sarah pushes for information. "Well, I'll tell you. They're holograms. Recordings. Ask yourself this, when you think of a classic haunted house; what does the house look like? What kind of house is it?"

Eric looks at us. We look at each other. Smiling I shrug and say, "Old, run down farmhouse out in the middle of nowhere." Sarah nods and agrees.

Eric sips his coffee and nods. "Right. Old farmhouse most often in New England. East coast type place, maybe the Midwest, not so much here on the west coast. And what almost always happens in these hauntings? Usually people hear some kind of spooky ghost voice, or echoes of laughter or they'll see a person in old civil war uniform walking down a hall. They might turn and then walk into the wall and disappear. In this case I'd say, look at the blueprints of the house, chances are you'll find there used to be a door there that got covered up or converted or something. And then, look at the physical structure of the house itself. Are they made up of sheet rock like our modern walls? No. They were thrown together with chicken wire, this paste-like cement and slate, etc, etc... all crude but highly mineralized material. In a lot of ways I'd say very large and crude but similar in material to what we might actually use to record something ourselves... like a tape, or record. You with me so far?"

Sarah and I both nod our heads.

"So, it might happen, one night out of fifty years or a hundred years living there, a storm comes in, an electrical storm. The air is humid, the atmospheric pressure is changing, like when a storm front moves in. The air is ionized with electrical particles and the house is swelling and expanding from the storm. Maybe a bunch of people are downstairs playing cards, laughing and having a good time and the conditions are so perfect that the sound is recorded, embedded, in these old plaster walls. One in a million chance but it happens. Now, because it's a really crude recording, some hundred years later, a storm blows in, the house expands and all the elements are right. Electrical wires running through the walls and the air is charged, maybe a storm front causes some kind of compression and out of nowhere... it plays back. But with the recording all fucked up, it sounds like a super fucking scary-ass ghost. Like there are multiple voices all screaming from beyond because guess what? It was multiple voices. And now there's this storm coming in, which lends to the old folk tales about haunted houses. So it seems like the classic haunting. Make sense?"

Nothing I can say to that. That actually seems possible. Way more possible than a dead person roaming somebody's house. Sarah nods.

Eric clears his throat and drinks some water then keeps going. "So, in the same scenario, you could say it could capture someone's image. Like an old projector only a bit more elaborate. It captures them walking down the hall, and then going into an old closet or bedroom. A hundred years later, you see this image of this woman in an old gown walking down your hall, and then turning and walking into the wall where there's nothing there. Of course it's stormy out and your scared to hell so you think it's a ghost when in fact... it never acknowledged you, there was no interaction of any kind at all... almost like it was a projection replaying when the conditions are just right, enough moisture, enough pressure to cause the walls to flex which creates energy... and that could trigger it."

Sarah laughs. "That's crazy."

I'm snickering to myself. I can see it too.

Eric smacks the table slightly, "Nine out of ten places that are supposedly 'haunted' are because of this. But you can certainly have a real, 'ghost', haunting where someone has died and they are trapped in this dream state. Think about when you dream, it's not always clear, things fade in and out and you can't always remember things that happened five seconds ago. They go to their house because that's the most familiar place to them. Or a graveyard... why? Because that's where their body is and they can't acknowledge that they're dead. They just feel like if they can get back in it they'll wake up from the dream they're trapped in. They don't believe they're dead and because they're removed from their sense of time all they know is things are changing around them but the same, like a dream, and it can be maddening. They drift in and out of awareness so they might act out by smashing stuff, scratching people... all the things you might hear from a really active haunting. But, they aren't thinking about it as clearly as you are."

Eric continues to tell us some stories about when he investigated haunted places. Some of them are chilling, others are strange, hard to believe they're possible but gripping, and compelling. Each story he intertwines how the entities were able to do things or how they perceive it.

We're captivated and I forget that he's crazy long enough to believe he can see flying energy shapes.

After a few hours we're tired of drinking coffee and ready to walk around again. We leave the Pig and Eric asks where Matthew is. I explain he's working and I begin to recite his schedule as best I can remember, when I stop and look around.

"Wait, we're actually really close to his work." I tell them he works only a few blocks over. Eric suggests we stop by and say hi. Without a car I rarely get a chance to drop by his work so I agree it'll be fun.

We do a slow drive-by of the studio. Inside he's painting the walls for an upcoming photo shoot. Sarah calls him on his cell phone and asks him to step outside. I smirk. You mean there's actually a good use for cell phones? Oh.. no wait, we could have walked ten feet and told him we were here. I hate cell phones.

Matthew comes out and sees Sarah's car, waves, and walks over. He reaches into the car and gives Sarah a big hug. Some people shake hands, Matthew hugs. If he could walk through the streets of L.A. and hug everyone he saw I think he would. They teasingly say their hello's. He hasn't seen her in awhile. Eric moves in the back seat but is quiet, he seems different. He has that air of intensity about him. He isn't used to how long Matthew will banter and take to say a simple hello. He's been trying for weeks to meet him, probably wants to finally be introduced. Oh crap, I do that, right. Catching myself I cut in and introduce Eric to Matthew.

Eric says a brief hello. He leans forward so Matthew can see him through Sarah's window. "It's been pretty hard to meet you. I started to feel like it wasn't gonna happen. You keep a busy schedule."

Matthew grins and agrees that he's wanted to meet Eric but, all these things kept coming up and it's been really difficult. He tells him that Justin talks about him all the time.

Huh. Justin never says anything to me. He's definitely Matthew's friend but it's weird how little Justin discusses it with me.

Eric nods and everyone goes silent. Matthew points back at the studio and tells us he has paint drying. We say goodbye and start to leave. Eric suggests they try to meet again.

"Definitely." Matthew tells him, nodding.

Has he really wanted to meet Eric? I know I've tried to introduce them. He hasn't said anything to me about being all that into the idea.

Must talk to Justin about it more.

Were you all that interested when Justin told you?

Hrmm. You have a good point.

Of course I do. The clear voice chuckles.

No you don't. You hardly knew anything at all. Justin's probably told Matthew a lot more, stupid. The grating voice moans in disgust.

Well, he may know more than I did, but Eric is hard to put on paper. Even now I go back and forth. His most fascinating characteristic is something I can't explain, but I know it's there. Only I don't know what it is. Either way, Matthew's always been more open to this kind of stuff. More like Sarah in a way. He should get a kick out of it.

We start to drive away. It was a brief meeting and I expected Eric to say more. He always says so much it's strange how little he said. We all feel a little hungry, so we decide to get something to eat. It's Sunday and every place we find is closing. We're in a weird part of town that I don't know. Sarah can't think of any place either. Suddenly, I recognize where we are. I tell Sarah to park and we'll walk over to a famous Mexican food stand I've heard of. It's supposed to be open 24 hours. Parking is a nightmare. It takes some time but Sarah finally finds a spot.

We walk over to the place which is little more than a small hut on the side of the road. I've never eaten here but it's very popular and famous for some reason. There's a long line. Sarah and Eric try to talk but the traffic drowns out all conversation. Cars zoom by less than five feet away. It's a busy street. I only catch a few words as they talk. Standing in line for ten minutes with Eric trying to talk to Sarah, I watch him start to grow irritated. A large truck rumbles by and Eric throws his hands up in the air. He turns to me.

"You know, I'm trying to get to know her and I can barely hear anything she says!" He looks around at all the cars and people and holds his hands out as if to say, 'what were you thinking?'

He struggles to find words. "You know?" He says, irritated, motioning to all the cars. He's yelling now to be heard. "Why would you pick a place like this where we can't hear anything we say over the traffic?"

I look over at the cars whizzing by. My heart sinks. He's right. My cheeks tingle. Does he have to point it out right in front of her? Everything feels awkward. It was my decision to come here. I put us here and there isn't even a chance to be social and talk. He put himself out there at coffee and told us lots of things about what he thinks and his theories and now he doesn't get a chance to see what she thinks. I didn't know it would be like this. That doesn't make it right. I should have thought about the traffic.

Idiot. You weren't thinking.

He's got a right to be mad. What does he get out of this? He gets to hear himself talk about things he's already thought. I hate repeating my own thoughts. I always like it better when people ask questions. He probably feels the same.

The traffic isn't going to work and I can't think of anywhere else to go that's cheap. It's Sunday, places are closing early. We decide we're all tired and hungry. Eric is irritated we drove around for so long only to end up at a place like this. We drive back to my apartment. He says goodbye and tells Sarah he hopes it's been an interesting conversation. Shrugging his shoulders he apologizes to her for getting irritated. She insists he has no reason to apologize. I sink lower in my seat. He shouldn't have apologized. It was my fault. He explains he doesn't know the area that well and isn't sure why I chose that place.

In her usually cheerful state Sarah tells him it's all fine and it was great to meet him. It's hard to get Sarah down, so I believe her. Sarah and I walk up to my apartment.

As soon as we walk in and close the door I ask, "So, honestly, what do you think of him?"

Sarah stares right at me, her smile drops, suddenly serious. "I have no doubt he can read my mind."

I feel the color drain from my face. What?! That's what she thinks? How can she say that? How is that even a possibility? Where did that even come from?? Gahh!

"Sarah... what?!" I put my hands on my face and throw them off to illustrate to what degree she's lost her mind and blown mine.

Who's crazier? Him or her? They are both insane!! The frantic voice cries out.

She's not crazy. She's just not thinking! I block the idea out of my mind and blow it off. Which one is further out there? Her or him? Where the hell did that even come from?

Sarah sees me struggling with the whole idea and adds a disclaimer. She also definitely thinks it's a cult. "California," she tells me, "is big on cults because everyone is so open minded! I mean think about this place, everyone's open to whatever and loves drugs."

I sit down on the futon and stare at her. Trying hard to convey the emotion I feel. I try to create the most dumbfounded expression I can. She's probably not feeling it. God, I'm not sure which idea is more ridiculous. Let's see, either he can read minds or it's a bizarre bookstore cult. Neither one makes any sense. Why would anyone try and bring people into a cult like this? Ugh! Why would she think that I would get sucked into a cult? Visions of group suicides with Kool-aid, mass weddings, or stockpiling huge amounts of weapons for Doomsday flash through my head. Weak. Really weak.

"Sarah," I say shaking my head in disbelief, "I'm sorry. People can say whatever they want but people only get sucked into psycho crap like that if they are desperately seeking a group to belong to, or are weak, naïve, easily controlled or impressionable or some combination of the above. I may not be the most worldly, street smart person ever but I'm not the kind to jump into some crazy cult. I don't plan on ever getting married so I don't have some wife to offer up as a sacrifice. I don't have money to give away. I hate guns. Suicide is the dumbest thing I ever heard of. So I don't know why anyone would bother with me, you know? Besides, most are crazy Christians anyway and I'm not about to go back to buying into Christianity."

I continue my rant that it could all be a matter of perspective. My church growing up was frequently called a cult because it was attached, however distantly, to the Mormons. It was out of the 'Christian mainstream'. In Springfield if you aren't a mad, Bible-thumping Baptist you could have the makings for a cult. I confess maybe that's why it's easy for me to dismiss the idea. It's something I've heard before.

Sarah doesn't give in so easily. Maybe I'm right but she's worried about it and I should be careful. I get frustrated. Feels like she's mothering me. Trying to keep me safe by controlling me. Only, my mother always gave me open reigns. She trusted my judgment Sarah needs too as well.

We sit silently. I relax and let my mind run. Pondering it a little more I take Sarah's feelings to heart. Her fear for me is unwarranted. I can chock that up to her female mothering instinct. I respect that she's a good friend for bothering to care. But let's say it is a cult. If it is there are going to be things they want from me. No point in running a cult if you don't get anything out of it. All I need to do is be more aware and examine things from that angle. If it is, I get an education. I get to see how it works and what they try to do. No harm in that and no harm in heeding Sarah's warning.

Then there's the mind reading part. That's so absurd I can't even begin to talk to her about it. Sarah leaves and I have mixed feelings about the whole day. Sarah is the only person I know who might have listened to Eric and not called me crazy. I can't explain to her why but I know there's something more there, under the surface. Neither of her explanations are anywhere close. No mind-reading and no cult. It's something else. Only, now that she's out, I'm really on my own to figure out what it is.

The next time I talk to Eric he doesn't bring up the way things ended with Sarah. Instead he brings up Matthew again. Now that Eric's finally met Matthew he's interested in meeting with both of us.

"When you teach someone in school," he explains, "you don't want to teach part of the class something one day and then the next day, teach the other half the same thing. Everything I've talked to you about I'm going to have to talk to your brother about. Why should I do it twice?"

Why should he do it at all? I wonder. What's in it for him? I know he wants to make his bookstore a school but it seems a strange thing to make a school for. What are people going to do with what they learn? It's not like they can get a degree. The whole student-teacher thing is confusing. Where can he go with it? What's the purpose? I'm sure he has an answer but I'd rather see it for myself than hear it. I know there's something about what he tells me that draws me in. There's something there, inside of it, and I want to know what that is. Does that make me a student? Has he ever said it? I've never thought it. It's a weird thing.

I don't see Eric for the next few days. Finally, Matthew has a night off, so we go to Tujunga together. Matthew drives, while I navigate.

We meet Eric at the bookstore. He gives Matthew a brief tour. I pause by the thermos full of Kona coffee. Fresh, hot, smooth Kona. I know from Eric's house he struggles to make ends meet. It would be wrong to take a cup of Kona without buying anything. Wouldn't it? I want the Kona, but I can't. Grumbling to myself I go watch the micro hamsters.

Eric decides he doesn't want to stay at the store. Matthew has the same inspired look I'm sure I had when I first saw the store. When I see his face I smile and nod. Something about this place, he feels it too.

We get into Eric's car and start driving. He tells us we're going out into the canyons. The night is warm, the darkness is thick. No lights along these roads. Eric swerves off the main road onto the rocky canyon floor. Grabbing the side of the door I squint out to see if we're following any type of road. It doesn't seem like it. Cruising right across the canyon floor in a Thunderbird. Waiting to hear the crack of a rock on the floor my nerves are on edge. Any time now... any time... the anticipation is killing me. He's driving too fast!

We finally park and never hit anything. I release my grip on the door handle. He must know his way around.

I get out and look up. It's a brilliant canopy of stars. I smile. All around us, inky black night. The dark outlines of the mountains are shadowed against the rich, blue starry sky. It's always so clear in California but you can never tell because the city is so bright. Out here I can tell. The stars are so alive. A warm breeze blows. I'm wrapped in a perfect blanket of summer.

The bottom of the canyon floor is littered with stones and pebbles. It's like the bottom of a dried up river. There isn't much dirt. Everywhere I walk the stones crunch under my feet.

Eric speaks from the darkness. "The sound of the stones. Each time you take a step. Listen to it. You can use it to put yourself into a specific state of mind. The rhythm of your walking. The sound echoing through your body, through your mind."

I crunch a few more steps. I don't know what he's talking about.

His voice travels through the night. He isn't talking loud but it echoes as if he's right beside me.

"I used to do it when I was younger. I would go out and walk and just clear my mind. The rhythm of my walking and the sound of the stones would put me in this deep, profound state. You can shift your consciousness by paying attention to the sound as you walk. It's also how you walk across the stones. It's the feeling of it." Eric's voice swirls around me.

He doesn't ask if I understand. I don't.

You should walk around and try it he tells me. I don't even know what he meant, but I agree. I understand the words, it's the context of what he's saying that I don't get. I try to put the whole thing together in my head. It doesn't really hit me. Still, I have the chance to walk around in the dark and feel the night. That's something I really enjoy so I'm happy to do it.

I start to walk away and he continues, "You've gotten a lot of time with me by yourself and this is the first time I've really had to talk to your brother. I need to talk to him in private like I did with you."

Why did he say that? He must think I feel left out. I nod my head to confirm I really don't mind walking around by myself. I want to. Duh, he can't see me nod. "It's cool." I assure him calling out. "I want to walk around."

I walk toward the mountains until I hear a stream. Following the sound I find a little mountain stream winding along the canyon walls. Sticking my arm in, I try to gauge its depth. It's too deep to cross. The smell, the wonderful refreshing scent of it, fills me. What music. The merry sound of it splashing on its way dances through my ears. There are so many variations of splashes. I smile. I sit and listen to it, mesmerized. Time slips away.

Slowly, I circle my hands through the water to feel the crisp wetness but not disturb the music of the stream. After awhile I get up and follow the stream in the direction of the current. A large grouping of tall reeds rises out of the darkness. The reeds seem really out of place in the desert canyon. They look like the kind you see in pictures of Egypt near the Nile. I start to walk through the reeds when my foot squishes softly. Using my foot to feel I shift it around. Sand! The whole area is covered in sand. Bending down I run my fingers through it. Silky, smooth and soft, I can hardly believe it! The reeds are about as tall as I am. It feels like a hidden oasis. A sanctuary that shouldn't be in this deserted canyon. My little secret place. I chuckle to myself, happy at my discovery.

Eric's yell breaks through my sanctuary. They're looking for me. I yell back and start walking toward the sound. It's an easy walk back. Stumbling out of the darkness I find them sitting on the hood of Eric's car.

"Have a good walk?" Eric asks.

"Yeah, I found a cool stream over there." I point in the direction of the stream.

"Yeah, we walked around some too." Matthew offers peacefully.

We sit quietly for awhile looking up at the stars. They sit on the hood of the car while I sit on a big rock.

"You know," Eric says quietly, "they have detected these giant shapes that shoot through the sky. You can't see them with the naked eye but they have cameras now that can capture them. They aren't sure what they are but they are about, I don't know, like maybe 6 feet long and they just shoot across the sky in big groups. They're basically like, energy organisms or something like that."

"Really? They have pictures of them?" I ask surprised. I've never heard of that. I can't believe they've discovered something like that and people aren't talking about it all over the place. I look up at the black sky and try to imagine these big streaks of glowing energy flying through the night. It's hard to imagine.

"It's just particles. Why couldn't something be moving at a higher speed, or vibration, and move through matter differently? Why does it have to be micro-size small to move through matter? They found that there are particles moving through the entire planet. Everything in the world has these particles beaming through it. Why can't something larger be moving at a higher frequency and move through space, or matter, differently?"

I guess they could. I never heard of it though. I'm really surprised they have pictures.

"Makes sense to me." Matthew said. Matthew is so much more open-minded, I think smiling. Why do I doubt so much? Why would someone lie about seeing pictures? Maybe a kid would but he's old enough to know I can look it up somewhere. It's good to be skeptical. I guess.

It's late so we decide to call it a night. Eric takes us back to our car and we head back to LA. Matthew and I are both pretty quiet. Finally Matthew says quietly, "I think he can read my mind."

An electric shock jolts through me. Not him too! What is going on? Why would Matthew say that? "What? Have you talked to Sarah?!" I gasp out.

"How could I talk to Sarah? She's your friend. Last time I saw her was when you guys came to see me at work."

I don't say anything. Matthew doesn't offer up anything else. It's pointless to ask why he thinks that. People can't read minds period. Why ask for proof for something that doesn't exist?

Walking up the stairs to our apartment I suddenly feel very protective of Matthew. It's one thing for me to meet with Eric but now Matthew's involved and he suddenly believes he can actually read his mind. It's ridiculous!

Maybe he's been a magician before. Some kind of trick or something. I need to find out who he is. I need to research everything I can. I'll also be more watchful and keep an eye on everything he does. Words are words. Actions rarely lie. Suddenly, now that Matthew's met him I feel a risk not present before. I have to keep him safe. Protected. I make the choices for my life but what if Matthew is following? I don't want him to follow me down a road if I don't know where it goes.

The conversation at the coffee shop with Eric and Sarah is where I clearly recall a big, fractured reaction inside of me. The lines were drawn.

There was a civil war brewing. The sides became more polarized each time I met with Eric. Our conversation at the coffee shop was the shot heard around my inner world.

Part of me had no doubt that Eric was totally and completely out of his mind. I wanted to believe that. Nobody else in the sane world, unless they're on major hallucinogens, says they see flying dimensional energy shapes moving through their waking reality. It defied everything any kind of scientist, medical doctor or any kind of technology allowed for. Black was black. White was white.

When I made my decision to turn away from God, I really turned away from anything having to do with my 'inner-voice', or Navigator. I refused to follow my instincts. They'd led me nowhere and I wanted stable, reliable answers. This created a very sarcastic, coldly logical, even slightly bitter personality. It was domineering, controlling, and smashed that little voice into the ground.

Eric's world called to that lost voice. It empowered my Navigator because he gave it logic, the weapon of my brain. He challenged many beliefs fundamental to my world. Namely, that all there is can be seen with my eyes.

This created a slowly rising inner turmoil. In the matter of a minute, I could swing from agreeing with Eric, to decrying him as a lunatic. I would swing from being intrigued, to not believing a word.

It was an inner duel.

The cold, rational part had spent five years in power. It had tried to kill every part of my instinct. Exterminating the part of me that believed in things I couldn't see. Condemning it as foolish, childish and naïve.

In the time I've known Eric, I've seen that this isn't unique to me. You follow your Navigator on enough wild goose-chases and dead-ends and you get burned out. The idea you have to 'grow up' and stop listening to the Navigator, that inner-voice, is a logical but ultimately unfortunate step.

Many people, once they push their Navigator away long enough, won't have the strength to ever reclaim it. Lucky for me, I had Eric. Like an arms dealer giving resources to my inner revolution. Without his direct intervention I doubt I could have ever read enough books, or heard enough lectures, to ever rise up against the tyrant I'd created. The amount of time and energy he had to put into me to do this says a lot about his true giving nature.

Few people would ever give so much, gaining nothing.

Once Matthew met Eric the tyrant gained power. It preyed on my instinct to nurture and protect him. Which is exactly the reaction Sarah seemed to have towards me. If I wanted to keep Matthew safe, I needed to have power over Eric.

My quiet inner-voice, my Navigator, was kicked into some cold, dark part of my mind. It felt something from Eric. It was given strength by him. And unknown to me then, my Navigator had a power I hadn't fully conceived. One thing was for certain, it wasn't going down without a fight.

... Oh, and those dimensional, energy things that move through reality? Well, I have seen them too. If that's crazy, it's the kind of crazy, my friend, I wish may one day grace your life. You can travel the world over and never know such a marvel that touches you so deeply. Truly, to experience such a sight is a blessing and a wonder beyond words.

have you ever noticed how much effort we put into rules and regulations? constantly shifting and changing them to fit our notions of what is acceptable? how we need to always...

Hunt for Reason

chapter eight

I've never investigated anyone before. It feels invasive. I always give everyone the benefit of the doubt. Wouldn't I want the same? Yes, but... I can't be naïve. There's no harm in taking a look. If I want to know something I have to seek it out, it won't be given to me.

I turn on my computer and wait for it to boot. I struggle to decide if what I'm doing is right. How would I feel if someone investigated me? It's all a gray area. Eric hasn't shown any ulterior or harmful motives. Forget it, I should play Civilization instead. It's a nice game where I get to start at the time when humans first started to settle down and create my own civilization. All strategy based but I build my own little world throughout time. Once I start building the Great Pyramids none of this will matter. Focus! Stay on target.

What are his motives?? Do we even know?? He teaches people for free, he gives his time away! Who does that? Nothing for nothing!! He wants something... he wants something! The frantic voice wails.

The paranoid thought triggers a moment of panic. No, don't go there. This is silly. He's passionate about it. Some people do what they love. It's not always about money.

Just get it over with!

Right. Get it over with. I'll always wonder if I don't look. Okay. Stretching out I get ready to crack down on the Internet. Time to play James Bond.

I begin searching the Internet for Eric Pepin. Hmm... nothing really comes up. I try different search engines. Still nothing. What about white pages, different places he's lived? Maybe he hasn't been truthful about that. No returns for any Eric Pepin in California. Fishing for random record search websites I start scrounging for any kind of bite at all. Hours later I've found nothing. Not one single mention. They all return the same totality of nothing. My eyes wander to my desktop where my Civilization game icon beckons me. Come on, that will be more fun. Kick back. Build a civilization to stand the test of –

Pathetic. You're going to give up already. Looks like he's going to win. Who's going to look out for Matthew? Not you obviously.

I scream out loud and bang my hands on my desk. "Fine! Shut up! I'm going to do this."

There has to be something on him. I will find something. Go broader. I start searching for Pepin. No mention of anything or anyone remotely connected to the person I know. The school? Go for Auxien. Thirty minutes later I have my first bite. It's a post on... a paranormal forum? It looks like Eric writing it. He's asking if anyone has ever considered the idea that the planet is a living organism. There's a brief summary of his idea and he mentions there's more information if anyone's interested.

I look below his post. There are no replies. Looks like nobody's interested.

"Crap. Maybe Sarah's right." I tell myself out loud. Maybe it's already out there and there's nothing special about it at all.

See, he's a fraud and you're a gimp for listening to any of it.
Or maybe... because it isn't mainstream nobody has the vision to see what he's trying to say. College flashbacks swarm inside my head.

Yeah, people always go with the flow damn it. I'd spent most of my college years fighting to get an education. All they wanted was for me to get in line and go through the mill, like everyone else. It pissed me off to no end. My freshman year I fought to get into senior and graduate level courses. They let me in, probably hoping I'd fail, to teach me a lesson. I did better in those courses than in my High-School-take-two, general education crap classes. Then they told me I wouldn't graduate unless I took all the classes they require.

"What a joke." I scoff at the memory. "Do it. Research his planet theory. See what's out there."

I psyche myself up for another round of Internet detective. I start to search for similar philosophies about the planet. Spiritual connections. How it thinks, how it functions.

Some time passes and movement out the window catches my eye. Damn, the street lights are turning on. I've been sitting here all day. I've found nothing. It's everything I remember from five years ago. New-Age Mother-Earth hug a tree because everything is alive and we're all part of the planet stuff. Sarah's wrong. There's nothing like what Eric's talking about out there. Not his details, not his levels of connections, nothing.

I rub my eyes and get up for a drink. What a surprise, everything in the fridge has been expired for three months. Closing the door to the frozen mold chamber I sit back at the computer and decide to do more research on Eric. I start again with the only other name I can think of; Justin. He's got an unusual last name so there's a chance.

Big surprise, nothing comes up.

Not satisfied I search for Auxien on other search engines and come up with a business that builds web sites. Finally, Christ, something. It's his business.

Now you've got him. Now you'll find something. The grating voice drives me on. Hungry to get something on Eric that proves he's nothing special or a fraud con-artist.

I look over his business website and see a list of clients. Maybe some of them have another connection to him. Every client listed I research. Nothing. Zero. Zilch. The most boring, normal websites imaginable. Oh... a horse ranch... wow, scandalous.

I think back to things he's said about himself. Rated one of the top ten psychics by some kind of institute, found missing people, tracked submarines. Desperate I search and search and search. There's nothing! Not one single scrap of evidence for any of it on the Internet. My back starts to throb, signaling it's time to take a break. "Well super investigator, what do we know?"

"Ugh!" I groan and rub my head. "Well, we know there's nothing good, bad or indifferent about him anywhere. He has a business with perfectly normal clients. And... we know his ideas aren't something everybody knows like Sarah said."

Who is this guy? Why the Hell is he giving time to me? Why is he teaching anyone? Why put all your time into teaching random people you don't know, stuff like this? Who does that? It doesn't make any sense! There has to be a reason, a why, a what for! The uncertainty eats away at me. Without an answer to why he's teaching me, and now Matthew, there's a vacuum that needs to be filled.

"Anything else?" I lean forward and stare at the floor. "Yeah, we know there's something here. There's something to all of this. Only we're not smart enough to know what."

That's right. You're not working hard enough, you're not pushing yourself. Take control.

Without answers I have no power. That doesn't sit well with part of me. It hounds me relentlessly. It feels like I have no control. Makes me feel overwhelmed and tired.

Pacing my room I go back over what I know. What he's given me. "He says he teaches people. He does have a nice bookstore. We know that. He says it's also a school. We know Justin and there's nothing wrong with him."

Actually Justin's got his act mostly together. I don't admit that to myself out loud. That makes it more real. "We know he thinks the planet is a living organism. That... we aren't the people standing right here, in this room, just our body. We're energy beings... energy... this eternal soul... a being made, formed of pure energy. That energy radiates out which is the aura. We know he believes God is the Force, which is a giant organism of energy... and when it created everything here it made the Darkside... which is like real evil."

Frustration turns to anger. Why! Why?! What is it? What's here?! It's so much information. All crammed in so perfectly connected. My brain burns through everything he's ever told me. I replay conversations we've had, again and again. Believes in past lives but thinks most are DNA. Doesn't believe in ghosts like Hollywood. See's flying energy shapes, in the sky even. Flaw, find the flaw in his thinking and you've got a crack. If he just read it in different places they should conflict. Different points of view, shouldn't match.

Grabbing my hair I scream out loud! Pacing in circles. Trying to find an edge, a moment. There's nothing. "God dammit!" I swear and grab a shirt off my bed to throw it at the wall. I've been rehearsing the same scenes and conversations for hours. Round and round. I can't find anything wrong.

I slump in my chair. Everything feels strange. Even though I've only been pacing my room my body is flush with sweat. I'm surging with energy like I could go out and run 20 miles. All his ideas and theories are spinning now, non-stop, through my mind. Universes, cosmic explosions, the beginning of time, the Force, God, energy bodies, red cells, white cells, micro... macro... my body is a universe... my consciousness in my body... God's consciousness in the universe... the planet's consciousness-

"Enough! I give!" I grab my head as if that will make it stop. I'm obsessing now. Need to stop. I go and sit in the shower for an hour and then give up for the night.

The next day, I'm back at it. For two days I scrutinize every angle. When I finish all I have to show for it is everything I learned the first day. He has a web business that I already knew about and a web forum posting trying to get someone interested in what he has to say. It's nothing.

I need more information. Start making mental notes of everything he says about himself. Every person he says he knows. Every job he's ever had. Every place he's ever lived.

I talk it out, to try and get my strategy clear. "My method will be simple. I won't judge and jump to conclusions. I will draw in data. All my practice writing will come in very handy. In order to write about something you must first study it. Right? I will study him - objectively." Part of me wants to make a judgment. It wants to reveal him as a fraud when nothing points to that definitively. Stressing impartiality I get my outlook back into check.

"Impartially, this way I won't expect any particular outcome and taint the results. Good, bad or indifferent all I need is data. In the end the data will speak for itself."

Seems like a lot of work just to know someone.

No. I can't think like that. He's not someone. We have to admit we've never met someone like him. He's weird. He's different somehow. "We have to watch how he treats people. Watch how they treat him. Write down any information he gives about himself or people he knows and research it. It's a simple process really and one that shouldn't involve doing anything wrong. We're not going to break into his house or anything harmful. We study him. If we want to know something what's the best way to do it?"

I get up and pace my room. To set my resolve. I feel like a general laying out his war plan. Must set the will to maintain the long haul. Forge the miles ahead. Patience. Know the goal. Like playing a strategy game... my course has to be clear. "Experience it. Life observations and interactions. Not what he says but what he does. Not what others say but my own experience. That's right. That's always the way. This is no different." Yes. It's a good course. Sure and sound. I will find the truth because it will come to me. It will come to the surface and I will be ready to see it for what it is.

A few days later I meet up with Eric. We go out for coffee at Rocky Cola, the little diner we'd been to before. On our way driving back to L.A. to drop me off he finally brings up Sarah and asks what she thought. I pause and think a moment. Well crap, what do I say to that? I could tell the truth and judge his reaction. Of course, Sarah may not want me to tell him that. She might be offended if I choose to speak for her. Oh come on. Sarah usually says what she thinks. If she were here she'd probably tell him herself.

"She thought it was really interesting." I say, still deciding which way I should go.

He nods. "I see, well, interesting is... okay. That's all she said? She didn't say wow, this is mind-blowing stuff! Or, gee, he really gave me a lot of great stuff to think about?"

"Well," I admit, "She did say she thinks you can read her mind."

He laughs. "Well, okay, that's something I guess." He lets it go quickly and doesn't ride on the idea. Someone looking for power should have ran with that. Try and make me think maybe it is possible, or plant some doubt to gain control. He barely acknowledged it.

I groan. I'm not sure how this next one is going to turn out but here goes. Guess we'll see how he reacts to this. "She also thought you were part of a cult."

I watch his reaction out of the corner of my eye. I can't be too obvious. He nods his head. "Yeah, I've heard that one before. I mean, any time you have a group of spiritual people who think alike and their philosophy isn't exactly part of the normal Christian religion, people want to throw, 'oh my God, cult!' Out there. As far as I'm concerned it's what the large congregation calls the small congregation."

He throws up his hand as if to say, 'what can I say?' There's nothing he can say. It doesn't matter one way or the other. I won't be swayed into thinking it is or isn't. Time will tell and his reaction is all raw information. Take it in, observe, and collect it for later.

He continues, "What she's really saying is cult in a negative context. Like, I mean last year Time magazine or something released the FBI's cult test, okay. And we figured, yeah, finally we're gonna know for sure." Eric grins and laughs. He wasn't taking the test seriously and makes it sound like an entertaining joke for them. He continues, "So we all sat down and took it and we failed. We missed it by like, I don't know, 10 points or something like that. Oh well, we'll have to try again. I'm joking but you get my point? Everyone has their own, you know, criteria for what they even think a 'cult' is!"

He flashes quotes with his fingers when he says 'cult'. I get his point, it has different meanings depending on how you throw the word around. Eric keeps going, "I mean, 1,500 years ago Christianity was a cult. The Romans fed them to lions. Now look at them! Most of them would happily feed everyone else to lions if they could! You could be a Christian in America and go over to India where everybody is Hindu and they'd say you were in a cult. Now if you're asking me, based on some of that criteria, if we're a cult the answer is yes. We are. We're a group of people, a very small minority, with shared spiritual beliefs. It's coming from a single source of knowledge, me, the so-called cult master. But the real question is does that make it bad? Well, it's really about not understanding something and the culture you live in and what's dominant in that culture and just, well, ignorance."

He nods his head to confirm ignorance is the main thrust of it. He raises his index finger, as if leaving at that isn't enough, there's more he wants to say, "I don't have an issue with being called a cult. My problem is, what they are really saying with that... what they are *really* trying to say is something really negative. That's where I get a bit resentful. Now, your friend Sarah, she seems nice, I really liked her. And it's like she met someone who she probably thought was pretty strong and came off really, like, intimidating, because I can seem really in your face and I was talking about things that maybe she never thought of. So it's the unknown for her. And for her to make a judgment, because that's what it is, to make a judgment like that without even knowing me or what I'm about I can't respect. But I think she's intimidated that there's someone you find interesting and it takes you away from her. Because it seems like she's the only one you know that you talk to this kind of stuff about and I think she's in love with you and afraid she'll lose that power. Now maybe she's not consciously thinking that but that's what's going on."

I grin and start to chuckle. "Sarah is not in love with me. Things have never been like that."

"Uhh, I don't know about that. I think you're being naïve. You know, men are usually pretty slow." Eric says sounding skeptical.

No way. Not Sarah. I've never had a moment with Sarah where I felt her approaching me sexually on any level. Are you sure? Think about other girl friends you've had who crept up on you with surprise feelings. Well, I can't say that about all my girl friends I've had but Sarah has always been pretty up front and straight.

"Nah, I've known her for a year now and nothing has ever come up. I mean, she might feel protective of me as her friend but she's not secretly in love or anything like that."

Eric slides a smile like he thinks I'm being dumb but doesn't know how to lay it out. "Well, you know... maybe. But that's women. Women are very protective because it's how they're built. It's in their programming you could say. They are meant to look after the nest and the young and they will also try to keep people they love safe. Usually by keeping them close. So, she may be intimidated that you're going into the unknown and it's a kind of love, a selfish love, but a kind of love that she wants to keep you close and safe in a world that she knows. She doesn't know this world so she wants to pull you out back into the safe and familiar."

Even that seems a stretch. Sarah and I come together by ourselves but rarely do our worlds really share the same space. Sometimes I'll go up to her house for a party but we don't really share social circles. Maybe he thinks we spend more time than we do and have more mutual friends.

Eric motions his hand like it's up in the air, or up to me what I decide to think about it. "But the cult thing, I mean, yeah, if you want to break it down... it is a cult. I mean, I see myself as a spiritual teacher. I have students. They come to me, one central figure, to learn. We can call it a school, or a group, or whatever, but it's a spiritual group with a minority view so what is that? It's a cult. They used to call Catholics a cult too. When that one guy there, the one who was killed, the big president of the United States..."

"Kennedy." I say getting an idea where he's going with it.

"Yeah, when he was running, he was a Catholic and everybody freaked out that there was going to be a Catholic in the White House. It wasn't mainstream or socially acceptable. Can you imagine them doing that now? That was only what, 30 or 40 years ago? So people throw that around when there's a spiritual group of people who think alike that they don't understand. When actually, when they say cult it's meant in a very specific, negative way. They mean the groups that kill themselves or stockpile weapons and have all these wives and, you know what? Almost all of those are Christian based. They use fear and fire and brimstone and huge control tactics and we may be a cult but we don't do anything like that."

Nervously, I check the road as Eric looks over at me more than watching where we're driving. His point makes sense. It's not like I didn't already see some of it. He asked what Sarah thought. Doesn't mean I think it. I consider telling him but can't decide how to interject since I started it in the first place. He probably feels attacked and wants to defend himself. I'd be defensive too.

"All of my students I tell them, 'Read everything about everything'. Every other cult only wants you to read what reinforces their philosophy. How many Christian pastor's are going out there telling their congregation, sure, go read a book about Buddhism or Hinduism... and then let's talk about it. I say know as much as you can about everything. And when you want to go and you think you've got nothing left to learn, then go! How many cults just let people leave? I don't make anyone do anything they don't want to do. Fuck, I even give people the boot I don't want to teach. I'm kicking people out! You know? That's a horrible way to run a cult. How many cult leaders you know tell people to get lost? It's ridiculous."

He continues on for a few more minutes. I don't get any more information other than a confirmation that there are others. He repeatedly says he has many students. Why haven't I met them? At least I know they're there. It's true what he says about control. The negative aspects of cults are fear and control. In that arena Christianity seems to have the monopoly. If Justin is any example, he goes and does whatever he wants. Peggy has more control over him than Eric. Everything else he mentions may or may not be true about booting people. That I'll have to see. Before he drops me off at home he hands me a tape.

He tells me it's about entities. "It's a lecture we recorded awhile ago. Listen to it. Have your brother listen to it too and then we can talk." I agree to listen to it and share it with Matthew. We say our good-byes and he drives off.

Later in the day I see Matthew and tell him about the tape. I put it in our stereo and get ready to listen to it together.

He gives me an, "Oh cool," which tells me he's not really paying attention. I look over at him and can tell he's stoned again. Ever since he and Peggy got the big brick he's been getting stoned more and more. Better to talk to myself than somebody stoned who doesn't have the mental capacity to really engage the material. I head to my room for the night. I can listen to the tape later.

don't conform, but fit in. be an individual, just like everybody
else. think for yourself, as long as everyone agrees with you.
choose the path less taken, only not without…

Social Security

chapter nine

A new project at work switches my schedule back to nights. It doesn't
take long for me to lose track of everything. Farah keeps me posted
and up to date on things. My little informant tells me Eric has begun
meeting with Matthew. She also talks about her floundering love life
with a younger guy she's chasing. He treats her bad. She can do
better and should get over it and move on. This isn't what she wants
to hear which is why she keeps bringing it up. She wants my opinion
to change… or something. My mind is more focused on Matthew so
her soap opera fades to background noise. I'm not around. There's no
other way I can know what's going on with Matthew. I'm lucky to talk
to him for five minutes before I head out the door to work.

One day I get lucky. I'm up and around getting ready for work.
Everybody else has the day off so they're hanging at the apartment. I
watch Matthew to see if he seems different. Main topic: sex. Woop,
woop, ohh yeaaah. Nope it's all the same. Maybe a change wouldn't
be so bad.

The next day I'm off so I find some time alone in the apartment. After
my 5pm breakfast I sit down in the living room. I don't own much,
but have a decent stereo. I keep it on a little wooden roll-away
cabinet along with a TV that was left behind by one of my old college
roommates. The tape Eric gave me catches my eye. Crap, I forgot all
about it. I flip the tape over to look at both sides. 'Entities side 1' and
'Entities side 2'.

"Well, not the most original titles but since it's about entities I guess that fits." I chuckle.

Sitting in front of the stereo I hit play. I'll give it a few minutes to see if it catches my attention. It starts playing fuzzy static. I'm sitting on the floor, leaning into a radio, listening to fuzzy static. I smile. Like an old radio show. Suddenly, I remember the big, old tape recorder Justin brought out when I first met Eric. Throwing my head back I laugh out loud to myself. "No way." This is what he was talking about, 'they want to record me.' They make these tapes to listen to. Awesome.

Eric's voice comes in and he starts off talking about things he talked about at the coffee shop with Sarah. The imprints in the walls. The contraction and expansion. What ghosts really are and how they work. His voice crackling through the stereo makes me feel like it's a transmission broadcasting from the past. A time before we had clear radio signals and recording equipment. If only he had his own sound studio where he would say 'ghost' and the soundman in back would make a spooky sound.

Even though it's a tape, there's something personal about it. The soft hiss of the tape. Night falling and me sitting near the speaker like a campfire. Feels real.

Then Eric starts talking about a particular experience he had. "I remember there was a house that was really, severely possessed. And it was abandoned. I interviewed two of the people that had lived there. Two different families, and they gave me different stories. The stories were intriguing and peaked my interest. One of the stories always kind of recurred to me and I always review this in my head all of the time trying to make sense of it..." You hear him barely chuckle through the hiss of the tape.

"So now, I'll damn you guys with the same thought. They lived in this house. The house is like right by the road. The road was so close to the house, like from here to the coffee table. It was the main road. So when they built the house they weren't really thinking. Nobody envisioned cars speeding through and stuff at that time period. And one story she said that her son, who was like 17 or 18 at the time, was there with his friend and one daughter that was younger was sitting out front doing something. And directly to the left about maybe the distance of 'this here' is a driveway that goes down and next to the driveway is this big patch of huge bushes." He makes a reference to something he can see but isn't clear on the tape. I get the impression if the house was built really close to the road the driveway has to be scrunched pretty close to the house as well.

The tape keeps playing with Eric. "And in New England we get, like, berry bushes and 'viney' shit and all sorts of stuff that grows. It's very green. And they're sitting there on a summer day, in the daylight keep in mind or it's dusk, it was like the sun was setting but it was still bright. And they said this black car, and they never really distinguished what kind but I've always envisioned it as being a very fancy black car like a Rolls Royce or something. I don't know why. Maybe they told me it was a fancy, big car like a limo or something. But this old, old fancy car comes rolling up very quietly and they were like, 'wow, look at this car', it caught their attention. And it stopped in front of the bushes and they say this little boy jumps out of the bushes, runs over to the car door, the door opens, he jumps in and the door shuts and it starts to drive away past them." Now it really feels like I'm listening to an old mystery-thriller radio show. Eric's voice comes through the soft hiss of the tape as I imagine an old farmhouse, stuck right by a road and an old classic, shiny car comes rolling up in some poor, middle-of-nowhere place, to pick some kid up.

"So now they're like, 'what the fuck was this shit all about?' and their minds are just blown by this. So the 18 year old has this sports car. And he and his buddy jump in the car and they peel out behind. They're watching this car go up over the hill and they're right behind it and they go up over it and the fucking car's gone... vanished."

I can tell Eric's younger than he is now. He sounds much younger. It's the tone in his voice and the way he talks. He swears more openly and freely which makes it sound like some guy from college is sitting around a party telling a crazy story. There are people in the background of the tape but I can't make them out. From what little noise they make they sound a lot younger.

The tape keeps playing, "Now, I know the route. It becomes a 'Y' eventually and it goes up. If they went to the right, they would've seen dust. If they went straight they would've seen it easily because it's a long, straight stretch. But, evidently, it vanished. So I thought that was a very interesting story. It doesn't really classically fit a lot of stuff but yet it kind of can. You know what I'm saying?" Having traveled down so many dirty country roads in Missouri I can picture the scene perfectly. A super expensive car comes up, picks up a kid they've never met, and speeds off. They probably had a Mustang or some kind of muscle car, jump in, because you get bored and when you see excitement you go for it. Then the car vanishes on a road you've traveled a billion times before and know like the back of your hand. Where I grew up, nobody could hide anything like that from me. You know the place too well. That would freak me out. It's also interesting that it stuck with Eric so long. I can see why. In his world ghosts can be real, but they're either from people, or they're projections like his recorded holograms theory. This is something outside, so what is playing the hologram?

The tape crackles. Eric continues. "In either case, other stuff that they had happen in there, like the kids would always hear stuff. They would see these two little girls or whatever. They would also see this guy who was, like, this gray colored guy, kind of balding. And he would look really mean at the kids down in the basement. After one lady told me all this stuff we did a little bit more research. We found out that a man actually killed and molested two girls in this house. And he hung himself when he got found out in the basement off of the wooden ceiling beam. It was very short, you could almost stand up. It turns out he was very short himself. And he had hung himself in this basement. So the story is now starting to be put together, but we still couldn't figure out what the fuck this car and this kid had to do with anything.."

Stopping, I realize I've slowly been leaning closer and closer to the speaker. His story is compelling. I sit up straight and keep listening. "But the neighbors down the street, who never had any hauntings and never really believed in any of this stuff, I spoke to them and they told me that when nobody lived there... there used to be these metal garbage cans. They were at the bottom of the driveway. Remember the driveway goes downhill. It's like mine almost just a little bit steeper and the house is built on a hill. At the bottom were these old tin cans. Nobody had lived there in a long time. The neighbors said they would get really pissed because in the middle of the night, it would sound like kids were rolling the tin cans up and down the hill. So they would get so mad, they were driving the car to go up the street to the neighbor's house to see what the fuck's going on and there would be the cans rolling like somebody just ran off but they would never see anybody. And this would happen at night at all different times."

It's interesting. It could be kids though. Doesn't seem reliable to base a haunting off what random neighbors who live down the road tell you.

"From what I understand, it was decided that the house was so old that the owners wanted to rip it down. And they didn't like how close the house was to the road and wanted to use the property to move it back some. They had a big, huge, yellow type truck thing to rip things down and a bulldozer. But they could never plow the house down. As soon as the truck would get close to it, it would stop. Like something electrically would short it out. They could do everything else but they could never get too close to this house." My eyebrows shoot up and I lean forward laughing.

"No way." I say to the stereo. If that really happened people would be all over that. A house that can't be bulldozed? It would be headline news!

The hissing tape plays on. "At this point, we move on to me going into the house. I've seen the man. I've never seen the two girls. They kind of steered clear. But the man really, really, really disliked me because he never met anybody who had balls." Eric chuckles and I hear people in the background laughing. Only knowing him a short time I can see him saying that with a cocky smirk. It's hard to tell if he's really arrogant or if it's more for show.

"I saw him sitting in the far corner. He was sitting in the chair staring at me. He could be very scary, I suppose, to most people because he was very pale, dark eyes and was just like angry. He looked like somebody who would work in a factory in the 1950s, you know. Like a 'wife beater' type shirt with a gray button shirt hanging open with denim type pants and black boots. And he looked like somebody who was just really angry. He would look at you like, 'hate'. Then he just faded after a few seconds. I went in there and I would bring students in to train them to feel things. I think that's part of the reason that he hated me because I would bring people there to train them. It started to turn into a classroom instead of people being afraid of him. Like this is where he belonged and this was his home and that's why nobody would move in and that's why he would make everybody leave. He would feel violated. Eventually, what happened was a level 5 entity ended up in that house. Or he became the level 5 entity. For those of you that don't know, a scale of one to ten, '1' is a basic spirit, '2' is a medium spirit, '3' is a spirit that can actually, physically hit you or attack you and anything higher is just more intensity of what they can do to you."

The description of the old dead man is spooky. I feel the chill, the strength of his hate, his eyes burning. It's still so unlikely. Not enough to make me afraid to be alone in the apartment, but it's a good ghost story. He never mentioned his rating system. It's intriguing that he's encountered so many entities he's breaking them down into levels.

The tape plays but it's not Eric's voice, someone else's voice cuts in from the background. "How does he become a level 5?" The guy asks. Sounds like a young guy. Could easily be my age or younger.

Eric's voice, closer to the microphone, answers him. "Pure hate. Pure rage. Pure absorption of Darkside energy."

The same guy continues asking another question, "Don't you stop when you die? Do you stay at that level?"

Eric's voice comes in again. "No, you can progress. Hate can drive you. It can actually will molecules and energy together to forcibly

192

strike somebody in this dimension. It's just by pure mental will. And he, obviously, was an evolved spirit from another time period. But it doesn't mean that just because you awaken you purely end up as good. You can become sick and twisted even as a thinking entity. It's rare, but it does happen. One of the times that was most amusing was with this other kid Josh. I met him and he was telling me about him and his friends who were into the Golden Dawn and how they would summon up spirits and entities and use the sword for the minor and lesser pentagrams and all this other stuff. They were kind of like playing a little ego game with me because somebody I knew wanted to introduce me to them and Josh became very interested in what I was doing. Anyway, so they were telling me how they dealt with entities all the time. And, I'm sitting there thinking to myself, 'not the kind of fucking entities I know' and they're like, 'oh, we handle powerful demons and Beelzebub and Lucifer'. And I'm like, 'oh, yeah?' And Josh is like making statements how he can control them and will them." Eric laughs lightly. I smirk. Seems like some kind of Dungeons and Dragons game. Everybody knows a group of kids who think they really have magical power. When I was younger I played Dungeons and Dragons. I dabbled in Wicca and magical rituals, but I never inflated what I could actually do.

Eric's voice grows a bit quieter, "Of course I'm younger at this time too. So, I turn around one day and I'm like, 'well, let's go to this place that I know where there's this entity that I go to.' And he was like, 'sure, yeah, let's go. I'll kick their ass.' So, I'm thinking to myself, okay. I just wanted to see what really happens. So, I bring him there and he gets out of the car and we walked into the back and we kind of get through the door and we go into the cellar and he's cool so far. I'm talking to him about different things in the house and stuff that I feel. I walk up the stairs and he comes up behind me and there's a third floor. And I'm walking like through the thing and he's coming up behind me and all of a sudden I hear, 'BOOM, BOOM, BOOM!' Like a six hundred pound man is charging over the ceiling to walk down the staircase over in this far corner to come down to deal with us! And it was an entity. The entity was really pissed and he was really powerful." The scene as Eric describes it feels so real. I imagine the whole floor shaking under the weight of charging steps. In my mind I see dust fall from the ceiling.

"So, I guess here we get to go, you know? Finally we get to see what you're gonna do. I'm already at the staircase and this thing's coming. I can already feel the presence. It feels like needles, like your leg's asleep. It's like something that permeates you. It's hate energy. And I'm getting ready to do my thing and I'm going to be entertained by this so I turn around to look and he's fucking gone! So I deal with it by just kind of willing it away and stuff and I go back down the stairs and there he is standing by the car. And he's like, working the door, trying to get in the car door but I locked the door, because I always do. I'm like, 'what's the matter?' And he's like, 'nothin... nothing.' 'Why'd you leave?' 'This is fucking serious shit...' And he was just, like freaking out. He literally peed his pants." People in the background come in laughing and I chuckle too.

It's always the way. The guy who talks the most crap can never back it up. Not that I blame him really. Who would've thought it was real? Only, I would've mocked that it existed at all, not that I could destroy it. Man, if I could experience something like that, then I'd know. I wish I could be so lucky.

Eric keeps telling the story, "I mean his pants were wet. I didn't even want him to sit in my car because I didn't want any piss on my seat. So I gave him a towel or something that I had. Anyway, to me that's what I'm used to dealing with ever since I've been a kid. I guess I've been indoctrinated into it. But it was amusing to see somebody who says they deal with that shit all the time, or that it's not a problem and no big deal. Then when they see the real thing, it's a different tune. Evidently, my friend Scott tells me that they actually got around to ripping down the house. So what happened, I don't know. But they tried for like, seven years, to rip this house down. And then finally, for some reason, they were able to rip it down."

Someone's voice asks a question in the background. They talk too soft to make it out.

Eric answers them, "It was probably gone already. That's one of the reasons why."

It's the same guy's voice from before. He talks louder this time.

"That's why they were able to tear it down?" Ah, he must have asked how they dealt with the level 5 entity. So it makes sense Eric said it was already gone.

Eric confirms his question, "Right. Or somebody went there and actually got rid of him instead of letting him stay there. But I could tell you guys fascinating stories. I mean, even the bible in there, how it got split right in the middle. I mean that was an entity that did that."

I know other people are in the tape, but it's always the same voice asking questions. He asks, "The bible got split right in the middle?"

Eric's voice comes through, "Yeah, the one that's right in there. That's my little history section up in there. Yeah, that's from 1825 that bible, or 1853 one or the other. I was asked to go and do a, I hate to say it, like an exorcism. It was sitting in the back seat and we pulled up in the car and all I heard was a loud pop. I felt like something just happened, psychically, I felt it. And it was this entity. It got pissed when we pulled up to the house and it knew I was going to fuck with it and that was its way of trying to intimidate me. It split the bible right in half like a laser hit it. Like somebody took a razor and perfectly knew what page, exactly where and sliced it in half. Wanna see? I don't like messing with it too much because I'm afraid that one of these days... it's getting old. But this was locked and if you realize this is like, very firm, it ain't going nowhere. This is what happened. It's just phenomenal. If you really look at it, you know."

He keeps talking, sharing more stories and what happens when you die, the process you go through and how powerful entities are made. Finally the tape clicks. Somewhere it had already flipped over. I've been sitting here the entire time, glued in front of the stereo. I didn't even notice. Oh, yeah, back... hurts. My back complains, shooting out little shocks of pain. My legs buzz like they're covered in ants. "Argh! Suck, suck!" Legs... asleep! It's been ninety minutes alright.

Smiling, my mood is lifted, despite the daggers in my back and the ants all over my legs. It was like sitting in front of a campfire telling ghost stories. I completely lost track of time. Totally, unexpectedly got sucked in.

Yeah, Eric, but come on... no way is any of that stuff real.

It sure is interesting to think about though.

"Yeah... that's true." The stories spin through my head. But how can he think it's all real? It's fascinating really, but only as stories. It's hard to imagine anyone actually believes all that stuff is real. But if he'd taken me into a house like that, then I'd believe. Who wouldn't? That's all he needs to do. Find more haunted houses and take people into them, then they'd listen to him. Somehow, listening to it has me really upbeat. I zing with energy. I decide to go clean my room and pick up the apartment.

My room looks like a tornado blew through it. A huge pile of clothes sprawls out of my closet, heaps around the foot of my bed, and then dwindles just before it reaches my computer desk. Between my bed and window is a round glass table piled with notes, papers, books, mail, every kind of junk imaginable. To make things worse, Farrah has stacks of milk carton crates filled with her stuff, from when she moved in, piled against my wall. My walls are barren, lifeless walls. Normally it doesn't bother me. I don't even think about it. But right now, looking at the mess, makes me feel insane. I want to take everything and throw it out the window, just to have it clean!

Disgusting dirty rat-man. That's what you are. Like a filthy nest.

I go into a berserk frenzy and attack the mess without remorse.

Later that night everyone is home. I'm exhausted from my battle with my room. The armies of Dirt-dor were beaten back but definitely not defeated. Toward the end I grew so tired I shoved all my clothes into the closet and closed the door. More of a band-aid than a true fix. But after it was done and I could see all of my floor, and the table was clear and clean... I felt so relieved.

Matthew, Justin, Peggy, Farrah, Lenny and I are all sitting around the round wooden coffee table someone left for garbage at an old house I lived in. It's in good shape except they painted it with a thick black lacquer. Hard to be picky when you scavenge.

I'm sitting on Peggy's bed which used to be our couch. It's a normal hangout night. Music plays in the background, everyone jokes and talks about their day. I don't mention the tape I listened to earlier. My mood is quiet, calm. I've had my victory and don't say much The conversation is a playful banter. It's fun to listen to at times and this is one of the times.

Unexpectedly, a knock bellows from the door. Everyone freezes.

For a moment it seems like everyone's instinct is to run like a bunch of scared prairie dogs. The only people who can knock on the door without being buzzed in through the gate first are residents. The only resident who ever knocks on our door is the landlord. I look around. Nobody's drinking. Matthew and Peggy are stoned but it isn't noticeable. The landlord likes Farrah. Yes, sweet, nice Farrah.

Farrah... that's Egyptian... he once told her. She giggled and batted her eyes. That was the first time she got us out of trouble. We'd worked on and perfected our strategy from there.

The sacrificial lamb. I squint my eyes looking at Farrah and signal by nodding my head and pointing with my nose to go get the door. She understands what this means. She rolls her eyes and sighs. It's required, so I don't take offense. You can't have someone nod at you to do something without some kind of protest. She gets up to answer it.

"Hi!" A familiar sounding voice says. "Is Eric or Matthew here?"

"Yeah..." Farrah says, sounding a bit unsure. "Come on in."

I don't need to look up. Content just to sit and watch. It's Eric. Other voices murmur in the background. The door closes and Farrah returns, followed by Eric and two other guys I've never seen. They look like L.A. guys ready for the clubs. One guy is really tall and lanky with short blonde, gelled hair. He shoots out a smile and waves to everyone. "Hey, what's up?" His smile is so genuine it makes me smile. I resist laughing. They wouldn't understand. Happy people make me happy. He seems really happy. Like a golden retriever but not in a mean way. In a good, honest genuine way.

Justin gets up to slap the tall guy's hand. "Hey, what's up guys?"

The other guy is shorter and has a smooth, pale pixie-looking, almost elfin face. His hair is a dark spiky brown, "Oh hey man! What's up? Didn't expect to see you here."

Eric introduces them, "Well, this is Jason." He points to the tall lanky one. Jason cracks a big grin. "And this is Peter." He motions to the darker haired one. "Hey, what's up?" Peter says to everyone. "And... I'm Eric. I don't know some of you."

I sit for a few seconds and wave hello. What a funny situation. Must resist laughing. Nobody will get your humor. It's sit-com material. Doesn't seem real... stuck in a movie.

Laugh and you'll look like an idiot. The grating voice warns.

It's hard, I want to. Such a contrast. I love it! A perfect painting. They all look dressed up to go clubbing. All bouncy and high positive energy. We have the lights all dimmed down and everyone is crashed out in lounge wear getting ready for bed. The strange contrast between the two is hysterical. It's a great moment. God, you can't ever explain moments like this! I can barely hide my grin. Justin steps in after nobody says anything and introduces everyone.

It doesn't occur to me that I should have said anything. Justin goes around and introduces each of us. "Yeah, hey, this is everybody... this is Lenny, and Farrah... she actually lives here..." Farrah is withdrawn on the couch. Normally, outgoing, lively, flirty Farrah. She says a quick hi. Justin goes on, "And this is Peggy. She lives here now too, well, for the summer...." Eric smiles and says he knows Peggy.

When Justin gets to Matthew, Jason and Peter both step forward to shake his hand and tell him, "Hey, it's great to meet you. I've heard a lot about you."

Justin introduces me as Eric and Jason leans forward to shake my hand. I say hello and then everyone falls quiet. Everyone probably thinks it's awkward but it's such a perfect awkward dance! I move my hands and pretend to rub my face. Really I use this gesture to hide my enormous smile. Why am I enjoying this so much?

Because you're sick? And... you need help.

God, that might be true. I wanted to say that out loud to myself in a room full of people. I think that is true. I keep my hands over my mouth when I'm done. Justin fills in the gaps.

"So, what you guys doing?" Justin asks them.

"Ah, not much. Just checking out the city and figured we'd stop by." Eric tells him.

"Yeah, just cruisin' around." Jason nods.

Justin asks, "You guys hitting a club tonight?"

"Nah, I don't think so." Eric shrugs. "Probably just get something to eat and then have some coffee, interesting conversation, that kind of thing. You know."

"Cool. Cool." Justin replies.

"So," Peter pipes up. "You guys just chilling out?" He talks really fast, seems hyper and full of energy. Something about the tone of his voice and his eyes. He's a wild pixie if anything. He looks around and then suddenly cries out, "And what are those things?!" He points to an ashtray on our coffee table and cackles hysterically. His laugh is ear splitting but immediately infectious. Nobody ever laughs so unrestrained like that.

It's not really an ashtray. Oh, if only that were true.

Looking down I inwardly groan. It should be so awkward but it's the stupidest thing. Nobody ever smokes inside the apartment. The smell of cigarettes drives me crazy and I've always found the whole thing pretty gross. For some reason one of the many visitors to The Hostel once decided to put a black ashtray on the black coffee table.

No reason other than they matched because we didn't need an ashtray. Someone else noticed the empty black ashtray sitting alone on the coffee table and decided it needed something in it. So, what's a guy to do? He put a condom in it. A Magnum condom.

It sat by itself virtually unnoticed until someone else put another condom in it. That's when the ashtray became the condom donation container. Perhaps unintentionally by leaving it out and being indifferent we'd allowed it to become, 'a thing'. None of the condoms have ever been used. I never gave it much thought. Until now, as Peter points it out.

Eric and Jason turn their attention to the ashtray and its contents. Everyone else laughs.

"Are those what I think they are?" Eric asks.

"Ohh my God." Farrah says. "That's too funny. I always wondered what the hell those were about."

"Whaaat?" Matthew says, trying to play it off as if every household in America has one. "Just a little decoration. We don't really use those!"

Peter can't leave it alone and notices the Magnum.

Oh God, it just got worse. Peter starts talking about the mentality of the guy who leaves something like this out. Like it's some subliminal suggestion. Just so everyone knows or thinks that someone living here needs the huge plus size condom. It's hysterical to him.

I can't believe it. Five minutes into having new visitors the main point of conversation in the apartment is, once again, sex.

This surprises you?

No, I guess not. It's an inescapable trap.

Luckily, the conversation quickly dies down. Everyone sits wondering what to talk about. Another few minutes and Eric stands up.

"Well, we're going to get going. We just stopped in to say hi. It was nice meeting everyone." He waves to Peggy and Justin. "Peggy, nice to see you again. Justin, I'll see you at home."

Peter and Jason smile and say their good-byes. Maybe I should get up to see them out. My body projects the effort required to move and I toss the idea. Nobody does that anymore anyway. Everyone seems too tired as well and they let themselves out. We sit in silence listening to the radio for a minute when there's a knock on the door. Two in one night? I strain my head to stare at the door. Jason pokes his head in.

"Hey." He calls from the door.

Everyone raises their heads up above the kitchen counter to see who it is. Like a big group of prairie dogs. I finally laugh out loud. Only Lenny gives me a weird look for laughing to myself. He mouths the word, 'psycho' to me. Whatever, he likes that I'm off-kilter. Jason walks into the kitchen with Peter behind him.

"Hey, Matthew." Jason waves Matthew over. Matthew sighs quietly as he exerts the energy and summons the willpower to get off the couch. He gets up and goes into the kitchen. The kitchen is little more than an alcove. I can see over the counter to where they're standing. When Matthew gets to them they both shake his hand again. I hear them whisper that it was good to finally meet him and they're looking forward to seeing him again. Matthew tells them how great it is to meet them and that he'll definitely see him around. He pats them on their shoulders in his usual touchy-comforting way.

Without saying another word Peter and Jason slip out the door and leave.

Those guys are so frat. I chuckle about the idea of Matthew being in a frat. He never even wears normal shoes. He always wears his sandals. Lenny gives me another look out of the corner of his eye. "Whatever. Like you don't hear voices." I tell him. He calls me a psycho and throws a pillow at me.

After a few minutes when everyone knows they're really gone the conversation turns to the guests. Is that Justin's roommate? Is that the guy I've been hanging out with? What was that all about? Why did they just drop by? The questions are pretty flat and die down once Justin answers a few. The one Justin doesn't answer and I don't ask is why they came back in to say how good it was to meet Matthew.

Maybe they felt he didn't react well to them? Probably didn't understand he's high. Tends to make him quiet like a clam. At least now I know Eric has other students. What does it mean to be considered a student of his anyway? Do they pay him to go to his school? Did they sign up? Is it just something for them to do? Even Justin might be considered one of them. Justin is at our apartment so much I don't know when he'd even have time to do anything with the others. I'm caught between feeling like I have to watch and be wary of everything they do because of Matthew and laughing at myself for ever thinking Justin and anyone like him could be part of some dark, evil cult conspiracy.

None of it makes any sense.

Do you know yet, what really drove me crazy? It's something I laugh at now.

It wasn't the whole cult thing; I'd heard all that before. I didn't believe what the majority believed anyway so what was wrong with being a minority?

It wasn't Eric claiming he could see things others couldn't, or any of his outlandish concepts, that made him interesting and intriguing. What really sent my brain spinning in those days was the whole 'student' concept.

It drove me nuts. There was no sense in it all. I was convinced they had it all wrong and didn't even mean what they said. Eric wasn't a 'teacher' and they weren't 'students'. They were all horribly confused, which baffled me.

Some parts of the world, or even social circles, might wonder how I'd ever be confused about something like this. It's pretty common in Eastern cultures to have a spiritual teacher, or a guru, or go out and seek to serve in a temple under a known master. They've been doing it for a thousand years. The relationship is intimate and dialogues, daily exchanges, are pretty standard. Like a school teacher. You have one teacher for a subject, you ask questions, they answer. Pretty easy to understand right? I must have lived in a cave.

I didn't think I did but... that would explain it. The relationship of teacher and student, in a spiritual context, was completely alien. Totally unheard of. Nothing like that ever existed, as far as I was concerned. The whole dynamic was bizarre!

Where I grew up... you went to church and sat in your seat while someone talked at you reciting passages from a book until they were done. No questions, no dialogue. You sit, you listen, you go. That's the 'proper' spiritual relationship.

If you did have a question, you'd ask it later on, after the speech. The answers were always, well, it says right here in this book... you don't believe the book? Well, it says here in the book... Still confused? Read this part of this book.

There wasn't any room for debate. The experience of God was prayer, reading The Bible and listening to people talk at you. No direct personal connection with God or any specific person who was trying to give that to you. Get with the program, there's nothing to learn. Read The Bible, recite passages. All you need to figure out is which passage to recite when asked certain questions.

My older brother, Chris, was the rebel. He fought, demanded real answers, refused to believe just because some book told him to, was confrontational and... it got him nowhere. Actually, it got him less than nowhere. It got him scorned, judged, and labeled all kinds of unpleasant things. I learned from what I saw as his mistakes. Though for me they were valuable lessons. If you want spiritual answers you don't ask people, you go read books by other people and see what they have to say. You gather as many opinions as possible and then sort it all out yourself.

To have a personal relationship where you ask questions and someone gives you answers based on experience instead of a book, where you learn from this person, well, it had no precedence in my world.

Without that missing link, I felt alone, without support. Like I was out on an edge nobody had ever been to before. I'd been thrown onto an alien planet. Forget their understanding of science, art or anything else... I was just trying to learn the language.

if only we could see time as a single living stream... allowing in our field of vision not only the present, but lessons of the past and a...

Glimpse of The Future

chapter ten

The next day Eric calls and wants to have coffee with Matthew and I. Only thing is... yeah, I don't know where Matthew is. I call Matthew and tell him I'm meeting Eric for coffee.

"Oh cool." He says. We both sit on the phone for a few seconds.

"So, do you want to come?" I ask.

"Nah."

That's it. He doesn't say anything about what he's doing. I don't ask. I get that he's already doing something else. Eric picks me up. We decide to go back to the Bourgeois Pig. Driving there, he asks if I listened to the tape on entities.

Yeah. Of course I did, I tell him. He asks me what I thought of it.

I shrug my shoulders. "It was interesting. A lot of what you said on there you'd already told me when we had coffee with Sarah."

He seems offended. "Well, sure. What if you had to tell people the same thing over and over and over again? Don't you think you might sound the same? You can only make it *so* different. I mean, how many times do you think I've explained that to people?"

My face drops. Why do people always think I'm judging? "I didn't mean it that way. I just meant it sounded familiar because we'd already talked about some of it. The other stuff was really interesting, but I mean, I don't know what to make of it yet. It seems a little out there."

He smirks and shakes his head slightly. "Always so resistant."

We sit outside near the door facing the street. The coffee cups here are huge. It's like Alice in Wonderland, gigantic with bright colors. Seems like every time I go out with Eric I get too wired. Staring into the cup I draw an imaginary line where I'll stop drinking. Eric asks what Matthew's doing. I tell him I don't know. I don't say it but I imagine he's stoned and doesn't really care.

"You should call him up and ask him to come to coffee." Eric tells me as he hands me his cell phone.

I let out a big sigh. If Matthew had any interest at all he'd be here. He's had enough conversations. He's been meeting with Eric while I've been working nights. His curiosity should have peaked. He should know what the deal is! Thinking about Matthew makes me confused and frustrated. Am I protecting him from harm or from change? Because change might not be a bad thing. It doesn't matter. I start dialing.

He's Matthew and he's only interested in things that make him feel good and are easy. This involves too much thinking... or something. Except he did come to L.A. Most people wouldn't go that far. And he has been trying to get an agent. Not an easy thing. Right, I know. I'm no better. See, God, this is why I hate imposing myself on Matthew. I start to feel frustrated, like I'm being put in the middle. The phone clicks and Matthew picks up.

"Hey... what are you doing?" I ask.

"Oh you know, chillin and hanging out. How you doing?"

"Fine. I'm with Eric at The Pig. We're going to hang out and talk, do you want to meet us?"

"Nah. I'm good. I'm just chilling at the apartment with Justin. You know what I'm saying?"

Do I know what he's saying? I don't know what he's saying, he always says that. He sounds stoned. Why does he have to be stoned all the time?

Why do you have to think he's stoned all the time?

I take a deep breath and try to let out the rising frustration. "Well, if you guys want to come we'll be down here having coffee."

"Cool, cool. Sounds good but we're just gonna chill, you know what I'm saying?"

"Yeah, I know. Okay, I'll talk to you later." I mutter.

"Cool, cool. Take it easy."

I hang up. There. I gave him another chance and he'd rather sit around and stare at the walls. I expect Matthew to act that way but I'm surprised Justin doesn't want to come down. Eric is Justin's friend and he even recorded Eric so he must consider what he says interesting. Justin never smokes pot or does any drugs. How is he entertained by sitting around with Matthew? Seems like he'd be interested in having a conversation.

"Well, what did he say?" Eric asks leaning back in his chair watching the coffee crowd.

"Nothing. He's hanging out with Justin at the apartment. They want to chill."

"Well, you could have made it sound more boring." Eric says sarcastically, sipping his coffee.

I'm startled. How did I make it sound anything? "What do you mean?"

"I mean you didn't make it sound like you were having fun or it was interesting at all! I mean, here's you." He mimics me picking up the phone calling Matthew. He talks in a dopey, slow drawn voice asking what he's doing and then tells him almost as if he's falling asleep that he's hanging out with Eric.

I don't sound like that! Besides it's not like I get exciting phone calls. People call up, ask each other to hang out and that's that! My neck starts to heat up. I can feel it tingle as I start to get mad. Normally, it's really hard to get any kind of reaction out of me. Somehow everything Eric says and does stings with incredible intensity.

Eric keeps going and throws his hands up. "You know?! You have to make it like, yeah, you know I'm hanging out with Eric and we're going to have these really stimulating, exciting conversations. He's going to talk about ghosts and entities and all this great stuff. You gotta remember, I've had more time with you than him. You need to help get his interest a bit more. He's not like you. He's not as mental. He works things differently. He wants things to seem, whooo! Exciting!"

"Whatever. I didn't sound like that. Besides I already talked to him earlier and he said he was busy. So he already knew we were going to talk about ghosts and entities from the tape."

"Did he even listen to the tape?" Eric asks.

"No. I told him several times but he'd rather just sit around or something." God, I even asked him to listen to it with me. He makes it sound like I'm not even trying.

"Justin tells me he smokes a lot of pot is that true?"

Damn, Justin said that? Well, maybe it's not just me. If other people think that. Justin probably knows more about what he does than I do. He's looking at something across the street which makes it hard to gauge what he thinks about it. I sip my coffee watching my imaginary line. "Yeah, I guess he smokes a lot of pot. At least lately. It used to be off and on but these days that's pretty much all he does when he's not working."

Eric slowly drinks his coffee and motions toward his phone, almost indifferently. "Well, you're going to call him back. Again." His voice is calm and matter-of-fact.

"I've already talked to him... twice!" I shoot back.

"I know. But you're going to talk to him again. And this time you're going to make it sound interesting." Eric says with an air of indifference.

Red heat flares and burns my whole neck and face I'm getting so mad. It's so pointless! Matthew AND Justin are sitting at home. Even if Matthew isn't interested Justin should be! Now Matthew is stoned so he's not going to want to leave and I've already talked to him twice. Like, five minutes ago! I feel used. I feel pissed! Everything Eric says stabs at me and cuts right to the core. Every calm word he utters makes my blood sizzle. If he wants to hang out with Matthew he needs to talk to Matthew. Matthew could care less about what I'm doing and when. Hanging out with me isn't any sell for him. I didn't make it sound boring. Now he's going to make me sound like an idiot salesman and call back! I keep my mouth shut. For what little Eric said nothing could enrage me more. My whole body fumes.

"You know," I seethe out trying to contain my anger. "He's still going to say no. He's probably stoned and Justin is there so I have to motivate them both."

Eric sits looking away at a building across the street. "You know..." he says idly. "You're probably right. But I'm not having you call back for now. I'm training you for the future when you have to deal with other people. You need to learn how to make this sound interesting. You don't know what you're competing with. Even people who are interested will be lured away. So, here's the phone," he hands me the phone again, "call him back, but *this time* make it sound like you actually enjoy being here and that he's missing out."

Pissed! I'm so pissed I want to scream. Part of my brain is crying out to swear. I want to swear. I want to cuss him out. God, I never swear but I want to now. I remember running cross country in High School. My coach was fanatical about not swearing. For every letter of a swear word you'd say the whole team had to do 10 push ups. I once heard about a guy who said stupid, God-damn mother-fucker. Even coach paused on that one. Still, he did push ups with everyone else. 190 push ups. In frustration, sometimes I would swear at him in my head if he pushed us for a long run. Eventually, I stopped swearing all together. That was then... and this is... I look down at the phone. God! Screw it! ASSHOLE! Assssshooooolle! I shout as loud as I can in my head trying to burn off the boiling rage. I can't believe he's making me do this!

I can't believe you're putting up with this! Smaaaash the phone!

No. You know what? I'm going to call him. That's right. I'm going to call him to show you that he's still going to say no! What's more I'm going to make this sound like the most fucking entertaining thing going on in all of L.A. and he's a total idiot for not coming. That way, when he still says no, you can't say shit to me!

I call back, my hands shaking slightly from wanting to crush the phone. Matthew picks up and I try to shake off the anger and get in character. I smile real big. Happy, exciting, thrill-ride!

"Hey! Yeah it's me again. Listen I think you're making a biiiig mistake!" I say cheerfully.

"Oh Yeah?" He sounds as bored as ever.

"Yeah! Eric's getting ready to talk about ghosts and entities and how they can push people around, where you can find them and some other real ghost encounters he's experienced. He had one guy piss himself when the entity was smashing through the upstairs floors." I use a story I remember from the tape. "It's going to be pretty interesting. Lot's of crazy stories." I try to play up what I know about Eric. He's always animated and says things that are interesting but crazy in a twisted logical way. "Eric's pretty worked up. He seems really animated today." Pushing back my urge to smash his phone into pieces. I use my past acting to raise my voice and give it lots of positive feelings. Sitting up straight I try to make myself feel as excited as I can so that it comes across.

Matthew pauses a moment. Then he shoots me down again and opts for sitting at home.

I close the phone and feel vindicated. There you go. Can't say I didn't try. I sit back feeling smug. Nobody could have sounded more excited.

You actually aced that. Tell him to eat it.

Eric takes the phone. "Much better. Next time sound like that." He says flatly.

That's it?! That's all he's got to say! ARGHHH!! The whole back of my head feels like it's being torched and I want to throw the table into the street.

Smash it all! Show him whose boss! Smash everything into little fucking pieces!!

Suddenly I stop screaming in my head, dumbstruck. Why am I so mad? I never get mad. It's like someone is shoveling coal right into me. Why am I getting so worked up over this? It's confusing. I replay the conversation to see why I'm reacting so strongly.

Eric distracts me, pointing across the street. "Do you know what that building is... across the street?"

I look across the street. A gray stone building sits, hidden by a tall brick fence with ivy growing on it. It looks like a college. "No. I don't." I've seen it many times before but haven't given it any thought.

"It's owned by a group called Scientology. Have you ever heard of them?" He asks, lowering his voice a bit and leaning in closer to the table.

"Nope. Never heard of them." I blurt out. I'm irritated that he won't leave me alone so I can figure out why I'm irritated.

"It's a new pseudo-religion. It was started by some science fiction writer guy, L. Ron Hubbard. He was big into science fiction, wrote a few books, then decided that the way to be really big was to start his own religion. He took lots of ideas from other religions, mixed in with Aleister Crowley, a guy that was into dark magic, and put his own science fiction twist on it."

None of the names he mentions mean anything to me. Staring at the building it's hard to think of it as religious. It doesn't look like any church I've ever seen.

"I've done lectures on them before. I know a lady who comes to my store who used to be involved with them. She's told me lots of interesting things about them. I did some checking into her stories and I believe her. They are very aggressive about keeping the people who come to them in the church. When she tried to leave the first time they came to her house, picked her up in a white van and took her back to their main center. They said they wanted to talk to her, to find out why she was trying to leave. But really they tried to coerce her into staying."

No way. There would be so many authorities all over that. That's kidnapping. How could that happen in the US in this day and age? I'm too baffled to say anything. Eric keeps talking.

"There are lots of secrets there. Lots of rituals that people don't know about. The interesting thing about the Darkside is that everyone expects to immediately recognize evil. Like they think they're going to walk around in black capes and declare their evil nature! Well, it doesn't work like that. People who are used and manipulated by the Darkside, most of them, think they're doing good. The Darkside always tries to mimic and make itself like a mirror-image of the Force. Only it twists it."

It's the most realistic example of the Darkside he's explained to me. When he'd said it before, I pictured the people marching around in black capes, which is why I find it so unbelievable. Manipulation, I get it. I nod my head and lean in, listening closely.

"Look at Star Wars for example. In Star Wars you have the Empire. Which we know is the evil Empire. We know they're the bad guys fighting the rebellion who are the good guys. But wait, let's look at the intentions of the Empire. They want to bring order to the universe. This way everyone will conform and everything will be safe. Do you think everyone in the Empire believes they're evil? Of course not. They see themselves as serving something good. They are restoring order to the universe by taking over all these worlds and systems. If they have to wipe a few out along the way, well, it's for the greater good. But somewhere along the way the Empire became corrupted by the Darkside. The nature of the Darkside is control and repression. The Empire wants absolute control. That's the Darkside. Don't expect everyone who's being manipulated by the Darkside to know it. Now, there's a lot I know that I can't tell you. It would only place you in danger or give you ideas you aren't ready for yet. Let's just say that one of the rituals in Scientology, now this is a secret ritual that few ever know or hear about, involves removing the light from around your body. Now they might look at the light as static, or chaos, or alien personalities that cause you to suffer but the truth is... the light they remove is the connection to the Force. What fills the void? The Darkside."

Light and dark. Good and bad. Black and white. It's too much like a comic book. A movie! It's too simple.

Looking at Eric his face is still and serious. His words, even though I don't believe them, are chilling. Part of me feels like it is the truth. It makes sense. It seems right but I can't explain why. I struggle because it seems so childlike. Things aren't supposed to be that simple. How can a Darkside even exist?

Eric lowers his tone and stares straight at me. His normal intensity is nothing compared to what I feel coming from him now. Everything else in the background, the rush of traffic, the frantic café crowd, fades away. There is only Eric and the weight, the gravity, in his voice. "I don't want you to ever, ever, go inside a Scientology building. Do you hear me? I give people total freedom. You do whatever you want but I am telling you this one thing, don't think about them or focus on them. The only reason I'm telling you now is so when the time comes you can say, at least I gave you warning. Do you hear me? The rest of the world is yours to do whatever you want."

He leans back and motions towards the gray building hidden behind the, now, fortress-like wall. "Part of your future is there. In the future there will come a time when you will do something with Scientology and you will need to be ready and know what it's about. There are people in their organization who are very skilled psychically. It's part of their training. You don't want them to become aware of you too soon, before you're ready. Now, I can't say exactly what you will do that involves them but the time will come. Just know this; everything is not what it always appears to be on the surface. So, I made you aware of them and now I am telling you to forget about them. Got it?"

I nod my head. It's a bit like a movie. Of course I get it but it's hard to take in. Another part of me finds it exciting. It's interesting to think that someone can feel into the future or that there are organizations that still have secrets the rest of the world doesn't know about or would find too absurd to believe. I wonder how much truth there is in what he's saying.

Looking over at the building I know I'm not curious enough about Scientology to go snooping around. I might entertain the fantasy of covert missions, or some kind of strange psychic war going on... but not enough to seriously put time or energy into seeing if there's any shred of truth to it.

I glance over at Eric but it seems like he's elsewhere. He lives in an interesting world; there are so many levels to things. There's always something going on under the surface. It's like a good novel unraveling. The way he presents things with such logic. It's hard to dismiss entirely. If nothing else it's fun to consider the possibility... what if?

Eric tells me it's time to leave. We get up and drive back to the apartment. I ask if he wants to come in since Matthew and Justin are home. He shakes his head no.

He turns away from me and up the street. "I hate to say this to you Eric but, you and your brother are a package deal. I can't teach one of you and not the other. There's no way for me to know you won't share my knowledge with each other. Everyone comes to me for different reasons. You come to me because you find the knowledge interesting. You enjoy analyzing, figuring it all out. You're starting to get that there's something here, only you don't know what."

I smirk. That's exactly the struggle. He nailed it good.

"Your brother, he doesn't work the same way but both ways lead to the same place. Make sense?"

Looking down I half-heartedly nod. I have no clue what he means by they lead to the same 'place' but don't ask. Then he asks what we're doing for the 4th of July.

I shrug. "Nothing planned that I know of."

He asks if we want to come to a barbeque and meet all the other students. "There's also... someone else I think you should meet." He has a weird smile and he's acting like he's trying to hide it.

"Who?" I ask suspiciously.

"Well..." he starts chuckling. "It's a girl. One of my only female students. She's a bit lonely, lives down in Orange County. She has a nice place. A big pool table you know, a nice bar. She's cute, blonde, smart, I think you two will hit it off."

I try and muster a laugh. Girls aren't real high on my list of important things. The idea of being hooked up is funny. I'm not real patient with girls. Relationships don't interest me much. "Uhh, whatever. I'll meet her but... I don't really date."

Eric chuckles. "Whatever, you've been single too long is all. Matthew should come too."

I nod and tell him that would be interesting.

He smirks. "You sure you can handle it? Might be some people psychically digging into you. Better be careful what you think." He tells me to watch them because some of the older students will be there. Some have trained for a long time. I laugh. He must be joking. I wave and thank him for his time. His car turns the corner and I'm still standing on the curb.

"He was joking wasn't he?"

Stupid. What did you just agree to?

"Ah crap."

Several years later I would finally, I mean finally, pinpoint the source of the strange, overwhelming bursts of anger, anxiety and stress that would occur around Eric.

It's Eric himself! Or, to be a little more specific, Eric's energy.

This was the first time I really felt the full frontal assault of Eric's "In the Zone" energy. Every time I'd met him before he was 'intense' but I never quite nailed down why. There was a quality to it beyond a deep conversation, or someone who's very serious and maybe intimidating at times. I'd met serious, intimidating people before. They feel more emotional caused by your own thoughts. You can tell after observation that the person feels like they do because of a reaction on your part. With Eric's 'intensity' you have these overwhelming sensations that are very physical, like your whole body is suddenly experiencing more of 'everything' than it can handle. This triggers an almost fight or flight instinct. If you don't run, internally, it can shift into a really strong emotion... anger, anxiety, bliss...

When Eric shifts his consciousness it becomes stronger, more noticeable. He can direct the energy into you and give you a little 'push', which is what I experienced at the coffee shop. Or it can simply radiate out like a pulse wave.

Working on another level tapping into the building across the street, he shifted his consciousness. I was operating on a slow, grind to a halt, unaware level and he pushed energy at me. Taking in all that fuel was like taking on, raw, uncontrolled electricity. I reacted to being pushed by getting seriously pissed off.

It might not seem strange to you but I never, ever, ever get really mad. I've never had a temper and anger's never been a real strong emotion for me. So, for me to get mad out of the blue, was insane!

I'd like to tell you that the more you're around him, the more you'll adapt, adjust and get used to this. Unfortunately, I've found the longer you're around him, the more hyper-aware you become, your sensory grows more refined, which means you'll only feel it stronger and stronger. To a point where I remember times he'd stand three feet away from me and it feels like I'm standing next to a bonfire there's so much physical heat. I'd crack into a sweat and want to push him away. Not only the heat but I feel pulse wave after pulse wave push through my body and all I can do is try to surrender to it so I don't have to run out the door.

Surrender, if that means anything to you, is the trick. Eric told me a story once, about how some of his students would try to, emotionally, get to him. They'd hurl insults, lies, spread rumors, steal his things, yell at him, do whatever they could possibly think of to hurt him. What they don't understand, he told me, is that they are throwing bricks at a ghost.

The person they're trying to hurt is an illusion. They sling the rocks, but it passes right through me. Like a martial arts master, they take their punch, only to find I've stepped aside, no longer there, fluid, the reed in the wind.

Internally, the more solid, grounded, structured you are, the more you firmly believe there is a person who can feel anger, who can be offended, that you are all that is inside your body... the more unwelcome, in a way, you are to energy. The more energy has something to push against. Something solid can break down. Fluid, dynamic, spiritual tonal.

When I surrender, let go, realize and release the solid nature of this person in this body, there's less for Eric's energy to hit, and like a ghost it passes through. Or, having lost the weight of the structured self, I can tune into and, in a sense, try to ride his energy back up to the place it came from.

This is hard to do, so most times I try to surrender and get out of the way of the bus. Back then, I didn't have that choice, I could barely restrain myself from grabbing tables and throwing them out into the street which is, let's face it, extreme for anyone. For me that was a walk into the unknown.

As for his glimpse into the future, well, all things in time.

have you ever received a gift that, at first, seems like the most plain, boring gift you've ever received? then it turns out to be your favorite thing in the whole world? because you judged it purely on...

Surface Features

chapter eleven

The fourth of July arrives. Matthew and I drive up to Eric's house. The BBQ isn't held there, but at the home of Jason and his girlfriend Bonnie. We get in Eric's car and drive over with him. Jason and Bonnie live less than five minutes from Eric's house.

After a few twists and wrong turns Eric pulls up to what he thinks is it. It's a small white cottage with a nice lawn, bright green bushes in front, and a long driveway on the left. Eric is debating whether he has it right when the front door opens and Jason leans out and waves. His tall lanky figure is hard to miss as is his big, friendly grin.

"So you found it?" He yells to us.

"Yeah, I took a few wrong turns. You'd think I'd know how to get here by now." Eric admits. Looking over at Eric I suddenly realize how down to Earth he is. He never tries to come off as perfect. For someone who says he knows how the universe began and how God experiences, it seems like he'd be more concerned with acting like he knows everything else too.

"What's up fella's? Good to see you again." Jason says flashing a big smile and shaking Matthew's hand.

Matthew pats Jason's shoulder and returns the big smile. "Yeah, you too, you too. Got a nice little pad here."

"Hey, what's up." Jason asks as I walk in behind them.

"Nothing." I say with a crooked grin.

As we walk in I immediately notice how clean the place is. I can't believe he can keep his house so clean. It has a very open feel. Looking at the edges of the room I know the house is old, it has the old style molding and paint build-up, but it feels brand new. There's a crispness to it. It's refreshing just standing in his living room.

"Welcome to my home." Jason happily exclaims as he opens his arms to the living room.

"Well, Bonnie's house..." Eric adds with a chuckle eyeing Jason. "Anyway!"

"Yeah," Jason laughs. "This is my girl Bonnie's house but we live here together so... it's also my house." Jason turns and gives a big goofy grin to Eric who is already walking into the kitchen. He says hi to a girl washing her hands at the sink.

"Anyway guys, the bathrooms are down the hall." Jason points away from the kitchen. "Bedroom's are down there too. Feel free to wander around and take a look. Our home is your home. The food and stuff is almost ready, we're all chilling out back. We got some drinks too if you guys want drinks?"

Still wary of the cult idea I figure if they are going to pull something it will be in the drinks. I decide to skip the drink. Freaking Sarah and all her conspiracy theories in my head.

"Nah, I'm good." I tell him.

"Yeah man, maybe later." Matthew says with a warm smile.

"You sure? Right in here?" Jason motions towards the kitchen. Just then Eric comes back out with a diet Coke in his hand and scowls at Jason.

"You know, why don't you be a good host and offer them some drinks or somethin', you know don't just keep them captive talking at them, let them walk around!" He finishes with a little smile so we know he's only giving Jason a hard time.

"What?! I just did! I was giving them the tour and offering them drinks! Huh guys?" Jason laughs, pleading slightly.

"Yeah, he offered." I admit.

Eric takes us into the kitchen and introduces us to Bonnie, Jason's girlfriend. She has bright chestnut eyes and long straight reddish-brown hair. She's as friendly as Jason with a big smile. Little freckles dot her cheeks giving her a strangely wholesome, Midwestern look. When they stand next to each other Jason is almost two feet taller than she is. Jason doesn't look like he's really that tall but somehow his lankiness makes it more pronounced. Bonnie offers us drinks which we decline again.

"Bonnie, you can make me something to drink." Eric tells her. The kitchen is cozy. There's a table along one wall on it is piled enough food to feed forty people. I wonder how many of them there are? Bonnie has a section of counter set aside with different bottles of alcohol. She starts making Eric a drink while Eric leads us out a side screen door that leads to the driveway. The driveway goes behind the house to an open parking area that's been cleared. A few portable plastic picnic tables are set up with a stereo playing music. There's a group of people sitting and milling around. Right away I spot Justin sitting near the stereo. I'm happy to have someone familiar around. He's not wearing his Gilligan hat which is strange. His bright reddish-orange hair is really visible, almost glowing in the sun, and sticking up all over the place.

We're walking toward the tables when one of the guys walks over to Eric. He's a little shorter than I am, average build with short, nicely combed brown hair. A thick goatee similar to Eric's outlines his chin. He's dressed comfortably and looks like a guy you would meet hanging out at a BBQ. A green polo shirt with khaki shorts and sandals. He turns and smiles at Matthew, extending his hand, "What's up guys. Hi, you must be Matthew."

"Yeah. How's it going?" Matthew shakes his hand.

"I'm Frank, it's nice to meet you. I've heard a lot about you from Eric." His voice is friendly but has a formality to it. He immediately seems more reserved than Peter or Jason. Looking him over I guess it must be because he's older, though I can't place his age. Maybe 28ish. Frank turns and looks over at me. A puzzled expression crosses his face. It's like he thinks he knows me. The look you give someone in a grocery store that you're sure you know, but can't place. I'm about to help him out and explain I've never met him when he comes to life. "Hi, how ya doing?" He asks. "I'm Frank."

We shake hands. Great, I'll probably be doing a lot of handshaking. "Hi, I'm Eric."

"Oh great." He says in a joking way. "Another Eric. Are you friends with Matthew?"

There's an awkward pause as I look over to Matthew with a little smirk. He grins back at me. "No. I'm his brother."

"Oh crap!" Frank says with genuine surprise. He looks at me and then at Matthew to compare our features. "I'm sorry dude. I didn't know there were brothers. Eric only mentioned Matthew. You guys don't look alike." Frank smiles a little sheepishly. I brush it off not really caring.

"Nah, don't worry about it. It's nice to meet you." I'm happy he mentioned we don't look alike.

Frank turns to Eric and I quickly glance at him more closely. If they are psychic they sure don't seem different. He could fit in anywhere. How am I going to know who's doing psychic things anyway? What would that mean? He seems like Eric in another way too, I can tell he's a sharp guy. Something about the way his eyes look.

"Eric you didn't tell me he had a brother!" Frank says snickering to Eric trying to deflect the moment's awkwardness.

"Well, I can't keep track who I've told what to. So, he has a brother, you met. Don't make a big deal of it." Eric waves Frank off and walks with us up to the table. Peter is there in a black shirt drumming on the table with his hands. He's sitting next to a girl that Eric prods to stand up and meet me. She has straight light blonde hair pushed behind her ears that falls down past her shoulders. Her skin is fair and either she's embarrassed or a little sun burnt, her cheeks are a little red. She makes eye contact with me and then quickly looks away. Yeah, a little shy. It's something of a forced introduction.

"This is Kathy." Eric explains to me motioning to Kathy standing there looking petrified. "Say hello Kathy." Eric says smiling.

With Kathy standing up looking at me all eyes are on us. The whole table is directly or indirectly watching the event take place. Peter is unabashedly grinning, enjoying the moment's entertainment. Not really knowing them or having much invested I don't mind so much.

Kathy tries to shoo Eric away, whispering crisply, "No, don't, shoo." She waves and pushes him away.

"Well, now that I've broken the ice, I'll leave you two alone because you'll have so much to talk about." He starts to walk away chuckling and Kathy seems relieved. Then he turns back, "Kathy, you should offer to get him a drink or something... you know, get things going."

Her eyes open wider and her face turns a little pink. She looks down embarrassed. I don't say anything. I feel for her but it was also the strangest introduction I've ever experienced so I find it a little funny. She should laugh it off. I know I can't lessen her embarrassment.

Breaking from a smirk to a smile I nod my head. "Hi, I'm Eric."

Kathy rolls her eyes and sighs loudly, still not meeting my eyes. "Yes, I know. Look, sorry about, well, the whole thing there. It's just this thing he does."

Chuckling I shrug. "It's okay. A bit odd but it's funny."

Peter pipes up. "Yeah, yeah guys. Don't worry about it Kathy. Sit down, relax, relax." His voice is high pitched but with a comforting tone to soothe Kathy. "Let's just play some cards, see?" Peter breaks out a deck of cards. He asks if anyone knows a game to play.

Now that the Kathy situation is over Frank pulls up a chair. "Okay. Here we are. Gonna play some cards huh?" He smiles and looks at Kathy. She glances at him then shifts away. Peter grins at Frank and starts shuffling. Resting my chin on my hand I feel like they're talking about me. Great, I'm being left out of a conversation happening right in front of me. They must know each other well enough to be able to read each others expressions and body language.

My only possible translator, Justin, is hanging out talking with Matthew by the stereo. The only game that comes to my mind is one I learned at summer camp.

"I know one. ERF."

They look at me puzzled.

Frank laughs. "Arf? Like a dog?"

Good one. Now you have to explain it. I look over at Kathy, now it's my turn to be embarrassed. "Uhh, well, no... it's ERF. E-R-F. It's short for, Egyptian Rat Screw."

Peter looks over at me. "Screw? Wouldn't that be ERS?"

I shift in my seat. "Well, it's not really screw, okay?"

Everyone laughs. "Nice name! I get it, so it's fuck! Egyptian Rat Fuck! What a great name for a game." Peter says chaotically.

Peter, Frank, Kathy and I play. Matthew watches grinning, shaking his head. I know, he can't believe I broke out a camp card game. Matthew bounces back and forth between us and the kitchen. He seems more comfortable than I feel. Of course, he's not on the spot trying to get hooked up and, well, he's Matthew. He loves socializing. I go through phases. This isn't one of those 'I like socializing' phases.

One of the key aspects of the game is flipping cards over into a big pile in the center of the group. If the cards match, like a Three of Diamonds on a Three of Spades, you slap the pile. Whoever hits it first gets the loot. When you get all of the cards, you win. You have to flip them in a way so you aren't able to see what the card is before it's flipped. So, no flipping towards you.

I clean up the first few hands, having spent many lazy summer days playing. My fingers getting slashed by fingernails. Everyone's laughing and having a good time. Peter's surprised how hard your hand gets hit. I grin and tell him Matthew and his friends spent one summer getting so into the game they started sharpening the ends of their fingernails. The intimidation factor. They spent most of the summer with little cuts on their hands.

It doesn't take long before the others begin competing well. Really well. Surprisingly well. They stop laughing and joking as much and start getting a little intense about it. Before I even think about moving my hand to slap they're already there. Even Kathy gets into it, though she complains when Frank or Peter smashes her hand a little hard. Normally girls are a bit gun shy because part of the game is psyching the other people out by being afraid of the pain of getting their hand pummeled. Her face turns serious and she keeps right up with the guys.

I start to wonder if they're cheating somehow. Signaling somehow to each other. They are quickly leaving me behind. Blocking out the whole 'psychic' idea I'm sure there's a reason they're learning so quickly. Before I get to flesh out my conspiracy theories Jason calls out there's food. Eric yells for Kathy to come help. The rest of us sit and wait.

They all act so nice and normal the anxiety of being around psychics who want to dig into my head quickly vanishes. The game was a fluke. Beginner's luck. They're all beginners so that would explain why they were all beating me. Or I'm disoriented from being in a new place. Not at the top of my game. The Southern California sun is bright and shiny as always. Not a cloud in the sky. The radio echoes in the little area where we're set up. There's a stand alone garage next to the house and we're in the parking area between the two.

Looking around I'm surprised at all the trees. Tujunga has so much more vegetation than L.A. The whole street is lined with trees. All the neighbors have big flowering bushes and plants. It's nice. The air is slowly starting to change as the time drifts near 6. I feel a slightly cool breeze blowing. Must be coming from the canyons. Never get refreshing breezes in the city unless you're near the beach.

Matthew wanders out of the kitchen with a can of pop. Looking over at him he looks all happy with his cool, refreshing can... I hate pop. Root beer I can drink every few months. That's it. Still, pop in a can is safe so I decide to have a look. Can't tamper with a can. I laugh to myself for the ridiculous thought that anyone would go through the trouble. Walking up to the kitchen, the screen door is propped open. I hear Eric and Kathy having a heated debate so I pause in the doorway.

"Go! Give him some food or something! You know, break the ice." Eric's urging.

"I don't know what he likes!" Kathy wails holding a plate with some food on it.

"He's a bachelor!" Eric bellows. "Anything will do!"

Bonnie, who is standing by as a spectator is aware I've walked into the doorway. She quietly points my way. Eric and Kathy abruptly quit talking and look over to me. Eric throws his hands up in the air and picks a drink up off the counter. Kathy, holding a plate in her hand, looks completely flustered. Beyond being embarrassed she looks like she wants to throw the plate at the wall and walk off. Instead she walks up to me and exclaims, "Oh, here!" as she shoves the plate into my hands and marches off.

I stand there holding the plate staring straight ahead not wanting to look at anyone. Holy crap this is really awkward.

I'm not quite sure if I should feel like I'm to blame for this or not. I feel bad for Kathy because she has no reason to feel embarrassed. God, what do I say now? "Um, I just came to see what you had to drink." I say to nobody in particular.

"I'm really buzzed. I gotta go walk." Eric says as he leaves the kitchen and walks down the driveway. I turn and look at him walking away and then look back at Bonnie. She tries to smile for me. Looking a my plate of food it all looks like she could have given it to me and I would have been perfectly happy. Maybe Eric's right, anything will do. I don't think that has anything to do with me being a bachelor, I'm just not picky with food. Beans, potato salad, hamburger. All good. I get a Sprite and go sit down to eat.

News of the outburst must have spread quickly. By the time I get to the table everyone is strangely quiet and giving me weird looks. Kathy comes back after a few minutes with a plate of her own food. Sitting a few seats away she keeps to herself. Peter, Frank, Matthew and Justin keep a conversation going until Jason and Bonnie come out to join us. The tables are pretty full and everyone seems to move past the incident. Frank looks around every once in awhile. He must be looking for Eric. He whispers something to Peter. Peter shrugs.

After eating I get up to throw my plate away. The trashcan is near the kitchen door so I make sure to listen for any loud talking before I get too near. Everything seems quiet so I toss the plate in and turn around. Turning to walk back Jason and Peter are almost right behind me. They walk straight up and tell me quietly they want to talk.

Oh great. Here's where they give me the protective speech about how I better watch myself with Kathy and then I'll feel like the incident is my fault.

In soft, hushed voices they apologize to me. I'm baffled. They didn't mean to make me feel excluded when they came back into the apartment that night. They didn't know we were brothers or that I was interested in Eric's stuff. They only heard about Matthew and thought he was the only one into it. Weird, well, that explains it. Guess it makes sense now.

I shrug it off. "It doesn't matter. It was dark and you guys didn't know all the people there." I feel weird that they feel bad about it. I guess they don't want to seem rude, but I hope they get over it. Seems like enough awkward stuff going on I don't need anything else. After I explain I don't consider it rude or strange the whole thing is settled and they seem happy.

Everyone hangs around in the driveway, playing cards and listening to music. It's surprisingly relaxed. They're all real down to Earth people. No candles, chanting or psychic duels. Anyone could walk up off the street and not think anything of it. Jason and Peter bringing up the apartment makes me realize how happy I am. Smiling, laughing, sincerely at ease. The night they came to the apartment, when all three walked in, I got real giggly too. At the time I thought it was something else, the contrast in how they looked or something.

Sitting back I let my mind wander through the memory. Could be it wasn't the contrast so much as something about them. It's almost like their presence, though it makes no sense at all, makes me feel good. I laugh off the absurd thought. No reason to it. These guys are total strangers. How can strangers change how you feel just by being around?

Almost an hour passes before Eric comes back walking up the driveway. Frank walks down and I overhear him ask where Eric's been. Eric rubs his forehead and tells Frank that he hasn't drank anything in so long he needed to go walk it off. He said that while he was walking he started scanning and went into stealth mode. He's surprised at how many dogs could still detect him. He hasn't had dogs or anything be able to notice him in years! He admits that he's really out of practice but he picked it back up really quickly. He makes a movement with his hands spreading them out like he is feeling the air.

What's scanning? What is he talking about? I try to remember if he ever said that word to me before. Nothing comes up. He's surprised dogs could detect him? My curiosity starts buzzing.

Eric walks up the driveway. "Are we all through here? Are we tired of the whole BBQ thing?" Everyone admits that they are. Eric nods like he's done with it himself.

"Well, you guys help Jason and Bonnie clean up and then let's meet at the school to meditate." Eric tells Frank, Peter and Justin.

They all get really excited by this. Matthew and I say our good-bye's and thank Bonnie. Eric decides I should ride over with Kathy.

Oh that sucks. I look over at Kathy. She seems uncomfortable with the idea but agrees. Like pouring salt on a wound. I agree as well hoping to find a way to make her feel better and get past the strange food spectacle. We get in her car and she doesn't have her radio on which intensifies the awkward silence.

"Do you meditate much?" I ask.

She's sits in total quiet. Either she's going to answer or she wants to talk about the food moment. She answers me explaining that she doesn't meditate as much as she should or would like to, but yes, she does. I ask her how long she's been meditating.

"As long as I've known Eric." She answers shortly. Maybe she doesn't want to talk.

Maybe you bug her. The grating voice jabs at my insecurities.

She finally speaks. "I had to think about it for awhile." She explains. "It's going on four years."

I'm a little surprised. That's a pretty long time considering how young she is. I think Eric mentioned she was 22 or 23. A little younger than me.

"Why do you meditate?" I ask.

She gets flustered. "Well, there's so much, you see... um, it's like... Eric hasn't talked to you about it?" She seems thrown off by the question, like there's so much to explain it overwhelms her. I was only looking for a simple answer. Meditation suddenly seems like a really intense, complicated thing. And now we're on our way to meditate with everyone? If it's so complicated what if I'm really bad at it? Kathy doesn't help. We continue in silence.

when you pray you talk at god and tell god everything it already knows. when you meditate you...

Listen to God

chapter twelve

We pull into the bookstore parking lot. Kathy exhales as if she's been holding her breath.

"It's like this," she says, suddenly calm. "It's like when you pray, you talk at God and you tell God everything it already knows. When you meditate... you listen to God. I meditate. I listen to God. That's why."

She looks at me, her eyes lock into mine. The weight of her explanation for why she meditates starts to hit home the longer I look at her open, honest tome of a face. There's no flair or fluff.. Gone is the shy girl who couldn't look at me for a second. I don't know what to say. Maybe I don't know what meditation is. I tried it before with visualizations and things I learned in books. It never was that big of a deal. Meditating seems like a fancy way to relax. The way she explains it, it seems like a very big deal.

Kathy gets nervous again and loses her calm expression. Oh crap, I've been sitting, silently staring at her for too long. Right, it makes people uncomfortable. I don't mean to. Her keys rattle. "I forget who said that. It wasn't me. It was probably Eric." She turns to open her door.

Inside the bookstore we find Matthew and Eric. Matthew is pulling the round café tables to the side. We help move the chairs and tables away making a large open space surrounded by bookshelves. From the back of the store Eric dims the background lights leaving only the main room brightly lit. The others show up and don't waste any time getting ready. Matthew and I sit in chairs against the wall while the others take off their shoes and start stretching. Stretching? What the... Why are they stretching? They look like they're getting ready to run a marathon. Wow, meditation must be physically exhausting I think sarcastically. I imagine someone sitting in a perfectly relaxed position, having to dab sweat from his forehead like it's a super intense sitting workout. A smile creeps across my face as I watch them stretch in all kinds of poses.

Matthew and I look at each other. He thinks it's funny too. We exchange looks like what are we supposed to do? I take my shoes off since that seems to be the thing. Matthew kicks his sandals off. We sit down with our backs to the bookshelves. Eric comes in and sits to the right of us near Matthew and I.

"Okay, everybody ready?" Eric asks.

They all switch into different positions and say they need more time. To warm up for... meditation marathon?

Be nice... sitting quietly can be a grueling task... The clear voice snickers softly.

"Enough already, let's move." Eric tells them. Justin and Jason try and get some last minute stretching in as the others scoot in closer to where we are.

"Um, I don't know what we're doing." I mention, since it seems like we're about to start.

"Don't worry about it. You'll catch on." Eric says quickly. He seems like a coach ready to get into the game. No questions, no dawdling. Catch up and do it. "Let's do some Oms first." He calls out sounding pumped.

Everyone slides along the floor even closer together and forms a tight circle. Matthew and I glance at each other again and then scoot inward.

"Come on, come on." Eric says somewhat impatiently. "Get in a circle. Knee's slightly touching." He taps on his knees so everyone knows to make sure they're touching. Kathy slides to the right of Eric and Matthew moves in on his left.

I come in with Matthew on my right and Frank on my left. When their knees touch me I shift uncomfortably. Not used to people touching me. Feels strange.

Eric corrects a few people, ensuring that everyone is facing the same direction from the torso. Our knees slightly touching the people on either side. The idea, he explains, is to visualize a bright ball of light right in the center of the circle. Like a big ball of energy. Everyone will project their Om into the center of the circle.

"Most people say Om, like Oh-mmm." Eric demonstrates with a quick "OHHHMMM". He raises his index finger to get everyone's attention focused. "I prefer, Ah-ummm. Hear the difference? AHHH, not, OHHH." I nod, though I doubt he expects a response. "Traditional people might nitpick and tell me I'm doing it wrong but my thinking is that they have no idea what they're doing or why. I'm really saying it better - so there." He ends with a little smile, a nyah-nyah kind if kiddish-ness. Everyone chuckles and shakes their head. I don't know the difference so I look away. Eric stops joking and explains that the Aum makes the sound he needs and serves the purpose better. He decides to demonstrate an Aum. He takes a deep breath in and lets out a long sound that resonates and shakes from his chest. "Aahhhhhh-uuummmmmmmmmm." It sounds like a chant I've heard in the background of music before.

Then for the sake of another example he takes a deep breath in and tells us he will do an Om. "Ohhhh-mmmmmm." The two are distinct. The endings are the same but the beginnings are different. I'm not sure what the point is or how it makes a difference but I hear the distinction.

"Everyone will do the Aum together. Try to last as long as you can. Try to har-mon-ize..." Eric emphasizes harmonize while holding his hands out to everyone like a conductor holding an invisible pointer.

"Focus on visualizing the white ball. Let's go!" Eric gives a brief shout. It's the final cry of go team! Almost in unison, everyone sits up straight and rolls their shoulders back.

I guess they've done this a few times... but what am I doing? My eyes dart around looking at everyone, as if it's going to help. They're all breathing in and puffing their chests out to catch more air. I take a deep breath in and look around again. They're sitting with their legs crossed but one leg is propped up inside the other against the knee. Their hands are folded, palms facing up and stacked on top of each other in their laps. Quickly, I decide to mimic at least the hand part. The leg thing is a mystery to me and I don't know if I can physically match it. It must be part of the whole ritual aspect of what we're doing. I hold my breath and wait to hear someone else.

Eric opens his mouth and slowly comes out first with the 'Ahhh'. I listen for a few seconds worrying that I'm not going to match their pitch. I suck at singing. It sounds funny, the whole group of them saying 'Ahh' like they're all at the doctor's office. I catch a laugh before it comes. If I start thinking about what everyone looks and sounds like I'm going to laugh. Starting my 'Aum' I try to mimic it while limiting my volume.

As soon as I start in everything changes. It vibrates through my throat and upper chest. But the sound... the sound changes so dramatically! It must be my ears. Closing my eyes and opening them wide I try to flex and pop my ears. I can't understand it... Before I started everyone sounded flat, empty. A group of people moaning... badly. As soon as I start my Aum I'm suddenly immersed in a rich, deep sound, resonating like a stereo surround sound system. I hear and feel everyone else like we're all in a little stone room and the Aum's are bouncing and reverberating all around us. It shakes and vibrates through my head. The sound feels three dimensional. My breath runs out quickly and I stop. The rich sound of Aum's that surrounded me are gone. Everyone sounds flat again. How can it make such a difference?

Everyone stops and Eric says that we need to focus. Justin and Peter are confused about exactly where they're supposed to focus. Justin leans forward, his huge billowing jeans make his legs look like they're 12 inches thick. He holds his hand in the center. "I mean, like, are we focusing here?"

"No, higher." Eric calmly offers.

Justin moves his hand about six inches off the floor. "So about here?" Justin wonders.

"Yes, yes. Right there."

"Okay everybody, we're going to focus right about here." Justin has his hand in the center of the circle about six inches off the floor. He moves his hand around in a swirl to demonstrate the range of the area, since we're supposed to visualize a ball. His voice is a tone I don't hear from Justin very often. More authoritative, like he's instructing.

"Now some of you are going too deep." Eric informs us. "It should be higher and try and match the pitch." Eric demonstrates again with a high Aum. "See? Simple! Some of you are really out of practice." He scowls.

He turns to Matthew and I. "When you have a really good Aum, you can hear this pitch, like ringing. It sounds like you're running your finger along the rim of a wine glass until it starts to ring. Have you ever heard that?" We both nod yes. "Well, that's a good Aum. When you can hear that ring and you can hold it, that's what you want. Let's try again."

I breathe in and hold it. Crap, I breathed in too early. Everyone else starts to breathe in. Eric starts again and everyone begins trying to match it. Paying close attention to each person as they begin to join in I notice it doesn't make any difference in the sound of the group. Each new voice doesn't change anything. It's flat and definitely nobody here is a singer. Sounds really off. I keep holding my breath. All I can tell is that it gets a little louder but it sounds like they're barely moaning the Aum out. It's so strange. It also sounds like it comes from the directions I'd expect. With people in front of me and on my sides that's where I hear it coming from.

I let out my Aum. WhooOOsh! It all floods back. The sound of the Aum surrounds me. It comes from behind me, above me, under me, inside of me. It grows in intensity the moment I begin. Their dull, flat voices are suddenly transformed. They're rich, vibrant. I look at the spot Justin marked and try to visualize a white ball floating there. It's a focus point. I did something like this when I practiced Wicca. You imagine things to help you focus. My breath runs out.

Everyone stops and Eric's pleased with that one. He decides we'll do two more. Each time I notice the contrast of when I haven't joined in and once I start. It's like sitting alone in an empty parking lot trying to groan out an Aum compared to suddenly being in a concert hall. Tingles of excitement surge all over me. What a cool thing! I don't understand how it works! I'm bouncing with a rush!

We stop, it's time to meditate. Like clockwork, no one speaks, everyone slides away and props themselves against the bookshelves or the couch. Eric tells Matthew and I to slide back and put our backs against the wall for support. We aren't used to sitting this way so we might need it.

Peter asks if we've ever meditated before and Eric tells him this will be our first time.

"No way!" He cackles in delight.

"What are we supposed to do?" I ask hoping they don't expect us to suddenly know how to meditate.

Eric looks over at us and shakes his head. "First correct your legs. Take one leg, and put it up on the other one." He shows us with his legs. First, he sits cross legged then he grabs one leg and puts it on top of the other, so that his foot rests by the knee of the leg underneath it. "This is called half-lotus. It helps keep your spine straight which is important for the flow of energy. Some people think they need full-lotus which is where you sit with both legs on top." He moves his hand up and down his spine to demonstrate how straight his posture is and how the energy moves up and down.

Peter pipes up, "Like this!" He quickly succeeds in getting both of his legs so that one rests on top of the other. He rolls backwards to show us that his legs are securely fastened to one another and aren't going to fly out.

"It's just overkill." Eric tells us. "You don't need to do that. Then you're going to breathe... who wants to show them how to breathe?" Eric bellows, his voice fills the room. Justin volunteers.

Justin assumes a very proper, older, authoritative position. Suddenly, he isn't the lax, laid back Justin I know. He watches the others as he explains how it's done. "First, you'll take a long deep breath. After that you will put your lips together like you're whistling. You'll be making a very small, pin-size hole. Then you'll try and force all of the air in your lungs out this very small hole." He demonstrates by taking in a very long breath then sticks his lips out in an exaggerated way to show us the pin-size hole. He strains his face as he tries to blow a full breath of air out the little hole he's making with his lips. His face quickly turns a bright red.

"Now you have to be careful not to do too many of these or you might pass out. Or don't do it too hard... it looks like he might be overdoing it." Eric warns us.

Justin finishes. His face looks like it might break a sweat. "Yeah, that's right. And you don't want to take so long that you're, like, blowing for a few minutes. You have to have a big enough hole you can get the air out quickly but with some effort. Now you repeat that three times and then you're ready to meditate."

Seems easy enough. "But how do you meditate?" I quietly ask.

Eric sighs. "It's simple, look at me." Matthew and I look at him. "All you are going to do is touch various spots on your body. The only thing you need to do is focus on the touch." He quickly shows us where we will touch. "I'll tell you when to touch each spot. So, focus on the feeling of the touch. That's it. If you can simply do that you'll be able to get into states it would take others 10 years to do, if ever. That's one of the reasons why even though all my students are so young, they've had more experiences than people who have been doing this their whole life. Just by following along you'll be able to absorb tons of prana, or energy. Now, your eyes should be closed and you shouldn't open them. When I give you an instruction you do it. I'll guide you while we meditate. Easy, right?"

His explanation takes a little over a minute.

I look around a bit nervous. At his prompting, do things and then do other things. How am I going to do this?

Doesn't matter. Keep your eyes closed! The frantic voices screams fearful of breaking the rules.

Right... eyes closed. I have no idea why. I guess it doesn't really matter. Have fun and see what happens. Resting against the wall I close my eyes.

Eric tells Peter to start the stereo. Right away I hear the deep, steady beat of trance music. It's the same tape Eric plays in his car.

"Louder!" Eric shouts.

Peter turns the volume up so loud it sounds like we're in a club getting ready to dance. Thump, thump, thump the bass on the stereo blasts. Follow Eric's instructions. All I have to do... touch the spots. After a minute or two Eric shouts out to focus and breathe. He calls out to move to the next step.

"Smile!" He shouts over the music thumping away. "The biggest smile you've ever had. Fill yourself with the feeling of love. Smile to the Universe! Let the Universe know the feeling of love you have for it. Project it out!"

Going with his instructions I start to smile when I feel my teeth exposed I pull back. Feeling embarrassed I make a big grin. Ever since I had braces I have trouble smiling big. Everyone has their eyes closed but... still I feel exposed.

"Don't feel foolish, don't hold back." Eric's voice echoes.

As Eric said, it's easy to follow along when he calls out instructions. Less than ten minutes later the music starts fading off as someone turns the stereo down. Wow. It went by in a blink. I open my eyes. The others are still sitting straight in their meditation positions or leaning over close to the ground with their arms stretched out before them and their heads folded into their laps.

"Bow when you're done." Eric tells me softly. I look at him not sure of the kind of bow he means. He points at Jason who looks like he's stretching. I look at him again and realize it could be some kind of bow. I reach out my arms and lean forward close to the floor letting out a good long breath. Looking around I hear Frank ask Peter how long the meditation was. Twenty minutes Peter tells him. Frank nods adding that it was a short one.

Twenty minutes? Can that be right? It felt like ten. Moving my legs to stand they tingle and rebel. They're both asleep. Weird, maybe it was twenty...

Eric's up and moving. "We'll meet you guys later on." He tells the others.

What happened? It went so quick. That felt like ten minutes. Probably less. My legs stop tingling and I stand up. Everything feels different. The whole bookstore, the floor, the paint on the walls... the couches... everyone here. No, it... it looks different. I look around at the lights. Can't be... still the same lights. Something's changed. There's something different. My whole body feels really strange. Curious, I pay attention to how I feel. Nothing solid, that I can say for sure. I can't put my finger on it. Everything seems so clear. Everyone seems so bubbly, happy, or peppy. I don't know what it is! It makes me want to laugh.

Matthew and I follow Eric out to the back parking lot. The night air sweeps through me. I feel like I could fly away on it. The scents of the canyons, of summer, flood my nose. It makes me smile. The night smells so clear, clean and rich! There are so many layers in it, like eating a rich cake, only with my nose! Sweet, succulent. I take another deep breath in. God, the air feels so good! I smile without trying to cover it up. My smile triggers a beam of warmth all over me and makes me feel even happier! It feels so freeing!

Wait... what's going on? Why do I feel like this?

Eric turns and looks at me. I suddenly realize I've been standing there just grinning, staring at the black mountains and the sparkling, lustrous sky.

"Feels good doesn't it?" Eric says as if he's saying more than asking. His voice sounds changed. It has a smoothness to it, like rich maple syrup pouring out over fresh pancakes.

I nod and then laugh. He knows! He knows how good it all feels! Talking doesn't seem to matter. I'm alive, and free and... at peace! That's it. I feel so content. Completely, wonderfully, wrapped in peace. God, it's such a strong sense of peace. I've never known a feeling quite like it. Magical... enchanting. So alive! Somewhere, in the back of my mind, part of me says, 'Yes. This is it. This is the feeling I have been searching for my entire life.'

Some inner nagging has let go. It's quiet. Then it strikes me. How can I try my whole life to feel a way I've never felt?

"Don't think too much about it." Eric cautions right at the moment I begin to analyze why the sensation feels so totally and unbelievably familiar and natural but I've never felt this way before. "Just hold onto the feeling. It will soon fade." His voice is soft, comforting, with a touch of sadness.

My heart sinks. Yes, of course. Nothing lasts. Wrapping myself in a mental embrace I cling to how I am, at this moment. I don't want to ever lose this feeling. It's perfect. I've never known something could be so perfect.

We walk to Eric's car and I crawl into the back. Suddenly I realize Matthew's been beside me the entire time. He hasn't said a word either. He must know, he must feel it too.

Eric drives away from the bookstore without saying a word. He turns down the hill in a direction I've never been before. It's in a direction away from his house and toward the mountains.

We wind our way through a residential neighborhood and drive toward the mountains. The road opens up to a park. Eric drives us all around the park which is basically a large oval. The park is pushed up against the mountains which loom like giant, ominous, hooded figures overhead. He parks on the side of the road. We silently get out of the car. Eric doesn't say anything as he starts walking through the park. Matthew and I exchange looks trying to figure out if either of us know what's going on. We don't. We follow him.

Eric moves closer to the heart of the park and stops, lingering near the playground area. Neither of us have any idea what to do, so we start climbing on the playground. I clamber up into the play fort and ride down the slide. Eric sits on one of the swings and seems strangely distant and still. He's normally so animated. I pause and watch him. The swing is barely moving back and forth. He's sitting perfectly still, staring forward. His mind isn't here at all. It makes me uncomfortable.

Matthew must have noticed it too. He climbs down off the play fort and sits on a teeter-totter closer to Eric. Suddenly, it dawns on me that we aren't here to play. Feeling foolish, I climb down off the fort and go hang on the pull-up bars.

When we're settled and quiet Eric reaches over and starts pushing the swing next to him.

"Some people think this park is haunted." He says, voice hushed. "What do you guys think?"

Searching the darkness I try to make out Matthew's face but can barely see it. The street lights surrounding the park dimly illuminate it but it is too dark to see his expression.

"I dunno. I thought it felt a little weird here. Why do they say that?" Matthew whispers.

"Well," Eric said. "I'm not saying if it is or isn't, only that other people have felt things here. They say it has something to do with a little girl that was murdered or something like that. I'm not saying I believe that necessarily. Just something I wanted to point out."

My desire to swing on the pull-up bars suddenly dies. My body goes limp. All I can hear is my own breathing. I look around the park. It isn't very big. I can see the whole park from one end to the other. A little distance away from the playground is a brick building that looks like bathrooms. It has a few trees hanging over it. I imagine a little girl playing here near night before the street lights come on. A slight chill comes over me as I picture a man watching her from the brush across the street at the base of the mountains. The park does seem a little foreboding.

Quit it. You only think that because he said something.

I look around again. It doesn't take much to make this place creepy. There are houses lining most of the park but everything is still and quiet. It's eerie. The houses are silent. I can hear the street lights buzzing it's so dead still. They give enough light to show off dark shapes and shadows but not enough to reveal any details.

"Come over here." Eric said. He gets up and we follow him to a small group of picnic tables hidden under some low hanging trees and blocked by a few big bushes. He sits on a bench facing the rest of the park, looking towards the houses, the mountains behind us.

We sit quietly for a minute or two before Eric speaks. "Well, do you feel anything?"

What does he mean by that? Does he mean cold, or something else? The question is confusing. The way he says it, makes me think there's a specific meaning I'm missing. It's not how it makes me feel emotionally. It's something else.

Matthew clears his throat. "I can't be sure. I mean, I think I feel something but... I don't know."

"Well, don't try to control it, just tell me what you think you feel." Eric says, a quiet depth in his tone and presence.

"Well, I mean, it just feels like... I don't know, like it feels uncomfortable almost. Like, I mean, I know it looks dark and stuff but, it feels like we're not supposed to be here. Like we're trespassing and you know someone wants you out or something. But I can't tell where it's coming from."

Eric nods in the darkness. "Good. Good." He tells Matthew quietly. Without moving his gaze from staring out into the park he asks, "And you Eric?"

What does he mean? What are they talking about? I struggle to try and get what Matthew was saying. Do they see something I don't? Are we supposed to describe how the park makes us feel, like creative writing or something? I look around the park. It is a spooky-looking place. That's it. I can read into the creepy look of it and make up stories or I can know that it's my limited vision and people are afraid of the dark and that's all.

"No." I shrug. "I don't really feel anything."

Eric nods again. His nod bothers me. It's like he's trying to say my reaction is expected.

"You're too structured. Matthew is going to have an easier time being aware of things because of how he is. He's more... " he seems to search for the words. "He's more fluidic. It's how he is and how his mind works."

Structured? What's that supposed to mean? How can I be too structured? I'm open minded. I have imagination and creativity. Just because I think about things before I jump into believing them, is he saying that makes me structured? I'm intelligent. Maybe that's what he means. That seems like something he needs to explain better. I open my mouth to ask him what he means when he whispers.

"Here... just listen and watch."

We sit in the darkness listening to the quiet of the night. Once again the overwhelming silence of the neighborhood makes me shift uncomfortably. It isn't right. It's still early in the evening but no sounds filter out of the houses. No televisions, or stereo music, no children or laughing, dogs barking... nothing. Typical of California there aren't any night insects either. All I hear is the occasional rustle of leaves in the trees.

Then one single sound breaks through the night. It's a car engine. It's a small car and a little rattly. From the far end of the park a Volkswagen bug appears with it's headlights on. It stops at the stop sign before the road that loops around the park and waits. A few minutes pass. Then it creeps forward and starts to circle the park. It drives under a streetlight. I can see that it's painted all black and I can't make out how many people are inside.

Slowly, it stalks along circling the park barely at a crawl with its engine rattling the way most bugs do. It comes to a dark spot between the street lights where it's almost completely dark. Its breaks squeak and it comes to a stop. It sits for almost a minute when it suddenly shuts off its headlights. Nobody says a word. We watch it for what feels like 15 minutes. Tension rises in my gut. It's like they're looking for us, like we're being stalked. How could they know we're here? Why are we hiding? What are they going to do? My breathing grows louder... every sound is magnified. My senses are on edge.

Sitting in the darkness. Nobody moves inside the car. We watch from the other end of the park, hidden in the darkness of the trees. There's very little chance they could have seen us or Eric's car. I look over to where he parked it. I can't even see it. It's behind the restroom which is also out of the bug's view. With the black mountains behind us and no streetlight they can't see us either.

What are they doing? Trying to squint and peer into the car I wait for a spark from a cigarette or a bowl from smoking pot. Something that will explain it. It starts moving again, creeping closer to our end of the park. Driving without its headlights on. The rattle of its engine is the only sound as it creeps closer and closer to where we are. If their eyes are adjusted to the dark they'll be able to see us when they come around. Suddenly, it flashes its headlights on and pulls away down a side street. In the darkness we sit listening to the sound of its engine fading into the distance.

Eric's voice startles me. I hadn't noticed how on edge I was. "Everything has a programming. It's energy. Energy draws like energy. In this case, darkness draws darkness." He said in a high-pitched whisper, still looking forward. "Do you understand?"

Without waiting for our reaction he explains. "Whether you want to believe this park is haunted or not, there is something dark, or evil, about this park. That's why people believe that. They feel it. That something, that darkness, draws other things to it. Things that are like it."

I look around the park again, trying to notice what they felt. I can't tell anything strange about it except it looks like a creepy park out of a horror movie. But I get his point. I nod and tell him I understand.

"Good." He says after Matthew and I both say we understand.

We walk back to the car and stop before we get in. He tells us to come around to his side which is closest to the mountains.

Eric's voice carries softly through the dark, "Look at the mountains. What do you see?"

I strain to make anything out. It's a little too dark I tell him. I can see dark shapes like bushes and stuff.

"Yeah, me too." Matthew says.

"No. Look in *front* of the mountain. Look at the surface of it. You should see what looks like, like, like a static." Eric says, his voice calm but serious.

I stare at it again not exactly sure what he means by look in 'front' of the mountain because there's nothing between us and the mountain.

"Oh, I think I see what you mean." Matthew tells him. I get frustrated. Matthew is saying that to be agreeable. He doesn't want to make him feel bad for not getting it or something. Matthew's answer prompts me to have him explain it again. I'm not sure what he's asking.

He points up at the sky. "Look at the sky. Look at the color of it. The stars. The dark blue that's almost black. The city lights reflected. Look at the texture of it. Now look at the mountain. Look at the different hues of colors from the light. That's not it. It's like, did you ever have your TV go out and you saw all the white and black static? It's like that but a bit more subtle."

I stare again at the mountain. Dark shapes of the bushes. Different shades of light. Then I see it. Little speckled shapes. I see speckled shapes everywhere! They're all over the place. I look up at the sky. Squinting my eyes I look harder. I think I see the specks in the sky too, only not as strong as the mountain.

"Yes, it is everywhere." Eric says as he notices me looking at the sky. "But it's easier to see in the dark or against black. It stands out more."

"Ah, I see it too." Matthew says staring at the sky. He must have seen it a moment ago too. Not only can he feel things better but he can see things easier. Eric told me exactly why Matthew will catch on faster, only, I don't get it. Sighing I let go of my competitiveness. I really can tell Matthew gets it more than I do. There's something to that.

"Now, if you look closer," Eric tells us, "you can see two different colors in the static. You can see like a blue and a red. That's prana, or energy. That's the Force, which is the blue static, and the Darkside, which is the red static. Both are everywhere. Both fill up and make this dimension. They are intermingled like oil and vinegar. It's like if you have a bottle of oil and you pour vinegar into it they float separately until you shake it up real well. Then they look like they're mixed but if you look real close you can tell they're just little bubbles that are still, like, separate but from a distance they look like they're one fluid. Get it?"

We nod our heads.

"So that's this dimension. They are in everything. Everywhere. Except in this dimension the Darkside is stronger. The Darkside is like, thicker here."

"If you can't always see it, how do you know which is which?" Matthew asks.

"You can feel the difference."

Eric tells us we can see it better in a closed room with no light. We can practice in a place like a bathroom.

We drive back to his house and walk back to his room in the garage. He closes the door and shuts off the lights. Suddenly the colors are extreme. Blue and red static fills the room. I don't have to try; it's completely obvious and distinct. I can't believe I've never seen it before. It's so easy to notice. If it's this easy surely someone else has seen it too. How does science explain this? What do they say it is? I don't ask the question. If I'm going to test his theory I have to take it at his value. He says it's dark and light prana. He says it's energy and one is the Darkside and the other the Force so that's what I'll call it until proven otherwise.

Forget what it is or isn't, how many times have I sat in a dark room and never seen that? I feel stupid. It seems so obvious he shouldn't have had to point it out.

We drive back to the school but the others aren't there. Eric calls one of them and asks where they are. They went out to the canyons but will be back soon, he tells us. We wait a few minutes until we hear them come in.

They're arguing about something that happened. They're talking about opening some kind of dimensional vortex. Frank and Peter say they did the most work. It was in some kind of concrete tunnel that went into one of the mountains. The temperature dropped so fast they almost froze and an entity came through the vortex filling the tunnel. It tried to make them all freak out. Eric gives Frank a questioning look. Frank tells Eric it was a pretty strong one and caught him by surprise. Justin and Peter start debating about who pushed it back and did the most work to fend it off. They get really worked up about it. I hear the words they're saying but I have no idea what they're really talking about. Peter tells Justin he needs to show respect for the older students and that he isn't a real student anyway.

That seems to be the tipping point. It's really noticeable Justin just got really pissed off, which is something I never thought I'd see. Must be some history here, doesn't seem like the first time they've argued about things like this. Frank steps in and tells them to chill out. He tells them it was a big entity but they took care of it. Frank decides that he and Peter will go back later to make sure they properly closed the portal.

None of them seem to care that Matthew and I are sitting here listening. Apparently there's nothing secret about it. They must feel comfortable enough with us to argue and fight while we're here. It makes me feel better knowing they can air things out in the open. Eric decides the night has been long enough and they must be getting tired so everyone should head back home. We catch a ride with Justin back to our car. It was such a strange day I don't know what to even begin to say about it. Matthew must feel the same because we drive home in silence.

What a journey it's been. I treasure so much, this marker, this moment. To experience such a thing for the first time... it's one of my cherished memories.

Part of you may wonder... why I've kept the description of the meditation so vague. If I learned it in five minutes why didn't I dedicate an entire chapter to it?

If you've ever learned meditation from Eric Pepin, or Higher Balance, you'll know it is not a five minute process. In fact, the current program for learning meditation is four hours long. It could be a book by itself. See, the truth is, I didn't learn meditation in five minutes. By this time, when we sat down to meditate, I'd known Eric about two months. We had countless conversations on consciousness, energy, Red Cells, White Cells, the Force, how everything works... seemingly unrelated but absolutely key in the process of meditation.

The real gem of Eric's meditation is not the technique itself but the understanding, the knowledge, behind it. To give you the technique and have you walk away thinking that's all there is... would cheat you.

There is a certain mentality that's all about how-to techniques. Tools, technology, pills, techniques... these are the things people expect are the real meat. The things that really work. My question is, when did knowledge become so underrated? Do we have so much information we see more of it as pointless talking and not what does 'the real work'? Why are we so quick to disregard knowledge like it's an instruction manual to a toaster? Who ever reads those, right? You know how to make toast, it's simple. Maybe you think you know everything in this book, all you need is the toaster, the technique.

Here's something you should keep in mind as you read this book. Pretty soon, things will start 'happening'. It's right around the corner. When you finish the book ask yourself how many times I meditated, that you read about. I'll tell you... a little over a handful, maybe.

It was not through meditation that I experienced what I did but through Eric's knowledge. Certainly, he was there to push me along and the influence of his presence cannot be denied. My point is that by pure realization, understanding of what he was talking about, doors opened in my mind and I shifted to those higher levels.

You can move through these other levels too, by the simple act of reflecting and working on understanding Eric's knowledge. If you think you get it but aren't experiencing some similar events... you're probably kidding yourself. Intellectually, maybe you get it. But you don't really 'get' it. What you can conceive you can achieve. Do not underestimate the knowledge. You will only be limiting yourself.

In those days Eric hardly emphasized meditation at all. His students were all too young and he told me he felt like it was too much work for them. He thought that if he pushed meditation they would see it all as requiring too much effort and would drift off. Keep that in mind as you may hear about experiences of other students in the future. Many of their experiences were not had through meditation but deeper understanding of his knowledge. The knowledge is essential. Vital. There's no substitute for reflecting, pondering, wondering trying to figure it all out. There's no shortcut there. No quick fix, easy stretch, or headphones to put on. Without that, the technique loses much of what it can do.

Now, what you should really know, that took me a few more months from this point to realize, is that when you start to 'get' what Eric's saying and then you add the meditation, with understanding, that's when the switches really flip and you see the thin thread that really separates now from whole other realities.

To do that is to experience life beyond your wildest, and I mean wildest, dreams... the greatest imagination cannot scrape the surface of what the Universe has set before us.

see the world now... with new eyes. all that lies before your sight is not all that there is.

The Secret Art of Scanning

chapter thirteen

Waking up I vaguely recall that yesterday was somehow important. Something special happened that I should still feel... or at least care about. But I don't. Yesterday is hazy. I remember everything that happened, it just seems like it didn't happen to me. Feels like another life, could have been years ago.

"Blech!" I shake my head trying to get rid of the whole sensation. Doesn't seem right. The day before doesn't seem real.

Everyone here at The Hostel has a movie shoot so they clear out early. With the place to myself, Unable to shake the feeling that nothing from yesterday was real I decide the best way to get over it is play a video game. Yeah, that'll help bring me back to life.

Ah, the game of Civilization... our other life...

Whatever, Civilization helps me think. It's gotten me through some tough times.

Eric calls with other plans. He decides to come down to LA tonight, even though Matthew won't be with us. I'll have to plot my new world another time.

When he arrives later, he starts joking to me about getting together with Kathy. Laughing, he plugs her many benefits. She has a car, she lives in a nice house in Orange County, she'll support a spiritual life, she's smart and looks good.

I can tell he's a little serious but I can't tell how much. Mostly, he says grinning, she needs a man and I fit the bill. Now he's just giving me a hard time.

Great, this space for rent. You're just a warm body. She's looking for anyone, not someone.

You can't judge her based on Eric. He's kidding around. But, maybe she is an anyone person. Might as well find out. Somewhere during my past I started breaking people down into two dating categories: the anyones and the someones. An anyone is looking for a person to fill or fix something about their self. They're lacking in some way, they need love, affection, entertainment... different reasons. They have criteria, sure, but mostly they're looking for anyone to fill the slot. The someones are looking for just that; someone in particular. They don't have any major pressing need to find a person, they want someone. There's a difference. Need or want.

Someone people are willing to hold out and walk away from anyone until they find that special person that enhances what they have. Generally, I try not to categorize people and let them do their thing but, once it gets stuck in my brain that somebody is an anyone person... I can't get it out of my head. Anyone people drive me crazy.

I tell him I'll probably call her and see what she's like.

Looking around the apartment he informs me having a woman around will help keep things cleaner. Now he's really joking. I laugh and say two girls live with us and it doesn't help a bit.

I don't take any of his suggestions seriously. I'm 24 and have no plans to ever get married. He grows bored joking about the Kathy plan and tells me to get my shoes on. We leave the apartment and walk down the hallway to the flight of stairs. The elevator is a painful experience and unless I have laundry I avoid using it. Clambering down the stairs Eric suddenly tells me to stop.

"Are you ever aware of where you're going, what you're doing or what's around you?" He looks at me like he's been hit with a crazy realization.

I look at him a little puzzled. What kind of question is that? Of course I know where I'm going. I tell him so. "I'm going down the stairs."

He grabs his head with his hand like he can't believe I just said that.

"No! Of course you know where you're going but are you paying attention or just automating?" His tone is patient but his face looks pained. What I'm doing can't be that bad. Can it?

His question makes me stop and think. Is automating a bad thing? I've walked up and down this staircase hundreds of times. Why pay attention to it? I have things to think about at the same time. My body can walk the stairs while I think.

He tells me to try something different. "As you walk down the stairs pay attention to every single thing that you can. Notice the color of the walls and if they change color as you walk down. Notice the smells, the sounds. Do the sounds change as you get closer to the bottom? Is one floor noisier than the other? Can you hear wind coming through the door around the corner?"

He clenches his fingers together in a point and shakes them at me, "Even pay attention to the sensation of your feet on the steps below you and what it feels like to descend. Do you get it? Aware! Awareness of your environment. Life!"

I walk down the stairs as he instructed. Trying to focus on everything I quickly find myself thinking about other things. What are we doing? Why are we doing this? Does he mean to notice the mark on the walls? What would cause a mark like that? It looks like someone tried to move a couch up the stairs. What idiot would do that? Oh, pay attention to other things. I quickly reach the bottom and he stops me.

"The longer you go the more you slip back into automating." He tells me solidly.

I think back. Yep. This is true. After one flight I found a way to automate paying attention without really paying attention. I tell him about how I found a way to automate being aware. He looks at me like he wants to punt me out into the street. Okay, fine, I've got to slow down. He's really trying to make a point.

Standing in the lobby of the apartment building, he starts trying to really emphasize to me that I need to listen. "Don't think about anything I tell you. Do this first. Think about your body. Think about how it feels. Stay focused right there on how it feels to walk." He points through the glass doors toward the stairs that go down into the street. "Walk up to the edge of the stairs and feel what it feels like to stand right on the edge knowing they drop down."

I start walking and push open the doors to the building. Cool night air rushes into the apartments past me. I hear the sound of the swoosh. Stepping closer towards the stairs, looking down at the street below.

"Don't use your eyes!" He cries out. "If you were blind how would it feel to know that it suddenly just drops off in front of you? Better yet, think of it like a video game. When you play a video game does the character ever move through the world or do they stay in the center of the screen and the world moves around them?"

"Well," I say, "they pretty much stay in the middle and the world moves around them."

"Good." He said, seemingly satisfied that I answered something correctly. "Now, imagine that those stairs don't really go down but they have been programmed to make you feel like you are moving in a direction which you interpret as down. Do you see? It's not what they do it's how they feel. You can feel that they are programmed to take you down. It's not that you can see it but you can feel it before you ever get there."

Unconsciously, I tilt my head sideways and then realize I tilted my head sideways. When did I start tilting my head to think? Then what Eric said hits me. It's starting to make sense. I picture myself in a giant video game. As I start to walk towards the stairs I think about it from a perspective, not of me moving through the world, but walking forward and the world scrolling by like in a game. It feels really strange. Kind of dizzying. I'm not sure that's what he intended me to feel. I get to the edge of the stairs and try to feel the sudden drop without acknowledging that I can see it.

"Focus," he reminds me. "Feel the feeling of down as you walk down them."

I start to walk down trying to feel the feeling of my body falling as I step down. It suddenly strikes me that's what's happening. I'm in a controlled fall walking down the stairs. I never paid any attention to it before! Once I feel my body drop I look at the remaining stairs and feel the feeling of stepping down each one and suddenly catch something. That's it. When I look at the stairs I feel the feeling of what it is to walk down them. It's like dropping but different. I can look at the stairs and feel that without even doing it. The stairs feel like going down. It has a feeling! I start to smile. It's such a weird way to think! It's fun in a way. Like thinking in some kind of bizarre language but different. I step down a few more steps and start to laugh. The feeling's so strong! Cool! I can feel it! Damn, the stairs always had this feeling only I never thought about it.

"You getting it now?" Eric asks from the top of the stairs.

"Oh yeah. It feels really weird to think about it." I say back smiling slightly.

"To be aware of it." He said. "Not thinking. Don't think about it. Pay attention to it. Be aware of it."

He walks down the stairs and meets me on the bottom.

"Now notice the difference facing up the stairs." He motions back up the stairs.

I look up the flight of stairs and immediately throw my head back in delighted surprise. "Awesome! They feel like they're pushing against me. It feels like walking up."

"Go ahead, walk up them. Feel them first. Feel what it is to stand before them and know that up and down, it all has a different feeling. Get used to paying attention to inside. What your body tells you."

I walk up and down the stairs a few times. Each time I notice little things I hadn't before. After a few tries Eric is done with the stairs. He waves his hands in little circles, "Enough already, let's walk."

We walk down the street. It's still early in the evening so I don't feel too uncomfortable. Still, in my neighborhood we are the minority and I always get wary looks from people during the day. I feel safe in my complex but the surrounding area always puts me on guard. A cool breeze blows through and I stick my hands in my pockets and press my arms against my body.

"You see," Eric explains, "early man didn't have the physical advantages animals had. We didn't have really great hearing where we could hear things hundreds of feet away. We didn't have super good smell either where we could smell without sight, or like claws to attack other animals... I mean when you look at a guy standing in a field naked you probably think sitting duck. We don't think, oh, that's a mean animal that can do some damage. So our ancestors, like, primitive primal man had to use another means of sensing trouble and finding food. Does that make sense?"

I nod. "Yeah."

"So like, well, first thing," he points to my arms, "take your hands out of your pockets. Always out of your pockets! Your hands are like what we used to feel our surroundings. It's like our antennae or feelers. I mean, hold your hands outside your body and move them around when you walk."

Pulling my hands out of my pockets we walk for awhile. It's all tall apartment buildings and the rush of the nearby freeway. I pull my focus away from what I can see to what I can feel with my body. The cold air rushes through my fingers. He said they are like antennae. It's hard to place but it feels different. Something has changed.

"Now, just, stick them back inside your pockets and ask yourself which makes you feel more aware? Which makes you seem like you are more connected to what's going on around you? Your hands, when you stick them inside your pockets, is signaling to your energy to withdraw. It's telling it to like stay close."

He holds his hands outside of his body and motions around his head to give me an example of his energy body. Then he sticks a hand inside his pocket and moves his other hand super close to his head. It's collapsing inward. He takes his hand out and pushes his other hand back away to show me what my energy body is doing when I take my hands out of my pocket.

"Get it?" He asks as if it should be obvious by now.

I nod again and chuckle. "Yeah."

"Your hands are like little, uh, satellite dishes. You have to have them out to retrieve information." He shows his hands to me with all his fingers stretched out so I can fully see how they look like little feelers.

We walk up the hill and he continues to explain how to feel my surroundings. He shows me how to feel buildings and cars. He leads me through connecting my mind to an entire hotel to feel who is inside it, what rooms are empty and what rooms have people in them. Going further he explains how to feel who those people are, what they're doing and the kinds of people that have stayed there before. We walk past several buildings and he has me move my consciousness into them to see how it feels.

"How it feels will also draw people who feel like it. Like attracts like." He looks at me out of the corner of his eye and I get a flash of the park. Darkness draws darkness. If a building has a certain energy, people with similar energy will be drawn to live there. Or worse... if you live in a place with a strong energy, it will influence you and try to keep you in its programming. The energy programming reinforces their programming.

We walk to a nearby Denny's and stop to eat. Even while eating his teaching doesn't stop. In every detail he shows me how they cut corners and how we're basically eating dog food. He can't believe how much crap American's put up with. It's because they're automated just like me. Nobody pays attention anymore to what they're doing or eating so places like this get away with it. The more he makes me notice the details of what I'm eating, the more aware of it I become, the less I want to eat it. Finally, I feel sick and can't finish.

After deciding he feels disgusted by their food we leave.

On the way back he reminds me again of everything we've gone over. How to walk, how to feel, how to not just look at something but feel it. Scan it. He calls it scanning after an old movie he saw called, "Scanner's", although the movie has nothing to do with what he taught me. It starts to sink in and there are little bits where it seems like I really can feel something. Nothing quite as noticeable as the stairs but I understand what he's trying to tell me. Only problem is I'm unable to do it very well.

As soon as we get to my apartment I start fast walking up the staircase again when he stops me. The apartment is so familiar I completely automated again and didn't think about it. He calls me back down to the first level.

"When you walk up," he explains, "feel the air. Smell the taste of the air. Pay attention to the sounds. All kinds of clues are hidden in your environment."

I start to walk up the stairs, confident I'm paying attention to everything. When I get to the second floor he stops me.

"You didn't notice it at all did you?" He asks sounding doubtful, already knowing I have no idea.

What is he talking about? I put on my best puzzled expression and shrug. He groans.

He tells me to do it again. I walk up and down between the first and second floor six more times. Each time I try to pay more and more attention to everything. Each time I have nothing to tell him. "Seems the same to me." I shrug.

He gets tired of me trying to figure it out. This time he walks up behind me. The staircase starts to turn to the second floor and he stops.

"When you walk up two more steps the sound is going to change. You'll go from faintly hearing the street noise to a muffled quiet."

I walk up two more stairs and right on cue I notice the background noise, though a little faint, distinctly cuts out. Eric tells me to go back down the stairs and try it again.

I try it twice more and on the last try I can't understand how I've never noticed it. It's so obvious.

"It's so loud!" I exclaim. It's more than street noise. It's machine noise from the elevator, it's wind blowing through the door... there are tons of noises and they all suddenly muffle as soon as I go two steps around the corner.

"Now, after two more steps the smell in the air is going to change." I walk two more steps and the air goes from slightly fresh to a stifled, stale smell of mold or mildew. I laugh and shake my head.

"Oh my God. How did I walk up and down this so many times and never notice that?"

"It blows my mind too." Eric said. "And don't think it's you, everyone is like this. They walk around barely noticing anything. I don't see what people get out of life! You're missing most of it!"

We continue walking up the stairs. We get to the next flight and he stops me again. Great, what did I miss now? It seems like I was really on it. No, crap, I spaced out again. Reflecting back I realize I'd stopped paying attention.

"You've stopped being aware already haven't you?" He asks knowingly.

Defeated, I nod my head. Harder than you'd think. Once I thought his lesson was over I got caught up in replaying it in my mind. I wasn't paying any attention. I'm too busy thinking about how I hadn't been paying attention.

"Everyone goes through life like a bunch of zombies! You know? Wake up! Look around. Life isn't inside your head. Take a break, get out of there once in awhile. Well, since you weren't paying attention I'm going to tell you this floor always feels different. One of your neighbors, down the hall and on the right, practices some kind of magic. It's got a twist though, like Voodoo or something. Kinda like pay me to remove the curse I cursed you with type stuff. It affects the energy of a lot of your building. It's something I've been aware of just thought I'd point it out in case you could notice this time."

Using what he'd shown me earlier I try to feel down the hall. I can't do it. I'm feeling down a hall I can't see, for a person I don't know... and I don't notice anything. Of course. It doesn't seem realistic. I like the idea that someone can feel an entire building but it seems like someone would just be imagining anything they feel. Noticing things around you is different. I can revert to my primal instincts and smell changes in the air and sounds. That's using my animal part. But feeling things around you that you can't see? How can there be anything to it?

I try again imagining this old woman sitting around in a dark apartment killing roosters in her kitchen. That can't be right. It's all imagination. We walk up to my apartment. Sliding my key into the lock the door pushes open. Already open? We walk in and everyone is not only home they're practically lined up at the door. Matthew, Peggy and Farrah are crowded in the entry way.

"Oh there you are!" Farrah cries out. "We were worried. You never leave and suddenly you've been disappearing!" She's joking around but there's an edge in her voice.

"Hi Eric and Eric." Peggy smiles. She looks up at me with a puzzled look on her face. Matthew beams a warm, I want to hug you all, smile at us. "You look taller." Peggy tells me.

"Really? Huh." I look down at Peggy. She's always much shorter than me. I don't feel any taller.

"That's because he's empowered." Matthew whispers quietly.

I shoot a quick look over to Matthew. Why did he call it that? Does he understand it in a way I don't? What does he mean by that? Farrah is talking to someone in the living room. Looking over I notice Lenny sitting on the couch staring at us.

"Well, I've had a long night. I'm going home." Eric says.

Matthew and Peggy tell him good-bye.

"Bye Eric, thank you!" I tell him.

"Yep, okay. I'll talk to you later." He tells me as he leaves.

No sooner has the door closed Farrah hisses out, "He gives me the creeps! I don't like him at all!"

"I have to agree with Farrah, as strange as that sounds." Lenny chimes in.

Farrah throws a pillow at him. "I'm serious! You just meet this guy and now it seems like you're always gone doing something with him! I don't know what it is! Call me closed-minded but I think he's up to something!"

Lenny jumps in again, "Yep, he's trouble. There's something about him. Besides, it seems like since he came around we haven't had a wine night and you've been, woosh!, off and awaaay! Where's Eric? Oh weee don't know. We're just his friends why would we know where he goes or what he does?"

They're being ridiculous. I suddenly feel really tired and don't want to talk to people. "Yeah, yeah. That's nice. I'm around as much as I used to be, sitting here all day long while you guys are out busy doing this or that." I mention defensively.

"Working! We're working!" Farrah and Lenny say together.

"Well, whatever you call it. You're there and I'm not working so I need something to do." I almost raise my voice but fail to find the energy. Not worth it. They keep ranting behind me as I turn my back and wave them off, heading into the bathroom. Matthew and Peggy don't say a word. Feels like I have two girlfriends. Feels like they're trying to control me or make me feel guilty. That drives me nuts. I can't stand it. I feel myself get defensive and put up walls. My mind is my own and nobody tells me what to do with it. Farrah's probably drunk. Lenny is probably in a pissy mood and feels like saying shit. It's not worth being mad about.

Farrah only wants me here when she's here. I'm a convenience. She needs to talk about her problems so it's easier if I'm here. If she's getting what she wants from some guy it doesn't matter if I'm here or not. They're all used to that. Come home, there's Eric sitting on the couch. Like I'm a freaking TV they want to switch on when it pleases them. Nobody's asking what the hell I want.

Suddenly, I'm exhausted beyond words and can barely think. Too tired for nagging. Walking out of the bathroom Farrah calls out, "Okay, good-night! Nice seeing you Eric!"

I've already blocked her out of my mind. I don't say a word. If we get into it her temper's going to flare and I'm going to get pissed. Only she'll be over it in an hour and I'll stay mad for months. Slow fuse but once it's lit I can't let it go. I'm not a convenience. Nobody controls me either. Closing my door behind me I'm too tired to battle it out in my head. I flop onto my bed and go to sleep.

does soil want to stop the seed from sprouting? or do they both have a part to play in...

The Force of Change

chapter fourteen

I'm in a bright green field. There are trees and radiant flowers. The Earth is spinning under me like I'm running on top of a ball. I'm running. Everything is moving really fast. I sprint forward and each stride carries me ahead at least 15 feet. A large structure appears on the horizon. It looks like a small city is being built. There aren't any solid walls yet... only the framework of buildings. It's speeding toward me.

The city isn't made of steel and iron it's all wooden beams. There aren't any people. I jump onto a beam and run along it. I leap gracefully to the next. The world is spinning so fast. I don't have any fear and jump perfectly from beam to beam. It's a giant wooden maze of construction.

Something catches my eye behind me. Looked like a long dark shadow. I glance behind me in mid-leap and see that everything looks burnt. I had just been running along the beams but they are cindered, and black. Even the grass and trees are charred and dead.

A movement underneath me. I look down beneath the beam I'm running on. The green grass is being swallowed in shadow. No. It's more like black goo. *It's moving fast. It's trying to catch me! My heart quickens. Fear triggers panic. It's trying to catch me! I'm being chased! It's destroying everything in its path.*

"Darkside." Something scratches into my ear. Grating whisper.

I jump faster. Each leap takes me ahead 40, 50, 100 feet. I'm practically flying. I look down. It's still right underneath me! I scan ahead and see the beams start to crackle. The cheerful, sun-colored wood fades to grey, splinters and turns black. It's ahead of me now. It's everywhere. A cold chill, like a stabbing icicle, shoots up my leg thrusting straight into my bone. A black tendril is wrapping around my leg. I cry out. Crouching low I push off the ground and leap up into the sky.

The Earth begins to fade below me as I rise higher and higher into the sky. The farther up I go the more I see. I finally see how much damage has been done. The blackness is everywhere. It's moving quickly over the planet. Everything is turning black and dying. Whole mountain ranges go dark like a cloud is passing over them.

I didn't mean to leave it. I didn't mean to fail. Sorrow. Grief. Despair. What could I have done? What was I supposed to do? I start to pass into the upper atmosphere. Everything around me flashes a brilliant, hazy white as I pass into space. I can see the whole planet now. Space is crisp and clear. The planet is dark. It's covered the whole world. I feel a cold tendril on my leg again.

It's still after me! Before I can fly faster it pulls my leg. It draws me into it with tremendous force. All around me. Black oil. Deathly cold. I try to struggle out but it's like freezing thick mud! It wraps itself around my arms and over my head. I feel it start to crush me into a little ball.

I can't scream. I can't move! What do I do!

White. I think of white. Like I used to... so long ago when I was young. I read a book on Wicca that talked about surrounding yourself in a giant white light. There's something else. It missed.

Peace. Fill it with the feeling of meditation. Such amazing peace. My fear begins to recede. A strange humming fills my ears. The white moves, flickers, strobes with the humming. The humming increases in intensity and harmonizes.

My whole body starts to hum. I feel it in my chest, in my stomach, my head. Wait. It isn't humming. It sounds like a million voices. They are all singing together. It is Aum. They're all chanting AAUUUUUUMMMMM. The coldness passes. I'm filled with incredible heat. The sound of AUM grows louder and the white light surrounding me flashes with it. As it touches the black tendrils they recoil and dissolve.

I break out and fly into space surrounded by a brilliant globe of white light. My whole body is vibrating with the incredible sound of AUM humming with such power it could fill the entire universe.

My body moves like I coughed in my sleep and my eyes open quickly. I look up at the ceiling. Something is happening. Everything is vibrating and moving. Earthquake! I roll over and touch the ground. Wait... no, the ground is still. Listening... everything sounds still, quiet.

I roll onto my back and let myself wake up. Everything looks bright, like there's more light in the room than there should be. My whole body slightly shakes. It's a quiet vibration.

I'm still dreaming. Or maybe I ate something strange. Suddenly the details of the dream come back. The sound and feeling of the AUM. Man, it's so intense. That's why my body is shaking, I'm still thinking about the dream. Pausing, I lie there paying attention to my body. What could cause this? It really feels like I'm vibrating all over. I try to shake it off. Reaching behind my head I grab my journal to write down the dream. It's a crazy one. So raw and intense. I'd been really afraid. Maybe that's what woke me up.

After writing it down everything is dark again and I can't feel the vibration. Huh, I was still partially asleep. "Now I'm awake..." I say out loud, trying to reassure myself that's really what it was. I was asleep. I throw my blanket over my head and go back to sleep.

The sun is shining right on my face and it is starting to make me sweat. I roll over and look at the time. It's 1:30. Holy crap - I slept so long! My head feels so thick. Thinking is hard. I feel groggy and exhausted. Everything feels like jelly. You'd think I have a freaking hangover. Staring up at the ceiling my body rejects the idea of moving. God, I'm exhausted, what did I do yesterday? Nothing except walk around with Eric...

Take care of yourself... go back to sleep...

Can't waste the day... what did I do last night? Trying to remember details my brain cries out. I don't want to think at all. My brain responds by throbbing. Mentally wasted. I'm completely wasted and my day hasn't even started.

Voices from the other room travel through the walls. The others are up. I wrap my blanket around me and wander into the living room. Farrah and Peggy are up and talking quietly. "Why, hello sleepy-head." Farrah says overly-cheerful. "You sure did sleep a long time."

"Yeah," I groan. "I don't know why, I feel totally wiped out. You'd think I ran a marathon or something yesterday."

"Well, maybe that's what happens when you leave the apartment." She taunts.

Maybe that's what you'll feel when I throw your smart ass off the balcony. I jab back in my head. It's way too early for her to start. I'm grumpy and so tired I'm a breath away from pissed off.

I go for my cereal. Digging around for a clean bowl but there aren't any. A Tupperware container calls to me. Yes, you will do...

"Hey, do you think Eric would teach me some stuff?" Peggy asks a bit bashfully.

"Oh my God no!" Farrah scolds in a hiss. "I have had enough of him! Nobody is to even speak that name while I'm around! That name is banned from this house. I don't know why you would want to do that Peggy. Honestly, he's up to something!"

I look over at Matthew still lying in bed with his head propped up against the wall. He rolls his eyes. Farrah can be overly dramatic sometimes. Frowning I look down at my empty Tupperware bowl. It's not that I totally disagree with her. I don't completely trust him either but I'm not going to be crazy about it. There's something there. Something that I can't put my finger on. Maybe he's the first intellectually interesting thing I've come across in a long time. I've never really met anyone like him. But... that's not it. That doesn't feel right either. Unsatisfying. I don't know what it is.

That won't calm Farrah down.

It feels so strong through. I know there's something there that I can't explain but I need to understand it. Until I know what it is I won't get sucked into her drama.

"I don't know," Peggy says smiling and trying to shrug Farrah off. "I was talking to Matthew and it sounded kinda interesting."

Farrah throws her hands up at the idea. "We'll see! We'll see who's right! Don't ever say I didn't warn you all!"

I shake my head at Farrah. She's never even talked to him. Any other day I might have tried to point that out but I can't get up the energy to even think about it. She's being too dramatic. I'm too wiped out for this. "I dunno Peggy. I'll ask Eric and see what he says."

Later that day I talk to Eric and tell him I've been sleeping in. I mention Peggy's interest. He wavers a bit and seems unsure of the idea. He likes Peggy, he assures me. He's always thought she was nice but he isn't sure if her interest is genuine or if she wants to do it only because everyone else is doing it.

Hmm. I can't say either way. I've never talked to Peggy about it but I was surprised she approached me about learning and not Justin.

Eric finally agrees he'll give it a try only if she makes the effort to read through all of the papers. After a moment he admits the reason for his reservation, "You know Eric, the problem is that often women don't take well to the knowledge. In all my years teaching, which has been a lot now, I've had less than handful of female students... and I mean, I've tried. But even among them it's rare to see any kind of success. Look at Kathy. She's been around going on 4 years, and is my most successful female student to date. But pretty soon, her biology will kick in and she'll start to feel the drive to have babies. There's the catch and it's a real problem." His voice is on edge. I can tell he's really driven himself crazy with it and sounds at a loss on how to deal with Kathy.

He goes on, "Men feel the sex drive too but want to go out and find a fuck and then get on with their day. Women are different. They want to draw you in, they want to build a nest and populate it. Biologically women are more tied to the planet because they're the ones who have to go through the whole process of carrying the baby, then nurturing it after birth and all of that. It's a real pull and pretty soon it will start hammering Kathy who will eventually slip away and lose all the progress she's made. To not fall into that trap she'll have to work twice as hard as a man would. If she goes with her biology she won't get another good run at it until she hits menopause. Women will do better later in life. As people get older men switch and become more passive and feminine and women become more masculine."

That part makes sense. I see what he's saying about the pull of biology. It's hard to go against everything your body tells you. Only... if someone wants to learn... shouldn't they?

I don't ask and let him keep talking, "I don't want to sound mean or discourage anyone who has an interest... but it's a numbers game. When you run the numbers a man, as bad as it may sound, when he is young, has a higher chance of success and therefore is better to put time into than a woman. Even now with Kathy, it's like this... if her need to have a baby doesn't run her off she could find a boyfriend who decides he's not into spirituality. I've taught Kathy well and she's become a strong person but she bends in relationships. She'll feel the need to conform to the man, because that's what women are taught to do in this society and off she goes until they break up. I can't fight so many things stacked up against me with the time I have. Right now Peggy's dating Justin. So, that works but what happens if they break up? All the time I've put into Peggy is gone... do you see what I'm saying?"

It's hard to take. I've always considered spirituality the only truly fair and balanced thing that exists. It's the only thing that seems to have no boundaries between races or sexes or anything. If someone wants to learn, it seems like they should be able to. Now he's placing conditions on it.

I'm silent too long so he says a little more, "In the end Eric, it's like this... think about how much time I've put into you. Multiply that by four years. That's a lot of time invested. My time. I'm giving that time to you... which is not something I have to do, get what I'm saying? Now, anyone I teach can give up, or fail in any number of ways but my job is to limit the amount of ways it can happen and put as much in my corner as I can to ensure success. Even to find a female who is interested, who has the desire and not because some guy is interested or she's after one of the other students, is hard but to take her farther while limiting all these other variables... it's a bigger risk."

Ah damn. I feel guilty now that he had to say it that way. It is his time, not mine. I don't know why he gives it but I know it's a lot. It also seems like he has a definition for success. Something he's trying to get them to achieve. He says they have a higher chance... a higher chance of what? Enlightenment? Is that even definable? It's hard for me to judge because he gives his time away. What if he spends time with all the rest of them as much as he spends with me? That's all your time. The biological clock part makes sense. If he's looking for some kind of dedication... that would be a big distraction. But what else do they have to do? You talk, maybe you meditate. I feel like I'm missing something. There's a point I'm not getting.

"I'll give her the papers and see where she goes with it." I tell him and leave it at that.

The combination of Eric taking me scanning the day right after I meditated for the first time, and saw the energy in the park... created what we call a, "Psychic Hangover."

Like a normal hangover when you drink too much... the psychic hangover occurs when you push yourself psychically or energetically too far from what you're used to. The resulting feeling is very physical and not much fun. You feel totally exhausted, even if all you did was sit around your room. Mentally drained, you usually feel like everything you experienced during your 'psychic high time' wasn't real.

It's the downswing of riding the pendulum up so high. You push yourself, or get pushed, up to a higher tonal than you're used to and then you come down. Because what you experienced was from a higher state of consciousness, when you come down to your normal, lower state everything you went through during the higher has a surreal, other lifetime, quality to it. Kind of like a night of getting wasted and you wake up the next day and everything's a blur.

Nobody ever spelled that out for me, which was hard because it can leave you in a strange place the next day. It creates emotions that are so mixed you're left feeling confused because you don't understand why. When you're there, in that higher state, you love it. So why are you so unsettled the next day? And why do you feel so detached from it? The uncertainty can leave you feeling farther and farther removed from the experience. Eventually, I pieced together things Eric told me here and there and saw a consistent process. After awhile, you adjust to the Psychic Hangover and they get easier to get through.

One process that isn't easy is the reaction others have to you as you change. Although I wasn't aware that I was changing much, the others were starting to notice. Farrah and Lenny particularly, were reacting. It wasn't that my habits were changing that bothered them. I was starting to act different in little ways. Even things that could be viewed as good, like not drinking as much, acting happier, not as grumpy... can spark fear in people close to you.

They knew me as a specific person. Because they liked that person, they wanted me to stay the same. If I wasn't the same, I wasn't their friend because that's who they knew! They didn't consciously do it, which is why I don't hold anything against them. It's only a simple fact that most people don't like change... the status quo is comfortable and safe. Why try to fix something that isn't broken? The more I changed the more they pushed against what they saw as the catalyst of that change... Eric.

The choices I found myself weighing were difficult ones. I once liked to think things could be every way I wanted it. Perhaps there were different ways I could have followed... but I have made my decisions. I have chosen my path. And I would do it all again... even the ones where I went wrong. For they have led me here.

Change requires choices. For better or worse, the last thing you want to do is stand still and not make them. When the seed sprouts, it cannot help but move some soil if it is to grow and succumb to... the force of change.

what do you want to become? the travels of an astronaut, willpower of an Olympian, help change the world... okay...

So You want to be a Meditator?

chapter fifteen

Curious and eager to recapture the feeling I had after the meditation I decide to try it on my own. In my room, I sit near the edge of my bed so my back can rest against it. I put on some nice classical music and get ready. I straighten my posture and do the breathing like Justin showed us. The first song starts playing and I use it as a warm up. Do some stretches, try and keep the legs alive... The second song starts. Okay, now it's time to meditate!

I do the first step Eric said to start with. My legs start to twitch so I shift around to get a better position. Cool, now I've got it.

My back feels like it isn't perfectly straight. I stretch my back and make sure I'm in the right position. Ugh, now my arms feel off so I shake them out and go back to the meditation. Quickly after, my neck gets a kink so I spin my head around in a slow circle then go back to meditation.

Focus.

I focus my mind on the music. God! I've been sitting forever! Restless, I open my eyes to peek at the stereo. I'm on the same song. I've been sitting for less than three minutes. Holy crap! No way. It seems like I've been here at least 15 minutes. I close my eyes again to refocus my meditation.

I wonder what's on TV? Shouldn't I be cleaning? I could start writing my script again. The bed my back is resting against doesn't seem comfortable. It feels like one mattress is sticking out farther than the other. I shift again. Let's play a computer game. This is boring. God, is this song ever going to end?! I can't believe it hasn't switched songs yet...

I start getting frustrated. Meditation is hard!

Opening my eyes I peek at the stereo. Barely over three minutes. This isn't right... something's wrong with the CD player... this is going too slow. It finally switches songs. Hrmm. Good. It was the song. That wasn't a good meditation song. Now I'm ready.

Encouraged by the new song I close my eyes and focus on meditation. Maybe I should turn the volume up. I wonder if I should face the other direction... is my back straight? I straighten my back, shift my legs, shake out my arms and take a few deep breaths. Okay, now I'm ready to meditate.

I open my eyes again to peek at the stereo. It's barely over a minute into the song. Damn, this song is taking a long time too! I can't do this. Come on, just do it. No... I'm not in the mood and can't get comfortable.

Thinking back to the school I don't remember it being so hard. Shaking my head I decide I need to wait for a better time. I should be in the right mood to meditate. Sucks. That didn't feel anything like it felt before. That was boring and irritating.

The next day before anyone else wakes up I decide to try meditating again.

I sit by my bed but make sure the two mattresses are perfectly straight. First I stretch my back out, then roll my head around to loosen my neck and finally do some deep breathes. Man, now I know why those guys were stretching before meditating. It must help.

I think there's a little difference. They said twenty minutes was a short meditation... you can't even do five. The grating voice mocks.

Shut up! Yesterday was a bad time, that's all. The small portable stereo in my room is loud enough for me to hear it but not loud enough to wake anyone up. I skip ahead a few songs on my classical CD to get past the songs that suck for meditation. Closing my eyes I follow Eric's instructions...

My legs start to twitch. I feel like going for a run. Damn, I haven't gone running in forever. Remember when I used to run 10 miles a day? Then there were those long summer nights where I climbed out my window and ran out into the night at three in the morning. Daydreams dance through my head. Yes, all the wonderful runs I used to have... oh... and the smell of dew as I ran through yards and fields. That feels like so long ago. I miss summers in Missouri.

Aren't you trying to meditate? The clear voice asks.

Crap! Right, meditate. I've been on the first part of the meditation long enough. I need to go to the next step. Moving ahead I change techniques to the second step.

Yeah, now I'm meditating! I'm on the second step. Now I'm making progress. I smile, happy to have made it farther than before. I wonder how long I can meditate for? Well, not too long, someone will wake up. I wonder what they would do if they walked in on me meditating? I feel a little panic at the idea of someone walking in on me and listen for sounds in the other room. Everything seems quiet.... except for the music. Oh music! Crap! I suddenly remember I'm supposed to pay attention.

I wonder if I'm doing this right. What's to do? It was so easy the first time, seems like you just go through it. Should I switch now? How do I know when to switch? Maybe you do it whenever you want. My back starts to hurt so I shift around.

Ugh, how long has it been? I open my eyes and look at the stereo. Three minutes... what the hell?! I never knew five minutes was so long. Frustrated, I take a few deep breaths. This is taking a really long time, you need to move on.

I skip ahead to the third step. There you go. You're getting it. On the third step now... My arm quickly starts to ache. I shake it out and go back to meditating. The ache spreads from my arm to my shoulder. Not to be outdone my back starts to ache in response. My whole body feels like it's really starting to hurt. I've been doing this too long.

Don't push it psycho.

I breathe out and relax. One eye peeks open. Damn. Barely 4 minutes. I close my eyes again. My body starts to ache from holding my arm. I guess you don't want anymore huh? I'm done.

Wussy. Weak little arm.

Don't push it or I won't do it again. I get up. Who knew five minutes was so long?

I continue my pattern off and on over the next few days. Each time I try to meditate for five minutes but can't. It always seems so long! I don't find myself getting overly frustrated instead I have fun playing around with it.

It doesn't make any sense... I can sit at a computer for hours but can't sit down and do meditation for a few minutes? What's that about? It seems funny. I no longer expect the experience to feel like it did the first time. Eric told me the feeling would fade. Now I'm not sure what to expect. Why am I doing this? I dunno. Curiosity maybe. It's not like it takes much time. It feels like learning something new. If it's hard it's got to be good! I laugh at myself.

I haven't heard from Eric in a few days. He's been meeting with Matthew but I also know he has to work at his bookstore. He seems to work when he wants though, so maybe I'm wrong. What does he do there anyway? I don't really know.

Justin shows up one day and tells me Eric asked to see if he could pick me up. If I want to go. I think about it. Yeah, I want to go. On the drive to Tujunga I remember the strange black VW in the park. There's something there, like a mystery lurking in the place. It's like an episode of Twin Peaks. I used to watch the show all the time. It was quirky. I loved it. It had this deep, dark mystery running underneath the whole series. Tujunga and Eric could be a bit like that.

Justin drives me up to the house. We're actually going to go inside the house. Justin tells me to come along but stops at the gate. He has me slowly walk in and lets the dogs look at me so they know who I am. One is huge! He comes up to me sniffing at my leg. I hold out my hand. He looks like a Doberman pincher on steroids. He's as tall as my waist but thick and stocky around the middle.

"That's Angus." Justin tells me. "He could do some serious damage you know what I'm saying? Once you get to know him he's really nice but make sure he knows who you are or that's it. The other one is kinda stupid so he's not a problem."

A little black dog comes running up from behind the house and sniffs at my shoe. He pushes his head into my hand and I pat him on the head. He's about the size of a coyote and even looks like one a bit although he has black fur. It's the first time I've had a chance to see the house close up. The yard is mostly sandy dirt. A row of bushes line the fence inside. Directly ahead is a low cover to a huge porch. It has a little stone wall with vines stretching up onto the roof. The house is made of the same large, shale river-rock type stones as the porch wall. They're multi-colored rocks ranging from a lush orange to rich brown and it gives the house a fairy-tale look. There's a colorful charm to it. I half expect to see Hanzel and Gretel walking out or the Gingerbread man.

From the porch there are windows with wooden shutters so you can see into the living room. The porch has a few chairs outside and a stereo. Justin and I walk into the living room and the dogs stop at the open door.

"They know not to come in." Justin tells me.

Once they realize they aren't going to be invited they both lay down in the doorway. The living room is simple and bare. There's a rock fireplace on one side with a few chairs. Some paintings and trinkets line the walls but nothing like the bookstore which is lined with relics. A black couch sits against one wall next to a cushy-looking lazy boy. The walls are an off-white which makes the room feel bright and sunny but not overpowering. The ceiling doesn't end in square corners; instead it's rounded and curves in. The ceiling dips again in a giant oval shape that goes up another six inches. Despite the bareness it feels welcoming, like a home.

A loud crash echoes down the one hall that leads back into the house. Eric appears with a large white bucket filled with cleaning supplies that he has knocked over. Justin calls out that we're here. Eric complains that we're a bit early and he hasn't had time to clean yet. He comes down the hall and tells me to make myself at home. Turning he asks Justin if he can help pick up a bit. He complains he's embarrassed the house is so messy. Justin dodges the question and tells him he needs to get back to LA. Eric sighs. Justin did bring me up so he should just go, he tells him. Eric asks if I want the tour, which I do. He waves around and explains we're in the living room. He points to the indention in the ceiling. He always wanted someone to paint a sky there so it would look like a giant skylight. You could sit in the living room and feel like you were outdoors. I look up. It would be a great place for it and would make the room really alive. I tell him it's a great idea.

In the hallway is a door on the left. Eric knocks on it and a voice yells back. Eric opens it and Frank is sitting at a desk in front of a computer. He's playing some kind of colorful game I've never seen before.

"This is Frank's room. You remember Frank?" Eric asks.

"Yes, I do. Hi." I wave from the hallway.

"What's up dude?" Frank asks. "This your first time here?"

"Yeah." I admit.

Eric steps in his room a few steps. "You want to clean up the kitchen? Are any of those your dishes in there?"

"Actually, none of them are mine." Frank tells him. "I don't ever really eat here. Sorry!" He chuckles.

"Of course, nobody makes any messes here. They walk through perfectly and disturb nothing. Ok then." Eric says as he closes the door.

"That's what Frank does. He plays computer games. Always on the computer. Always playing that game. It's a new online game. Do you play online games?"

I shake my head no.

"Good. You probably shouldn't start. They can be addicting."

I think back to my wasted years playing online games. Nazmorghul. Yeah, addiction is exactly what it was. So much time I've lost forever. Never want to go back there again. It took so long to fully withdraw and recover. Mine was never that colorful either. It was all old school MUD text crap. The colors seem like they would be even more addicting. The easy reality escape-hatch.

Straight across from Frank's room is the kitchen. It's a single room and a little small. It has a little table stuck in the corner piled with so much stuff I don't see how anyone ever eats there. The cabinets look like they've been freshly painted. Eric explains that when he bought the house there had recently been a fire. The whole roof had to be ripped off and rebuilt. Most of the house was destroyed but the foundation remained intact. They did it all themselves.

One of his students had some experience in carpentry so they rebuilt all the cabinets in the kitchen. I nod my head. From what I've seen the house doesn't look damaged. The cabinets look new and fit in well with the kitchen. Then I see the sink. It's stacked, over the top, with dishes. Pots, pans, plates, glasses, everything. I'm suddenly struck by how strange it is that nobody wants to do the dishes for Eric. I don't exactly understand their relationship to each other except they're his students. Of course, I don't really understand what that means either. To me a student is someone who pays money to go to a school and the teacher is paid by the school to teach. If they're starting their own school for spiritual teachings then they aren't doing much else. It's hard to believe he's some kind of sinister cult master. He can't even get people to do the dishes for him. How is he supposed to do anything else? If he's a cult master he's a really bad one.

I hear someone say something behind me. I turn and a young, latin guy is standing there with two bowls in his hands. I realize he needs to get by so I move aside. Eric watches him go over to the sink and fill his bowls with hot water. He sets them on the side. He turns to walk away and Eric asks if he's going to leave them there.

"They need to soak." I barely hear him mumble.

"Well, why don't you clean some of the others while you're waiting?" Eric asks him.

He's slowly slinking his way closer to me. He has long dark hair that covers his eyes and I can't make out his expression. "None of them are mine." He quietly replies.

"Of course! Nobody in this house uses any dishes." Eric throws his hands up.

He slips out and walks down the hall. That was weird. Where did he come from and where is he going?

"That's George. He lives in the basement with his girlfriend." Eric tells me as if reading my thoughts.

"This place has a basement?" I'm a little surprised. "Nobody in California has a basement."

"Well, wait until you see this basement. It's more like a cellar. His girlfriend's name is Ana. You might see her too but they won't talk to you. They don't talk to any white people." He laughs. "Or anyone else actually. I'm the only one they talk to."

"Oh. That's strange." People living in a cellar under your house who never speak... I've seen horror movies like that I think.

He shows me around the rest of the house. The hallway turns to the back of the house into a long dark hallway that has no walls. Eric tells me it hasn't been finished in the construction and is being used as a giant closet. Eric informs me they build as they have money and recently nobody has had any. Something catches my eye between some hanging shirts.... it's sunlight.

The wall at the back of the house is barely a wall. It's some plywood pieces nailed in a big sheet with slits between where they meet. That's when I notice the bathroom door at the end of the hall is crooked.

We walk out the front door around to the back of the house where Eric stays. Separate from the main house is a standing garage that's been converted into a room. It's my first chance to see it in the day. Part of the roof in the corner is burnt black.

Eric points out the burnt roof. "The garage is the only thing left intact after the fire." He tells me. "It scorched the roof but that's all."

The back of the house is a giant construction set. They haven't finished building the back wall of the house because they hope to extend it. Instead, they have a big, flat boarded porch covered in tarps. Big flat pieces of wood lie across beams that make an area to sit on large enough for a big group of people. Eric tells me after they finished tearing apart the burnt part but before building everything back up, everyone was pretty wiped out. Then he ran out of money and can't afford to build the rest.

Like a giant tree house...

It reminds me of a sophisticated tree house you might build when you're a kid. You find bits and pieces and hammer them all together. I'm surprised how good it all looks but once you notice the details it becomes obvious how much they're struggling without money to put into the place.

Beyond the porch is a little yard. There are some trees and bushes with an area of grass. Angus runs past me. The dogs are running around sniffing everything circling close to Eric. Eric points to steps leading down under the porch.

"That's the basement. It's one little room but that's where George and Ana stay." Eric apologizes for the mess but I wave it off. Our apartment is always wrecked. I'm not one to judge by those standards.

He says that with so many people living there it's hard to keep it clean the way he likes. Still, he firmly believes that your home is your sanctuary and you have to always keep it like that. Of course, without all the people living here he could never afford to have it at all. It's his first house. Shrugging he believes he's a bit old to never have had a house before. He's never had many possessions. Most of his time and energy has gone to his spirituality and teaching others. It's made him rich in other ways. Right now, he has to focus on the bookstore and the school, neither of which make much money but it's what he's always dreamed of doing.

I can tell by walking through the house he certainly doesn't make much money from it. The house has a charm but it's simple. Humble. I like it.

He needs to finish cleaning in case we decide to eat there later. "Do you want something to drink?" He asks me.

Sarah's voice jumps in my head. *'Always cults in California. Open minded, too trusting, California, he can read my thoughts'.* Ugh, shut it. I decline the drink. The thought borders on ridiculous but better safe than sorry.

I sit on the couch in the living room and wait for him to finish cleaning. After about 30 minutes my throat feels parched. Great, I'm thirsty. Walking into the kitchen I see him with his shirt pulled up to his elbows scrubbing frantically at an enormous stack of dishes. Cinderella. He's doing enough dishes for a small naval base. God, they don't even have a dishwasher. At least we've got that... not that we ever use it. He turns and asks what I need.

"Water. Just a glass of water."

"Oh sure," he jokes, "now you're making a mess too and not going to help." Ashamed, I turn my head slightly. "I am joking. You're a guest." He assures me.

I nod. "I got that one." I'm starting to get his humor. His voice throws me off. It's hard to tell. It's the tone he uses that is confusing. His voice hides whether he's joking or not. Still, I feel like I should help, nobody should clean up such a big mess alone. I scan the counter for the bowls George left. They're gone. He cleaned those too. He even cleans up after them. Seems like he's getting a raw deal.

With my water in hand I head back to the living room and wait. Eric finally finishes cleaning and comes to sit on the couch. He looks around the room.

"You know, after cleaning it all, I don't feel like being in here. Let's go to my room. I need my inner sanctum!" I can tell he's tired, his face looks drained. Like the tired you get when you clean house for a whole day and want to stare at the walls when you're done. We go to the garage.

The garage room looks more like the bookstore. A big black hutch with a glass display case on top of it has a few interesting objects inside. One is a crumbled black book... now way, it's a Bible. The Bible from the entities tape. Chuckling to myself I shake my head. I can't believe it's real. I can't make out the other objects and don't want to snoop. His bed is tucked away in the corner with a desk and a computer. A single dresser and a small couch are pushed against the wall farthest from his bed.

He motions to the couch and tells me to have a seat. Sighing in weariness he crawls over to his bed and sticks his face in his pillow. Rolling over he looks at me.

"Well, have you tried meditating since the barbeque?" He asks.

"Yeah, I've been trying it a little at a time. Not as easy as I thought it would be." I grin sheepishly.

Nice way of saying you're so weak you can't do five minutes...

Snickering through my nose I hope he doesn't press for details. That would be embarrassing.

He smirks. "Well, of course. You were being carried by our energy. No way is it going to be the same. I told you that."

What does he mean by being carried by their energy? Nodding my head I make a mental note to remember it. It will probably make more sense once I understand meditation better.

"Well, let's see how you've been doing. Stand up." He gestures for me to get up.

I stand up and take a few steps so that I'm between the couch and the foot of the bed. It doesn't look like he wants to move. Briefly he turns his head to stare at the ceiling. He has the look of someone convincing himself that he has to get out of bed but wants to hit the snooze button instead. Groaning he pushes himself up and sits against the wall.

"Okay. Here we go. Take off your shirt." He instructs wearily.

I pause, waiting for him to give a reason. No reason comes. "Take off my shirt?" I ask doubtful.

"Oh God. Yes, yes. Your shirt. It's not like I'm asking you to strip. Right, I have to explain every little tiny detail with youuu. I need to see your causal energy clearly. Your shirt makes it harder to look at.

I don't know how else to say it." He pushes his glasses up with his hand and rubs and presses his fingers against his eyes like he's trying to relieve pressure.

"I'm tired, I'm trying to put some time and energy into you when I don't want to. I don't say that for you to feel bad, I'm only being honest. I'm not going to keep teaching you until I can see it. So, you decide." He says as if he's straining to continue speaking.

I know how he feels, the kind of tired where you want to shut down but... what is he talking about? None of it makes any sense to me. What is causal energy anyway? What does that even have to do with anything? Before he said he could see the aura around a person. Why doesn't he look at that? How do clothes block anything? I don't want to be difficult unnecessarily but if he's so good and advanced he should be able to look at whatever he wants. Panic starts to grip me ever-so-slightly. I stand motionless in thought. I say nothing.

"Uggh!" He moans. "I'm so tired of using kid gloves with you! You're so shy and scared of everything. How do you get through life? You need to be back in the days when men would bathe with the full long underwear on, you know? Like, when women had to cover their entire bodies and all that. It's pathetic. Haven't you ever gone to a pool? I'm not asking for something crazy here. It might be a little unusual, you come to a guy's house and he asks you to take your shirt off but if you go see a homeopathic doctor they might ask the same thing and work out of their house. Look causal energy is your core energy. It runs up and down your spine. To scan it I need to get a good look at it. I can look at your aura but that only tells me so much. Causal tells me more about where you're going, who you have the potential to become, what are the highest peaks you've hit in your past lives. I mean, for Christ's sake, you might have been sent here by the Darkside. I'm not saying that's the case but I've got to be careful, you know? So, if all that helps, there you go. Men go walking around without shirts all over the planet, I think you'll live." He flops his head back on his pillow and stares up at the ceiling pressing his palm on his forehead. He must have a headache, though he doesn't say it.

I think about what he said. I take it all in. Let it soak.

He's saying you're shy. You're shy and scared. The grating voice digs into me.

I'm not shy! I haven't been shy since high school! God, I used to be so shy it was crippling. So much fear. Petrifying fear. Skipping school for a week to avoid standing up in front of the class and read a report. I barely spoke three words during a day. What's worse, I'd have to quickly take my shirt off during gym only when I was certain nobody was looking. Why was I like that? I don't know why. I was skinny.

Skinny little nerd. Strange, quiet, afraid little kid. Nothing's changed.

No... that was in the past. I conquered that long ago. Didn't I? Look at me. Here I am. Thinking myself a grown man feeling fear, true panic and fear, about taking my shirt off. I start to sweat. My knees are shaking slightly. I'm trying to keep it together. Why am I so afraid? It's the same. The panic I used to experience. Some part of me freezes. Totally controlled by this crippling shyness. I don't want to be exposed. I don't want to feel vulnerable. My clothes hide me. They're my safety.

"Well, I'm waiting..." he says looking beyond bored staring at the ceiling.

Is he doing this on purpose? Does he even need to see me with the shirt off to see this 'causal energy' or is he pushing my buttons? He said he was tired of the kid gloves... He pointed out my shyness.

He's doing this on purpose. He's pushing you.

Well, that's not his fault. I'm the one afraid. It's you Eric. You're afraid. I stop and pay attention to how I feel. Fear and adrenaline race through my body. Over what? Here I'm saying I'm not shy and yet I'm paralyzed. For what? A shirt? Is it control? Am I afraid he's controlling me? What if I went to see a doctor? Crap. The last time I went to a doctor I almost freaked out too. I have been to a pool. I used to go running without it on.

That's when I went to the gym and had muscles. Now you're skinny and weak again.

Is that what this is about? Is that where this came from? I used to like my body. Now I don't. Because of that I've let it all come back. Damn it! I start to get mad at myself. My old weakness that controlled so much of my life is exposed, out in the open, clear.

What's the worst thing that could happen? The clear voice asks.

You could DIE!! The frantic voice answers.

Always to the extreme... I think sighing sadly...

Yes, I could die. And is taking my shirt off going to kill me? No! In five years, is it going to matter that I took my shirt off? No. In ten years will it make one shred of difference? Will I even remember? No! But will I remember if I fail? Yes, I will remember that. Will I be content to know that fear was the deciding factor? That fear made the decision for me? When I am dead and gone which choice will make the difference? Will whether or not I took my shirt off make any difference when I am dead and gone? No. But to know what he knows. To understand what this is all about. This is life. I will live it. I will not shy away from it! Screw fear! I work myself up. I become angrier at myself. Ashamed of not having any courage and trying to hide from life. Disgusted to let my shyness cripple me once more. Enraged that I'd let it regain control.

I reach down and take my shirt off.

"My God, that was painful, wasn't it?" He says with a slightly hidden smirk.

He's making fun of me. That's fine. For me it's victory. I will not live in fear. His reasons don't matter. I found fear and conquered it. Any victory over the self, no matter the size, is still just that. I stand, content with myself.

"Okay, now that we finally have that over with…" He lowers his glasses and looks over them to see me with his normal vision. "Stretch your arms out." He instructs.

I stretch each arm out as far as I can to each side.

"Hrmm." He says after a few seconds. "Do this for me, take your hands and make your fingers like this." He raises his hand up and shows me a way to position my fingers. He gives no explanation and, thinking it more of a ritual than anything, I don't ask. I put my fingers the way his look and stretch my arms back out.

He lowers his head again to see over his glasses. "Good. You can put your shirt back on." He sighs again as he moves to sit on the edge of his bed closest to his black hutch.

"What kind of music are you listening to when you meditate?" He asks facing the floor as if he's thinking.

"Uhh, classical." I say as I put my shirt back on.

"Classical?" Sounding a little unsure of my choice.

"Well, it's the only music I have without words." I explain.

"I see. Well, classical's no good really. It's just one of those things. It depends on the kind and maybe it can get you by but there's much better music to use."

He bends down and opens a cabinet on the bottom of his hutch. Digging through it he finally pulls out a tape.

"Here." he says handing me the tape. "It's an album I put together for the students. They tell me it's really good. We made a bunch of copies and that's my copy."

"Thank you." I say eyeing the tape.

"Now, it goes in songs of three. Three songs for each part of the meditation, got it? It's 15 minutes long. Don't do more than that, okay? If you push yourself too hard you'll burn out and you won't want to meditate. So when you meditate use that. It's kind of Celtic, tribal with some deep drums. You need something strong to shake you up. Get you out of your timid routine."

I nod absently. Christ! What am I going to do with 15 freaking minutes! I don't want to explain I'm fighting to do 5. It's going to take me months to listen to the whole tape.

"Now, where are you meditating?" He asks looking at my face as if my response is going to tell him something important.

"Umm, on the corner of my bed in my room. Kind of like, closest to the window." Picturing my room I don't want to admit it's the only clean spot in the place.

"Okay..." he nods like he's trying to see it in his head. "Do you feel comfortable there?"

"Comfortable?" I ask, not sure what he means.

"Yeah, comfortable! Like you sit there and you feel like you're ready to meditate. Does it make you feel like you belong there? Listen, why did you decide to meditate there?"

I think about it. Did I decide? Did I even think about it? I could have cleared some clothes out but... it was an open place... "I'm not sure. I think I rolled out of bed and that was where I landed so I just kept using it."

"Yeah, great. There's a book you should read sometime. It's all about this guy Carlos Castenada and his teacher Don Juan. Anyway, in that book they talk about finding 'your spot'. It's a spot that feels most comfortable to you in any given place. In the book Don Juan tells Carlos to find his spot. Carlos doesn't know what he's talking about so he rolls around this whole place trying all these different positions but can't find it. He keeps complaining to Don Juan and he tells him to just do it basically. Finally, Carlos becomes exhausted, gives up, and falls asleep. When he wakes up Don Juan is there and he tells him, hey, good job you found your spot! Get it?"

I nod even though I don't get it. His final question makes it seem like it should be obvious. I will get it... eventually... only not now. Later might not happen either. Huh. I should get the book. Then I'd get it.

"So, go to your apartment. Walk around and try different places. Sit in them. Meditate in them. Whatever. See where you land and what feels right. The real trick, which they don't say in the book, but it's all made up anyway, not that it really matters, anyway!" He shouts out to stop his train of asides and shoots me a smile. "The real trick is pick a spot and stick with it. Make it your meditation spot. Every time you sit down to meditate and do it in the same place your energy and tonal saturates everything around you. The better your meditation the better the energy. When you sit down to meditate again because that spot is radiating that good meditation energy it will be easier to get to the same place. It's like an energy bookmark. Also, psychologically your brain will relate that spot to meditation. You'll train it to be like, okay, now we're sitting in the spot so now I've got to go into the meditation zone. Get it? It's about using the same spot because it trains your brain and conditions the energy. Makes sense right?"

I nod because I get it this time.

"Of course it does!" He grins. "What you think I make this stuff up as I go along?"

I laugh. I wonder if he could be that good. Eric is too tired to drive me back to LA so he calls Justin to pick me up. I thank him for the tape and say good-night. I'm eager to try it out. Why didn't I think that the music would make a difference? All this time I never switched my music! It feels like I have a new toy to play with and I'm excited about what it might do.

Later, Eric would be proven right again. I would discover not only is energy harder to see through clothes but that it's easier to see with bad vision.

Eric describes how the eye is curved, so your forward vision and peripheral vision are a little different. It's easier to see energy out of the corner of your eye. This same principal applies to bad natural vision. Whenever Eric would look at energy he'd lower his glasses and use his natural eyes. Whether he did this for practical reasons or as confirmation for me that I should try it, is a different topic.

Since my eyes were also bad when I finally started to acknowledge and study my own aura I would practice seeing it in the morning or at night, without my contacts. I remember the days when I could take my contacts out, go meditate, and everything would come to life. Swirling vortexes, auras, it was all so much easier to observe! The details, intricacies and colors!

Until the day came... that I got laser eye surgery. Somehow they left off the brochure for Lasik that it would impair your ability to see energy and dimensional fluxes. All joking aside, it reduced my ability to see energy by at least fifty percent. It makes a difference.

Clothes are a bit different. I think Eric was trying to demonstrate a few things that night. One is that energy can be obscured by physical matter. Only once have I clearly seen energy within, not around, someone's body. There was another student sitting across from me wearing a button shirt and had it hanging open at least 5 inches below his throat. I started by observing his aura and then noticed an incredibly clear line, like a brilliant blue neon sign tube, running from the center of his forehead down his face, throat and on down his chest. It was following his spine. The fact that it was 'inside' his body made no difference, it was phenomenally clear.

As soon as it hit his shirt it was completely shrouded. I couldn't make it out.

I'm sure if you saw this enough to study it this could provide useful information, which is what Eric was after. At the time I was too excited by actually seeing it to get much information.

The second thing Eric was starting to pick at with his "kid gloves" was my deeply embedded fear. Fear would gradually play an increasingly larger role in my development... or lack of. It's hard to tackle something like that overnight. Eric started attacking it from every angle he could find. Enough to make me aware of it without making me lock up and run.

Soon, you'll see my fear in action and part of you will agree with it. Think it natural. If you could switch to a different timeline, into the past and farther into the future, you would see the degree and depth that it controlled me. Like driving around with the emergency brake on.

Loud, unpredictable, at times seemingly arrogant... all these traits obscure the part of Eric that lies hidden, ever-present, watching. This part is a masterful surgeon. His skill at stepping aside and letting this aspect conduct its operation is flawlessly subtle and a testament to his ability as a teacher. There's a reason Enlightenment is sometimes described as liberation. Freedom. Release of your bonds.

What did I feel that night? A quiet victory... The loosening of a weight, whose string was snipped by scissors without matter, phantom hands without name.

I have found many times, the obstacles you believe to be ahead of you are nothing more than the baggage you are dragging behind.

is it so hard to believe in yourself? your strength, uniqueness...
purpose? does being different have to create a...

Super-Hero
Separation

chapter sixteen

Morning. My excitement is gone. Flushed away in the night. In no
hurry to struggle through another meditation I decide to finally go out
with Kathy instead. We've talked a little on the phone, mostly failing
attempts to arrange something to do. Orange County is a long drive
when you include time to sit in traffic. Not having a car doesn't help.
Yeah, there's that too. I call her and we decide to go see a movie.
She'll drive.

She picks me up and we decide on a place we've never been. There's
an outdoor shopping mall in Century City I've driven by but never
visited. We hop in her car, a little white Honda that's pretty nice and
clean, a big contrast to Justin's car. Even though I rode in it after the
barbeque I must have blocked most of it out. It was the food incident.
Walking in on her and Eric arguing about what kind of food to give
me.

I chuckle involuntarily. Kathy shoots me a quick look out of the
corner of her eye. Crap. I freeze up. She's going to think I'm
laughing at her. She isn't even asking me what I'm laughing about.

That's not a bad thing idiot. You want to bring up what you're laughing about?

Right. That would be a real smooth way to start things off. So Kathy, let's go back and talk about the last time we were hanging out and you were really embarrassed! Way to go.

She clears her throat nervously. Now I shoot her a quick look. She brushes her hair behind her ear. Must be a nervous habit.

"Uh, how was the drive down?" I ask trying to make her more comfortable.

"It sucked. The traffic was fucking shit!" She quickly glances at me, her eyes large with fear. "I shouldn't have said it like that. I'm sorry! It was bad, that's all."

I laugh. "Don't apologize. I don't care. Talk how you want to talk."

Despite my trying to laugh it off she goes dead quiet. We ride the rest of the way to the mall in total silence. Wandering the Century City mall before the movie we start to talk about the only thing we have in common; Eric Pepin.

I try to control my eagerness; she's the first student I've talked to alone. Except for Justin who, for some reason, doesn't really count. It's hard relating to Justin as a student because I've known him as something else for so long.

Jumping right into it I pepper her with questions. How long has she been a student? How did she meet Eric? What does she think? How many students does she know? There are so many things I'm curious about. She stares at me with 'you've got to be kidding' eyes. Hrmm. My excitement isn't shared.

Little by little I whittle a picture of her story out of her. It takes a lot of coaxing. She's quiet but firm, which brands an image of her as a librarian... which she kind of looks like.

She's been a student of Eric's for four years. Wow. Four years. It's strange. She's so young! I look at her and try to guess her age... Eric told me but I forgot, maybe 22 or 23. She must have met Eric when she was 18. Her introduction to Eric was a stranger affair than what I'd gone through. She was at a coffee shop with her boyfriend. They were playing cards, not doing much. Eric walked up to the table and asked if he could see their cards. They didn't know what to think so they handed him the cards they'd been playing with. Eric flipped them over in a pile so they were all face down. Looking straight at them both he said the name of a card and flipped the top one over. It was the one he called out. The pile didn't need to be shuffled. They'd been playing for awhile without any kind of order. Eric started calling other cards and flipped them after he'd said the name. Each one was right. Eric started flipping card after card as fast as they could read them. He got the whole deck right.

Soon after her boyfriend became a student. She began learning through him.

When they eventually broke up he went his own, separate way, and she remained with Eric. My mind tries to formulate the right way to ask the question I really want to ask. Is she going to be offended? Are there rules about what I can ask? If there are, I don't know them. It would seem controlling and I've never heard of any controls, sooo...

Screw it. DO it you little freaking pansy.

"Have you experienced anything?" I ask after a pause.

She let's out a little groan. It seems like the question bores her.

"Are you serious? More than I know what to do with." She mutters. "Why, haven't you?"

My mouth opens to talk but nothing comes out. I close it again. Not only has she experienced things but she sounds like it's happened so often that she's tired of it.

"Um, no. I've only really known Eric for two months or something."

"So?" She makes it sound like I should have experienced something already. Her manner is short and really to the point. Maybe I'm not asking the question correctly. I said it wrong somehow. She doesn't know what I mean by 'experiencing' something.

Okay, so clarify it. The clear voice quietly suggests.

Actually, I'm not even sure what I mean.

"No, I mean like, well, like…" she could help me out here. She remains quiet staring at me with little expression. God, she's hard to read. There you go, have her ask the question. "What kinds of things do you mean you've experienced?"

"I don't know." She pulls away with her body language and turns her head. The question seems like it flusters her. "You name it. I've seen cracks of light appear in a room. They looked like they were being drawn in the air and these white, energy-like balls flying around. I've seen entities, which, I can't even sleep on my back now because of this one entity…" Her voice trails off quietly. Suddenly she's vulnerable, even a little scared. It's out of place and I start to laugh.

"You can't sleep on your back!?" I cackle out, in disbelief.

"Well, no." She shoots me a dirty look. She looks like she really doesn't appreciate that I find humor in this. "Hey, you go through what I've gone through and see how it changes you buddy!"

Whoa. She doesn't mess around. Her firmness comes across. "All right, okay, I'm sorry. You just seem, you know –" Tough. I want to say tough. When she said she can't sleep on her back her whole air changed. She seems too strong and tough. Suddenly I realize telling her she's tough won't go over well either. "You know, that you could like, sleep… wherever." Reflexively I smile at her. She warms back up.

Her face softens a touch and she shrugs one shoulder. "I'm too paranoid. It doesn't feel secure. Well, tell me how you'd feel. I wake up one night lying on my back and I can't move. It felt like someone was sitting, sitting right on top of me, holding me down." She pushes her arms into her chest to show me how much weight she felt on top of her. No way! Justin! Suddenly, the story Justin told me with the floating head comes to my mind. The guy in that story couldn't move either. I forgot all about it! How could I forget a story like that?

"I saw like this thin, hazy outline, some kind of shape, it looked like energy. I struggled and fought but it wouldn't get off me. The harder I struggled the tighter it held me. What was I supposed to do? Something is there, I can see it, I can feel it holding me down, I can feel the weight but I can't move." Her eyes are distant like she's withdrawn into the memory. Her strong, firm presence fades into a small, vulnerable, shy girl.

Oh my God. Somehow, coming directly from Kathy, having experienced it herself, it seems so much more real than Justin's story. Maybe it's because I've heard Eric talk about entities and listened to the tape so now I have a better idea of what she's describing. But to see one, to have one on top of you... fear is evident on her face. It sends chill's through me.

"Did you scream?" I ask no longer finding humor in it.

"Well, yeah I think I did. I tried to anyway. I couldn't though. Wouldn't come out. But then I got a little mad. I was mad this thing was trying to control me and make me afraid so I got real, angry, and I threw all my energy at it and it flew off." She showed me her mad face and threw her arms out to demonstrate how much force she felt. Even her mad face isn't too far from her normal face. She doesn't express a lot of emotion. Kinda like me I bet. "That worked... for whatever reason. It went away. Only now I feel... I don't know. It sounds stupid..."

"No..." I assure her shaking my head. Whatever she feels it sounds like she's justified.

"I feel vulnerable, exposed or something, sleeping on my back. Ever since then I started sleeping on my side!" She says bluntly.

She's so matter-of-fact about the whole story. Her conservative demeanor doesn't leave any room for drama or flair. She gives me the

299

facts and acts like it's something she went through and not something she'd want to experience again. I get the image of her lying on her back getting pissed off and then being even more pissed that she has to sleep on her side. I start to laugh.

"That's so crazy." All I can do is shake my head. It's not possible... is it?

"Yeah, well, I've seen more. Now I don't mess around. I feel them come in my room sometimes or at the base of my bed and I throw energy balls at them." Her face hardly changes at all. She could be telling me she runs track she's so casual about it.

"Really?!" No way! She's seen more than one!

"You're lucky. Eric doesn't train students that way anymore. Used to, everyone would have to go through that... he'd send entities to test you. Like final exams or something." She tries to smile but it doesn't seem natural. Catching my shocked stare she looks away and pulls her hair back behind her ears.

"No way. Eric sent it? He can do that? He's never said anything like that..." I'm baffled. If it's that easy... why doesn't he do that to everyone? Then they'd believe everything he says about entities. At least then I'd know they're real.

"My God, you're so young." Her look seems condescending. "Give it time. You'll see it all too."

I'm sure my eyes are sticking out past my face. Her comment belittles me. Internally I withdraw. I'm older than she is but her tone suggests I'm a little kid who doesn't know anything. She turns to look at me and then looks away.

"No, I mean, I didn't mean it like that, like in a bad way." She shifts uncomfortably. Embarrassed and nervous. She must have caught my reaction. Her eyes glance down and her face drops away. It's strange to watch. When she told me how I'm so young she was so certain, so confident, and then she switches to insecure and unsure. The switch is sudden. I forgot that we're on a 'date' and we're supposed to behave a certain way and impress each other. She must feel like she offended me. She hasn't really...

Whatever. You feel put down.

Maybe... her tone surprised me.

"No, it's okay, I'm not offended or..." I try to explain.

"No, look." She insists seeming more bothered than anything. "It's just, well, look I don't know whether to envy you or pity you. I mean, you're only now starting out. Everything's new and so exciting when you start. It's so much fun to learn about it all and experience it! It's great! It's like, this whole new world. But then when you experience so much you forget, or get all tied up into everything and then you don't know what to do with it! I've seen all these things and I can do things with entities, and dimensions and know how the Universe thinks but what do I do with it all? Once the newness wears off you start asking, what? What is it all for? Why? Why me? Why do I know all of this? I mean, kids my age are out drinking and partying, going to school, and having fun. And that's most of my life!" It's the first real strong emotion I've seen from her. Her eyes have a helpless, almost pleading, sad look. Even her arms move around a little like she wants to shake me and make me see what she's saying.

"Then I go hang out with Eric and everyone and it's entities, dimensions, the Darkside and saving the world! What do I do with that? Most guys I date want to drink beer and watch sports. They don't want to know the girl they're dating fights entities and can do all these psychic things!" Her voice raises slightly but she keeps it under control. She doesn't let it out but I can feel the intensity of what she's trying to express. She keeps it all wrapped up. It's all locked inside.

So much strength. She's the strong Kathy again. I'm absorbed by what she says. The tone she used to tell me how young I am suddenly makes sense. She's right. I'm older than she is but for what we're talking about she's the senior. If she's been doing this for four years I can't assume to know what she knows. I can't presume to even be able to relate. If we were in college I'd be the clueless freshmen. She'd be the veteran graduating and she's right to suggest I'm clueless. I am. The way she describes it all... it's such a reality for her. I'm fighting to think of it all as real and for her there's no doubt. She's experienced it. She's even bothered or bored with it. I can't pretend to know what that's like.

I've never been bothered by someone being above me, or having a position over me, male or female, as long as they deserve it. Kathy acts and speaks as if she's earned the position. Without making an issue of it, I accept her role as the senior in Eric's world. There's a lot to learn from her.

We walk around and I lose myself in thought. The silence isn't comfortable for her. She tells me she's having a hard time lately with Eric and everyone else. She's felt so isolated from it since Eric moved to Tujunga. It would be better to talk about something else.

I agree. I don't want to make her uncomfortable, but all I want to do is pick her brain about what's she seen, done and known. It's a familiar world to her. I'm still trying to get a feel for Eric, who he is, what he wants, what the whole group is about. Is it really real? She takes for granted all the things that have my mind buzzing.

We go in to watch the movie, The Summer of Sam. She's surprised I pay for her. Nobody's ever done that for her before.

Now it's my turn to wonder how young she is. That's unbelievable. I want to tell her how bizarre it is that she's experienced things few people on the planet ever have but she hasn't experienced things everyone else has. I don't want to make a big deal out of it so I play it off, "It's the way I was raised I guess. Treat people you're with right. Not that I'm all old fashioned or think women can't take care of themselves!" I put up my arms defensively, joking that I don't want any ultra-feminist action.

She laughs and starts to blush. "No, I'm not like that. It was nice... so, that's all. Thank you." She turns away after thanking me. I chuckle. She's uncomfortable telling me thank you but she'll throw energy balls at entities in her room.

"Good. Because I've opened the door for a woman before and gotten cussed out for it." Kathy laughs until I tell her I'm serious. She's shocked. I try and lighten things up by telling her about the sad, sorry social maze guys are in these days so she needs to be nice to me. We joke around before the movie and I steer clear of any talk of Eric and the others.

Afterwards we wander through the closed shopping center. Most of it is outdoors and the sky's lit up with the lights of L.A. Not sure what to do next Kathy suggests grabbing a six pack of beer and going back to my apartment.

We hang out on the little balcony drinking and the conversation drifts back to Eric. I start trying to ask questions to understand what he's about. What does she think of him? What are the other students like?

Kathy looks pained and conflicted whenever I bring up the others. After awhile I start to understand. After knowing Eric for four years she can't dispute the knowledge. It's real. It works. She's experienced it first hand. All the students have. What she struggles with is trust. She doesn't really trust Eric. To hear her say that shocks me. How can that be? How can she have the experiences she's had and not trust the person who led her to them? How can she trust the knowledge he gives her absolutely but not trust the person who gives it? Somewhere in the back of my mind I've been nursing the idea that if I could experience just one thing, one thing I couldn't deny and see for myself, then I'd know. Right now I don't know because I haven't experienced anything. Seeing is believing. All I want is to see and then I will believe.

Kathy is suggesting that it isn't enough. She's so young and seen more than most people could ever dream of seeing but she doubts. I feel conflicted with it. I don't get it. I try to tell her as nicely as I can that it's strange to not trust someone after so long and so much.

She thinks about it. "Eric would do anything for me. There's no doubt in my mind about that. He's already done a lot for me. Probably more than anyone I've ever known. If I was ever in trouble, or needed something, he'd be there for me. What I doubt and struggle with is why. Why is he teaching me? Why am I a student? Out of all the people he can teach, out of all the people in the world, why me? What are his motives in singling me out? I don't feel special. I don't seem to fit. And his reasons for teaching me seem to change. Am I here only because my boyfriend was a student? Is there another reason? That's where I'm confused and feel like things don't make sense. And I shouldn't be telling you this... see... this is why I didn't want to talk about it. I mean, you're new, you should figure things out for yourself. I don't want you to be like... negative about it because of me..."

Eric told me she was the female student who has made it the farthest. She's the best so far. I tell her what he said.

This seems to make her a little upset, although she hides it well. Her eyes narrow and she shakes her head. "But why? What for? What's the purpose for it all? I know all this stuff and I've had all these experiences... but why?"

We fall silent for awhile. I see why she's made it so far, her thinking is intense. When we start to talk about Eric or her experiences her eyebrows scrunch and she speaks with an edge of strong emotion. Normally she's almost as stoic and detached-seeming as I am. Like a librarian. But inside she can tear things up with a fiery intellect. I smile at her as we sit on the balcony. She sits quietly in the chair with a beer looking a little distraught from my endless, nagging questions, and I stand there with a simple, probably dumb looking smile. She looks up and catches my smile then quickly looks away. She's so shy! How can she be so confident at one moment and so uncertain the next?

"What?" She asks looking away.

"Nothing." Some things I never say out loud. I expect people to be able to read my facial expressions which probably all look the same.

So hard to tell people things... what exactly you feel... I wish they could just read my face and know. To me they feel different. I like Kathy. She makes no pretense and doesn't try to hide who she is. She is who she is and that's it. Conflicted for sure but she has depth.

Being with her makes learning from Eric feel safer. Her doubts, her experiences, her knowledge and her other, 'normal' life. It's so muddled and rich she couldn't have made it up if she tried. Kathy could be anyone. She could be someone I knew in college or high school. She just happens to have experienced things most haven't dreamed of. Here I've captured a glimpse of how that's shaped her, set her apart and how she's trying to deal with it. Makes me wonder about comic book superheroes. Even Superman had to go to work. Kathy has to live in a regular world and live a regular life right alongside one that isn't. Somehow, knowing that, makes the things she's telling me more real.

We sit and talk late into the night. After awhile she gets tired and I realize what a long drive she has. Maybe I should invite her to stay the night? Part of me freezes.

Are you sure you want to do that? The clear voice cuts in.

I haven't touched or kissed a girl in two years. What if that happens? What would I do? Do I even want that? I'm not sure. I like Kathy but my emotions come back and reject the idea. I need more than this to want to touch someone. She doesn't make me feel that. We aren't there. If I don't feel it I don't feel it. Another reason creeps in. If I date Kathy and it doesn't work out, will I lose my connection to Eric? I'm not sure what that connection is but shouldn't I find out before I ruin it on a girl?

How do you know if you even like Kathy in that way yet?

I guess I don't know. I'm getting a little ahead of things.

I decide to proceed cautiously. I offer her some coffee for the drive home. She declines and we agree to see each other again. As she leaves I smile when she doesn't even move to hug me. She's so like

305

me in some ways. We're both very cautious and have solid boundaries.

The days pass. I talk to Kathy on the phone and we try to see each other again. It happens once or twice but not often and never for long. Each time her dilemma becomes a bit more clear. What she knows and what she's seen makes her different.

It also makes her special.

The problem is... she doesn't believe she's special, or can't. What's more, she spends most of her time down in Orange County. She attends college, goes to parties, and works her job like everyone else. Only she isn't like everyone else. Rather than feeling empowered by her experiences, she feels isolated. She's different in a way that nobody relates to. It makes her separate. It makes her alone.

As I realize this I think about Kathy a lot. I try to feel what it would be like to be her. I can't quite relate. My whole life I've felt different. Ever since I was young I've felt like I wasn't like everyone else. I was searching for answers nobody understood or cared about. I didn't know why but I knew in every part of my being that there was more to everything than what everyone else knew. I was already alone. I had friends, family, plenty of people who loved me. But a part of me always felt separate. If I experienced what Kathy had, even a fraction, I might still feel alone but at least then I would have proof. I would know there really was a reason.

To me that would be comforting.

Then I think of Eric. From what he says, his whole life he hasn't felt different, he's been different. He lives in a world nobody can understand. If everything he says is true... how does that make him feel? Kathy talks about her experiences and makes everything about Eric. Why is Eric teaching her? Why is she having these experiences? She doesn't ask why she's learning. But then I wonder, a question I've had myself, why is Eric teaching? He gives his time away. Maybe this separation is a reason Eric's teaching. Imagine having abilities and things happen to you that no one understands. How alienating would that be? At least Kathy has Eric and other students. Maybe Eric teaches so people understand him, so he's not the only one. Would I be any different? If Superman could teach other people how to fly... wouldn't he? It's a big sky. As great as flying would be, it's also got to seem a bit lonely being up there all alone.

Of course, it's hard to judge it all. I haven't seen what Kathy has seen or known what she knows. I can barely conceive it as reality. If I can barely conceive it then it's hard to guess how it would change me. Maybe I would be like Kathy. Despite her certainty that I'll soon have experiences and see for myself... I'm doubtful.

Kathy. I regret that I never told you how much you truly taught me.

Everyone Eric teaches becomes a strange hybrid of him. Each emphasizing certain aspects of him you may never have recognized in the source.

My hope is that you haven't made any quick judgments about Kathy. It's very likely; you too may suffer the same fate as she.

Though I doubt she ever realized it, Kathy gave me wisdom and realizations that profoundly changed my direction. It wasn't her conflicted nature, loneliness and feeling of separation that really made the difference. The true gift that Kathy gave to me is yet to come and we will speak of it a little later.

Of her sense of separation and loneliness, those I could see to a degree and would go through similar phases myself in time. I can hardly believe there is a White Cell alive that hasn't wandered some of that lonely path.

The times my steps carried me to places where the separation seemed impenetrable the candle of Kathy's memory helped give me the resolve to go on. Not for those reasons, would I lie down. Inspired by a strange sense of duty to not fail her and others like her, I found strength.

Eric has often repeated that, as White Cells, we are guests here in this world. Reflecting on this, the meaning of it has changed many times. At first it increased this sense of difference, lonely separation, even abandonment. One who must live in the home of another, having none for himself.

Many guidelines came with being a guest. Rules, he'd lay out, on how we can intervene, influence and direct reality using our spiritual abilities. In some aspects of the world, like politics, it's not for us to meddle. These are some of the founding mechanics for how things are run. You do not write the rules for how your hosts run their house.

Starting to understand where my role was not, I searched for where it was. It's then I found another term, similar to guest, but which removed my feelings of alienation; steward. One who looks after the property and affairs of another.

You see, the steward is not of the place he tends. Like the guest, he exists in the home of another. Unlike the guest he has a role... to care for, look after, and protect that place. It is everything Eric always said a White Cell was here for. When I stopped focusing on the differences, instead realizing the importance of the role Eric stressed so much... I accepted it... and found my peace.

if you know how you will get to your destination then why seek? if you're certain of what you will find then why wonder? it's a maze of mirrors built by your mind, only seeing what you know. to enter the unknown you must first...

Break Expectations

chapter seventeen

The lure of Eric's mediation tape calls to me. Why am I putting it off? I look at my glass table sitting by the window. There it sits resting on top. Little black tape. I was so excited to try it and now it's been days. What do I think is going to happen when I listen to it? It's not like everything's suddenly going to change.

"Or is it?" I throw my head back and let out my best maniacal laugh.

Whatever psycho.

Walking over to the table I pick it up. I flip over each side. It looks like a normal black tape with a label, writing in green marker. Wandering over to my bed I start to sit down then stop myself.

Find your spot stupid.

Eric said you need to find a spot, are you sure this is it? I reach up and scratch the back of my head. It doesn't itch, it helps me think.

"No, actually, I'm not sure." Looking around my bedroom I can tell right away there's no spot for me. My computer desk where I play games, surf the Internet and pretend that I'm going to finish my screenplay. At the foot of my bed is my closet, the doorway to laundry hell. A giant heap of dirty clothes is always there. Near my window my round glass table is stacked with junk and underneath it are Farrah's boxes of stuff. There's no spot in here.

I wander into the living room. Nobody's home. The entryway isn't any good. Scanning the living room my eyes fall on Peggy's bed.

"Peggy's bed?" Are you sure? Meditating where someone sleeps? I shake my head to myself. That's no good. Walking into the living room I stop in front of the coffee table. If I move the coffee table out of the way it would be perfect. It's a large open space.

It seems right, or feels right.

Yeah, feels right, isn't it supposed to feel right? What does that mean anyway? Pausing I scrunch my eyebrows in thought.

Like scanning maybe. It should feel a certain way.

Images of me sitting down meditating in every nook and cranny of the apartment flicker through my head. Which is the right one? Where shall be the promised spot? Deliver to me the all great knowing spot. My brain crashes as an image of me hanging upside down in my closet meditating like a bat jars me into frustration.

"Crap, this sucks! How can you tell?" I ask out loud hoping a part of me will answer.

Calm down. Try it and see how it feels. The clear voice answers.

Okay, okay. I'll do it. Stupid brain. Upside down meditation, I'm so sure. Grabbing the coffee table I slide it across the floor to the foot of Matthew's bed. It leaves a large open space surrounded by the futon where Farrah sleeps, Peggy's bed which is another couch and Matthew's bed. I'll sit with my back to Peggy's mattresses facing the TV and stereo.

There. I fold my arms, satisfied. It seems like a good spot.

I get Eric's tape and put it in the stereo and hit play. Quickly, I rush over to get in place. It starts to play and I take a few deep breaths in. Crap, no remote control with a tape. Closing my eyes I take a few more quick deep breaths in and adjust my legs trying to get into the half-lotus they showed me the first time. Pain, pain, pain! My body screams at me. I quickly take my foot away and sit cross-legged. Straitening my back I smile laughing at myself. Pretty lame.

The music starts to pick up with some loud drums. It sounds tribal with a Celtic twist. I focus in and start meditating. Three songs. Remember the songs. Everything is going well. It isn't like listening to the classical at all. Time isn't dragging. My body feels energized but calm. It's a strange mix. I go through the first two meditation steps hardly thinking. It's easy to focus on the music. My body doesn't complain much... nothing's really happening or feeling like the first time... but it's not going bad so that's become good.

Pretty soon I'm starting on the last three songs. Suddenly, bright rings of light pulse through my vision. The rings start small, as if I'm looking at them from a great distance. Then they quickly expand and shoot at me. They come quickly, one inside another. Each time a ring grows so large and reaches the point where I would pass through it if it were a real thing I feel a tiny, physical buzz on my forehead!

Surprised, I open my eyes to see what's happening. The room's the same. The music keeps playing. The light from the afternoon sun is shining through the window. Looking around the living room there isn't anyone home messing with the lights. I look all around me. I'm not touching anything like a cable, or wire. It's only carpet and the mattress. Weird. I close my eyes and start meditating again. The same blackness I always see when I close my eyes with some other not-quite black colors thrown in because of the sunlight. Shrugging it off I go on meditating.

Less than a minute later the rings start again. Zip, zip, zip. One after another, they fly at me. I feel my head buzz with each expanding ring, like a little twinge of electricity. Strange. I open one eye to see if I can see the rings in the closed one. No luck. I can't see the rings anymore with the other. No head buzz either. The room looks the same. I continue meditating, this time waiting to see the rings. If I catch them before they happen I can find out what starts it. Maybe I'm crossing my eyes and it's bursting the light or something. Sitting, trying to meditate and watching for the rings the other two songs fly by. Damn. No rings. Paying attention to how I feel I'm a little disappointed I don't feel like the first meditation so I blow the whole experience off. It's nothing. Strange little body thing. More important I made it through the whole tape! Fifteen minutes! My victory over the five minute barrier encourages me.

Later that day Eric calls. He suggests Matthew and I come up and stay in Tujunga for the weekend. We can take his truck out and see the upper canyons. His truck? I didn't even know he had a truck. I'm fine with it, I tell him, but I'll have to ask Matthew. He's already spoken with Matthew and he wants to go. It's all set then, we can drive up when Matthew gets home.

As I begin to hang up Eric clears his throat and I realize he's still there. "Yes?" I ask.

"Well, aren't you going to say anything?" He says abruptly.

Pausing I wonder what he could be talking about. It seems a pretty self-explanatory conversation. Should be over. "About what?"

Eric pauses, then asks uncertain, "Didn't your brother tell you?"

Tell me? Has Matthew told me anything recently? Wracking my brain I come up blank. "Uhh, be more specific..."

"Huh. Have you seen Matthew smoke pot recently?" He asks a bit unsure.

I start to tell him of course, Matthew's always smoking pot but then I stop. Wait. When was the last time I saw or smelled pot? I can't recall. Weird, it's been awhile. "You know..." I tell him still trying to remember, "I can't remember the last time. Seems like it's been awhile."

"Good. Well, I thought he would tell you but I might as well; he quit." Eric says casually.

"What?! No way! When did that happen?" I am shocked.

Eric pauses, "Hrmm, maybe a week. A little over a week ago."

No way. Nobody said anything. I wonder if everyone knows. "Wow. How did that happen?" I ask in disbelief.

Eric picks up on my stunned uncertainty, "You know Eric... you've never really done drugs or pot. It's hard for you to see where Matthew's coming from. I think because you've never had an issue with it... it's easier for you to judge than be supportive."

What? I've never judged Matthew! My mouth opens so I can tell him I've never...

Haven't you? In your own mind, in your own way? A little self-righteous?

My mouth shuts. Damn. He's right. Swallowing my own shame and guilt I stay quiet. I believe I'm better because I don't do stuff like that. Always kinda hoped he'd grow out of it but I judged him and never tried to help him... other than nag or show my disapproval.

I'm quiet for too long so Eric starts talking again. "I'm not saying you're overly judgmental but... you don't know. People always talk about how pot's not addictive and come on, they're full of shit. This may surprise you, or not, but I hope you don't make any judgments about me for it but I used to smoke pot too. A lot of it."

"Really?" That is surprising. Eric's out there but he seems too smart for something like that.

"Yep. And ask anyone who smokes a lot of pot to quit... and we'll see how nonaddictive it is. It was hard for me to quit and right now Matthew's made a decision and making a sacrifice in a way you haven't had to." Eric's voice is softer now. It rings of compassion, understanding.

"Why did he quit?" It all seems so out of the blue. I didn't even know he was trying.

"Well," Eric strains, "I laid it out for him. Told him what I think of it, what it's going to do to his life and is already doing. It alters how you think. It makes it okay to be bored and sit on your ass and that's a bad thing. Look at people who smoke a lot of pot and see how they think... it's all very similar. I told him that I could teach him some of what I know but that pot would prevent him from reaching any level of real awakening or enlightenment. What's more, I would never teach anyone who uses drugs like that any advanced stuff. It leaves you too susceptible to influence. You're easier to manipulate in that state... by the Darkside or others influenced by the Darkside. Plus, you lack true control. You are not the master of yourself... the plant is. I think pot uses people to propagate itself."

Pot, a plant... uses people? He must have meant something else, "Huh? What do you mean?"

Eric sighs like I'm not keeping up. "You know how trees grow fruit, like cherries so birds come and eat the cherries, which have the seeds of the tree? And then the bird flies away and craps out the seed... so then you could say the tree had a means of propagating and spreading itself?"

"Okay..." I mumble out... still trying to connect the dots.

"Okay, so that means that pot uses people kind of like that. It gives people something they want, which benefits the plant because they grow more of it... spreading the seed. It's like the pot has an alien intelligence, meaning different from the way a human thinks. But in a way you could say it's enslaving people to do what it wants. It's using them to ensure its survival and so I think people who smoke pot are slaves to it. What's more, pot crystallizes your consciousness. It freezes your energy mind in... like a stasis, and you can't grow. So I told your brother all this and said hey, I'll keep teaching you but look at what it's doing to your life. And now you've got this opportunity to experience something really amazing and it's going to hold you back. I told him I'd help him quit because I know how hard it is. So he decided to go for it."

I'm blown away. I'd always wanted for him to quit but I never imagined he'd try it. Eric's helping him and now it's been a week. I'm speechless.

Eric continues, "So, it's going to be hard for him. It's really a big part of who he is right now and for him to give it up shows a lot. He needs you to be supportive and if you see or hear about him smoking you should tell me, because he'll probably relapse before he goes all the way."

"Okay." I blurt out, unsure how to express any form of gratitude or thanks. It's one of the greatest things anyone's ever tried to do for me. Given my brother his life back. How do you thank someone for that?

"So, I think that's it. I'll see you guys this weekend and we'll cover a lot of ground. He needs to stay busy on constructive things." Eric says openly.

"Cool. See you tonight then." I say quietly, still in disbelief.

I put a few things in a backpack and look around the apartment. Part of me is glad for a chance to get away for a few days. Another part doesn't like the idea of being around someone else's environment. I like being able to do what I want. Imagine Farrah's reaction to us being gone for a whole weekend. I chuckle to myself. "Poor Farrah." Maybe I should leave her a note so she doesn't freak out. She's been hanging out with a new guy anyway. She'll barely notice.

Matthew and Justin come home to pick me up. I ask them about leaving a note for Farrah and Matthew laughs. He's already called her. Matthew lies down on his bed and closes his eyes. Justin rolls up on Peggy's bed.

"Are you waiting for me?" I ask.

"Nah," Matthew says, "just taking some chill time."

I go into my room to give them space. We don't get much alone time in the apartment. Having only three of us here is as close as it gets most days. I know what he's after. Computer on. Time to build a glorious civilization to rule for all time. Once more... for the thousandth time. After a few hundred game years pass I wander into the living room to see Matthew and Justin sleeping. Okay then, keep conquering. It starts to get dark. We should be leaving but... I don't want to nag. I'm not in a hurry but I don't like telling people I'll be somewhere and then purposely show up late. Lateness happens as a matter of course. Finally, a light flicks on and Matthew starts putting his things together. He finishes and Justin drives us up to Tujunga.

We arrive as the last shreds of red light are slipping away behind the mountains. Justin needs to run by the bookstore so he drops us off.

Matthew and I walk up to the gate and then stop... staring. I pause and look at Matthew. He's thinking the same thing I am I bet...

"Should we go in?" I ask him.

"Yeah, should be cool." He smiles. "You scared of the dogs huh?" He grins at me. He doesn't need to ask that one, he already knows.

"Umm, yeah!" I say sarcastically to hide my nervousness.

"Nah, they should be cool with me." Matthew says confidently.

He cracks open the gate just enough for the dogs to see him. They run to the gate barking as he coo's at them.

"Hey little puppies. Hi, heeey, remember me?"

I smirk. He's nervous too. Neither of us are sure they won't try and tear us to pieces. They sniff through the cracked gate and wag their tails. Bravely, he sticks his hand in.

"Good doggies." He looks up at me. "See, they're all cool."

"Man, you got so lucky."

Frank comes out and yells at the dogs. Matthew is sliding through the gate. Frank laughs about his caution and tells the dogs to take off. They run off jumping at each other. He walks into the house in front of us calling for Eric. The distant sound of a vacuum shuts off. After telling Eric we're here Frank goes into his room and closes the door.

Eric is cleaning again. This time he's vacuuming and dusting the whole house. He apologizes again for it being so messy. He's trying to clean everything up so we'll be comfortable for the weekend. We're going to have to stay in the living room. We can flip a coin over the couch but the other has to sleep on the floor. I volunteer for the floor. Matthew offers. I know he'll take it but I like the floor. Ever since I was a kid I would skip the bed and sleep on the floor if I had trouble going to sleep. Matthew either remembers that or doesn't really want to sleep on the floor because he doesn't ask if I'm sure.

Eric knocks on Frank's door and asks if he's going to stay for dinner. Frank yells back yes then asks if someone else can stay for dinner.

Eric looks at us and pauses. "Yes, she can." He tells him. "We're having guests. Better not be trouble!" Eric yells at him.

I tilt my head to the side so Eric can see I'm wondering. I can tell there's someone in Frank's room but I also know there's a story we're missing. Eric shakes his head and tells me I'm better off not knowing. Matthew and I sit in the living room until Eric brings the vacuum in from down the hall. Looking over at Matthew I notice he's looking at me. We both stand up and ask if he needs help cleaning. Eric waves us off insisting he's fine and likes cleaning.

"It's satisfying cleaning your own home and knowing you did it. You feel like you made your place, your abode better. It actually relieves stress for me." He assures us.

I'm skeptical. One look at Matthew tells me he doesn't really buy it either. We play the courteous guests and do as he asks. We sit talking while he spends over an hour cleaning his house with small conversations in between. During that time Frank and George pass through with quick hello's but neither look remotely interested in helping Eric. After Eric cleans the house and kitchen he begins cooking dinner.

Matthew and I move to stand in the kitchen doorway to watch for awhile. It isn't cooking like I'm used to. I cook from a box. He makes a salad from scratch. Frantically, he washes all the vegetables moving with incredible speed and precision. He swiftly goes from washing the onions, bell peppers, carrots, tomatoes and lettuce to cutting them all into perfect bits. It's like watching a cooking show.

He apologizes that dinner won't be much. Money is tight and he tells us that the only way he can afford to feed such a large group of people is pasta. We both laugh. Having fresh vegetables and a salad is a luxury. It's more than we're used to. Once he starts in on the pasta and making fresh hummus I wander back to sit in the living room.

It isn't long before Eric calls Frank in and asks him to set up the patio. Frank goes to get George and they start putting together a table for us to sit at. I go out to help. In the middle of wiping down the end of the table Eric comes out and sees me. He looks at Frank and asks him why he's making me help. Frank starts to explain but I interrupt and explain that I offered. Eric looks at me, to see if I'm covering for Frank. He tells Frank that I'm a guest and he shouldn't have let me help. In no time we're all sitting down outside on the gigantic patio. There's enough room at the long table for eight of us to sit with room to spare. Justin shows up just in time to eat. The dogs sit at the edge of the dark but I can still see them. Cool night air sweeps down from the mountain. Insects buzz in the still warm darkness. It's summer. I smile. This is how summer should be.

Eric's dinner is fantastic. His salad is full and fresh with so much variety and flavor. It looks like something I'd get from a restaurant. Frank comments that it's a shame Eric never made it to culinary school. Eric tells us he had once thought about being a chef. It makes sense, he's really good at it. They have fresh bread, pita bread Eric explains. With hummus he made fresh. I have a brief flash of memory. I tried hummus in college. My brain reports to me it isn't something I should try again. I decline the hummus. Eric asks if I've tried it.

"No," I admit, "but I've had it before."

He assures me his is the best and he made it himself.

"No thanks," I shake my head, "I'll pass."

He tells me I don't know what I'm missing. Everyone else eats it up. Eating at the table is Frank, a girlfriend of Frank's, as well as George and Ana who, true to what Eric told us, say nothing the entire meal. Ana looks really young too. She has long, wavy black hair and she looks down a lot so I can't make out her face because I don't want to stare. They both seem really shy. Eric also made the sauce fresh which surprises me. Dinner is completely satisfying.

After it's over Frank, Justin and George start to clean the table. Frank buzzes from one task to the next with lightning speed. I laugh at the sight. He's so fast and precision quick, it's strange. Justin tells me Frank was in the military. Frank laughs but says nothing. I watch him. It's like watching a perfect human robot he's so... efficient! After clearing the space in record time Frank takes over washing the dishes from Eric.

Finally Eric gets a chance to relax. Matthew and I sit out on the porch with him talking idly about the dogs and Tujunga. Eric tells us about a haunted house he'd investigated in the area. He'd been highly skeptical but went to look at it anyway because it was so close. It turns out it was a very unusual house. The entire house was built with a single, large pillar through the center of the house. The pillar was as round as a large tree. It went into the basement and came directly into the center of a table of Moses.

Matthew and I both sit there saying nothing. He glances over and then sighs.

"Do either of you even know what that is?" Eric drones sarcastically.

We look at each other and laugh. "No." We say in unison.

"Why don't you ask what it is then?" He suggests. "Be a little engaged, you know?"

"We're both too full." Matthew tells him.

"Well," Eric says smiling at Matthew's comeback compliment, "I guess that's what I was going for. Anyway, the table was covered with inscriptions from the Book of Moses. It's something I used when I was very young. I was living with a girlfriend in her basement when I found it. I played around with it a few times to see what it could do. One time we had some, let's just say, interesting results." He cracks a grin and then sits back as if enjoying the memory.

"I remember she had this large rug on her wall and the rug had these dangling tassels. Well, I spent days getting this thing ready from the book. I drew like this large circle with all these really intricate symbols and it had to be exact. I mean, I took this little drawing from the book and made it into a circle that had to have been... let me think, oh, 10 feet across. When I started in on it the first thing I remember is she suddenly got real excited and said, you know, Eric look! And she's pointing at the carpet on the wall. The tassels were all swaying in unison. They were all making these perfect circles and swaying back and forth all synchronized. There wasn't any air blowing down there or fans or anything, not that they would create that effect but, you know what I'm saying. Pretty soon everything got real hazy, like a thick fog filled up her basement. Then this spot on the wall started, like swirling." He moves his hands in a spiral to show us the slow motion of it. "Pretty soon these giant whitish, like, blobs came floating out of it filling up the room."

My mouth drops open and I shout, "No way!"

Eric tries to hide a smile. "You have no idea."

"Do you know what they were?" I ask entranced by the tale. It's everything I tried to do in my childhood but never pulled off. I'd always suspected something like this was possible.

"Well, I didn't then but I do now. You know, I was still young then, like 18 maybe. But yeah, there were a bunch of them all floating around the room. And large, you know, maybe as big as Angus. It was something!" Looking around for Angus I can already imagine the size. He's an enormous mix of Doberman and buffalo. His point is clear, they were big.

We talk awhile longer. My head buzzes from the story. The possibility of it. What if the story is true? What if such things are possible? If it's possible how is it practical? How could such a thing be done? My memories drift back to my own youth when I was experimenting with Wicca. It was supposed to be white magic. I tried different rituals that were supposed to do different things. The last one I remember I lit 16 cones of orange incense and practically choked to death. All I could smell was orange incense for a week. In that moment, as I was performing the ritual but before orange incense filled my room like a chemical weapon. I did feel something. It felt like there were other things in the room, aware and watching. I wasn't frightened. I didn't feel like I had any reason to be scared. It seemed like they were curious, if anything, about what I was doing or what I would do. It was nothing as dramatic as Eric's story but... what if. Maybe it is possible. I remember being aware of something... it felt like intelligence. Something intelligent was there. Only I didn't know or couldn't see what it was. Maybe it was my imagination. His story places doubt in my mind about disregarding my own experiences.

Eric stretches out in the chair. "Okay... it's time to go to bed."

Matthew wastes no time in wandering into the living room and plops right on the couch. I pull a thick sleeping bag Eric gave me up on the floor. Lying down I notice how everything feels strange. There's something very different about sleeping here. I can't put my finger on it but it feels safer. More like a home but... there's something else. Maybe it's the quiet of being away from the city.

Maybe...

That day, I began to learn something about expectations. While meditating I saw the rings until I stopped openly experiencing them and started expecting them. Sitting and waiting for their appearance I clamped my mind into a box. My mindset was... the rings are coming. This is what they will look like, feel like and be like. That state of mind is nothing like the open, meditative state that allowed me to shift my consciousness and experience them in the first place. My expectation killed the experience.

The expectation of what Eric is like as a person and a teacher can also kill the experience. Forget even Eric, the expectation of what a 'spiritual teacher' is supposed to be like, act like and look like can kill your growth. What does it mean... to be a teacher? Some people who come to Eric see him as holding a position of power and authority over them. That he is above them.

The strategy I used to understand Eric slowly led me to a different realization. I removed what I thought of Eric and simply observed without expectation. Separating his words from his actions. No opinions, anticipation, or solid judgment.

He constantly surprised me. What I found was not one who believed he was above those he taught but one composed of such humility he was constantly serving them. When Eric teaches he's giving to those who come to him. Even when he's not teaching by giving knowledge, Eric serves those who ask for his help.

He would clean the house for everyone. Do their dishes. Cook meals. Scrub the bathroom, on his hands and knees, after teaching them for hours on end... in service. He would go over to the homes of his students and clean. I can't count the number of times he's visited me and cleaned my kitchen, picked up my entire home, done my laundry and cooked dinner. In all the years I've known him he's been consistent in this, without fail. Many people who have a concept of a spiritual master from books, who rarely engage in such mundane matters, or real life figures may be surprised to learn this... the levels and degrees which Eric Pepin gives.

Seeing, time after time, how nothing was ever beneath Eric forged my trust in him.

All other abilities and knowledge aside, I have never met one such as Eric, who puts so much time and energy into the betterment of others without seeking gain for himself. He has never asked anything of me in return except to treat him as I have been treated and be true to the Force.

There is such strength in his presence, his will and conviction it is too easy to believe he feels he is above you. All the while overlooking, or taking for granted, every service offered and given with no expectation of return.

I too have been guilty of taking for granted his goodwill and giving nature. Thinking it is somehow owed to me for the struggles I have endured under his guidance. Never considering the struggles were my choices in an effort to better myself and become what I wanted. This feeling that something is somehow 'owed' to you is not unique to those who come to Eric Pepin. Many people, on the path, feel as if their awakening is their right and owed to them by the Universe. The sense of purpose instilled within them by the Force is mistaken as a feeling of rightful destiny. This quickly leads them to assume Eric must give them whatever they desire.

The truth is, just as you can choose not to seek to awaken, Eric does not have to teach. It is given by his will. He made the choice to step into that ring. You too, must make a choice, to stop waiting for your destiny and awakening to be handed to you... and enter the arena to take it.

imagine all you want. watch to your heart's content. but you
will never know a thing until you...

Enter the Arena

chapter eighteen

I wake up to the smell of eggs and coffee. Eric's cooking breakfast.
He comes in and tells us to start rolling around, he has breakfast
ready. Matthew groans in protest. I feel the same.

"What time is it anyway?" I croak out.

"I don't know, eight something. I let you sleep in." Eric says.

I laugh.

"Oh my God," Matthew says looking at me through bleary eyes, "he let
us sleep in?"

"Yeah, I know." I chuckle. Extending my body, I stretch as far as I
can to help me wake up. Crawling up from the floor I walk out to the
porch for food. Matthew stumbles behind me.

Eric apologizes for the bare meal. They're short on food. He has eggs,
bacon and toast.

Looking at the plate piled with food I'm troubled to think what not
being short on food would be like. It's twice as much as I would
normally eat. Definitely nothing to apologize for. The eggs are
scrambled and mixed with some kind of melted cheese. I've never
had eggs that taste like this. The cheese is crumbly and bright white.

Absently poking at the cheese with my fork trying to analyze it Eric offers, "Feta. It's feta cheese with a few other spices thrown in. You like it?"

I nod my head in agreement. I can't remember the last time I had a breakfast in L.A. that wasn't cereal or oatmeal.

Matthew lifts his head and smells. "Is there coffee?"

Eric smirks, "Of course. I didn't think you could get up at eight and be able to speak without it. It's in the kitchen."

Matthew grins, "Yeah, pretty much." He comes back with a huge, bright yellow coffee cup filled with steaming coffee.

I can't stand the taste of coffee but oh, how I love the smell. Closing my eyes I wait as the aroma drifts past my nose. Once I catch it a smile stretches across my face. I love breakfast.

"The others won't be up for hours." Eric tells us.

Who can blame them, I think. I'd be right there with them.

"I don't get it. It's a waste of a day. Look around you!" He says as he waves his hands around the porch and motions towards the sky.

The fresh, invigorating smell of dew still lingers in the air. There's something about early mornings. My mind drifts back to my childhood. It's summertime. I'm barefoot walking through the still house. Wandering out into the back yard my feet brush through the soft, wet grass.

Even the trees seem quiet. Still asleep. Looking out across the lawn I start walking to the far end near the honeysuckle vine. The tops of my feet are wet. Looking down I see the droplets of water and little blades of cut grass all over my feet. Glancing back I see my dark, green footprints imprinted in the silver-brushed grass.

The way it sparkles. Shines. I lay down to be closer to it. Breathe it in. There's magic in it.

A little smile crawls across my face as I come back to breakfast. Matthew gives me a sideways look.

"What are you doing?" He wonders with eyes that tell me I'm acting crazy.

Eric chuckles. "Yeah, I wasn't going to say anything. He's just sitting there staring off with a weird smile on his face."

Shaking my head I wave them off. "Nothing. I like mornings. That's all. It's been awhile." Not sure how I could tell them anyway. How do you share moments like this? No perfume ever smelled as sweet as dew, but damn I hate getting up for it. Tangled vines climb up the sides of the porch. Their leaves sparkle with little drops of moisture reflecting the light of the sun. Delicate, miniature flowers poke out and somehow their color seems brighter. The dogs lie still and quiet, not quite awake themselves.

The world stands still. Peaceful. Everything has an air of possibility.

"The day is so young." Eric says softly, "You can do anything with it. By the time they get up, it feels like it's almost over. I hate sleeping that long."

Eric tells us today will be a training day. "There's so much to teach you guys and this is the first time I have both of you together for a few days. We've got to cover a lot of ground."

I guess he's right. We haven't all been together for any length of time. We quickly clean up after breakfast and then sit in the living room.

Matthew is still in his pajama's and I'm in jogging pants. We move the chairs against the wall to clear out a big space. The off white walls shine with the morning sun coming in through the windows. The room echoes with a solemn brilliance, a quiet sacredness.

Eric sits in front of us on the floor. He takes a deep breath in and his presence is suddenly transformed. He seems like a martial arts teacher now. Strong, intense. I can't pin down why he seems different. Maybe it's because he changed his posture and sat upright.

In a calm, almost serene voice he tells us, "Look at your hands. When was the last time you really looked at them? Look at the lines in the palms of your hands. Examine the grooves. Look at all the skin lines. See how your fingers attach to your palm. Notice how your four fingers all move in the same direction but how your thumb sticks awkwardly out to the side."

As he speaks he holds his hands out to us. He turns them, displays them in the light. The way he looks at them, curious, examining, and the tone in his voice makes me think he's talking about something separated from himself. Like a biology teacher displaying a frog or a cat. Impartial but familiar. A strange feeling twists in my gut. Opening my own hand I examine it with this strange sensation.

Eric shakes his hands at Matthew and I. "I mean, don't just stare, really, really look at it! Now turn it over and look at the back. Look at your fingernails. Most animals have claws there. Real claws. Useful weapons. Look at our pathetic nails. Look at your knuckles and the hair on your fingers. Look at the hair on the back of your hand..."

As he tells us all of this I analyze my hand. I turn it and peer into the details. The lines, the grooves. I imagine the structure under the skin. The bones, veins, muscles as I twitch my fingers. He's not kidding. What is this thing? I look at the lines in my palm. What did they look like when I was a little kid? They must have changed. What will they look like when I get old? Then it catches me as funny when he mentions the thumb. I picture my hand without my thumb and it seems better shaped, like a long claw. More animal-like. The thumb comes back in and it looks dumber somehow. Probably too many jokes with friends about our pet dogs and cats being screwed because they don't have opposable thumbs. Only, now it isn't funny. It feels very distinct. Yes, it's the thumb that made us different.

When we flip our hands over the smoothness of the palm is suddenly contrasted with the hair. The reality of our primitive origin hits me, I feel a little sick. God, we really are apes. The hair is so thick, and noticeable and... everywhere! The palm's so smooth and clean. The lines give it such character. Now I'm an overgrown intelligent furless ape.

I stick out my tongue.

"It's the hair right?" Eric asks.

"Yeah." I'm like one of those furless cats. Bare, pink shaven naked ape.

He laughs. "I know, that always gets me too. Makes you feel like an animal when you start to become aware of it doesn't it?"

Matthew chuckles. "That was getting me too."

"Okay, we can't get stuck here..." Eric says asserting a seriousness back into the conversation. "It's good to acknowledge that, yes, this body is an organism. It's an animal and we are animals. But there's something else. We have used our hands since the very beginning. Our hands have helped us make tools and stay alive. I mean, look at our fingernails, we know it wasn't the sharpness of our claws that kept us safe. So, somewhere in the back of our minds, we know our hands have power. We know our hands can do things, they can shape reality and that's how we've transformed."

He asks us to flip our hands back over so the palm faces up. "Close your fingers now... and then open them. See how that makes you feel. That means, internally, see, notice, be aware if it feels different. There's a shift. It's a way to shift you."

I open and close my hand rapidly to see if I notice anything. Eric stops me. "Slowly. Slowly." He stares at me so he knows he has my attention and speaks slowly, assuredly. "Everything there moves slowly." The tone he speaks with tugs at my curiosity. His eyes shine with silent certainty.

It's like he's speaking in code. There's something there, a mystery.

There? There? How are we supposed to know where 'there' is?? The frantic voice asks with an edge of panic.

I don't know. I don't know where 'there' is. It's a weird use of the word related to opening your hand.

Eric goes on to explain how the outstretched palm is used as a spiritual symbol for a reason. "It's a symbol for awakening. It has an effect on the brain. Like, subliminally. It's a back door past the part of the brain that controls us and keeps us locked in this reality. Because the brain acknowledges the power of the hand as a tool. If we do something with our hands it accepts that the hand can change reality. It's a back door, like a secret way in. Get it?"

It starts to make sense. It's a way to fool the brain into doing something. What, I'm not sure.

Matthew clears his throat and looks up from staring at his hand, "I can feel a difference. Like between when my hand is closed and when it's open and my palm is outstretched. It's almost like a tingle inside my chest or something." Matthew's hunched over, his hair still messed up from sleep. His arms are thin but have thick hair.

We even look like a bunch of monkeys. All hunched over scratching our heads staring at our hands trying to figure out what they are.

"Good." Eric says encouraged, his eyes brightening behind his glasses. "That tingle is a shift. It's shifting your consciousness and you're going to feel it."

I look up at him, uncertain. I shake my head. I can't be sure but I think I get what he's saying. He shakes his head and tells me, "Eric, you're thinking about it too hard. You need to stop thinking and feel it." He cracks a little smirk. I feel a sharp twist in my gut that he might be laughing at me. It quickly changes as the look in his eye says something very different. Patient. Incredibly patient. Even seems a little caring. It's the strangest look. He should be irritated I'm not catching on as fast as Matthew. He has to work harder to make me get it.

Feel this, feel that, feel, feel, feel. What does he mean by that? He keeps saying 'feel' it but he doesn't mean it like touch, or emotional feelings or in a way anyone else ever uses it! How am I supposed to know what he means!?

Try not to be an idiot. Matthew gets it. What's wrong with you?

What is wrong with me? Eric said Matthew would catch on faster because of how he thinks... but now he's telling me not to think. If Eric notices my confusion he says nothing. I start to get frustrated but something in the tone of his voice, the way he speaks, soothes me and calms me down. Eric wants me to get it. He's being patient and really trying. Like a parent teaching a kid to ride a bike. You want to laugh because it's the easiest thing in the world but to the kid it's almost impossible. I quietly snicker through my nose. That would explain his smirk. Can't get frustrated. I can figure it out.

Eric brings our attention back to his hands. Holding them in the light coming through the window they're haloed in brilliant white sunlight. "When you're trying to wake up inside your dreams, they always say, look at your hands. Look at the palm of your hand. This is a way. It's a signal to the brain that you are in control. It signals that your hand is going to do something and the brain must obey. This puts you in control."

Eric speaks more about our hands and what they're used for. He talks about their power and how the brain responds to that power. Then he tells us about primitive times, how we were dependent on our hands for survival. They were our advantage. He explains the reason he is covering all of this is to show us how to use our hands to affect energy.

"I've already shown both of you how to see aura's right?" He asks looking at us.

I look over to Matthew who nods his head. I nod my head too. When I first met Eric he showed me. How did it go? Look at the head... and.... suddenly the image of Eric surrounded in a fiery bright golden glow crackles through my memory. I saw his aura! Was that real? I keep forgetting about it...

Or repressing it...

Eric continues, "The aura is the energy body. You have your physical body and then your energy body. Your energy body isn't perfectly contained inside your physical body. It isn't restrained by physical matter. It extends about 32 feet beyond your body."

Matthew and I nod our heads. I remember him saying that before.

Eric turns his head slowly and looks up, out the window. Normally fiery and passionate he's being so still and serene I'd swear he's a completely different person. The only similarity is that strange undercurrent of intensity. Even passive Eric can't seem to get rid of it.

Pulling his eyes away from the outside sun Eric looks back to us. "So, like a lamp it goes beyond the bulb inside. Now, you can take your hands and reach out away from your body to feel things, right?" Although easy to understand Eric extends a hand away from his body, farther than would be natural to make his point as he really stretches, and touches the carpet.

Mathew and I mumble our agreement.

"In the same way, you can reach out with your energy body to 'feel'," he puts his fingers in quotes, "things or feel your surroundings. The problem is most people aren't used to using their energy body. So it's stiff and inflexible. It's solidified. You want it to be limber and fluidic. I'm going to show you exercises to move it and push it around. If you do these exercises, consistently, they will help you feel things more and be more fluidic. You guys with me so far?"

"Makes sense to me." Matthew says confidently.

I glance over at him and the way he's smiling I believe he really gets it. "Yep." I say quickly. It makes sense but I really don't get it. Better to keep things moving so it can all snap together.

Eric holds one hand out straight to us so we can see his palm. "A big part of doing these exercises is using your hands. They will be the tools you use to move and push your energy. Your brain will accept this easier because of what we talked about earlier, the power of the hands, secret back door, right? But your hands alone aren't enough. You have to have absolute will. Like a kung-fu master who is about to smash through a pile of bricks. You can't have this attitude of, well, maybe I'll give it a try. I'll hit the bricks and see what happens... No way! Do you know what would happen if you had that attitude?"

"You'd be seriously hurting." Matthew says with a chuckle.

"Damn straight. So your attitude has to be," Eric takes his hand and folds his fingers so that his index fingers point up toward his chin and he holds it right near the center of his chest, "this is my will, and it is already done." He pushes his breath out and moves his hand in a chopping motion toward his waist.

It sends a chill up my spine. All the hair on my arms stands up straight.

His eyes are slightly closed and something about how he looks or what he's done triggers a response in me. I smile and look at Matthew. He's grinning too.

I understand this. I don't know what he means by feel this or that but the idea of willful discipline is something I've always striven for. I respect people who can harness their will to achieve great things. If you put your mind to something, no matter what, you can do it.

"Do you understand?" Eric asks serenely. We both agree quietly.

"No, let me hear you say it. Nodding is different than saying it out loud. When you say it out loud you're also speaking to yourself. You are making it more real. Like writing it down." His voice is quiet, calm, certain.

"Yeah. I understand." I say with Matthew.

"Okay then, stand up!" Eric says enthusiastically. We stand about five feet away from him and apart from each other. Enough room to move around and not hit each other.

Facing us Eric holds his hands down near his waist. "The bulk of your energy is going to rest and settle right around here." He motions with a hand a large area surrounding the lower stomach and groin. "That's all useful stuff you've got to get moving around but it's not going to move unless you really want it to. You've really got to will it to start churning, in a way."

Taking one hand in combination with his breathing he demonstrates how to pull the resting energy towards the top of our body and then push it back down. As he pushes it back down all the hair on my arms stand up again and my skin tingles with goose bumps. There isn't any kind of wind blowing through the room. I take a quick glance at my arm. Right, like that'll help me figure out why all my hair stood up.

"This is how you start out. Simple movement. It's the warm up just to get that sleeping energy moving around. Got to stretch it out some. You two try with me this time."

Eric has us mimic his movements. Matthew and I begin moving our hand up in unison with our breathing. Eric reaches over and lightly smacks Matthew's hand. "Too limp! Is that how a kung-fu master would do it? Be willful with your body and your mind but flexible."

I grin. My hands weren't very firm and willful either. Matthew's always so gentle and easy going I can see him having a hard time with being strong and willful. Picturing Matthew working up the testosterone to chop a brick with his hands makes me chuckle.

If Eric hears my snickering he lets it go and continues. "Many martial artists are too physical and inflexible in their thinking. Their whole focus is body, body, body. In trying to be willful they become rigid in their mind. Be like the wind. The wind is strong, certain, but fluidic. Be like the reed in the wind. Make it so. Think it is already done. Do you understand? Your physical energy is, by nature, lazy and stagnant. It's been used to sitting around, unused, your entire lives. Now you're going to make it do something?" He makes a face as if the idea is ridiculous. "Pffft!! Your energy will laugh at your pathetic attempts to move it!" Eric puffs out a breath of air in contempt at the idea. "Please, it's not going to want to do anything. Only your will and desire will make it move. You have to be certain. You have to be commanding." He places his palms together near the center of his chest and briefly flexes his arms to illustrate the resolve. Moving and projecting the idea, he suddenly feels physically intimidating. Like he grew a foot taller. Not that I'm afraid but he quickly loses his bookworm physique. I'm suddenly aware of just how big Eric actually is and it shifts to where I think he could do some damage if he wanted to.

"Now, do it again." Eric challenges.

I begin again. This time I try to reframe my thinking as Eric suggests. It's like breaking the brick. It is not a question of maybe. It's already done. I move to execute what has already happened, there is no way it cannot happen. My mind is already set. The movements are physically simple. Light and easy. Inside I summon my will and visualize my lazy energy body moving and twisting around.

"In time with your breathing. Synchronize the movements with your breathing." Eric tells us.

I follow his simple movements. As he pulls his hand up, I pull my hand up with will and determination. Something surprises me. I feel a bead of sweat trickle down my forehead. Stopping I stand up straight and wipe it off. My finger is covered with sweat.

Eric sees me and smiles. "You're hot huh?"

"Yeah." I say a little confused.

Matthew fans himself by pulling his shirt away from his body. "Yeah, no kidding. I wasn't going to say anything but I'm dying too."

Eric nods. "That's your energy. When you move your energy you start to shift and you're going to get really hot. It's different than a psychic sweat which usually feels cold. Of course, it helps that you two have me helping to push your energy around." He grins.

What the hell. Freaky. I can't believe how hot my whole body is. We've barely been doing 10 minutes of movements that are about as difficult as lifting a pencil. I should be able to do this for hours and not work up a sweat. It's still so early in the morning the living room isn't hot.

"Don't worry about it." Eric tells me. He turns his back to us and looks over his shoulder. "Now we're going to move on to actual exercises. You need to shadow my movements. This way you won't have to reverse it. Follow the way I move."

Eric places his hands away from his body. Taking a deep breath in he brings his hands close to his chest. He loudly exhales so we can hear his breathing as he pushes them away and takes a step forward. I mimic his movements awkwardly.

With his hands held in front of him he turns his body to face us so that his hands are being held to one side but behind him. "Now, with your hands like this we're going to do what I call throwing the log. Imagine you're holding something heavy, like a log, in your hands. Also try to keep in your mind an image of your energy body. It is all around you, like a globe. When you push your hands through it the movements affects all of it. Like being in a swimming pool and pushing your hands through the water, it ripples out and pushes through all of the water right?"

"Right." I say quickly getting the idea. Matthew fans his shirt out and agrees he gets it.

"So, what I'm going to do is make a big arc with my hands. I'm going to have them behind me like they are and I'm going to move them over my shoulders like I'm throwing a log forward. When I do that it's like pulling all my energy behind me and pushing it in front of me. That's going to move all that energy in its path, okay? Now watch."

With unexpected grace for someone his size Eric smoothly throws both hands in an arc over his shoulder as his back foot slides forward. When his hands move in front I feel a wave of heat pass through my entire body. It's like someone just opened up a steam vent.

"Ugh." Matthew steps back and fans his shirt frantically.

Eric laughs. "Did you guys feel that?"

"Yeah. Big wave of heat going to make me start to stink. Sorry guys." Matthew admits, not having taken a shower for a few days.

Cracking a grin, "Even I felt that one." I confess.

"Good. You two won't notice each other quite that much but you'll get there. Now let's go through it."

Eric has us go through his 'throw the log' exercise a few times before he sets us loose and tells us to try mixing up the routine. "Don't mimic my movements, do your own. Try and feel what you need to do and where you need to push your energy then do it. Your senses will tell you how you need to move to get your energy flowing. Don't question it, don't feel stupid, just go with it."

Matthew and I begin moving on our own. I slide my arms around my body taking steady sliding steps. Sweat starts sliding down my back. You'd think we were doing aerobics. It's hard to tell if I'm hitting the right spots or not. Rather than worry about it I concentrate on trying to feel some kind of energy. After awhile Eric seems satisfied that we've gotten it. He tells us to sit back down and take in what we've covered.

After we sit for awhile Eric tells us to think about our bodies. "Feel yourselves sitting on the floor. Feel your breath. The heaviness of it. In and out. Your chest rising and falling. Now take your hand and grab your leg." I reach down and place my hand on my leg. Matthew does something similar.

Eric rolls his eyes. "You're both so timid. It must be a Missouri thing. No, take your leg and grab it!" He declares. He takes his hand and grabs a good pinch of his leg and shakes it so that we can definitely see he's grabbing his leg.

Reaching down I grab as much of my leg as I can and shake it.

"That's it, now you're feeling it. Now, that is you, right?" Eric asks a bit doubtfully.

Yes, we assure him.

"Is it? Is it really you? Isn't it just a part of you? Isn't it just the biological, roving machine that YOU, the real YOU is in?"

Ah, of course. He says the body is only a vehicle for our real self. The energy consciousness.

"No, it's just a part." I say.

"Right." Matthew agrees.

"Now, you can say that it is but just because you say it doesn't mean you really get it. It doesn't mean you really conceive it and understand. Neither of you really get it." Eric says this simply as if it's something we need to accept and move on.

Matthew glances at me and I look back at him. I guess he isn't wrong.

"But that's okay, because you're going to do this exercise that I'm about to show you, twice a day. It's going to seem silly at first and you'll probably think, oh why oh why did Eric tell us to do this? Because it distills. It separates. It creates awareness. You two walk around like everybody else in life. You relate to your body as you. The only you. The body gets burned you get burned. The body feels good you feel good. You don't see any separation. Well, how can you start to think and be aware of something separate if you're only aware of one thing, your body?" He raises his hands and shoulders to suggest it's idiotic.

"Huh? How can you? The answer is you can't. If you don't acknowledge something you can't be aware of it." He continues, telling us about the process of awareness. He explains how the difference is subtle and that we aren't used to paying attention to subtle things. To slowly note that there is a separation, however small, gives a place for awareness to grow. Once we become more aware the difference will seem larger and larger until finally we won't be able to believe we never noticed a difference in the first place.

"To begin to be aware of the difference is a simple thing." He assures us. "Take your body as you did before, and then label it. Say, out loud, ME! This is ME!" He grabs his chest, "ME!" He declares. He grabs his arm, "ME!" He grabs his leg, his stomach, and his head, "ME! ME! ME! It's all ME!"

Then he stops, takes in a deep breath, holds up his index finger and points at himself. "Now... I. I?" He asks himself. "IIIIIIIIII." He drags the word out slowly. "ME!" He grabs his leg again. Then pauses and holds up his index finger. "I. ME! I. ME! I. You see, they feel different. When I grab my body and say 'me', I can feel what I'm talking about. It's very easy. It's familiar. When I say, 'I', it's as if my brain goes in search of the thing I'm trying to label. I'm questioning, 'I' where is the 'I'? I've told it where 'me' is. 'Me' is the body so it can't go there. When you say, 'I' and you wonder, it feels different. Your brain is searching for it. That creates a separation. Your brain realizes it can't find it but it distinguishes it from your body. It's an interesting thing to feel. It really makes you realize there is a difference. The two things have a distinct and different feeling. But, like I said, it's subtle. Try it."

We spend the next few minutes grabbing our various body parts and declaring, 'ME!'

"Louder!" Eric encourages. "Be certain about the 'me'. Let your brain know you have no doubt your body is 'me'. Be firm. Grab it. Let it know every part you can grab is 'me'. There's no doubt in your mind."

"ME!" We shout louder grabbing our arms and legs.

"Now, go in search of 'I'." Eric says reverently holding up his index finger near his chest.

Then we both pause and take a deep breath. I hold my finger up as Eric did and ask, out loud, 'I'? IIIII. I tell myself. He's right, I feel silly. I grab my leg again, 'ME!' Then I say, 'I'. Stop. I really feel something. The 'I' is different. It's like the question spins inward, and inward and inward. I don't know where it's going. When I grab my leg and say, 'ME!' it feels more there. More present. The 'I', even when I say it, feels like a question. It feels like I'm trying to remember something. It's like digging into my brain, expecting something to pop up but I already know it won't. It's an answer I don't know. It's strange to feel a contrast. Eric's right, it is subtle but it's a subtle I can actually feel! I can feel it! I smile happily.

"What is it? You can feel a difference?" Eric asks.

"Yeah, it's cool. It's slight but I can feel like the 'I' kind of spins inward like I'm trying to remember something."

Eric nods and then smirks. "Good. Now the thing to wonder is if you would have felt a difference before you did the energy movements?"

I grin and lean forward. He has me there. Using his logic the energy movements make you more aware of your energy body because you're using it and pushing it around. It helps you feel it more. The 'I' is your energy consciousness. Even though the only thing I noticed with the energy movements was feeling hot his explanation makes sense. It all lines up.

Eric is quiet for a moment. We sit listening to the stillness of the house. "The brain is a product of this dimension, this reality." he explains. "It will try to keep you here. Keep you from acknowledging or even noticing things, like feeling the heat of moving your energy.

The brain will lock you out of shifting into dimensional consciousness. Why? Because it is designed for this dimension. This place. It is a product of this dimension. But, as I said before, there are back doors. Back doors are like things computer programmers have. They code in certain ways to get around security measures so they don't get locked out of their own programs. There are ways to slip past the brain and make things happen. Bend reality."

He goes on to give us examples and tells us how they work. "Magick is one kind of back door." As soon as he starts talking about magick memories of my youth come swirling back.

"There's very little truth in magick and for the most part it's all junk for the ego." He says off-handedly. "But with the use of all the tools, designs and rituals with your hands it is possible for it to get through the back door. It's the long way around and very indirect but it can work. I mean, why light all those candles, inscribe runes, chant all the nonsense, wave your wand around in the air when you can go straight there with your mind?" He rolls his eyes and tosses his hand up as if to say we'd be crazy to do all that pointless work.

From all my past experiments with Wicca what he says makes sense. "That's funny you mention magick. When I was younger and looking around I played with Wicca magick. I, um, even had this little statue that was supposed to be a representation of me." I snicker quietly to myself. Seems silly to talk about it. Hard to believe I ever bought into that stuff, but what if there was something to it now? "I tried these different rituals from a book I'd gotten at a local store. I forget what I was trying to do but one time I accidentally spilled some red candle wax on the statue. It dripped on the statue's right eye. Didn't think anything about it at the time. Afterwards, I went to bed and woke up the next morning same as always." The memory of the wax dripping across the statue flashes through my head. Still so crisp. Right in front of my window. Summer breeze coming through. Room flickers with dim candle light. Lifting the candle above my head. There was too much melted wax. It spilled out over my hand onto the statue's face. I still have that statue.

"Of course," I admit, "it wasn't the same as always. When I tried to put my contacts in the next morning I couldn't find the right one. Freaking searched and searched all over the place. For almost an hour I scoured because contacts were so expensive. I gave up and went into my room to get my glasses and that's when I saw it staring right at me. My statue still sitting there, red wax dripped across its right eye. The representation of myself, red splashed across its right eye and me missing my right contact. I freaked out! I didn't know how or why but I was certain the wax affected it so that the sight in my right eye would be hampered which resulted in my lost right contact. Man, I felt lucky it didn't blind me or poke my eye out. After that I was convinced magic worked and never used it again because I didn't know what I was doing."

Eric laughs. "Well, I can't say what caused you to lose your contact but you get the idea. The ritual created belief. You were using your hands to move the candles around and whatever else you were doing and I'm sure you had an influence. All your tools and statues helped slip little bits past the governor."

We talk for a time about different tools like Tarot Cards, runes, and things that Eric knows about that neither of us have ever heard of. He explains what works and why. "The reason why is almost never the tool itself. Rather it's the effect the tool has on the mind."

It isn't long before we realize it's late into the afternoon and we've had nothing but breakfast. I feel dirty and need a shower too. We stop and Eric lets us relax around the house.

Evening comes. The sun dips and illuminates the tops of the mountains. It makes me think about auras. The sun is behind them but light still spills out. Sitting out on the porch I watch the light flicker and spark, hypnotized by the slow but sudden movement of the sunset. I'm strangely content.

Eric decides we'll take his truck for a ride into the canyons. The only time I've been to the canyons was the night I found the stream. This time he wants to go high into the mountains to a place he and Matthew found before.

Matthew and I go out front and wait for Eric. It's then I realize what truck he's talking about. In the front of Eric's house is a truck. Truck isn't quite fair... Mechanical-Godzilla-Monster of total off-road domination is better. The tires are enormous and come up to my chest. It has a huge antennae and a mean looking grilled front end. It's always been in front of his house but I never imagined it was his.

He comes out and calls the dogs, Angus and Duncan. With a little help they make it into the truck bed. Scrambling up the side I climb into the back seat and we start off. It isn't long before the faint lights of Tujunga vanish. One turn into the canyons and everything's swallowed by blackness. The high mountain walls hide the remaining light. The canyon roads are winding and it's more noticeable in the tall truck than Eric's car. Eric pulls out a CD and slides it into the player. It sounds like a strange country bluegrass. Almost like twangy, pioneer music.

Clicking through he finds the song he wants. It starts with a deep, haunting violin. It has a melody that's awkward but suddenly, quietly, takes me into myself. I don't want to talk anymore, or think. The canyon air blows through the back. I lay down looking up backwards at the sky we're passing beneath. There's something magical in this moment. Something I can't capture. My thoughts feel constrained. Closing my eyes I take a deep breath in. Inside I'm invoked to dance with a phantom of the past. I sit and enjoy... feeling the movement. It reminds me of being in love for the first time. Your head spins, your heart whistles, everything takes on an air of newness. Your whole body is in rhythm with your emotions. Life is active, alive, vibrant and oh... oh how everything sings. Such a song man cannot make himself. All the world, renewed and awake, joins you in your love. I don't know why but I feel a taste of that. It isn't strong but... it's been so long since I've felt this breath of freedom. It's an adventure, into new territory of some winding canyon road. I enjoy going off into the unknown. It's always called to me and I'm happy to answer.

Eric finds the road he's looking for. It's almost straight up the side of a mountain. There's no pavement. I barely make out tire tracks that mark it as a road. Large rocks cover the whole road and it's more gravel than dirt. It would be easy to slide over the stones, or be rocked the wrong way and tumble off the edge. Eric switches to four wheel drive. He notices me watching the edge not 2 feet beyond the wheels. Assuring me I have nothing to worry about he tells me his truck was used for racing down in Baja California. It was used to pull the other trucks out if they got stuck in the mud. It's got great grip and won't slide off. I'm not convinced...

After driving twenty minutes a yelp echoes through the night. Quick snap of the head behind me and I count... crap... only one dog, Angus. Eric skids to a stop and asks what the yelp was.

"We're missing a dog. I don't see Duncan." I tell him.

Eric groans. "I can't believe he did it again. Dumbest dog ever. Duncan has a death wish and always jumps out of the truck."

He runs back to try and find him.

"He isn't there." He hurries back and turns the truck off. Matthew and I jump out and Eric calls for Duncan. I look down over the edge. The cliff is steep and dark. I can't see more than five feet down. It doesn't look like ground. It looks like it keeps going. A long way down.

Everyone wanders off in different directions. Matthew goes up the mountain and Eric goes down. I stay with the truck. Nothing could happen to him. Dogs can be dumb but they try to hurt themselves.

You're kidding yourself. Your dogs ate cat poop...

Where did that come from? That doesn't make them dumb. Throwing yourself off a cliff and eating cat crap are totally different. I try and think of dogs eating cat crap in a funny way but it doesn't work... I'm nervous. The thought of the poor dog falling off the cliff, down into the darkness on the sharp rocks... is almost sickening. There's nothing we can do...

Eventually Matthew come backs. He shakes his head. Nothing. No sign of him. We wait. Twenty minutes later Eric comes back up. He's breathing hard. Duncan's nowhere to be found. Eric always acted like Duncan was a retarded dog but his face is strained. He is genuinely concerned.

As if reading my thoughts he tells me he always jokes about what an idiot Duncan is, but he's Eric's idiot. "I take care of the things under my responsibility. I don't have a flashlight so we'll have to go back to the house to get one..."

We all fall silent. Not a single noise anywhere. If Duncan were out there... conscious... you'd think he'd make some kind of noise. I can tell Eric isn't going to give up. We'll be here until morning. Eric walks to the edge of the cliff. Instead of looking down he stares out into the distance. We all become strangely silent. I start to move but suddenly feel as if I shouldn't make a noise... so I freeze. Matthew is perfectly still as well. Eric stands quietly at the edge of the darkness. I'm not sure what Eric's going to do.

At that moment I hear panting and Duncan comes running up the hill. Holy crap, I don't believe it.

Eric calmly steps away from the edge and calls him over and checks him. "Dumb ass dog. He's perfectly fine." Eric pets him on the top of his head and rubs his back.

Where the hell did he come from? "Well, he must have run the other way, before he realized he was going the wrong way." I wonder out loud. Staring down the road Duncan ran up I'm not sure if that's true. Something about it doesn't seem right. Everyone laughs. The anxiety is gone. Duncan is pretty dumb. Eric looks happy to have him back. He lets Angus down and the dogs run behind the truck.

We drive to the top of the mountain. Eric parks the truck at the peak. All around I see the other peaks in the Angeles Crest. Far away in the distance the twinkling of Los Angeles steadily glows. It's far away, a dim nightlight on the horizon. We sit in the back of the truck.

Matthew was smart enough to bring a sleeping bag. The air this high up is colder than I expected. Complaining out loud at my own stupidity for not bringing anything warmer I can't believe any peak this close to L.A. gets high enough to change temperature.

Eric tells us that he's found snow on a few high peaks. Once, he was up on a high peak, in a mountain glen with tall pine trees and saw a wolf.

"Really?" I ask amazed that any wild animal would live within 500 miles of LA. These mountains must get more remote than I thought. "What did you do?"

He looks away into the distance. "Nothing. He came into the clearing. I looked into his eyes, he looked into mine and... we shared a moment, you could say. Then he trotted off."

It paints an interesting picture.

The sky is smooth and a rich clear black. The kind of sky you almost think has a texture you could reach up and feel. The stars are the brightest I've seen in a long time. Radio towers blink red lights from nearby peaks. Everything is quiet and still. The dogs roam around near the truck. Their sniffing noticeable, almost loud. On one side of the mountains lies L.A. Its fake electrical sunrise shining up over the peaks. The other side is a plain of darkness lit by a few twinkling lights. It's the desert. I breathe in deeply and look out to where the ocean should be.

Then the entire sky flashes white.

I blink and shake my head slightly. What happened to my vision? I look over at Eric and Matthew who are in the truck bed with me. They make no sign they noticed anything. What did I just see? For an instant, the whole sky flashed a perfect white. It was as if, like hitting a light switch, night had become day for a moment.

I look over to L.A. and see the same hazy, steady glow. Search the sky for clouds. None. I've never seen lightning in L.A. anyway but so near the desert... it could have been a freak lightning strike. It's cloudless. For miles and miles there isn't a single space where I can't see the stars perfectly.

Then everything flashes white again. The whole sky and everything around me goes from the dark blackness of night to completely, brilliantly illuminated white.

I rub my eyes. "What the hell.." I say out loud to see if I can get a reaction from either one of them without sounding crazy right away.

Matthew starts chuckling in his warm, cozy sleeping bag. I look at him and he's looking at me, a half-cocked grin on his face. Eric's grinning at me too.

"What?" Eric asks a little too innocently.

Ah crap... might as well ask. "Did you guys see that?" I ask pointing to the sky. "It happened twice."

"See? See what?" Eric asks again with a slight tone in his voice that I know means he's having some fun with me.

I sigh. "The sky, it flashed white like –" suddenly everything, not only the sky but everything around me, flares with a bright white light. I was looking up at the sky before but it's everywhere!

"There!" I shout pointing at the mountain and then at the sky so they don't think I'm pointing at a bunch of rocks. "There! It just did it! Did you see it?!" They had to have seen it! It wasn't soft. The whole freaking sky lights up bright white!

They are the perfection of calm and indifference. Matthew looks, oh-so-casually, at Eric and I can tell he's having a hard time not laughing. I don't get it. Can they see it too? If they can why aren't they saying anything?

"The whole sky flashed white?" Eric asks me.

"Yeah! It's flashing bright white. It's done it like three times now."
"Probably a search light from L.A." Eric suggests somewhat coyly.

"No!" I say excited by what's going on and growing frustrated by their lack of response. "It's too bright, I mean L.A. is over there!" I point at the dim glow over the mountains. "It's the same, it's too faint. This is bright!"

"Hrmm." Eric thinks out loud. "The radio towers?"

"Radio towers? Uh..." I ask forgetting for a moment about the weak little blinking, red, radio towers. "What? No... look at them." I say looking towards the quiet radio night specks. "It's... it's so bright..." I wait, listening to my breath.

Whoooosh! The whole sky, the mountains, everything around me, goes white. This time everything seems slower. I pay attention to how it looks. It doesn't look like daylight. It isn't bright like daylight is. It looks paler. Less color. It almost looks like an electrical white. It's bright but void of color. What's more, when it flashes, I can feel it flash through my body. For a moment, my entire body buzzes with it.

"There it was again..." I say quieter, confused, uncertain.

"Maybe," Matthew suggests, "it's lightning." He chuckles.

"No, no, no. I got it. A weather balloon." Eric says. They both have a good snicker.

Now I get it. They're giving me logical explanations. They're making fun of how they think I'd take it. They think I would dissect it and cast it off with the best scientific explanation I could find. Damn it, am I that bad? Matthew's always been more open to things.

Am I critical or narrow minded? I think back to the night in the park. When Eric explained things and asked us to feel them Matthew had an easier time. I can't figure out why exactly. I'm trying to understand but can't seem to catch on like he is. They must both be able to see this. He's taking it in such stride. Maybe he's seen it

348

before. They said they found this together. I sit forward and smile, laughing quietly through my nose. It's something I'd learned to do when I was young and didn't want to smile with my teeth showing.

"I get it. It isn't a weather balloon, it isn't the radio towers and there's not a cloud in the sky. But I give up. What is it? I'm ready to listen." My voice humbled by the event.

Matthew looks over to Eric. "Well," Eric starts, "you guys have been around me so much lately you're starting to tune into my frequency more. You're seeing things more how I see them. You're starting to operate on a higher level. What you're seeing is the planet shift. When the planet shifts it flashes white for a moment. It goes through everything, not just the sky. Kinda like a heartbeat I guess you could say. You know, like the electrical pulse that goes through your whole body. Well, the planet has something sort of like that. You're tuning into that."

I nod slowly letting my brain air the shock of acknowledgment out. Holy crap, it makes sense. I grin and shake my head. It's insane... totally insane. I picture the electric wave that goes through my body signaling my organs to function. Imagine my poor cells crying out to each other, 'Dear god! Did you see it flashing white?' It's exactly like Eric explained the first time I met him. Micro-macro. Electricity moves through my body as a signal. It moves through Gaia. Part of me starts to spin trying to come up with other, more reasonable, explanations. Inwardly I laugh at myself. Good luck. His might not be reasonable but it makes sense.

Inside I feel incredible friction like part of me wants to explode.

Oh my freaking God!! He said *starting* to see things the way he sees them! If this isn't it how else does he see everything?

Calm... be calm. The implications... the suggestion. Overwhelming. What else does he see? How does the world look to him? Christ... we're not living in the same reality. Don't go there... just enjoy it. I breathe out and watch my breath float through the night sky. My desire to rationalize the experience floats away with it. Let it go...

It's amazing. Such a mystery. Who would have known such a thing existed? Who would have known a human could witness such a sight? It's a wonder! Oh my God! My mind spins. Life is a mystery. An incredible mystery. I've never been able to see something that goes on every single day. It's been here, the whole time. Yet, I've never seen it. I complain the world is mundane and boring but here it is! Magical, mysterious with all its hidden secrets. Who knew? How could we not know? Right here... before our very eyes. There's so little I know... incredible...

We sit quietly awhile longer. My speech is driven from me. Sitting, staring, I'm captivated. In total awe there's nothing any part of me can say, or think... or deny. There it is. The world... as it is... hidden in plain view...

We eventually drive down off the mountain... though we are quieter than when we went up. I go to sleep that night unsure of the world I live in. Uncertain if what I can touch and hold is truly all there is... and all the while wondering... what does Eric see...

I didn't understand that inside I was going into the unknown. It was this internal journey, this shift to a place in my consciousness that I had never been to. This was my real adventure.

Eric told me after our first meditation that I was pushed by the group's energy. This happened again on the ride up the mountain. He calls it, 'riding his coat-tails.'

It's a main benefit of being in the direct presence of someone with a higher tonal. Using Eric's meditation you raise the vibration, or frequency, of your consciousness. If you meditate with someone who has a higher tonal you can ride along on their vibration. As they shift up into higher frequencies they radiate that tonal which makes it easier for you to shift into it.

The same is true even if you aren't meditating. Being around Eric when he was in a higher, shifted state, all day tuned our frequencies closer to his without even meditating.

Once you've been to a 'place', or a specific frequency, it's easier to get back there. In the beginning I learned to shift by being pushed from Eric's energy. He would shift our consciousness to places and eventually we learned how to do it, without ever having to consciously recognize it. We knew the feeling of it.

This ride up the mountain was the highest frequency I'd been too. As Eric started shifting we were carried along. It was a place that filled me with peace, love and... as I'd soon learn... mystery.

no life without death. no courage without fear. no safety without risk. with every warning a choice...

Do or Do Not

chapter nineteen

My eyes open to meet the morning. Restless and eager. There's something I want to do. Excitement drives me from sleep. I haven't been excited to wake up at the crack of dawn since I was a kid. The whole house is blanketed in the quiet that only hovers before anyone has stirred. I sit up and look at Matthew. He's passed out fast asleep.

The morning is yours. Take it.

Creeping out of my sleeping bag I sneak into the bathroom. Wash my face and scrub my teeth clean with my fingers and some toothpaste. Forgot my toothbrush. It helps me feel like I'm awake and ready for the day.

The porch. I smile. Yes, the morning is mine. I felt something last night I can't describe but neither can I shake it. I have to know what it is.

More willful. You will know what it is. It's already done.

Yes, like Eric said. Making sure I don't make a sound I sneak out to the front porch. It's clear except for a little wooden table with a stereo and a small round table where we eat breakfast. Eric brought the CD we listened to in the truck and played it before we'd gone to bed. I sift through a small stack of CD's and find it. The music is part of it. It framed the moment. Captured it. I want it back, that breath of mystery.

353

I put the CD in and turn around facing the yard. Everything is gray. The half-light before the sun has climbed over the mountains. The dogs are still sleeping too. I adjust the volume so it is just loud enough for me to hear. Closing my eyes I take a deep breath in. The air is moist, untouched. The music starts playing and I bring my hands up to my chest. I picture Eric in my mind from the day before. Imagining him before me on the porch leading me through the movements. Step by step I begin as he'd shown. Yes, that's it. This is how it was. My movements are clunky. It's hard to remember exactly. I try several ways before it feels right. My body triggers a memory that I have found the right way.

After a few songs I feel like I'm starting to get it down. I open my eyes to watch my hands.

The secret. The secret is in your hands. Breathe with your movements. Breathe in time and move.

Oops! My energy. I have to be aware of my energy body. It's not enough to do the movements. I have to try and be aware of what they're for. I forgot that step. I couldn't feel anything anyway, makes it hard to remember to push around energy that I can't tell one way or the other if it's there or not.

But it's important. If you're going to test it...

Yes, of course. I know it's important that's why I remembered. If I'm going to test Eric's theories I have to try it as he says it is. Suspend my own beliefs. He tells me I have an energy body and I can move it. That might be true. If it is true there's only one way to find out; do what he says and test it. Don't discredit something before I try it.

I smile at myself. Who am I trying to convince? I get up at the buttcrack of dawn to do this and now I have to convince myself why I'm doing it?

"Always gotta have the council weigh in." I whisper to myself out loud.

All the different personalities in my head. Stupid council. Sometimes seems like there are so many voices it drives me nuts. Always this and that and on and on about everything. It was worse when I was younger. Over analyzed and thought about everything. I recall a day I stopped thinking all day long in my head, I freaked out and thought something was wrong. Now I wish they'd shut up most of the time.

The song Eric played on repeat starts in. The strange harmonics bring me back to the drive. It brings me back to the moment when the sky flared white... I felt so strange then. I felt so... alive.

Maybe that's what it was.

Chills run up and down my spine and I straighten up. Willful. The kung-fu master. You must be willful. Don't think about moving your energy around. Move it. I stand up straight and then begin rehearsing Eric's movements. Slowly at first I move with my eyes closed and then open. When I get distracted I focus back on my breathing and close my eyes again. Songs start moving by. I go away from Eric's steps and try to do what I want. It feels like playing. It's fun!

Since I can't feel my energy I try to visualize what it would look like. It's bright and radiates from inside my body. I take my hands and pull at my visualized energy body. I breathe in and make huge globes of energy then lurch forward and shoot the energy globe out across the yard. I grin at the thought. That's more fun. Taking a deep breath I think about pulling more energy into me. Spinning around like I'm about to karate-chop someone behind me I pull my energy into another giant energy globe. This time I make it more like a ball. I move the ball back and forth between my hands and roll it through my body before launching it at the gate.

The CD stops and I start playing it again, this time switching the CD to repeat. Moving all over the porch I visualize stretching my energy into more shapes. I swoosh it into an arc over my head and then shoot it like a laser into the sky. Soon, I visualize little balls of energy pulling and following my arms like sparkling, trailing comets. By the time the song we heard on the drive up the mountain starts I notice my whole chest feels warm. The rest of my body seems cool. I'm not sweating like I was the day before, even though I've been doing it much longer. But the feeling of it... I can't tell why but it feels right. It's what I wanted. I want to laugh and dance. I want more!

I whizz from one end of the porch to the other, spinning and making slow, steady slides with matching movements from my hands. By now Angus is awake and stumbles over to the edge of the porch. He plops down and watches me.

I'm not thinking anymore. I've stopped analyzing how I'm moving or why. I stop trying to mimic Eric's movements perfectly. It's happening by itself. My body is moving where it wants to move and I let it. All I can see in my mind is what my energy might look like. Visualize how it flows and changes. It doesn't matter that I can't feel it. I don't know what it would feel like anyway. I don't even know what this is supposed to do really. I don't care. It feels good, so I keep doing it.

Four repeats later I hear a door inside the house shut. It breaks my concentration like someone blew an air horn right in my face. Frozen in my tracks I pause and listen. There's only silence. It must have been Frank. His door sticks and closes with a lot of noise. I turn the stereo down and go inside to check the time. I've been out there almost four hours.

People will be getting up soon. Might as well take a shower. I shower and clean up. Finished, I creep quietly down the hallway in case the house is still asleep. Voices talking from outside. Walking towards the front door, I hear one voice, it sounds like Peter, "Why is that? Fear?"

Then a voice that's clearly Eric's carries down the hall, "Of course fear. Fear is huge. It limits almost everything. It's an abyss. You can't explain your way over it. You can't talk yourself out of fear. You either make the jump or you let it rule you all of your life."

Not wanting to stand there eavesdropping but not wanting to interrupt I poke my head out of the open door so they know I'm here.

They both look up from the small table they're sitting at on the porch. Peter's eyes light up. "Ah, it was you up so early."

I grin. Busted. We say our good mornings and everyone falls silent. It seems their conversation is over. Interrupted. Should have laid down and let them talk.

Peter looks over to Eric and motions to me. "What about him?"

Eric looks at Peter like he's ridiculously insane. "Him?! Are you kidding! He's so full of fear he's already got one foot out the door. He's more afraid of everything around him than most people. He's like a cat creeping in somewhere new. One little sound and voom he's gone. I've got to use kid gloves with him."

Peter nods in understanding. What am I afraid of? How am I supposed to respond to that?

Kathy. Kathy said Eric sent the entity to her as part of her training.

Maybe that's what they're talking about. How would I react to that? Please, if such a thing exists and he can send it I'd be happy to see it. That would prove something at least. Well, one way to know I guess. I clear my throat. "What am I so afraid of?"

Eric smirks. "The same thing as everyone else. Everything. The unknown. You're just more afraid than most. You ever seen that one movie, on the desert planet..." He concentrates trying to remember, "Dune! The sleeper must awaken. It's got these giant worms."

I saw it a long time ago. I still remember some of it. "Yeah, I've seen it."

"Well, one of the great lines from that movie, which you should see again after you've known me for awhile, it will make a lot more sense..." he grins, "Anyway! One of the great lines from that movie is 'Fear is the mind killer'. He says it I think when the one head lady, his mother's teacher, goes to test him and puts his hand in the black box. You remember that?"

It's been so long. Yes, the lady dressed all in black, some kind of witch, comes to test him. She tells him to put his hand in a black box but he doesn't know what's inside. The whole scene starts to replay through my head and I nod.

"Right, well, she has him put his hand in the box as a test right? And he starts feeling like his flesh crawl, and this burning pain like his hand is being burnt off but what happens if he succumbs to fear and removes his hand?" Eric asks.

"Oh, right. She has the needle by his neck and she pricks him with it and he'll die." I answer.

"Right. It's her way of testing if he's controlled by his 'primitive' instincts. All the pain and feelings are all in his head. Fear will make him break his concentration, his willpower, everything. Fear is the mind killer. Same thing with spirituality or psychic states. If you are afraid you will not progress. It's like, your brain keeps doorways in your mind hidden from you. If you can access these secret doors you'll find this whole new perspective and all these experiences are suddenly open to you. How does your brain hide these doorways?"

"Fear?" I ask, certain it must be the answer but his thinking is so strange at times it's hard to tell.

"Exactly. I mean, you can probably think of even small examples. Have you ever been afraid, I mean really afraid, to do something but then once you did it you found yourself changed?"

I don't have to think about this one. "Well, my whole life I was pretty afraid of heights and roller coasters. When I was 14 my grandma once tried to get me to ride a roller coast for 6 year olds but one of them told me it was scary so I chickened out. Then when I was like 17 or 18 I got a chance to go skydiving and I was so mad about being afraid of heights I made myself do it."

Peter starts to laugh, "Really?"

Eric shakes his head, "I'm not even sure I'd do that. But, go on, so what happened after you did it?"

"I felt invulnerable. I felt immortal. I became so confident about everything. I mean, you said earlier when I came out how scared I was and... you know, maybe you're right because I used to be so shy and scared of so much it was pathetic. But after that I couldn't find anything to be scared of. Once I felt afraid of something I'd make myself overcome it. But, I mean, I felt like I could conquer anything after that." I chuckle. Man I miss that feeling... invulnerable... no fear.

"Good. Right." Eric said. "So, that's a good example. It's more of a social or psychological example but it's right. Once you overcame your fear all these other avenues of acting and being opened up. What I'm talking about is a bit different but it's kinda the same in how it works. I'm talking more about how every fear of the unknown begins to confine you. What you can't see, how you think the world works, or how you think the universe works. Maybe thinking about the vastness of the universe overwhelms you because it makes you feel small or powerless. That's all fear. That fear imposes limits on what you allow yourself to see in your mind and achieve. Fear of the world you grew up with. Fear of things being as your parents told you, or society. You're afraid to think differently. You're afraid of breaking down the box that you have lived in your entire life. And sometimes you do what you did, break it down. Because you can't think beyond your own fear. There was no way for you to think what it would be like to jump out of the airplane and have it affect you the same way. Am I right? I'm sure you thought about jumping out of it before you did it? Was it the same at all?"

I smile and shake my head. "No way. Nothing could have prepared me for it."

Eric nods. "So, it's the same. People want to sit around and think, philosophize and yak all day long. Well, I already know about this or that, they might say, I've read all about it. Sorry, reading and thinking won't do crap. They aren't the same. Either you're going to experience it or you're not. Only way to know is to do it. That's the only way beyond the doors."

Eric taps the side of his head.

Yes, the doors of limitless possibility. I've always believed the human mind is capable of anything. It's only our thoughts that limit us. Fear makes perfect sense. Fear keeps them locked. That sucks. I laugh out loud to myself and they give me weird looks.

"That sucks," I confess, "Because fear is so... scary." It's kinda funny, fear is so scary. It has to be right because it's so perfect. Fear is the freezer. At the root of it all I will find fear. Part of me, ever so quietly, seems to confirm that. It's the truth.

Eric throws his hand up in the air as if to say, well, it is what it is. "Well, if it were easy...."

Peter finishes his sentence for him, "Everybody would do it." He nods to himself, lost in thought. After a few moments of silence he adds, "Breaking down walls with wrecking balls..."

We sit for awhile talking about fear and how it will take you right out of spiritual states and prevent psychic abilities. My mind drifts back to what Eric said to Peter when I first walked out. I am full of fear. More so than most. Am I? I feel cautious maybe but it doesn't seem like fear. Still, he made an observation that I'm not aware of. He could be right. I have to watch myself.

We wake up Matthew and Eric makes us breakfast. Eric decides we should watch Dune now rather than later. If we watch it with him he can explain parts of the movie from his perspective. Holed up in Eric's small garage room we watch the entire movie.

I've seen the movie before. Granted, it was at least 5 years ago but it's strange, I can't believe it's the same movie. There are so many parts I'd grazed over and never contemplated the details involved. There's a point where the Guild Navigator, a giant floating worm, moves an entire space fleet across the Universe. It isn't explained in detail how this happens.

Eric pauses the movie and tells us about an old legend where magicians were said to be able to move armies across vast distances instantaneously. "They would march the army into a thick fog or mist, someplace where they couldn't see clearly what was around them. Then these magicians, which I think would be more like spiritual mystics, would do their thing which was really folding space. When the fog cleared the army would be hundreds to thousands of miles away from where they were! Now, it's not that I believe every legend but I think there's truth in that and Dune is saying the same thing. When they prepare to move the entire space fleet they all enter the giant metal tube. This blocks out the surrounding stars from everyone inside their ships. The Guild Navigator creates an image in his mind where he wants to go. Then he projects that out and folds space. It's not about size or distance. You have to think in non-linear terms. Everyone inside the tube can't see out, so they aren't so strongly connected to the outer grid, and they accept more easily that something is going to happen. Now in the movie the Navigator's do this using spice but, you get the point. It's really a spiritual concept. The Navigator is taking reality inside him and turning it out. Using his consciousness to fold space and time."

It's an interesting concept and we end up talking about it for some time. At the end of the movie the main character performs the same action, according to Eric, when he brings rain and water from his homeworld to Dune, a dry desert planet. He folds space in his mind and transports the water onto Dune.

Through the whole movie Eric talks a lot about dimensions and awakening. That there is some part of us, a dimensional consciousness, locked in hibernation and that is what we're trying to connect to. I never considered that when Eric says awakening I have no idea what he really means. Seems like a normal thing people say about spirituality because it sounds nice. Like you're growing and maturing. The point of meditation is 'awakening'. Hmm, isn't that nice. Now it seems like it's more technical. He has details I was not aware of.

Between Eric pausing to discuss things when they come up and Matthew taking smoke breaks it takes about 8 hours to watch it all. There are themes Eric already discussed. The hands... the palm of the hand as a signal to awaken. Remembering past lives. Moving through time and space with your mind. My brain spins trying to crunch all the data. It's hard to take it all in. To piece it together. By the time we finish it's night. Eric drives us back to L.A. When we get closer to our neighborhood I start to feel different. I never realized how tired and heavy it makes me feel. Maybe it's the fresh air... if I can call Tujunga air that... but it all feels dirtier and unwelcoming. I can't be sure why.

Eric turns, pulling down our street and slows down his car.

"The time is coming when you are both going to have to decide if you want to continue learning from me and I will have to consider if I am going to continue teaching you. This isn't about me calling you guys up and asking you guys to do this or that, it's fifty-fifty. You have to meet me half way. You need to call me up and tell me you want to learn and you're ready to learn. I've given you both a lot of my time and you need to appreciate I could be relaxing. I could be helping my business. I have a school full of people who want to learn from me but I can't teach them and you guys because you're just starting out. You both get it?" His voice is stern but quiet.

I nod my head and tell him yes. Matthew remains silent then says yeah.

"There's something else you guys need to consider. You need to think about it, seriously. You hear me?"

His tone changes to very serious. What is he about to say? Why did he change all of a sudden?

"Yes." I tell him. Matthew agrees as well.

"Now, if I didn't tell you this you might come back years from now and say to me, 'well, you never told me it would be like this,' or, 'why didn't you ever say anything?' You have to take this knowledge seriously. You have to understand – it will change you. You cannot un-know what you know. You cannot unlearn what you learn. Maybe you'll change a little, subtly, or you could change beyond recognition. Much of that depends on you and what you do with it. However, and listen to me, once you begin you cannot help but change. Once the seed is planted the flower will grow. You may find that you cannot relate to the people in your life the same. You may find you cannot relate to your friends, or your family, the same. That may cause you pain. The people in your life now expect you to be as you are. When you change that, they may very well not want you to change, and they might reject you. Change can be as scary for those near you as it is for you, get it?"

We both nod.

"Once this knowledge removes you from this, your world," he waves his hands around all the buildings around us, "it's very hard to go back. The habits you keep now, the things you do, the interests you have, it may all change. Right now you want to become an actor and this may change your whole life direction. I don't want you coming back later saying that you were going to be an actor and instead I changed your life and took it away from you. You know, you want to be a writer or make movies or whatever it is you want to do but it could all change. You both have to review your life and think about what you really want. Now, you may doubt what I'm saying now, but listen to me. Listen – to- me. I am warning you. I am telling you. Consider your decision carefully. Make it with clarity. That means think about all the possibilities. Decide for yourself."

He stops and we pull up to our apartment. We sit silently for a few seconds. I feel the gravity of what he's saying. I can already see the tension with Farrah and Lenny. But then life always changes you. You can never be the same. More than that I know there's something here. I don't know what it is but I know if I let it go I will never have peace with myself as long as I live. To think that fear of change would keep me from knowing... I couldn't forgive myself.

"That's it. See you later." Eric tells us. We climb out and say good-bye. Neither Matthew or I say anything as we climb the stairs back to our apartment. Both deep in thought, we go to bed.

walk in the steps of those ahead, learn from the mistakes of the fallen... by example, trial and error you begin to...

Find Your Way

chapter twenty

The meaning in Eric's warning is not lost on me. I decide it's been too long since I've hung out with Farrah. She's been chasing a guy who's playing games and her head is spinning so... we do what we've done in the past. We go to Barney's for some happy hour drinks.

Thirty minutes. Thirty minutes, one drink and I'm done. The feeling of a buzz starts to creep in on me. One beer and I can feel it already? I scrunch my eyes unconsciously as I try to think why I can feel it so much more. Maybe I just notice it more. I clench my hand into a fist and open it again. I can feel it in my hands already. Smiling I think about the open palm signaling the deep recesses of my mind to awaken. Farrah leans forward and asks what's wrong. Looking up I wonder what she means. Her large brown eyes framed by her thick black hair really do make her look Egyptian. Maybe our landlord was on to something and it's more than her name. You'd think she'd know it if she was. Suddenly I realize she looks genuinely concerned and wasn't making idle conversation. I feel a frown on my face and change it. I smile and tell her I was only thinking. When I concentrate too much my face bends into a frown.

I don't like the feeling. I don't like drinking. Eric's warning comes to my mind and I push it out.

This knowledge will change you... can't relate the same...

It's my mood. I'm not in the mood and that's all. We have more drinks and then leave for some food. McDonald's has specials on hamburgers where we can get several for less than a buck. It's gross but it's cheap. After enough beer I don't care. Plus Farrah loves their ice cream.

Farrah drives us up to the drivethru and the grating mood comes back. She keeps talking about the guy she's trying to see and all the things he does, how he contradicts himself all the time, and the parties she goes to. We've been through it three times... today. That doesn't count all the other days we've talked about it. She talks about it for awhile and then loops back and starts over. Makes it easy to keep up, I guess.

My mind is somewhere else, though I lose track of where. It's gone. Usually there's a slight sexual tension when Farrah and I go out. We talked about it once and decided nothing would ever come of it. Still, it lingered and was always a point of conflict for me but kept things interesting at the same time. Now, that's it. That might be what's bothering me. It isn't there. Looking at Farrah I don't feel it. If I don't feel that, what do I feel? I smile to myself as Farrah leans out the window of her car placing our order. I feel like meditating.

That sucks.

Not that it matters. I haven't had sex in two years. It would only screw things up. Still, it gives me something to look forward to. Not much... but now I want to meditate instead of thinking about having sex? There goes the warning.

What's the purpose of this? Why am I doing this? What will this do? Is that what my life is supposed to be? Am I supposed to spend my days drinking, eating and talking about people's sex lives? Love lives?

No, it's about sex. It's always about sex.

Our whole group, everyone at the apartment, sexually repressed. My mood swings to dark. I sigh out loud. Farrah is talking but I'm not sure about what. She puts my hamburgers in my lap. Now I remember why I don't like to drink, this happens. I start hammering myself about the meaning of my life. I look out the window. Perfect blue sky. Always. We live in a giant freaking aquarium. L.A. always has bright, clear skies. My mind goes back to the night on top of the mountain with Eric and Matthew. The whole sky flashed white. It felt so strange. How could that mean anything here? What did that mean anyway? Was it even real? I start to fight myself over the memory. Part of me wants to forget it even happened. I don't want to acknowledge it. Another feels a deep ache for it.

It's buried, the part that wants it... It also feels painful. Like remembering the loss of some loved one. I wonder, staring up at the sky, at the strangeness of it.

Kathy pops into my brain. God Kathy, maybe this is what she meant. She's seen all these things but it doesn't matter in her day to day life. How does she make the two happy? Is what I saw all that fantastic? So, the sky flashed white. What's the big deal? The emotion of it doesn't feel as strong as when I first saw it. Maybe it isn't a big deal, it's not so incredible. It isn't like the sky opened up.

What are you saying? Do you even know what that means?

No, I don't know what it means.

Isn't that something?

Yes, it is something. It's a mystery.

That sends chills through my body. Yes, a mystery. That's what life should be. I look around the car and at Farrah happily eating her ice cream cone. This isn't a mystery. I've lived this day over and over and over again. I know each time we go out what's going to happen and how it's going to play out. I could be doing this same day for years. And that's my life. Shouldn't there be more? Is this what I'm here for?

We go back to the apartment. I brood for hours debating the meaning of it all. I want to dismiss the flashing sky I saw over the weekend as nothing. It was a visual fluke and meant nothing. Another part of me aches when I consider it that. There's something there. I can't explain but I yearn, not so much for the sight of it, but how it made me feel.

I think about Eric's warning that we won't be able to relate to our lives the same. He said that a few days ago. At the time it didn't seem realistic that I couldn't do both. Now, I'm not so sure. I'm starting to notice a contrast. How I felt over the weekend and how I feel living at the apartment is very different. It's a difference I can't completely put my finger on but it's there. There are so many questions but I don't know how to verbalize them. I need a shower. My escape capsule. I sit down in the shower staring ahead at the water dripping over my eyes.

Let's do the 'ME' and 'I' exercise Eric showed us.

Fine. That'll snap me out of this. Doing the exercise out loud it doesn't take long for Farrah to open up the door and yell if I'm okay. She thinks she heard voices.

"Of course," I tell her, "just talking to myself again." We're beyond the point where either of us think that's strange. She knows I talk to myself and I know she knows. I go back to the exercise.

The next day comes and goes. It's been weeks since I've been called to work. Things are slow and all the projects are being given to senior employees.

Eric calls me in the evening. "Hey, Jason and I are almost there."

I'm confused, "You're almost where?" He acts like I should know what he's talking about.

"Your apartment. We've been down in L.A. and want to know if you guys want to get coffee."

Holding the phone to my ear I look around the apartment like he could see my sarcastic expression. Yeah, I'm alone. There is no 'you guys'. "Matthew and Justin are out with actor friends. I'm not sure what they're doing..." I drone out a bit grumpy.

He tells me to be ready.

Nice of him to ask if we even wanted to go.

Please, like we would have said no?

Right... good point.

I walk down to the sidewalk and they pull up in a bright, shiny red car. I look in the window and see Jason driving. "Nice car." I offer.

Jason beams his big, friendly smile. "Thanks."

Eric rolls his eyes as he opens the door. "Please, he acts like it's his. It's Bonnie's car. She let him drive it for the night."

I hop into the back seat and watch Jason and Eric interact. Jason strikes me as different this time. He's so tall and lanky his head hits the roof in the small sporty car. Like a giant teenager. Despite his young appearance he seems older. His blonde hair is shaved pretty close to his head but I don't think that's it. It was pretty short before. He's not even acting different. It's in his presence. They joke about something I don't know about. Eric doesn't seem as serious around Jason. He's lighter and more relaxed. It's like watching two good friends going out for a night on the town. They start hounding me for somewhere cool to go that's close.

"Well... I know mostly bars, so let me think about coffee shops. There's a place I've heard about in Los Feliz. It's an 'eclectic neighborhood'..." I finger quotes around a phrase I got from L.A. Weekly, a free local paper, "and there's supposed to be good places up there. Since I'm not really part of the whole 'car crowd' I only know how to get there from what I read in the paper." Not that it matters... as long as I've seen a map once that's usually enough.

We drive around Los Feliz looking at different shops, houses and restaurants. Eric decides he likes the place and if he ever moves back into the city it might be in an area near here. Not that he can afford it he jokes. We settle on a place that looks promising; Fred 62.

It looks like a revamped diner out of the 50's. Everything is white and green. We settle into a nice long booth. Eric and Jason have been talking quietly since the last few minutes of our car ride and into the restaurant. Their tone turns more serious which triggers my attention. I'm sitting in the corner against the wall next to Jason. Eric notices I came out of my wondering head and moves his hand to tell Jason to stop the conversation. Jason turns to me and smiles.

"What's going on there buddy?" Jason asks.

Jason's shiny grin feels so genuine it's hard not to like him. I'm suddenly struck by how very nice he is. It makes me want to laugh. Knowing he would probably take that the wrong way I control myself and smile back at him. L.A. has made me so jaded I find any smile suspect. I shrug my shoulders. "I guess whatever you guys are talking about." I tell him with a smirk.

Jason laughs and looks at Eric. Eric waves me off with one large hand. He looks me over and then turns away. "Nah, you wouldn't be interested in what we're talking about."

He must be baiting me. He even went through the trouble to turn his head. Like a cat brushing you off. He's been joking with Jason so much I think he's playing. "Ah, come on. I don't have anything else to talk about." It's the truth but I act like I'm joking. I'm in a broody, quiet mood. Thinking of a conversation point is more energy than I want to muster.

The waitress drops off water and coffee. Eric picks up his water and takes a drink. From my angle I can see the ice cubes reflecting in his glasses. Even through the liquid image I can make out his sharp gaze that suddenly turns serious. He raises his eyebrows, "Well, like I said, not that it would interest you but we're talking about vampires."

He's still playing with me. I grin at the joke. "Vampires, huh?" I look at Jason who's looking at me like he's about to crack up. "What?" I say to him sarcastically.

Jason bursts out laughing. He looks at Eric. "You were right. He doesn't believe you at all." Eric shrugs.

"It's not going to make sense in his world. There's not much use in telling him except to confuse him." Eric says indifferently. His face is straight and the way he sits staring at me I don't feel there's much of a joke.

I stop pouring cream into my coffee. "You guys are really talking about vampires?" I ask somewhat snidely to let them know I won't leap into their joke. Maybe they're measuring how gullible I am. I shake my head. "Like, real vampires?"

Eric nods. "That's why we're down here tonight. I know a place where some, what you could call vampires, do business. I'm debating whether or not to take Jason there." Eric assures me they aren't like the vampires Hollywood created but there is some truth to them and for all practical purposes vampires are real.

I sit there stirring my coffee. Damn it, how do I tell if he's kidding? He always tells me stuff that sounds crazy at first then makes sense later. "Okay, maybe." I tell them. Jason has a huge grin on his face. If they're making all this up I'm going to feel really stupid. "But, where do they do business?" I ask thinking the lack of details will bring the joke out.

"Believe it or not, they have a little pizza place, though I'm not going to say where." Eric says seriously.

I laugh. It sounds too much like the movie Lost Boys. "Really? A pizza place?"

Without missing a beat Eric gives a confirming nod. His thick goatee doesn't even twitch from any kind of chuckle or smile. Jason laughs slapping the table and says the whole thing is awesome.

I have to come out and say it. "Are you guys joking or serious?"

Eric smiles and his face changes. He assures me that he is, in fact, serious. "I've debated taking you along but you're still too young of a student and you wouldn't be able to conduct yourself well. They aren't a spectacle to gawk at and I don't think you could keep it together. You need more training. Even Jason, who's one of my best students, I have doubts about taking."

Jason turns his head and looks at Eric when he mentions he's one of his best students. The waitress comes and takes our order. They order food and I stay with coffee. Eric asks if I'm at all hungry but I insist I'm fine, which I am. I know he doesn't have money either. I'll eat cereal or spaghetti later.

Eric called me one of his students but that doesn't make sense to me. What does he consider a student? What does it mean to be a student? I'm not going to their school or bookstore, whatever they want to call it. I don't attend any of Eric's classes that they talk about from time to time. It's something they say a lot but I'm not sure how they figure it. When I went to school I had to pay for it. There were grades and tests. They talk about promoting the school and getting more students but if I don't know what they mean how will anyone else will get it.

Eric and Jason go back to talking about what they were discussing in the car. I realize they're talking about Jason's relationship with Bonnie. Eric wants to know how it's going. My chance to talk about vampires is gone. Probably for the best. Seems completely absurd, what would the point be?

Jason opens up that she's having some trouble with a restaurant she owns with her ex-husband.

Eric suddenly appears a little concerned. "I'm worried about you balancing your relationship and your spirituality. It's a difficult thing to manage and few people can really do it and make much progress."

Jason seems to understand what he means. He describes their relationship and Bonnie's willingness to work with his spiritual interests. "She doesn't understand it or necessarily share my interest, you know? But she gives me lots of room and is really supportive for me to do it."

After some discussion Eric is satisfied that everything is as Jason explains. "You know, I've always liked Bonnie and I have to say, you have, so far, balanced your two lives better than any of the other students. But, to keep that balance will require constant attention." Eric warns hitting his index finger against the table. His main concern he admits, is Bonnie's age. She's at the 30 mark. Her desire to have kids will kick in soon. Jason coughs and waves his hands around as if Eric set off a fire alarm.

He howls and laughs refusing any thought of having kids. "Nah, nah, nah. No kids. That's, like, the last thing that will happen and she knows that."

Jason's younger than Bonnie but he's hard to place. He looks really young but acts really old. I guess he's about my age, maybe a little older. Cutting in I ask, "How old are you anyway?"

Jason laughs and Eric stops stirring his coffee and points his spoon at me. "Guess. How old do you think he is?"

Staring at Jason I jokingly squint my eyes. "I'd say my age. Twenty-four. Maybe a little older but he looks young."

Jason's mouth drops and he turns to look at Eric. "No way! I'm not like that am I?"

Eric rolls back into the booth laughing. He quickly holds up his hand, "You said he looks young though. So you think he's that old because of how he acts, right?"

I can't tell by Jason's reaction which way I guessed wrong. Either I placed him way too young or too old. "Yeah, it's how he acts and talks. How he carries himself. He's very certain, I don't know, together. Comes off a little goofy sometimes." I turn to Jason and crack up. "I'm joking!"

After a good laugh Eric turns to Jason and motions to me. "See? That's kind of a compliment. So you gonna tell him?"

Turning to me with his long neck Jason zero's right in and says with a tone of confidence, "I'm twenty-one. Just turned."

Sliding back a little farther into the booth images of me at twenty-one burn through my head. Holy crap, how did I fall so far behind?

Too much wandering. Always running off and starting over, place to place.

Could that be it? Those seemed like huge growth lessons if anything. How many people leave their homes and lives and move where they don't know anybody? It was hard but I learned a lot. I've always seemed older than people my age but Jason, he's really with it for 21. When he's my age. I shake the thought out. No use comparing. I try to give a grin for Jason, "Unbelievable. That's crazy. You're so freaking young!"

Eric and Jason chuckle about how a year with Eric is worth four years of college. Under that system Jason's been in school for eight years. When he talks to people his parents age about spirituality they can't believe how old he is.

Eric turns serious again and brings the conversation back to Bonnie and children. He leans in and tells Jason he better listen. "It doesn't matter how many conversations you have or what she says, her body will tell her something different. Look, she might not even want to have them. She may tell herself no way but her biological clock is her clock and there's nothing she, you, or anybody else can do about it. It'll kick in and you better be ready to deal with the pressure she'll apply when it happens. And, trust me, there'll be pressure!"

Eric turns the conversation toward their sex life. He's mostly interested in how often they have it. I shuffle somewhat uncomfortably in the booth. I'm getting a front row seat into Jason's personal life. Having never even had a one-on-one conversation with him before it's a little strange. If it's strange for him he doesn't show a single sign. He seems perfectly fine with discussing whatever comes up. Damn, so mature. I almost want to ask for his license because I can't believe his age.

From their talk I gather having sex on a regular basis is a bad thing to do. It drains your energy and slows spiritual progress which requires energy. Even living in the same house is a risk. She can claim too much time for herself and the relationship, depriving him of spiritual time. If the boundaries aren't clearly set, the little things can end up taking big chunks of time. Little by little his spirituality could be whittled away. Eric keeps stressing openness and communication as a big key.

Jason is adamant that he explains everything to Bonnie and she understands the dynamics very well and is willing to work with it. "I mean, we have separate rooms so we spend most of the time sleeping apart. Sometimes we sleep together but, you know, makes it special and it's balanced."

Eric nods.

"She knows that if we're gonna have sex I have to be meditating. She understands about energy and she's really cool about keeping sex balanced and not having it all the time. Plus, there are times where I want to be more spiritual so we cut out the sex and she's really chill with that. I treat her good and make sure she's happy, you know? And it works."

In the end Eric tells Jason he can have his cake and eat it too. "But there's a price. The cost is that you'll have to spend twice as much time and energy on your spirituality than someone who refrains from sex and a relationship."

Rubbing his hand along his head Jason laughs, "Yeah, I know that part."

"Truthfully," Eric tells him, "I have nothing to complain about. Only as your teacher I'm obligated to point out potential risks. Get it? If I didn't do that, I'm not doing my job." After a few bites Eric looks over at me and asks if I learned anything. I nod my head yes. A few minutes go by as they eat and I sip on my coffee. Without any reason Jason sits up straight and cocks his head.

Eric smirks, "What?"

Jason turns to Eric and, with a puzzled expression, asks him, "What was that?"

Eric raises his eyebrows and smiles. "Oh, you felt that did you? I'm surprised. I didn't think you'd catch it."

I look at them both. What are they talking about now? I've been sitting right here and they've lost me again.

Jason explains, "Yeah, I was like, sitting here eating and then I felt this crazy, like buzz, and this energy wave wooshed through the whole restaurant! Does that make sense? Is that how you'd explain it?"

Eric nods. "That's good, very good. Your senses are right on. I'm really surprised you felt it though, I thought you'd miss it. Your meditations are going well."

I think back to the moment before Jason sat up straight. I can't remember smelling anything weird or hearing anything. Nothing happened at all. I look around the restaurant to see if anyone else is looking around strangely. Nothing. Everyone else is eating and talking as if nothing happened at all. Only these two are talking like some major event just swept through the whole place and nobody noticed except them.

Eric looks over at me searching the restaurant for clues. "Don't even bother." He tells me. "You're about as aware as a brick."

Aware? I've been paying attention. It's ridiculous to think these two can somehow see or feel something nobody else can.

Here we go... back to flying shapes again.

Right, all the shapes flying through the walls... only... what about the flashing sky? I could see that, why couldn't I see what they're talking about? Eric starts to explain to Jason what it was but I dismiss the whole thing. It's frustrating being told I'm as aware as a brick when I'm paying as much attention as the next person. If I could see the sky I should have been able to see what they saw. I feel intentionally left out. It must have been nothing. The fact that nobody else reacted to it at all tells me it's something only they think is important to notice... like a rush of cold air.

Matthew would've felt it too.

Screw off! I don't need that crap.

They finish eating and Eric decides it's been long enough. If they're to see the vampires they need to get going. On the drive back Eric picks up a piece of the conversation from earlier. He reminds Jason about the look he gave him when he mentioned he was one of his best students. Jason remembers. Eric feels it's important to tell him, especially in front of me. "You and Peter," Eric says, "are my greatest works to date. You're my top students. How many years have you been studying? You said two earlier right?"

Jason gives it some thought and replies it's been a little over two years.

Eric nods and laughs. "That long huh?"

Jason grins broadly. "Doesn't seem like it does it?"

From the back seat I can see the satisfied smile on Eric's face as he nods his head. "You've done well. I have no complaints with either of you. You and Peter, for the most part," Eric grins, "do what I say and listen to me. You've made good choices and have made a lot of progress." Eric turns to me in the back seat. "If you're going to model yourself after any of my students Jason and Peter are the best. My other students..." he pauses and let's his sentence trail off. He seems unsure how he wants to express himself, "It's not that they've failed necessarily, but they reached their limit. I consider it more a failure of myself as a teacher... although, I can't say that completely but, you know, I have gotten better over the years. You know, just because I awakened at a very young age doesn't mean I've always known the best way to show others. I've refined over the years. Many of my early students were limited by my ability to explain to them how I knew what I knew. I tried lots of different things and they weren't always right. You know, I was a very strong figure in those days."

Jason laughs and hits his hand against the steering wheel.

"You laugh, you know, but I'm strong now but I mean... well, you know what I mean!" Eric yells out smiling.

"Oh yeah," Jason nods grinning, "I've heard the stories."

"What stories are you talking about?" I ask wanting to know the joke.

Eric doesn't want to discuss the details but by the glowing look on Jason's face I can tell they're good. Ahh! So many secrets!

"You know," Eric's voice becomes more serious, "they made decisions based on what they saw in me. You can't... you know..." Eric struggles, "I am who I am and you can't pursue your spirituality like I do. This is for both of you, do you get it?"

Jason says yeah and I nod, though I'm not completely sure.

"It's like, I can slack off and be a certain way because I can rebound faster. I know how to get back there like that." He snaps his fingers to show how fast. "You guys have never even touched that place so you have to do what I say... not necessarily as I do." He frowns and then smiles and shrugs. "I know that sounds hypocritical but it is what it is. Once you get there, you'll get it. But until you get there... you have to struggle. But... back to the point!" He declares. "I'm very proud of where Jason and Peter are. They're the next generation." He laughs. "Like Star Trek! They're new and improved! But really," he turns to Jason, "I look at you and Peter and I feel very satisfied. Keep up the good work."

Jason's face is lit up. I can tell it's an emotional moment for him. For whatever reason I also feel very relieved. I pause to think about it and then understand why. It feels like I'm not alone. I feel like I have help. Eric... I feel like I have to question and analyze everything he tells me. To say Jason has gone through that process of questioning and analyzing and come out on top gives me a resource of experience. He's made mistakes and seen what works and why.

It's comforting to know there are people who have been down the road I'm traveling down and can give me advice. I can look at Jason and Peter and see where they succeeded and understand from them what success means. It gives me a way to measure things. Eric seems unrealistic. I can't relate to a lot of things he says. Shapes flying through the air, entities and universal consciousness. I don't get it. Jason's about my age and somebody I can relate to.

Though Eric doesn't say it I can also learn from the students who failed. Why have they failed? What choices have they made? Failure is as important as success. I'm a recovering perfectionist. I went through a time when I had to embrace failure. To make mistakes meant I was trying. When I stopped failing I stopped trying and that was the only true failure.

I have to find out which students he's talking about and figure out where they went wrong. I never thought about the other students before. I don't know why, maybe it's because I'm never around them. But now it seems like there's a lot to gain from them. Kathy's the only one I ever speak to. Sometimes Justin but the only time I'm around him is at the apartment where the topic isn't really accepted. Happy to know I'm not alone on the crazy journey I say good-night to them both.

As they drive away, I wonder if they're really going to look for vampires...

Often, I look back on what I was aware of when I first began... and I laugh in delight.

It would be too perfect to travel back in time and visit myself and talk about everything that would come to be. What I would see and experience. If only to see the expression on my old face. I wouldn't believe myself.

At this time, talking with Eric and Jason, I hadn't put the pieces together of how Eric's use of the word 'awareness' worked. I had trouble separating it from paying attention, to scanning, to shifted consciousness. In my mind, it didn't matter, once I understood something and experienced it, like the world flashing... nothing should bar me from seeing it again.

I didn't understand that awareness required both an active sixth sense awareness and an energy consciousness tuned into a higher frequency. To me it felt like more of a mind game than a reality. They were excluding me only because I didn't understand their special, inside vocabulary or language. The words they would use often seemed like they had multiple meanings.

Less than two years later I'd be sitting outdoors at a coffee shop on the sunset strip with Eric and a new student. The sunset strip in L.A. is an active place with lots of things to feel. I was actively scanning the area, sending my awareness through the coffee shop and up and down the busy street, and into people. The new student saw things very differently. Eric and I were both sitting there, dead silent, staring off into space doing absolutely nothing.

He openly complained about how boring we were. He told us we tried too hard to seem mysterious by never speaking. We'd gone to all these places and we were always the same... staring off saying nothing. Eric looked at me and I knew he was scanning too, although not on my level. I felt he was plugging into different frequencies. We both cracked up laughing.

Suddenly reminded of Eric and Jason in the coffee shop that night I told him the story to try and help him understand we were doing anything but passively sitting. He didn't believe me and it was all the more beautiful – I wouldn't have believed me either!

I confessed to him it wasn't something I felt was possible to explain. Eric told him about scanning and how your awareness can give you more information than all the other five senses. While he seemed to get the theory, the concept is far from the reality.

how would you tell friend from foe if you could not see them, touch them, or hear them? without these things the unknown is often greeted as an...

Invisible Invader

chapter twenty-one

Kathy and I make more attempts to see each other. She finally finds another chance to visit me in LA. We go to get something to eat and talk mostly about our lives and try to feel each other out more. Little by little I veer the conversation toward the other students. I can't help it. I've had so little time with them. The more I know, the more curious I become. They're also the only thing we have in common so far. She's hesitant to talk about Eric. But she decides she doesn't mind talking about the others. She and her ex lived with Eric and some others down in Costa Mesa.

"Where is Costa Mesa?" I ask trying to visualize what it looks like. I've never heard of any town like that. It could be out in the desert or something.

Kathy's looking down at her plate and only moves her eyes up to look at me over the top of her glasses. Her face is so expressionless. It's like I just coughed too loud in the library and she's giving me a disapproving stare. I know her enough by now to know she doesn't mean it like that. Her facial features don't match what she's thinking. It makes me laugh.

Kathy raises one eyebrow at my random outburst. "Umm, where are you from again?" She quips sarcastically. "Must be from somewhere where they don't know much... Wisconsin... or Michigan..."

Immediately dropping my smile I give a dead-pan stare. "Whatever. Exactly, you can't even think of the state I'm from. You Californians are the center of the universe so you don't know anything about the outside world." With an evil smirk I dip my finger in my water and splash it at her face.

That breaks her game face and she jumps back laughing. "I know. I'm kidding." She recomposes herself straightening her back. With a nervous movement she brushes her blonde hair behind one ear and quickly glances at me. "It's Montana." She says dryly.

Taking a deep breath I reach down and pick up my whole glass of water. Trying to raise one eyebrow I give her a look to let her know it's going to happen. We've raised to Defcon 3.

She stares blankly at the water glass pretending to not know what I mean. I don't buy it and pull my arm back slowly into launching position. Quickly holding up one hand she shows a slight smirk. "Joking. Joking. It's Missouri."

I sigh and look at the glass. I wonder what it would take to actually make Kathy scream. Not a frightened scream but the kind of surprised yelp you let out without reservation. Like, for a moment, you lose control. She's always so reserved and controlled. The water in a restaurant would definitely be going too far. Sadly, I put the glass back on the table.

"So, where is Costa Mesa?" I ask again.

"It's by the beach. South. Orange County." She's being a smart ass using terms she knows I know. It works. I get the idea.

"It was in this really enormous house and there was a huge group of students living there. It was kind of overwhelming at first because I didn't really know them. I moved in with my boyfriend and knew him but everyone else was still new. Eric was teaching all the time. It's really different now. I'm not sure I know everyone who's around now. I know Peter and Jason but I know Peter better. He lives near me in

Orange County. I don't see him a lot but he can be a bit much sometimes."

"What do you mean by a bit much?" I ask unsure of how to take it.

She says matter-of-factly, "Peter is a boiling pot of wild energy and can be a bit crazy at times." She laughs. "Then there's Justin..." she says with a slight groan. I notice her change in tone and ask what the deal with Justin is.

"We dated for a really brief period." She says quietly blushing as she rolls her eyes.

I laugh not so much at her as how that must have gone. I can't see it at all. The combination in my head is Kathy sitting, very serious, trying to eat with her hair up and glasses like a school teacher. Then Justin with huge baggy pants, his Gilligan hat on, dancing all around her.

She starts stressing, almost pleading, how brief it was. I keep joking with her until she shuts up and looks a little angry.

"Sorry, I wasn't trying to be mean..." I mutter.

"Well, you could've fooled me. I'm not going to say any more if you're going to rub it in." Kathy mutters clamping down.

Damn. She's so direct it shuts me right up. It's a quiet kind of directness, even a little cold. Not aggressive and in your face but it has the same effect.

"Right, I know, really I didn't mean to, okay?"

Now she looks even more frustrated and her cheeks turn red. "Okay! Okay! Now stop! Stop..." she's waving her hands around in frantic little circles, "making a bigger deal out of it. Let's forget it. Forget I told you that."

Nodding my head in a stilted motion I want to make a funny comment about her reaction but keep it in check. My sense of humor definitely needs to be kept in a box until I get to know her better and she loosens up. She reacts so strongly to things.

"Okay, so... what about Frank?" I ask thinking another student will take us away from the uncomfortable Justin incident.

Kathy throws up her hands a little and let's out a loud groan.

I can't help it, I bust out laughing. "What? What did I say now?" She rolls her eyes at me like I'm an idiot. I'm holding my hands up totally confused.

"Nothing, nothing, it's not you!" She motions for me to calm down. "Frank... Frank is always trying to come on to me or something."

Restraining myself I hold the laugh and grin. "Not gonna go there huh?" I ask innocently.

Kathy rolls her eyes around her head again. She may as well keep them there. "No. No I'm not. After Justin I made a rule to not date any more students."

Her comment sends a giant question mark popping up over my head. Aren't I becoming a student? If not, what happens if I become one? She's right in thinking it would be awkward to date someone then break up and have to be around them because of mutual friends. Suddenly I'm in a dilemma. Is dating Kathy worth jeopardizing what I can learn from Eric? Am I even dating Kathy?

If I'm going to find out what Eric's all about should I date someone who's been around longer? If they have to choose between me or Kathy they'll choose Kathy. Can't be friends with your friend's ex. Doesn't work.

Intellectual curiosity or... sex?

Wait, do I want to have sex with Kathy? I haven't felt like I do. I haven't touched another person in two years so why start now? Kathy's interesting but is most of the intrigue the experiences and knowledge she's gained from Eric? Don't I also want to know what those are really about?

Stop, this needs to be simplified. Don't over complicate it. What do we know?

Okay, I know that there's a strong pull or something, an indescribable drive to understand Eric's knowledge. I don't know why or how come or what it is but it's there and I've seen things that are... hard to understand... or explain...

Doesn't seem like much of a choice then.

Kathy notices my long period of silence and asks about it. I laugh it off as spacing out and we continue talking. I'll think about it later.

The next day only Matthew and Justin are home in the apartment. It's a first in a long time. We're waiting for Eric so we decide to meditate together. We all sit in my bedroom. Matthew and Justin with their backs against my bed and I'm facing them with my back to the wall. I put in the tape Eric gave me and we start meditating with the music low. About halfway through the first song the whole room fills with a rush of crackling, static energy. My whole body reacts to it and surges with this strange heat and what feels like a rush of adrenaline.

I suddenly recognize the intensity of it. Only one person gives off that kind of intensity, it's Eric. Eric must be pulling up in his car four stories below.

I open my eyes to see Matthew staring at me grinning. I look at him with a puzzled expression, not sure why he's meditating looking at me. No way. He feels it too. My expression changes and I grin back.

He nods his head yes. "Eric's here." He whispers out loud.

How can we feel that? I have to know if we're right. It's really strange he feels it too. Too much of a coincidence. I leap up from the floor and run to go look down out of the window. Sure enough, Eric's walking away from his car toward the front door to buzz. I buzz the door below to let him when. Smiling to myself I'm happy I noticed something Matthew felt too. He always seems to feel more than me, maybe that's what it's like to be Matthew. It's amazing we could tell. How did we know? How could we feel him like that? It didn't seem subtle at all.

There was a charge like someone turned on a giant electricity generator in the room. It was like the balls with the sparks spinning through them and when you touch it the sparks move to your fingers or jump out to meet your touch and make all the hair stand up on your head. What does it mean that we could feel it? How does it work? I want to understand the mechanics of it! My brain starts trying to crunch how it happened.

We leave with Eric and don't mention anything about feeling him arrive. He liked Fred 62 so he drives us up there again for coffee. Parking's hard to find. The area, Los Feliz, is quickly becoming a popular spot and new cafes and restaurants are sprouting up everywhere.

After driving around for about 30 minutes we finally find a place and have to walk 7 blocks to get there. About three blocks away Matthew and Justin are leading and I'm walking slightly behind Eric. Out of nowhere, Eric stops walking and looks up at a red brick building. Confused, I stop and look up at it too, trying to see what caught his interest.

It looks older, like an old brownstone. Plain red bricks with iron balconies. It's an apartment building. There's a glass door and people are walking up the main steps. I look over at Eric and he turns his head toward me.

"Are you looking at it or feeling it?" He asks with a knowing gaze.

My heart drops.

Failure, you didn't even try.

Not even sure that I can feel anything anyway... so there isn't much point in trying. But how can I say it doesn't work if I don't try? To not try is the only failure. Not being able to feel it is a minor obstacle. Something caught his attention. I turn to look at it again and try to take the building in as a whole. Imagining my energy going out of my body and plugging into the energy of the building like it's a person. Images pop up in my mind as I visualize what there is to feel. I let out a sigh. I'm making it all up, I can't feel anything.

"Can't get anything huh?" Eric asks as if he already knows the answer.

I shake my head. "I can't tell." I confess.

"About as aware as a brick." He says plainly. "You think about it too much."

How can I not think? What else am I supposed to do?

Try. Practice makes perfect. Don't make your failure more than it is.

But his argument of thinking too much doesn't make sense. Our brain tells us what's going on so how can we not use our brain? Even feeling emotion seems like you know it through your head. You think about what people feel.

See, that's thinking about it too much again.

I sigh to myself. Part of me is being really annoying... but I suspect it's right. It's like the steps. Feel the steps before you walk down. Like they were programmed in a video game. Going down has a feeling. That wasn't emotion. Right, I don't know what that was, a new language. Only that was the programming of steps. This is a whole building!

"Neanderthals." He says with a fake sad sigh prodding me. "Too bad. There's someone in that building that's interesting. Second floor from the top. He's into some dark stuff. He has some ability too and hasn't been afraid to use it. I've got a lock on him now though. I'll have to have a talk to him when he goes to sleep." I'm frozen. Eric's tone is eerie, his suggestion dizzying. Eric says everyone has a unique frequency, their energy. Like a fingerprint that can't be duplicated. So now he has a lock on this person's energy... that he picked out from looking at an entire freaking building... and now he's suggesting he can go into this person's dream? He says the whole planet is all one big energy grid. It would be like knowing someone's phone number, call up their consciousness and you're in. Electricity travels that fast. Why not energy?

I look at him, my eyes a bit wide. What if... He turns and looks at me and I almost jump. "I shouldn't be telling you this but I know you're afraid enough that you won't try anything."

My heart drops again. Ugh, failure two, I'm too scared of everything. Why does he keep saying that? It's not true. Matthew and Justin notice we've stopped and come back.

What would I try anyway? I wouldn't even be able to tell who it was and if I could what would I do? Doesn't seem to matter. What does dark stuff mean anyway? Images of a serial killer come to mind. Or someone dancing around their apartment practicing some kind of dark rituals that involve killing animals like the guy at my building.

"Anyway," Eric says looking around the area, "I've got his frequency now so I'm sure if I get bored I might do something with it." I smile to myself. When he says he has a lock on them he did mean their frequency. Finally starting to understand.

Eric looks down at the sidewalk and points at the ground. "There are signs hidden around the world you walk in. Signs that look like one thing but mean another, like that one there."

We all look down at the ground. There's graffiti spray painted on the corner. It looks like a stencil in blue paint. It's hard to make out what it is as the image looks like one layered on another. It's a cross between a face with a gun or some kind of pointed device underneath it. My mind flashes with different possibilities to determine the secret meaning behind the image but it looks like random L.A. graffiti. Aimless nonsense that only makes sense to some stupid kid or idiot thug marking his territory.

I look up at Eric. I'm skeptical but want to understand what he's saying. Justin mentions he thinks he's seen others like it before.

"None of you are paying attention. These things are right out in the open so it's not going to be obvious what it is if you just look at it. It's a way for them to communicate with one another. The message is really underneath the picture. You can't look at it and think you're going to figure it out. It's not that kind of code. It's what is underneath... beneath the picture. That's the message. Look, I'm hungry so let's get going but I am telling you there is more to that thing than meets the eye. It's what is embedded within it that tells you what it is and you need to be aware of things like this. There are signs all around that hold a different language. They mean one thing on the surface and another under it."

Eric starts walking down the sidewalk. We all turn and look down at it again. I pace around it trying to see it from different angles. Picturing it with different layers taken off so I can see what's underneath as Eric suggested.

Matthew says, "Huh." As if he suddenly understands and starts walking away. Justin follows after him.

My brain burns, a little frustrated. It's three feet away. Matthew and Justin probably got it, what's wrong with me? I can see all the lines they can and even tried looking at the blank spaces and not the lines themselves to see if that makes any sense. It's random graffiti. If he knows it meant something he should have pointed out what the picture was. Ah crap, I have to store this one in memory. I'm not going to figure it out now. Maybe later it'll make more sense. Maybe there's something there, maybe not.

Walking towards the café I'm confused. Why did Eric really stop at the corner? Sometimes he seems deliberately vague and mysterious and doesn't make any sense.

Doesn't he make sense?

Sighing I look up at the others walking ahead. Of course he makes sense. More sense than anybody I ever met. It's coded... the sign and his meaning. He means something by it only I don't understand what.

We talk for a long time over coffee. Eric tells us a few stories about his youth and working as a psychic. He started doing psychic readings for people when he was about twelve, telling people their future. As long as he can remember he's had paranormal experiences. God, imagine being 12 years old and telling people their future. If some 12 year old told me my future and ended up being right it would freak me out.

Eric talks about awareness and how hard it is to remain aware. The conversation we're having will make us aware but as soon as a dish crashes or some cute girl walks by we'll lose it. Most of his job, he explains, is to keep us on our toes. It takes constant care and attention. Even the act of simply listening to the stuff he talks about helps but the Red Cell world is a moment away. In the beginning you have to stay close to the teacher, to the source, to keep you aware. Awareness has a lot to do with energy. In the beginning its all about energy and who you keep around you has a big impact on your energy, your vibration.

Eric continues and explains how the consciousness of others creates a web, a program, around us. It's the box that holds us in. When we stay around people with a low tonal it's harder to awaken. He stresses the importance of spending time with him, other students, or other spiritual people who have a higher tonal. It will help us as we start out.

He takes a fork from the table. "The fork", he tells us, "is a tuning fork. It is idle by itself." Now he picks up his knife. "Until you put it next to a tuning fork that's already vibrating. What happens when an idle tuning fork is placed next to a tuning fork that's moving?"

"It begins to vibrate." Matthew and Justin say almost simultaneously.

"Right." Eric demonstrates hitting the knife against the table and placing it next to the fork. "If it was a tuning fork it would move to the knife's frequency. Now you, the fork, are vibrating. But what happens when all you hang around are idle tuning forks?" He puts the fork on the table near his spoon and coffee cup.

"The spoon starts vibrating?" Matthew asks with a little smirk.

"Maybe. Mostly they disperse the energy, or vibration, you had and you slow down." Eric states.

Eric points out Matthew's behavior of hugging everyone as an example of a quick way to disperse energy. He likes that Matthew's compassionate and feels like expressing it but every time he hugs someone they're sapping some of his energy. I think about that. Matthew hugs people all the time. Every person he meets or says hi to. Always touching them, arm wrapped around people, very affectionate and warm. It's hard to imagine him changing that.

Eric keeps talking, "By being around me his tonal has increased. But by running around hugging every person he sees he's giving it all away and it will be harder for him to stay aware. The Asians have it right. They don't shake hands really or touch when they greet someone. They do what?" Eric asks.

"Bow." Justin and Matthew say together.

"That's right. No loss of energy but they acknowledge each other. I don't even like shaking someone's hand because it's like a direct conduit between your two energy fields. They can just suck off energy unless you know how to hold it in. Imagine being a politician and running around shaking hands, hugging people, kissing babies all day. Just doing that would make you exhausted because of all the people sapping your energy."

Eric talks at great length about energy and how others affect it. He tells us about the energy of where we live, the area we live in, the consciousness of all the people around us and how that affects us, everything. It starts to become more clear to me. I can see the connection he's making even if I can't feel it. It still seems so abstract. He's saying all this stuff about energy loss and high energy but what does it mean really? Does he mean a positive attitude or being happy? I know everything is energy and we're supposed to have energy bodies but I've never felt drained from hugging someone so to a certain extent what he's saying doesn't make sense. When he explains it I understand much better how it's supposed to work, only I have no evidence or proof it actually works that way. After awhile we start to get the shakes from too much coffee. We walk back to the car and Eric takes us home.

When we get home Matthew goes to the porch to smoke and Justin heads out to talk to him. I turn on the TV to see what's on. After a few minutes I feel irritated. What's bothering me? Suddenly a distinct feeling comes over me. It feels lethargic, sluggish and depressing. My whole brain feels like ooze. I keep watching TV as I pay attention to the sensations until it grows stronger. Is it the TV? My finger blitzes to the remote, quickly turning it off. Shaking my head I try to get rid of the feeling. It's gross! I laugh at myself for thinking that would make a difference. How come I never noticed before how it makes me feel? I've slipped into a habit of watching TV all the time and never realized that it makes me feel like I feel now. I'm alarmed but excited. I finally noticed something! I'm aware! I'm no longer a brick!

Stopping I sit and pay attention to how I feel, internally, with the TV off. The strange oozey sensation of being doped up starts to change and I feel more normal. Unbelievable! When people say TV makes your brain mush I didn't think they meant it literally. It's crazy! Inside I bounce with excitement and encouragement. After so long of watching TV aimlessly! I retreat to my room to pace and think about it. As I pace I think back to the sluggish feeling I noticed and I shake my whole body. It makes my skin crawl to feel that way. Madness! Total madness! Why hasn't anyone ever pointed that out before? I can't be the first person to ever notice it.

I go to sleep with a smile on my face. Happy that I was finally aware of something by myself.

The next day everyone at The Hostel goes off to work on a movie. They won't be home until late. I spend the day on the computer. When night falls I decide to treat myself by heading down to the local Denny's to eat dinner. We haven't gone to the grocery store and there's nothing left to eat. Not even a potato or can of soup. On my way back I'm walking briskly with my hands in my pockets to stay warm when I remember Eric telling me never to walk with my hands in my pockets.

"Right, sorry." I say to Eric as if he were there reminding me. I quickly take them out. God, that's going to be hard to do, I always walk with my hands in my pockets.

Do you want to be more aware or less aware?

Remembering how it felt to notice the TV the night before I know it isn't a real question. I want to be more aware.

Well, if you want to be more aware it's going to take a little work. Eric said it isn't easy but if you don't try it's not even possible.

I stop to hear myself out.

"No," I say to myself out loud on the sidewalk, "I know it's possible." It's dark and people rarely ever walk in my neighborhood at night. Part of me becomes self-conscious and looks around. So what if they hear me talking to myself, everyone else does it here. It helps me think.

"Well, if it's possible then that's all there is to it." I say confidently.

That's right. That's how you have to look at it. The clear voice encourages.

"Yes, if it can be done I can do it. I just gotta practice."

With my hands out I start walking the way Eric showed me. I take a deep breath of cold air. Not caring about whether I'm as successful as when I was with Eric or not I take pride in knowing I remembered to do it. Even remembering everything, he said to me, is hard. As soon as I walk into the entryway of the apartment complex I bolt automatically for the stairs and then stop at the doorway and throw my head back and laugh.

"Ahhhh! I'm a robot!" I shout out loud. I'd fallen back again and went on auto-pilot right where I did before. As soon as the cold air is gone and I was in the warmth of the building I stopped trying to be aware. I shake my head and grin. I am Eric, the human hamster, watch me run the maze. It's funny. I slow down and force myself to walk up the stairs like Eric's walking behind me, ready to pounce on me the moment I automate.

By the time I get to The Hostel I really feel like meditating. I'm buzzing and energized. It'll feel really good to sit down and try it again. It's been several days since I tried to do it. The apartment is dark so I flip on the kitchen light. I walk into the bathroom leading to my room and turn that light on as well. Stopping I decide not to turn my bedroom light on. The light from the bathroom sends a beam right by my bed where I'll sit and meditate. That should be enough light. I kick off my shoes and pop the meditation tape in. I want to be able to hear if anyone opens the door since I'm meditating with my door open so I keep the tape volume low.

Pushing my back against the mattress I start to meditate. Right away, everything feels really good. Less than a minute into it the sound of squeaking metal and sudden, gushing water makes me jump. The sound's coming from the bathroom!

I open my eyes and quickly look toward the source. I'm sitting directly in front of my bedroom door about eight feet from it. The sink in the bathroom is in clear view and it's gushing water. Hot water. A cloud of steam rises from the sink and clouds the mirror.

What just happened? I stand up and walk into the bathroom to stare at the sink. The water is rushing out full blast so much that the water is hitting the bottom of the sink and splashing up onto the counter. The billowing cloud of steam has completely clouded the mirror. It doesn't make any sense, how could it turn on like that? We've been in The Hostel over six months and never had any problems with the water. The plumbing is a little old but nothing ever happened like this. And how could it turn on full blast, shouldn't it leak first? I was in here not even five minutes before and the sink was fine. I didn't even use it but I would have heard the water leaking or seen it.

I turn the knob to shut off the hot water. My surprise cranks up a notch as I keep turning and turning the knob. It'd been turned up the whole way. I finally shut it off and grip it firmly with my hands. Grunting, I twist it as tightly as I can. If it leaks like that when we aren't home it could flood bathtubs full of water. There has to be some logical reason. There must have been some kind of pressure that surged through all the pipes. Maybe something happened in the laundry room. Wouldn't that affect both hot and cold though? And how would that turn the knob all the way? Wouldn't it just spit water out? I imagine the washing machines shaking simultaneously and shooting water through the whole complex causing everyone's pipes to burst spitting water.

I frown. I don't know anything about plumbing but I've never heard of anything like that. We're on the fourth floor too. Could it carry that much pressure that far? I'm not satisfied but it makes the most sense. Suddenly the thought crosses my mind that someone's in the apartment with me. It feels like someone walked into the living room. I spin to catch them but nobody's there. Well, that would make sense too. Someone's playing a joke. The music was so low I would have heard them walk though. Everything in the old place creaks and it's even less likely someone's here. The apartment's too small. I can hear everything that goes on in it. No, it makes more sense that something happened to the whole complex.

Ah, just check anyway.

I search through the apartment checking the closets and cabinets. I check the porch and front door, both are locked. It takes less than 3 minutes to search the whole place. There aren't any places to hide really. Satisfied I've turned the water as far as it could go and searched the apartment I shrug it off and go back into my bedroom to meditate. I'll start wherever it's playing. The tape is still going so I sit, take a few deep breaths, and go back to meditating.

Less than a minute passes when the sound of squeaking metal grates against my ears. My eyes shoot open and I spin my head to look in the bathroom. Steam is flaring out of the sink from the hot water gushing, full blast, out of the nozzle!

"What the hell?" I swear out loud and jump up to go turn it off.

I quickly start turning the knob and find it's been opened as far as it can go again! How the hell could that happen again? My memory replays me turning the knob minutes before. I turned it as hard as I could. My memory confirms it. I turned it so tight I couldn't turn it anymore. This is ridiculo- I immediately stop thinking as the sudden awareness that someone is standing right behind me sends a shock through my whole system. I twirl around as fast as I can to confront them.

I stare at nothing.

My mind races. My whole body is on edge. I can feel my feet touching the carpet on the ground. I feel my jeans hanging against my legs, my shirt partly away from my body and the air between my clothing and my skin and the air moving through my nose. My eyes slide quickly around with no movement from my head scanning wildly for any visual clue.

I can feel, without a single, shred of doubt in my mind, that someone is standing two feet in front of me.

If I took a person and placed them right in the doorway to the bathroom it would make sense. I could see the person there. I could feel them, their presence, physically there. If they suddenly became invisible I could still feel them. I stand, staring into nothing. But it isn't nothing. Someone is right there in front of me. Only I can't see them.

Not someone. Something.

That single change in thought sends terror and panic slamming through me. Holy shit, it's an entity! My whole body locks up in horrific fear. A wave of cold shock seizes me. No! No! No! No! I'm screaming inside my head. I don't want to believe it. I can't believe it. They aren't real. They don't exist. It's so real. It's so present. There's something right there, feet away from me, and I know it. Every part of me screams to shut down. I want it to not be there. I can't deny how real it feels. I'm so scared I can't do anything. I can't scream, or defend myself... or run.

Then something kicks in. Adrenaline shoots through my system. My mind comes back to life, shouting inside my head, 'Shit! Run, FUCKING RUN!' I'm too frozen to scream out loud. My whole body runs by itself. It knows what to do. Forget fight or flight there's only flight.

Every instinct in my body kicks in and I run. I run for my fucking life. Running for the door my coat sits on top of my shoes. I grab them and run. I don't stop to lock my door. I don't stop to even wonder if I have keys or a way to get back in. I don't stop to put on my shoes. I don't even think about being aware of where it is, what it is, or anything. My body does what it has to do. Distance equals safety. Run as fast and as far as I can. There isn't a single thought going through my brain. It's pure, adrenaline pumping fear.

My shoulder slams open the stairway door and I jump down the stairs. Four, five, six stairs at once leaping from one flight to the next. Crashing into the walls to catch me. I fly through the front door to the complex and almost trip down the stone steps. When I reach the end of the block I stop, completely out of breath, and look back. My mind's racing. Every Hollywood horror movie is subconsciously slashing through my memory. Frantically I throw my coat and shoes on.

The possibilities of what might be real and what might not be real overwhelm me. Reality isn't safe, it isn't certain. Fantasy is colliding into my world. I can't feel the walls of what is and what isn't. Every possibility starts to rise from the depths and with every thought that could be I smash them down into dust. It didn't happen. What happened didn't happen. It isn't real. I repeat to myself again and again as I run to Denny's. It isn't real. It didn't happen. Forget about it. Forget about it. It's nothing. Nothing, nothing, nothing.

I sit in Denny's for four hours feigning to drink coffee at the counter. Every once in awhile I take a quick walk back to see if anyone's car is parked on the street to signal someone's home. After a few hours I start to calm down. I push the memory away and make it unreal. Finally Matthew's car is parked on the street. Cautiously, I go back to the apartment and find everyone there laughing and joking. I linger with them in the living room late into the night, never saying a word. They'll think I'm crazy. Worse, they might believe me. It isn't real. They shouldn't believe me. Don't think about. Stop thinking about it. I succeed and stop thinking about it. When I'm finally so exhausted I can't help but sleep I crawl into my room and lie down staring at the ceiling.

An image of Kathy telling me about her encounter with an entity and how she never sleeps on her back flashes through my head. I roll over so fast onto my side I almost hit the wall my bed is pressed against.

Don't sleep on your back, don't sleep on your back, I repeat to myself until I fall asleep...

growing up, every house has doors that are not to be opened until you're older... never does reality hold up to the fantasy... or does it?

Secrets of the Psychic

chapter twenty-two

A few days later Matthew and I visit Eric. Eric wants to speak with Matthew alone so I wander into the main house. Walking into the kitchen I stop in my tracks. There it is... again...

A sink full of dishes.

More dishes than any one person should do alone. No doubt Eric will come in here and have to do them all again. All the time he spends with Matthew and I, he must have put in ten times that with the others, they've known him for so long.

I stare at the pile of dishes thinking about every meal Eric's cooked for us, every new place he's taken us and every bit of advice and knowledge he's shared. The only thing he's ever asked in return was for Matthew to quit smoking pot, which is a gift in itself. The house is Eric's. At the very least he's given these guys a place to live. I'm sure they pay rent but it doesn't mean he has to clean up after them. Eric told me Jason and Peter are his two greatest students. Why do the others fail?

Laziness maybe? Ungratefulness...

My brush with the entity makes everything Eric ever told me more real. It gives it weight. Part of me is still trying to deny the entity was ever there. It's trying to repress the whole event and block it from my mind. I can't. The very realness of it is so... shocking. I never expected it to be so... *there*. So present. When Kathy told me about her entity I thought it would be like a movie. I thought it would be some glowing figure and would be somehow fantastic. It never dawned on me it would be like it was. To feel it so close and know with such certainty that something I couldn't see with my eyes was there. To know my eyes are so undependable and other levels of reality exist. It's hard to take. But, it holds true to everything Eric's told me.

Looking at the dishes, I know what I have to do.

I walk to the sink. Picking up the sponge I set to work. Burning into my mind with willful execution I lay out laws... I will not be lazy. I will not be ungrateful. I won't allow someone so giving to be used like this.

If they won't do their own dishes I'll do them. What would Jason and Peter do? Jason threw a BBQ at his house for everyone. He never asked anyone to help with anything. They would do the same. I finish all the dishes and put them away then go sit in the living room. After awhile Matthew and Eric come in. We sit and talk casually about life. After awhile Eric asks me how I'm doing with things and if I have any questions.

Leaning forward I feel my thoughts intensify. Do I tell him? Do I ask? Will it freak Matthew out? Well, Matthew will probably believe it. Of course, they'll both believe it... crap, will that freak me out?

"Oh my God, you're so slow. You've been sitting here the whole time and you're just now thinking of questions?" Eric's question has a certain intensity to it. I don't say anything about the dishes. He has a point. I've been thinking about this for a few days, I should know whether I'm going to say anything or not. Inside my head I start screaming – ARRRGHHHH!

Shutup! Just spill it.

"Okay, well, so... something happened." I mumble.

"Okay..." Eric says already sounding impatient. "Well, don't sit there, feel free to tell us."

"Right. Um, well..." I start struggling and throw my head back and laugh out loud.

"Come on freak show." Matthew jokes giving Eric a hopeless look like he can't help explain my actions. "Why don't you be more random about it?"

They both make fun of how long it takes me to say anything. I can't hold it anymore. There is no grace in my delivery. I have no lead-in. I don't even know how to begin. I immediately start rambling about how I'm not nuts but something crazy happened that seems crazy but I'm absolutely certain it did, in fact, take place. They both look at me like I'm on drugs so I start rambling about meditating, and hot water gushing, and someone in the apartment but nobody is there and more water.

Eric finally puts his hand up and tells me to stop. "What the hell are you talking about?" He says very slowly. "I don't think either of us get anything you're saying. Do you know what he's saying?" He asks Matthew.

"Umm, no way, I think he needs to stop smoking crack though." Matthew says with a confused grin.

I laugh. Yeah, it probably does seem like I'm on crack.

"Well..." I start then stop myself. Don't ramble on again, hold yourself together. I want to spit it out and get it over with. "Entity!" I blurt out. "It was an entity... in the apartment."

They're both quiet for a few seconds. Matthew looks completely surprised. "What?!" He says slightly stunned.

The flood gates open. I spill the story. What I believed happened with the missing clue of the ending. I keep going giving them everything, even my shameful sprint out of the apartment, shoes in hand, and hiding out at Denny's for hours. Trying to grasp the intensity of the encounter I start to wave my hands around and push against Matthew sitting next to me so they understand how real it felt.

"Had I reached out, it was so real... you don't understand... I could have felt the thing!" I explain growing desperate to hear a reaction.

Eric and Matthew look at each other and Eric starts cracking up. His face turns a cheery red and they both have a good laugh picturing me fleeing for my life out of the apartment. Neither of them can believe I've sat on the story for days and said nothing. Trying to explain, I tell them how I've tried to repress it and ignore it. My fear was first that I'd be ridiculed, or that people would think I'm crazy or unstable. Then, I started to be afraid of confirmation. If they believed me it would be harder to ignore or neglect and I'd have to confront an even greater fear; we aren't alone in this reality and my eyes are useless like locks on the doors! It makes my chest start to constrict and it's hard to breathe. I feel incredibly vulnerable and insecure.

"They could be anywhere!" I exclaim. "They could do anything at any time and I'm helpless to do anything! I can't see them, or lock them out, or defend myself!" It took everything I believed. It took my entire reality. Everything I ever believed to be solid, isn't. Everything I ever relied on, science, technology, other people for my safety like the police, are completely and totally useless.

"I'm alone! Totally alone and exposed and I've been forced to reevaluate my entire view of life and what is. It freaks me all the hell out. No warning, no reason, no understanding, no safety, no defense!"

Eric stops making fun of me and becomes more serious. "Look, I completely understand. Completely. First, let me say this. Don't panic. You're going overboard. Way, way overboard. Calm down. Okay, do you think this is the first time I've heard anything like this? Huh?"

Shaking my head, I admit, "No, I've heard stories from you about entities and I know some of the other students have run into them before too..."

"Exactly. So, why are you so worried? I mean, you should have told me earlier I could have saved you a few days of panic." He chuckles and shakes his head slightly like he can't believe I'd freak out for days and not say anything.

He leans back in the chair, "It's not true to say that you have no defense. It is also not true to say you can't fight back. You can. Absolutely you can. But let me say that you have to remember, and I've told you stories before, I've been tormented and tortured by entities since I was very young. I mean, I don't even want to tell you half the stories that have happened to me. Try being six years old, you barely understand anything anyway, and you've got things throwing you out of bed. Who are you going to talk to? Everyone thinks you're a kid who's imagining stuff! Okay, you think I'd go through my whole life putting up with that?"

Matthew and I chuckle. No, you'd probably go insane first.

He points at me and continues, "You? Please, at least you've got me! I've got answers for you! Now let me make one thing clear first. It's not like Hollywood. I keep saying that and the reason I do is because that's what you're going to base all your assumptions on. It has nothing to do with you. Okay? It's not like this thing picked you out of a crowd and is going to keep coming back. It's curiosity. That's really what it is. Imagine you live down in the darkest depths of the ocean. There's very little light and everything is different shades of grey. Suddenly, off in the distance you see a flicker of light, like a neon fish glowing, swimming through the water. As an intelligent being is that going to get your attention? You bet it is. Are you going to check it out? Sure you are."

Taking a deep breath in I nod my head. I'm following. I'm a neon fish and it's a curios shark coming to eat me.

"If you are a being of pure energy, an entity, that's how you're going to see this reality. This dimension!" Eric spreads his fingers out and waves his hands to show that he means everything. "You don't have eyes like we do so you aren't going to see walls, buildings and colors. You're going to 'see' frequencies of energy. Everything on Earth pretty much stays in the same frequency. It's the DOE you know? The tonal and vibration of the planet. Slight variations but you guys get what I mean right?"

Matthew and I nod our heads.

"So, when you meditate and you start raising your consciousness, pushing your energy higher, your tonal is going to start vibrating at a higher frequency. To something that views everything as energy that's going to look different. You're going to stick out. Remember not all meditations do that. That's why I meditate the way I do because it raises your consciousness. Plus you've been working on your psychic senses. Going out scanning, that's psychic sensory. You're going to be able to feel things beyond your five senses. Now, if I'm an intelligent being, cruising through the area and I pick up on something different than everything else, well guess what I'm going to go do?"

I smirk. "You're going to stop and look at the strange little bug?"

"Well, don't make yourself out to be so small, you have more power in this dimension than they do. But yeah, it's kind of like that. They have no interest in you personally. What's more, look at what it did. It didn't push you against the wall... or throw things at you like in some kind of movie. There was nothing threatening about it at all. It turned on your water. Guess what? It was trying to communicate. It was trying to get your attention. You get me? You can't see it. It knows you can feel it. If only it could ring the doorbell so you'd wake up and answer. So it rang the doorbell and what happened?"

Matthew laughs. "He answered and ran out of the house screaming."

I start laughing too. It sounds stupid when it's explained rationally. Takes some of the edge off the fear.

"That's right. You answered. You felt it and then you freaked out but that's experience. Just because it's different doesn't make it bad.

Every person on this planet has different personalities, intentions, desires. Other kinds of beings aren't any different. It's actually very rare to run into something that has bad intentions. Most are neutral like meeting a person on the street. We just assume anything unknown is something to be afraid of. Now, here's something to consider. Think of the possibilities of what you could have learned from it had you been able to communicate. How it thinks. What it's experienced. What it could have shared. It will probably be awhile before you're able to do that but, thought I'd throw it out there." Eric gives me a knowing look over the rim of his glasses. At times Eric suddenly seems much older than he looks. The feeling in his voice takes on a kind of gravity. His last statement hits me with a weight.

I missed a chance. Fear and ignorance. I've been driving myself crazy for days and I never once thought for a second about communicating with it. Why didn't that ever occur to me? He's right. How incredible would that have been? Like talking to someone from another galaxy.

Eric leans back into his recliner. "Don't beat yourself up over it. That's what experience is about. You learn and grow. Fear is powerful when you're confronted with something like that. The important thing is for you to feel safe. Even though most entities don't mean any harm there are a few exceptions. Usually you have to go looking for it but I can teach you guys how to protect yourselves. I've been through all this shit so I'll give you the radar and the Uzi and tell you everything you need to know. You think I went through my whole life and simply put up with it? Please. They tried to scare me into not awakening. They wanted to freak me out so bad that I would never pursue my spirituality. That's what happened to my brother. He was shaken out of sensing things by fear. No." He shakes his head with a resolved look on his face. "They made a mistake with me. Rather than making me frightened they made me pissed off. They didn't make me run away they trained me to become a bad-ass. They made me a fighter and trust me." He puts his hand on his chest, "Trust me. When I started figuring out how they worked and that I could hurt them the tables turned very quickly. I started hunting them down!" He shouts. "I went and tracked down every haunted place and entity I could find and I tore them to shreds. Now I have to hide my energy. I wish they came at me the way they used to. I get bored now. Now it would be great if I had something to play with. When they feel my energy move into the area they all take off right outta there!" He says laughing. His laughter makes me feel at ease.

He smiles at me, in a calm, you've so got nothing to worry about way. "But I'll teach you guys how to defend yourselves and take on entities. You can use the same techniques for psychic combat and defense, which I've had to do my fair share of as well, though not as often. Okay? All my students go through this and they all survive. It's a good thing. Really."

I nod, smiling. His confidence makes me feel secure.

All his students go through this?

Suddenly reminded of Kathy's entity story I open my mouth to speak and stop myself. She said he sends entities to train his students. Did he send this one? Is that something I should ask? Eric stands up out of his chair and stretches. His hulking form reaching up to the ceiling. Searching his face his eyes seem to twinkle with a touch of amusement. It's hard to say if I'm putting that emotion on him or not. He does find it funny. Doesn't mean he sent it. How can someone be so casual about something so unbelievable?

How can you seriously ask that question?

What? You're telling me that entities exist but there's no way to have one go visit somebody? If we're going outside reality then we're outside. Eric opens the front door. Better not to ask. An entity is an entity no matter how it came to me. I'm partly afraid to ask because I don't want to consider Eric has that kind of ability. If such a thing were possible it's too much for a man. Energy beings roaming the universe is fine. Energy beings being called on by a person is another story.

We all get up and start to walk out onto the porch when Eric stops us. "Hold it." He says raising his hand. "Do this. You guys have been around long enough to know that when I start teaching you your consciousness starts to rise. You shift. That's what we call it. We call it shifting. Your mind starts to move into higher lanes of consciousness and you start to feel like, everything starts to feel good but different. You know what I'm saying?"

I nod my head yes. The ride up the mountain is what he's talking about. Shifting into higher consciousness and boy does it feel good. Even thinking back to the place I remember how wonderful it was and I want to feel it again. Matthew agrees that he knows what Eric's talking about.

"Good. I want you two to see how fast you can move yourselves there. We're going to walk to the garage and by the time we get there I want you to be shifted and ready. Got it?"

We're both ready. Eric starts walking at a normal pace. A little shot of panic. What if I fail? What if I can't do it? It's such a short distance, only behind the house.

Shutup! You're wasting time. Do it! Don't screw up!

I try to make my brain quiet down and focus on my body. I think about energy all around me and pay attention to my breathing. Walking by the kitchen now.

"Don't let your brain babble away!" Eric says from the front. "Concentrate and become aware. Stay calm and allow your mind to shift."

It isn't happening. I'm not doing it yet. Racing my mind pulls its focus down to the first spot in the meditation. There you go, I assure myself. I put all of my attention on the first step of the meditation so that it's like I'm meditating as I walk. My brain calms down. I start to feel the sensations and tag them as 'shifting'.

I'm at the garage door. Eric opens the door and we walk in. Angus and Duncan are behind us and start to follow us in. Eric tells them to not even think about it and they back off. The old relics in his display case are hidden in slight darkness but my eyes are drawn to them. There's so much mystery there that takes on a whole new light.

Before they were nothing but props. Simple belongings that had no real magic or meaning but were more for effect. Now, I don't know... there could be something more to them. Everything's an unknown and I have to reevaluate it all.

I sit on the larger black couch while Matthew sits on the smaller one closest to the door. Eric stands by his computer desk and looks around. He sits down in his black office chair and reclines staring at me. The room immediately begins to intensify and thicken like it is suddenly filling with water. Surprise triggers a little panic. I never noticed before but I'm certain it happens often with him. So much more alive. Like feeling the entity. There's a realness to it even though I can't see it. It's there, some kind of thing. Instead of trying to deny it or ignore it I watch it in the back of my mind. The longer he sits quietly the more intense the feeling becomes. It's so thick it begins to be uncomfortable. Like sitting next to a huge power line and hearing and feeling the hum of electricity you know is saturating the whole area. It's intimidating and exhilarating at the same time. Energy. It's his energy. I'm giddy inside. I never felt energy but maybe this is it, that's what I'm feeling.

If I can notice it then it's something. If it's something it deserves observation. I take a deep breath in. Part of me struggles to push it away. I try to recollect my thoughts.

"Everything okay?" Eric asks with a knowing smirk.

I look up at him and smile. He must know what he's doing. There must be some way to control it. A light bulb goes off in my head.

Of course there is, stupid. He showed you energy movements and said they help you get more control of your energy.

Of course! God! How easily I forget all this stuff. Another light bulb goes off in my head but it's more like an internal thud. A heavy realization in a potato bag. Yes, it's easy to forget this stuff. Too easy. I have a very good memory.

Eric clears his throat distracting me. "All right, don't go off too far. You guys have that shifted spacey look to you."

Matthew and I laugh. I could sit here for hours and let my head spin. It feels so good. Like it's nourishing.

Eric begins, "Now, I'm going to say a few things to both of you and... I don't know how you're going to take it. It's a little different than what you've heard before. I want you both to know the seriousness of what I'm about to teach you. Right now, the truth or the weight of it isn't going to hit you. Get it?" He leans farther back and looks at the ceiling. "It's like; I need you to grasp the weight of what it is I'm sharing with you before you understand what it is. In order to make sure you know I'm going to have to make sure you have at least a grasp of what it is I'm going to show you! Do you guys kinda get what I'm saying?"

I feel lost and stare blankly at Eric hoping Matthew will say something. I'm not going to say I do because I don't, but I'm not ready to say I don't because maybe I kind of do.

Matthew nods his head slowly. "I think I kinda get it."

Eric leans forward and puts his arms on his knees. He sighs and I can tell he isn't yet satisfied with his presentation. I feel better because I have no idea what he's really trying to say. "Okay, I'm going to show you both techniques for psychic attack and defense. This is not the kind of shit you play around with. This is serious, powerful stuff that you two don't have any appreciation for, okay? Everyone else out there practicing magick or O.T.O. or any of that crap all go through these elaborate rituals that are time consuming and for the most part useless. Understand? I'm telling you the other stuff is crap because I know neither of you have any experience with anything else. Somebody could come along and tell you what they know is ten times better and you'd believe them. It's not, believe me, I've seen and done it all. There is nothing out there that compares. You'll see it in time. They're all kidding themselves with ego boosts. They can play with their junk because it doesn't work. Do not, I repeat, do not play with this stuff because it does work. Get me?"

We both nod. His tone has taken on a serious intensity. The room has a weight that makes me feel a little sick. Do I want to know what he's about to teach or is it too much? Before I would have brushed off my concerns with indifference. Now I have to consider what he's going to say as very probably true. That element of truth makes the responsibility and the effect of it a little stressful. I can't un-know what I know.

"It's like you can do one kind of psychic attack and it might take you an hour to get it ready, then another few hours to execute it, and it will have little to any effect. Or you can do it my way and in an instant," he snaps his fingers and the sound cracks through the air like a board splitting, "it's already done. By the sheer activation of your will, you have done it. That's power. It's taken me years to perfect it and I'm still not going to tell you all of it. This will be enough. You both get what I'm saying?"

We both silently nod our heads. I glance over to Matthew who looks a little pale. I feel the same way.

"Now..." he takes his hand and wipes his palm along his forehead. He looks hot. It's cool in the room but he's starting to sweat. "I'm not teaching you this form of... psychic attack so that you can go out and hurt someone or show off how powerful you are. I don't think either one of you have that in you anyway and if I thought you did I certainly wouldn't teach you. Get it? That's not the reason I'm showing you. I don't intend for you to use it like that. I'm showing it to you because it has other applications. Like fighting entities." He motions to me. "Or if you ever are psychically attacked, because you know how to do it, you will understand better how someone else can do it and better defend yourself. If you think these things don't happen... I mean, please, trust me. It's out there. The more you get into this the more you'll see. It wasn't too long ago I was in a restaurant in L.A. I go to a lot, Canter's. Well, a group of people who were well-trained in psychic abilities came in all wearing military-like uniforms. Okay? Eric, you kinda know who they are, I showed you their church across from the coffee shop we were at..." he says looking at me.

I think about it and remember the place. I nod my head, "Yeah."

"Well, I'm telling you guys this so that if you see them you'll know they aren't with the military. Their uniforms look very military-like but they aren't. There's a lot there you guys don't know but let me just say they picked up on me and I picked up on them and they took it to that level." He moves his hand above his head to suggest the higher level. They took it to the psychic realm.

"There was about six of them and they engaged me, psychically. We started kinda throwing down, you could say." He laughs. "When things happen on that level, psychic level, unless you're aware or trained you'd never know it. It's not like it ever interferes with things on this level." He moves his hands in front of him to suggest this level of reality. "Needless to say I was a little surprised how skilled they were plus there were a lot of them. Well, I shifted up a few notches and let's just say they were the ones that became a little surprised. In their understanding of the world someone like me isn't supposed to exist. I took it to a level they'd never even heard of and when I go to that level it's like psychic stuff becomes child's play. So, it's kinda like there's this intense struggle and once I go to that place I yawn and it's more than anything they can handle. Psychic abilities just can't touch that place. So they took off pretty fast and I'm sure it gave them a lot to think about." He laughs.

I have no idea what in the world he's talking about. There's so much in what he says. I'm sure of it. I picture every detail of his encounter. Him sitting there getting ready to eat his sandwich. Group of military-like people coming in. The radiation of the psychic intensity and both groups acknowledge each other and start to fight. There's as much in what Eric says as what he doesn't say. He said there's a place psychic abilities can't touch. That means there are levels of knowledge beyond anything he's told us about yet. The suggestion of all these other places and that they could be real makes me think we're little babies who haven't even taken our first step. A scary prospect.

Eric speaks slowly, with intent, "I tell you that so you understand, it does exist. There are people out there who have abilities and not all of them will use them for good. Now that being said, I don't believe there is a group in the world who has better skills or training than my students. Now, maybe my students don't always practice as much as they should. Still I know if I ever needed to pit any one of my students against anybody else, hands down my student would come out on top. Might take them a bit of effort to rise to the occasion but they would do it. The depth and breadth of their knowledge and understanding can't be found anywhere else. For the most part though, it's nothing you guys need to worry about for now. There are other uses that are much more practical. In other words, don't get caught up in the big 'go out and beat somebody up psychically' stuff. It's about what it can do for you spiritually. Spiritually, these are the tools that are going to get you there."

Eric tells us about the possibilities of the technique he's about to show us for psychic attack. You could give someone a heart attack or harm them physically and it wouldn't matter where in the world they were. Distance is no factor. Someone could cause headaches, make someone sick, even affect physical objects. He tells us a story he's a little ashamed of.

"Most of my students are very young. This is good because you can make the most spiritual progress and advancement when you're young. The older you get the harder it gets. It also allows them to become leaders in the future with so many years under their belts. The downside is that, like you guys, they're young and often lack wisdom and experience. Having psychic abilities doesn't mean someone is spiritually advanced. Don't mistake the two. One can be had without the other. Now, there was this time two of my students got into a... dispute, you could say. I kinda left it unchecked waiting for them to find a resolution on their own. Instead it escalated and they started using psychic abilities. They didn't use them directly on each other because they knew how I'd feel about that. They knew that was the line they couldn't cross. They shouldn't have been doing anything at all but they got into it and were willing to push the line. What they did was screw up each other's day, making little things happen here and there. Harm electrical equipment like computers when they had no access to them, and then eventually they started psychically damaging each other's cars so that they wouldn't work."

I grin and start to laugh but quickly stop myself. Eric's face is stone cold. He doesn't find anything funny about the story. It seems humorous to me that someone would go through the trouble to develop psychic abilities and then use it to disable cars. I picture them staring at the other ones car zapping it with their mind and the car starts smoking. It's comical but I keep my mouth shut.

"It was at that point I finally stepped in and put an end to the conflict. I also learned a lesson. What I'd taught them was more than they could handle. They couldn't be trusted with it. I had to place a cap on their minds to limit their psychic abilities. I could no longer allow them unlimited freedom without restraint."

My eyes widen and grow a bit larger. Place a cap on their minds? Holy crap. It's one thing to say something like that with an air of confidence or even arrogance but Eric said it with such casual ease it makes it even worse! I rub my head. He might as well have been talking about the weather he said it with an air of such normalcy! My brain twists. Before the entity I would have enjoyed his story as just that – an interesting story. Now I have to admit to myself that everything he says contains the potential to be true. There are two paths to everything he says. One path is to a purely imaginary place where it's interesting but theoretical and only a thing to think about. It isn't real. The other path... which makes me want to freak out but I need to come to terms with, is that everything could be true. It isn't like reading a textbook that's never going to be more than food for thought. It could be freaking real.

To think... that someone has the ability to tear up someone's car, with their mind, to the point that it won't work and do it from anywhere on the planet! But what the hell? Eric says he has the ability to place a cap on someone else's mind and limit what they're capable of. Holy freaking crap! I take it in. It's true first. Innocent until proven guilty. Possible until proven impossible. Don't think the other way around where things are impossible until proven possible. If it's possible it will only be proven impossible if I fail to do it. Everything he's telling us we can try for ourselves. I'll try it and then judge. It shouldn't be for him to prove to me the possibility of things. He's showing me how to do it. It's for me to prove to myself what can be accomplished and what can't.

"There's something else." he tells us. "There's a universal law that you must each swear to uphold. The main reason to use a psychic attack is to defend yourself. When I was younger someone pulled a gun on me. The person was a few feet away from me when he pulled it on me. It was basically right in my face. I was really certain that was it. I was going to be killed. Without thinking I reacted psychically and broke the mechanism of the gun. The guy pulled the trigger, I saw his finger pull it, I heard the gun click but it didn't fire. Needless to say I took right off and escaped, okay?"

Matthew and I laugh nervously. Glancing over at Matthew his mouth is a little open. I'm sure he's thinking the same thing... I would have freaked out!

Eric gets quieter, "Much later I'd think back and wonder what would have happened had I not interfered and instead trusted the Universe to protect me. You see, there's a rule about using abilities and that is to never use them on others who don't know about or possess any abilities themselves. The guy with the gun had no psychic abilities. But, I was younger then and didn't know what I know now. The Universe has a way of self-regulating itself. In a way you should consider them Universal Laws. When we use abilities on those who do not possess abilities the Universe will let you know." He laughs and insists that we should trust him on that one.

"The Universe evens the score rather quickly." He tells us. "It doesn't matter how little of an ability they have as long as they try to act on that level. Even someone using magick is willingly trying to reach you on that level which means you can act." He makes us swear that we understand and will respect this law, even if it means we could be harmed ourselves.

I'm not sure about it. "If I have the means to protect myself by using my mind shouldn't I do it regardless of what someone else is aware of or not?"

Eric nods. He holds out his hand to show me his index finger. "If I place my finger on a hot stove what would I do?"

I don't need to think about it. "You'd pull it back."

"Pretty fucking fast too right? I wouldn't even need to think about it would I?" Eric says leaning back in his chair again. The tone in the room lightens a little, as if we'd been staring at the barrel of the gun and now the threat has passed.

I shake my head no.

"Instinctually our body knows when it's in danger and will react before we are conscious of it. We just have to let it." Eric raises his eyebrows as if to ask if he's right or not.

I agree. It makes sense. I've been burned before and never had to think about taking my hand away.

"When you move into these higher regions... When you meditate and start to raise your tonal and come closer to the Force, you become a part of it. Instinctually the Force will protect itself. Like a hand being burned it will move to protect it. Had I trusted the Force to protect me I might never have needed to interfere. Maybe the gun wouldn't have gone off anyway. It should have been up to the Force to decide how it would protect me. When you willfully act and push your will into reality..." He takes his hand and spreads it over his forehead and then clenches his fist like he's grabbing energy from his mind. Then he throws his hand at me like he's throwing a ball. "It's very solid. Forceful. It affects the Gaia consciousness or grid and that has repercussions. It's a bit more than you can understand right now. Better to say, don't do it. Trust the Force. The Force is more powerful than anything you can imagine. If only you can trust enough to step aside, and let it act on your behalf. Get it?"

I get it. I swear to agree to never use what he teaches us on those without an awareness of psychic abilities or any ability of their own. He's satisfied that we understand the gravity of what he's about to teach us.

First Eric explains the practical use of his method of psychic attack. He has us imagine thin strands of energy attached to us and stretching out in all directions, like telephone wires, connected to every person we've ever met in our life. "When I talk about Gaia, I also call it the grid. Other people refer to it as the Web. There's some truth to that. We are plugged into the Gaia Mind through these connections. It's what keeps us wired in. If we meet someone during the day... that person, whether they know it or not, gets our unique frequency. Like a fingerprint or telephone number. Whenever they think about us they send a mental signal along this energy strand and it hits us."

He explains the phenomena of sitting at home and thinking about someone and then minutes later they call. They think about calling us, which sends a signal to us, we pick up on it and then they call. Or, he said, we're thinking about them which moves a signal to them. They pick up on it which makes them think of us and triggers them to call us.

He leans forward in his chair and motions with his index finger pointing at Matthew and I. "We're all connected. What most people don't realize is that there is a way to cut this webbing. There is also a way to momentarily take yourself off the grid - completely. When you cut the webbing it weakens their link to you. If they think about you on their own all they have to do is think about you and they lock onto your frequency again and they have the strand back but it's not as strong. Many times when you begin meditating and start spiritually raising your tonal it's like sending powerful energy signals through all the webbing connected to you. It's like jangling all your lines and people you haven't spoken with in 5, 10, 15 years all of a sudden come out of the woodwork and call you or track you down. I've seen it happen with everyone I've ever taught. Once they raise their tonal all these people come back into their lives.

When you raise your tonal and grow spiritually you start to move yourself off the grid. You raise your tonal beyond the DOE, the tonal of the planet. The DOE is a mechanism. It's an energy that reacts and like an automated process has a way of keeping you in the machinery. Signals sent through the webbing, that you are connected to, causes the whole machine to react, ensuring you are kept in place within the machine."

He continues for some time detailing the way the connection works and relates it to our connection to the grid and Gaia. Each passing minute increases this background sense of a kind of static intensity. It's very calming, relaxing and peaceful but at the same time feels like a pressure, like taking an exam. It's physically and mentally fatiguing but also stimulating. More than the process of learning new information I feel exhausted beyond any college cram session I've ever done.

Neither Matthew nor I can even think of a question to ask. Eric's explanation is so detailed going over every aspect of how it all ties together and functions there's nothing to ask. If a question pops in my mind, I hold it there wondering if I should ask it or try to figure it out on my own. I always hated people who asked questions without thinking first. Instead I always exhaust my own means of questioning and thinking first. Never ask until you try to know. Still, I don't want to forget my questions. It doesn't matter. Within minutes Eric has the question answered without me having to mention it. Every picture he paints and analogy he expresses adds to a movie slowly unfolding in my head. His words seem to not only register in my ears where I hear them but inside my mind as if he's speaking in images.

It feels like little bubbles of light slowly bursting in my brain like soda pop. Everything he's ever said about energy connects to what he tells us. This connects to what he's ever said about the physical universe and the Gaia mind, or the soul, and Red Cells and White Cells. It all fits together in ways that seem separate at first but make sense after he pulls back enough and shows the broadness and depth of it.

After an hour I can tell he isn't even giving us everything there is. It's just a taste of what we can handle. The possibilities of what he describes are limitless. He isn't giving us a simple technique and saying that's the end of it. He's telling us a few possibilities but every suggestion and tactic he relays never comes to an end. Never once is there a hint of an end or limit. My mind reels from the magnitude of it all.

Finally, he senses we're both at a breaking point and he stops. My eyes feel glazed over. It's such a strange feeling. Just by listening it's given me a deep sense of contentment. It's as if I'd achieved something by doing nothing more than listening. I laugh to myself. Like I ran 10 miles and knew I made good time.

He wags his finger at me, "I warned you this knowledge was addictive! I see that wild-eyed grin on your face like, wow!"

Laughing I nod my head. It isn't too far from the truth. I don't know about addictive but I want more. We air our brains out for a few minutes until we feel rested. Eric doesn't seem to need a break. He's doing all the work but he's restless to continue! As soon as he senses we can handle it he starts talking about the defensive technique.

"Okay first things first is how to defend yourself. I call this 'The Pyramid'. Remember when we watched Dune and they used those energy shields? They look like they encase them in crystal but it moves with them? Well, capture that image in your minds. Clear. Crystal-like. Perfect. That's only a starting point because your brain needs something to latch onto. It needs a structural, physical thing to grasp the technique." There are several objects in his room he has us hold in our hands. We feel them and turn them over and observe their structure, solidity, and weight.

Once we've had a chance to physically feel them he has us visualize the shapes we held in our minds. It's trickier than I thought it would be. I keep wanting to move it around and make it rubbery. Not solid and firm.

Eric turns his head and looks at Matthew. "What is it?"

Matthew puts his hand up to his head and laughs. "Ahh! I can't! It's like, it won't stay straight."

Eric chuckles. "That's why I had you hold them in your hands first. Have you ever tried to use a sword or something straight in a dream? It usually bends and moves like butter or something. Like your mind won't allow it. This is kind of the same thing. People who are more mechanically-minded would have an easier time. All I can say is don't get frustrated. Picture it slowly and methodically. Practice makes perfect."

After we practice visualizing he explains how to fill The Pyramid with energy. Its activation is instant. As fast as we can think of it and fill it with energy it's there. Once our energy is in it we have an invulnerable shield against anything energy related.

The greatest importance to me is how it will defend against entities or any kind of energy. The beauty is its amazing simplicity. "Even as simple as it is", he tells us, "there's nothing, absolutely positively nothing that can penetrate it once you've activated it."

A relief washes over me. There's been a slight, but constant, tightness in my chest ever since the entity. A kind of anxiety that everywhere I go I feel totally vulnerable. Nothing is solid and energy is energy to an entity. Walls are useless. Here at last Eric offers instant safety and security. My guard comes down and for the first time in days I feel relaxed.

After discussing the activation of the technique and different ways it can be used Eric asks us to sit on the floor. Matthew and I sit next to each other, about five feet apart, in front of the couches. Eric pushes his chair away to the other end of the room and sits facing us.

"Now, I'll walk you guys through using The Pyramid with what I call The Sword. The Sword's as easy as The Pyramid and now that you understand psychic attack it will make sense to you. In this case we aren't going to learn about using it for attack, but you'll understand how to do it. We're going to use them together to remove the energy webbing connected to you from every person you've ever met and take yourselves off the grid momentarily. Knowledge like this, relating to energy attack and defense I call High Guard. Technically this is High Guard level 1 but I don't really teach anything past this anymore because you can take this pretty far as it is." He turns off the lamp directly above him on the desk. With the added darkness I suddenly notice the air looks like it's filled with white, static dots. It's the energy he showed us before but I can't see any color. I only notice it's like watching television on a bad channel without cable. Little dots all over the place.

There's a thick charge in the room. I swallow in anticipation. We all breathe in together and a little wave of heat washes over me. Eric begins to lead us through the techniques.

"The Sword is similar to The Pyramid in that you'll create it and draw it from your own energy body. You'll need to visualize it to start with until you can feel your energy more and pull it from there. The closest thing I've seen to what they really look like are Light Sabers from Star Wars. More like pure energy than an old steel sword. Something that glows and hums with power and can cut through anything. If you study seeing auras you could get to the point where you can see them."

Great, now we're making Light Sabers like we're Jedi Knights or something. Instantly a part of me feels foolish. What kind of sensible grown adult would be caught dead sitting on the floor cutting, 'energy webbing'? It sounds so New Agey and hokey I feel a little ashamed. One week ago I would have rolled my eyes and laughed at myself.

Another part of me quickly jumps in and yells at me for being so lazy and uninquistive. How will I ever know the truth of it if I don't try? Am I supposed to assume I know it all? I laughed about entities too.

I don't know everything. The only way to know if it works is to try. My mind leaps back to where Eric and Matthew are. Eric has us activate our Pyramids. He walks us through becoming aware of the webbing. For a moment, it almost seems like I can feel something really connected to me. I brush it off as my over-active imagination. Next we create The Sword.

With The Pyramid still active we use The Sword to cut the energy webbing. In the middle of performing the Sword technique I feel a slight, but noticeable lightness. My head cocks unintentionally to the side as if it'll help me answer the question. What just happened?

It's there, I can still feel it. Almost like a physical weight suddenly gone. Like I'd been carrying a backpack I didn't know I had on and just took it off. That isn't a satisfying label for it. I keep digging in deeper trying to nail down exactly what the feeling is but I can't pin it on anything. It isn't like anything I've felt before but it feels familiar.

It's relieving. Makes me feel lighter but in a way I can't rationalize. My posture hasn't changed. The air in the room hasn't changed. I'm not expecting anything to happen. Eric didn't mention at all what it would feel like or if we were supposed to feel anything.

We go through the rest of the sequence and stop. Matthew and I both sit in silence. Matthew's stooped forward a little with a slightly confused look on his face. God, I probably have the same look. I feel that my eyebrows have been furrowed as I analyze what took place. I stop and let them lift. Well, note to self, that was... different.

Eric lets us take everything in. "Well, how was that?"

What do I say? There's nothing I can tell him. Hard to describe.

Matthew rocks back a little. "I could feel, I don't know what, but, I could feel something. Like I could really feel a change when we cut the strands."

Eric says nothing but turns and looks at me. "Eric?"

Slowly shaking my head I explain, "Yeah. Me too. Don't know how to describe it."

Quietly Eric clears his throat. "Good. Don't think about it too much, you'll limit yourself. You guys should do that at least once a week starting out." He pauses for a moment. "There's one more thing. I've been debating in my head this whole time, having, like, a side conversation to myself about whether to show this to you guys. I've decided I'm going to show you both how to do something else. Here's the condition. You both have to promise... no, swear. You both have to swear to me you will never, ever, ever tell anyone else how to do this. I don't care if they are a student or your mother or you're on your death bed and I'm long gone and you figure, what the heck, it doesn't matter now. You must never tell another living soul until I give you permission otherwise. You both understand me? And I am being so serious you have no idea."

"Because if either of you ever broke this promise I would never teach either of you anything, ever again. I would ex you so fast you wouldn't know what happened. You get me? Not only that but at the moment you started telling someone how to do it you'd feel a little sharp pain in your head, and get like, a little headache... and then you'd kinda shake it off and you'd be like, now what were we talking about? And just like that." He snaps his fingers in front of his face. Eric has a slight frown and a scowl to show us how serious he's being. "You'd have forgotten it and most everything I ever taught you."

I chuckle at the thought of someone suddenly being so dumbfounded. It's like an old wizard cartoon.

"You think I'm joking?" He says deadpanning right at me. The intensity of his gaze and tone of his voice wipes the smile right off my face.

"You're not joking?" I ask him naively.

He forces a smile and shakes his head no. "You have no idea." He says matter-of-factly. "It would happen just like that. And the fact that I'm telling you now and making you aware of the repercussions means I wouldn't think twice about it. If you don't think you can handle it then tell me now and I won't teach it to you. You'll learn everything else I know, in good time, and your knowledge will be safe. It won't change whether or not I'll teach you from here on or not. What I am giving you is an opportunity that I don't share with all of my students. That opportunity comes with a price. I can take the memory from you in less than a second and you wouldn't even know enough to know you'd forgotten it. It would just be gone. Poof!" He blows through his hand to illustrate my memory vanishing into the air.

Despite the suggestion of what would happen I don't feel threatened by Eric. I take his threat in stride and I don't doubt he would act on it. After everything he's told us about psychic attack I realize the possibilities. It's hard to completely believe he could do it but it's possible. What I do know is that I don't feel threatened because I believe in his judgment. He wouldn't do it without good reason. You promise to keep something important that could cause harm if it were given to the wrong person you have to keep it. His motives and his intentions feel like they're in the right place. That being the case, I have nothing to fear. If I ever break a promise he'd be right to do what he's saying he would do. It's a little unsettling to think he could do what he's saying but... it's safer and more comfortable to think about it from a perspective of right and wrong. If I break a promise I'd be wrong and he wouldn't be harming me, he'd only be reclaiming what he'd freely given.

It's hard to tell what Matthew's thinking so I try to explain my thoughts to them.

He nods and motions his hands to say, well, there you go. "Yeah, that works. However you want to look at it."

Matthew stays quiet and we both look at him. He weaves his head back and forth and starts to say, "Ehh, well, yeah... I mean, I get what you're saying and all..."

What is he doing? Is Matthew going to say something against the

grain? I put my hands on my chin. Matthew is about to disagree. He's always gone to great lengths to never disagree with anything.

"It's just..." Matthew strains.

He doesn't want to say it whatever it is. God, this has got to be painful for him. I shift my head to look at Eric who's rolling his hands to get Matthew to spit it out.

"It's just what?" Eric said. "Come on, just say it. I'm open to whatever you have to say. Never do something because I say it. Always question everything including me."

"Yeah. I know. You say that a lot and stuff but... like, well, it's like... just, um, I mean I don't want to, like, agree to something without, you know, like, really knowing what is the thing I'm like, generally agreeing to. You know what I'm saying?"

Eric turns slightly to look at me. "Not really. Do you know what he's saying?"

"Uh," I think I get the gist of what Matthew's trying to say but he didn't give me much to go on. "I think like, he's saying that how can he promise something without knowing like... um... the general context of what it is he's saying he'll keep secret... or... something. Right?"

I turn to Matthew for confirmation.

"Yeah, yeah, like, you know, if someone comes to you and tells you, like, hey I gotta tell you something but like, you gotta promise not to be mad, then you're like, well, hell no I can't promise that. I mean, does that make sense here?"

Eric nods his head. "Yeah, I get it. That makes sense. I think that's reasonable too. It's a fair thing to ask."

Eric explains he'll show us something we can practice on our own that will dramatically accelerate the development of our psychic abilities. What's more, by practicing it regularly, we will postpone and hold off the negative effects aging would have on our abilities and progress. The older we get the harder psychic development becomes. If we use this little trick of his we'll give ourselves a lot more time.

Eric asks if Matthew can agree to keep such a thing secret. Matthew agrees that he can and promises that until Eric says otherwise, he'll never share it. Eric asks me again to promise and I do.

I'm afraid, my dear reader, that to this day I have not been released of my promise. This is one thing I must keep from you. Rather than skip over the subject entirely I thought it best to tell you that even here there are secrets and things we may not speak of. I, at least, want to be open and let you know where I have kept doors closed until such a time that they are ready to be unlocked and the light of day let in.

When Eric finishes showing us the exercise he gets up out of his chair and stretches. "You know, there's going to come a time very soon when I have to decide whether or not to keep teaching you two." His statement comes out of nowhere. Why would he say that? "I mean, how long has it been now?"

I think for a moment. "A little over two months." I look over at Matthew, "Well, for me anyway."

"So, two months… still, that's enough time for you both to know whether or not you want to pursue learning. It's a two way street you know. It's not just if you want to learn it's if I want to teach you. I have to feel an honest desire from you and you need to tell me that you're excited to learn. Because if I get the feeling you're here because you're bored and you've got nothing else to do, well, that's not the right reason for me to show you all the things I do."

I feel as if I've done something wrong. That, in some way, we've offended him and not been thankful for the time. Eric never struck me as someone who wants attention or needs people to suck up to him but he has a very strong sense of being properly appreciative and respectful of people in your life. He's never asked for anything in return for making meals or taking us places and talking to us about what he knows. I try to think when the last time I thanked him was. I've tried to be good about it.

"If you don't pursue me and the knowledge, if you don't come to me and say wow Eric, you've really opened my eyes and I'm grateful for that or come to me and tell me how you want to learn… then, if you don't feel the need to do that then, like, maybe this isn't for you."

I frown. Eric is almost always the one calling. He's always the one saying we should get together. He seems to enjoy it himself so I never thought about it being work for him.

"I've got to make a decision then if you're worth putting time into. I've never asked either of you for anything to learn from me. I give freely. But there is a reason I'm teaching you." Eric sighs as he sits back in his chair.

Oh crap. Now it's going to come out. The reason he's teaching us and giving us all his time. Now comes the price. I feel my stomach turn. Blind-sided. Out of nowhere. All this time he did want something. What could he possibly want from us? Leaning forward I start to feel flush from sudden stress.

"I'm looking for people who can do something with this knowledge. I'm looking for people who will take it far enough that they can teach others in the future. You know, not now or anytime soon, you're just getting started. But you're only good to me if you can teach. That's all I ask. Later on give as you have been given to. But there's only so many people I can give my time to directly so I have to make sure I'm making the right decision. You're being given an amazing opportunity, only you don't know enough to know it, so I can't really blame you. In the future, things will be very different. There will be a lot of people seeking me out to learn what I know. Too many for me to handle alone and... I may not even be around. I need to know I'm making a wise investment... and that you aren't going to take what I'm giving you and hoarde it for yourselves." He pauses and a quiet descends on the room.

That's it? That's the big price? When am I ever going to have to worry about that? Seems like teaching anybody this stuff is jumping a little ahead. I don't know what to say. I feel as if I've been impolite and taken him for granted. It's hard not to as he makes everything so easy. Then another thought creeps into my mind. Matthew is sitting still and staring forward at the floor. I'm not sure how Matthew's taking any of this now or even before. He always believes things so much easier than I do. He's been so much better at it than me. I take for granted that he isn't struggling in different ways. There are many times he goes somewhere with Eric and I don't go. While I'm polite and always try to say thanks maybe Matthew's rude about it. I think about the possibility of Matthew being rude and it doesn't fit. Matthew would never be rude but he can be indifferent and that could be read as rude. He could also be struggling with quitting pot. Or maybe he doesn't get the attention he wants. Maybe Matthew doesn't really care one way or the other. It's hard to imagine the whole thing is so intriguing but Matthew always seems to be indifferent. Doesn't mean he is. People read me the same way.

I feel a heaviness come over me that makes me tired. It's the same reason I never pushed him to quit smoking pot. I love Matthew but I don't want to make his life for him. I'm not his parent, I'm his older brother. He has to make his own decisions. It's hard sometimes but I always want for him to find himself. If I have a role in it he'd only find me. The thought of pushing him and trying to inspire him makes me want to sleep.

Eric breaks the silence and waves towards the door. "That's it. I'm tired. You guys can go."

"Bye Eric, thank you." I say trying to assure him I appreciate the things he has shared with us.

Eric acts indifferent waving his arms for us to move faster. "Yeah, yeah, I know. Think about what I said, drive safe, lock the gate, take care, get going."

We hustle out the door and Matthew calls back and says thank you as well.

Neither of us speak on the drive back through the winding canyons. I don't believe Eric will stop teaching us. Maybe he wasn't even talking to me. He was bringing up some other conversation that I don't know about. I have to put aside taking his comments so personally. I'm sure I can be resistant and stubborn at times. They even make fun of my overly logical analysis, but at the end of the day there's something so compelling and irresistible about what he talks about he has to know my interest is real. I look over at Matthew and wonder if he's excited by it. He doesn't have to believe in something to want to tear it apart and see how it all works. My mind drifts away from Eric's last comments to the rest of the evening. I think about the pyramid again and rehearse it in my mind. I don't want to forget a thing. That will keep me safe. It will keep me from worrying and being afraid.

I chuckle. How stupid. A grown man afraid of going to sleep at night because of some invisible boogey men. I lean my head against the window. Yes, it's all a bad dream. Only now I've got a way to stop the dream... don't I?

while an important driving safety feature, what if you were to slam on the brakes every time something moved in front of you? while moving forward restraint becomes as important as activation...

Pyramid Power

chapter twenty-three

The next day I wake up to a phone call. It's Sarah. Her friend that I met at one of her parties awhile back has been trying to get in contact with me about a new job. Although I still work watching movies, officially, it's been a slow season and Sarah knows I'm ready to move on. Actual work is sporadic but more than that the hours really take a toll. It's good to see the light of day and be on the same hours as everyone else. Working through the dead of night isn't natural. Longer projects really hit hard and I'm not looking forward to another one.

Sarah's been a big advocate of me finding other work. Last week I went to a party at her house in the Hollywood Hills. One of her friends, who works at a temp agency, told me I could find a job in days but I wasn't sold on the idea of being a temp. Selling me with her usual excitement Sarah convinces me her friend found a really good company that I have to check out. An hour later I call her friend. She's been expecting my call and even held off other applicants because she knew I'd be what they're looking for and will do great. The company is basically these two great guys who started out in their garage and recently moved into a new office. They have a ping pong table, a laid back environment and an old arcade machine in their lobby! What else could I want?

"Well, other than playing ping pong and arcade games what do they do?" I ask trying to understand the kind of company that let's you play ping pong.

She tells me it's some new thing I probably haven't heard of. They're an Internet company and do something with the world wide web. She isn't exactly sure. I pause for awhile thinking it over. Then she explains the hours are nine to six with an hour lunch. Monday through Friday. They're by the beach and have an awesome office with lots of light. I grin. Sarah must have really filled her in on what to say.

"Okay, I'm in." No darkness. No late nights and by the beach. It'll be hell getting there but at least I'll have something to do.

Part of me struggles with the idea of working at a 'normal' company. Am I giving up on my dream of doing film? That's why we're in L.A. isn't it?

No, we're not giving up. We need stability so we can finish the script.

Makes sense, how can I write when everything's always up in the air and I sleep until evening when I do work? I'm at my best when I write in the mornings. Besides, it feels right. Some part of me is eager and restless for change. This could be what I'm looking for.

Eric calls me later in the day. He's made a tough decision. He's closing the bookstore. Will I be able to help move or pack? Whoa. Change, it turns out, is in the air. I don't know much about the bookstore or the school. Eric's life outside of hanging out with me isn't something I know a lot about. I've seen fliers advertising classes for the school part of the bookstore but never heard about any being held there. The bookstore always has so much expensive stuff I've always assumed it pays for itself.

Of course I'll help I tell him. Whatever he needs me to do. I toss around in my mind whether or not to ask him and finally decide to. "Why are you closing it?"

Eric is quiet for a second and he sounds frustrated when he responds. "We've thrown our lives into this thing. I mean all of us. You wouldn't believe where it was when we started. I mean, most businesses don't turn a profit until they've been around two or three years. Bookstores usually won't run in the black for at least five years! This turned profitable in a year but it's too much. It's too draining and isn't turning out like it needed to."

He tells me the area, Tujunga, isn't too into the metaphysical. The local economy is bad and it's becoming a major meth hub. He knew that going in but it also meant cheap rent. He went for the cheap rent hoping to lure people outside of town into the store. It relied too much on foot traffic which has been non-existent. His real dream, of having a school and place to teach from, hasn't done much better. The locals are either too strung out on meth or too dense to be interested. It's also too far from L.A. to draw from the larger population of the area. He sees now where it's going and knows it isn't going to turn out the way he wants. Rather than drag it out he decided to pull the plug and move on.

He laughs about how much better the building's improved since he's moved in. Many of his students put thousands of dollars into the store and it's hard to see it go. In another five years, he jokes, from all the good energy that they've generated in the store, the whole town will probably be booming but it'll be too late.

I sit and listen. I shouldn't bring the subject up again. He's trying to be positive about it but he also sounds defensive, like I'm judging him for closing it. It doesn't sound like he thinks that but maybe it's hard for him to close it down. I can't really tell what he feels about it. He makes it sound like he wants it closed but is also upset about it at the same time. We hang up arranging a time later in the week when I can make it up to the store to help pack.

Looking around the apartment is empty. Nobody's home. I start to get ready for my morning shower. Walking into the bathroom I look at the tub. There's an orange ring along the bottom and I notice, for the first time, how grimy it looks. Nobody's going to clean it, sighing to myself. Why shouldn't I clean it?

Damn I hate cleaning but now that I've noticed... I can't stand thinking of taking a shower in something that dirty. The grime starts really bothering me. After finding a sponge I scrub the bathroom clean. Time goes by quickly and I barely think of anything while cleaning it. Happy to see it bright and white I get a craving to take a bath. I smile. Yes, a nice hot, relaxing bath. The tub fills up and I turn on some Beethoven in the background. I leave the door slightly cracked so the music can drift in and I can hear if someone comes in. Stepping into the tub I try to resist jumping around from the hot water. Got to let it sink in, keep it in. When my body adjusts to the temperature I rest my head back on the edge of the tub.

My eyes are slightly cracked. I stare at the whiteness of the bathroom. With my eyes slit so narrowly I can't make out any details and it looks like I'm surrounded in bright white light. I sigh contentedly to myself. "God, I love you shower." I say running one hand along the edge of the bathtub.

I love you too Eric. I pretend the shower whispers back.
I snicker. "Of course you do." The shower has always been my sanctuary. My escape. When I need to think I always take a long shower where I'll sit, talk to myself, and think. I feel the hot water surround my body. The feeling of the split between the surface above the water and underneath it becomes pronounced. My mind drifts to each place where my body comes out of the warm liquid. My knee, my chest, my arm. I become aware of each one simultaneously and laugh out loud.

"Like a womb." I say out loud to myself, grinning.

Let me serve you. A voice whispers through my head.

I quickly open my eyes all the way and lift my head to look around. Straining my neck to look at the crack in the door I can't see anyone. "Did I think that?" I ask myself out loud. My thoughts can't place thinking it. "Oh great, I'm losing it." chuckling again taking a handful of water and splashing it on my face rubbing the heat in. "Here we go Eric. We knew it was going to happen someday." I say to myself.

I look around again trying to hear if anyone is walking around the apartment. "Relax freak. What are you worried about?" trying to comfort myself. I feel strange. Part of me feels peaceful, relaxed, even bubbly happy but there's something else going on that makes me restless. Leaning back I pull my knees up so my head can slip far enough underwater that I can blow bubbles. Part of me tries to break the tension I feel. Coming back out of the water I rest my head against the edge of the tub. Closing my eyes I feel the surface of the water rise and fall with the breathing of my chest. The line where the surface is rolls along my skin. Slitting my eyes I think about what it would feel like if I wasn't in a bathtub at all but floating in white light.

I will be your servant. A thought echoes through my mind.

Now I know you. Now I remember. Recognizing where the voice came from, my mind rolls back to my youth...

The shower water is pouring down. Sparkling water spills down the front of my face. It captures the light and reflects hundreds of colors. It shines and dances like magic. Solid light. I sit and watch it as it pours down my face. My head tilts down so the shower can beat on the top of my head. My knees bent as I sit on my legs. My hands are in front of me, placed together, praying.

I press them to my forehead and lean forward so they are both flat on the shower floor. My head bowed reverently. "Let me serve you." I whisper out loud. "I will be your servant. Tell me what to do and I will do it. Tell me how I can help you."

A song rises in my chest, in my heart, through my being. I don't know what it is, there are no words, only feelings. It sounds like a Native American chant. I'd never really heard any but that's as close as I can think of what someone hearing it would think. God knows what it means. God understands. It is God I am singing to.

The memory begins to fade. I feel sad, mournful... as if there is something precious I've lost.

So long ago... I would sit in the shower, praying, singing, chanting for hours. I was so young. My eyes open and I'm back in the present. So long ago. So naïve then. How great to be young and naïve. The memory makes my heart ache and I feel a twinge of longing to be that young, innocent kid again with nothing but the love of God in my heart. Never thinking to doubt or consider there's nothing there to hear him.

Whatever. Even then we were doubting.

I know. You're right.

It's true. It was about that age I started to look at other religions. I loved God but I wanted to really know God. I wanted the truth. I didn't believe the God of the Bible was the God I felt calling to me in my heart.

Closing my eyes I take a deep breath in and start to sing. It feels so foolish now but I let it go. I hit a low note and my singing changes into an Aum. It stretches out and reverberates against the shower walls. Like an echo chamber it rings through everything. The sound sends a chill down my spine. I take another breath and this time let out a long Aum. For five minutes I rest for a few moments soaking up the hot water and sing out Aum after Aum.

Something catches my attention. Everything feels strange and I'm not sure if I'm alone. My body freezes. Every part of me tunes in to catch the slightest sound. There's only the normal noises of the apartment. I quickly wipe the water out of my face and reach out to open the door farther.

"Hello? Anybody home?" I shout out into the apartment.

Only silence answers. I look into my bedroom. The light from the window pouring in. It doesn't come in with a straight beam though. It looks like my whole bedroom is filled with light. I sit up and strain to look out into the living room. Everything looks so bright and filled with light. Only... I look harder... the light's moving! The strange feeling increases. It feels light and the feeling of the water in the bathtub slips away from me. I can't feel the water. Panic and fear grip me. It's not a normal feeling. It feels like I'm becoming aware of something else. There's something going on and it's intensifying. Everything's too bright and it's fluttering. I'm becoming less aware of my body, like I'm floating away from it, and suddenly I can sense beyond the walls. It's space. Everything feels open, hollow. Entity! My memory of the entity comes into my safe little bathtub world.

Pyramid! Use the pyramid! I scream in my head.

I instantly throw up the protective pyramid. Almost immediately I can feel the hot water surrounding my lower body again. The apartment looks normal and the brightness is gone. "It's okay, everything is fine and normal." I assure myself keeping the pyramid active in my mind. Everything returns to normal. The pyramid works. The pyramid works. I have no idea what happened but feeling vulnerable sitting naked in a tub I quickly get out and dress.

Memories and thoughts of everything Eric's told me about reality come crashing at me in a flood. The flashing white sky is the pulse of Gaia. Gaia is a conscious organism. I'm living in the body of another living organism, who lives in the body of another conscious organism... and it keeps going... and going but through it all is another consciousness. Energy. God, it's all energy and like a video game... hologram... it's not real. Not solid. Energy beings are aware but not physical... they could be anywhere... the mind can move anywhere. Eric can lock onto anyone's frequency and move into dreams. You can plug your consciousness into anything, draw out information, scanning... I'm not even physical. Aura is my energy body... who I really am...

"No, no, no, no." I whisper quickly to myself. Got to get away from there. Those thoughts will draw the entity to me. Stop, stop, stop. I need to distract myself so I jump on the computer to play a game. Soon my mind is absorbed in the game and the thoughts of that other reality slips away.

What a way to kill your evolution. When you begin to learn how to shift, or raise your consciousness into higher frequencies, you reach a point where you start to hit dimensional levels. Having Eric as a tuning fork I reached that point quickly.

It is common for everything to appear brighter, clearer than it normally is. This light won't be like normal light it will flicker, or flutter, like a strobe. Your consciousness is shifting into these higher lanes and you can see it, feel it.

When this first started I had no idea what it was but it made me so afraid I'd always throw the pyramid up with the purpose of stopping it. Which it did. As much as I said I wanted to see to believe, or embrace the unknown, the truth is I was petrified of it. I wanted the unknown on my terms where I was safely in control.

There were so many times I could have experienced something profound but I allowed my fear to kill it. Over the next month I'd feel the lightness, the expansion, see the fluttering time and time again as I began to shift dimensionally. Each time fear would seize control and I'd stop it.

Eric was right to attack my fear, constantly point it out.

Looking back, many times I wish I'd never learned the pyramid when I did. That I'd been forced to experience beyond my fear and see that nothing bad was going to happen. What I did eventually gain was disgust for all the experiences that I missed. When I built up enough I started to go out of my way to experiment with everything I could to conquer my fear.

Fear is the mind killer. It does its job very well. Never realizing your goal of awakening should terrify you more than anything you might have to face to gain it.

The Extraordinary Tales of Evil Richard

chapter twenty-four

A few days later Matthew and I go up to Tujunga to meet Eric. He's been busy working on closing the bookstore and needs a break. He wants us to meet one of his oldest students; Richard.

When we arrive at Eric's house he quickly ushers us into his car and we start driving over to Richard's. With a grin Eric confides that he's also known as, 'Evil Richard', and then laughs maniacally.

Eric's worked hard to find a house in Tujunga for Richard and his family and finally found one close to his own. This was a few weeks ago and they've already started to move in. The house needs a lot of work but has a huge yard, bigger than his.

As he talks about the many features of the house, how hard it was to find and how he has a strange knack for finding good gems I keep wondering when he's going to let us in on the most obvious and pressing question.

"Um, what's with 'Evil' Richard?" I say as soon as he pauses.

Eric laughs. "Well, it's like this. Richard is one of my oldest and most advanced students. Of all of my students he puts the most time into practicing and dissecting my teachings. Almost obsessively at times. Unfortunately, his motives for doing this aren't exactly... let's say pure. I mean, Richard's seen things nobody on Earth, living anyway, has ever witnessed. Incredible, amazing, your head-could-explode-if-you-saw-it stuff! Rather than inspire Richard to achieve greater and greater things he has this... thing, where it drives him to try and 'figure out' how I do the things I do so that he can master these abilities, or powers as he sees them, himself. It's like a power struggle. Richard knows what I'm capable of but can't fathom the obvious. He sees it as power and he wants to wield it himself."

I'm not sure what the obvious is that Richard can't fathom. Matthew isn't asking either so maybe he knows or is as lost as I am.

Eric chuckles shaking his head and tells us if the other students knew he moved Richard up to Tujunga and is talking to him again they'd tie him up in a chair until he comes to his senses.

Still not sure I understand anything I restate my question, "But, like, what makes him evil?"

Eric's expression becomes more serious and he shrugs. "Well," he explains, "Richard's done some evil shit to me. He's broken into my house and stolen things from me. He's lied and tried to get friends and students to turn against me. For instance, once, I left for a week when I was living with a house full of students. During the week I was gone, Richard went to all the students and tried to orchestrate something of an uprising. Okay? A great coup! He started trying to convince them that I was actually evil and dark, and when that didn't work, that I was keeping secret knowledge from them and holding them back. I was the reason they weren't getting everything they wanted. I was keeping them down. And that is truly closer to what Richard believes. Of course," Eric says in a serious tone, "I am keeping knowledge from Richard and stopped teaching him many years ago. But that was only after he started all this shit. Richard's shown a very dark side and until he comes to terms with it I won't give him any more knowledge. I try and help him any way I can... but teaching is no more."

Matthew and I nod our heads understanding.

Eric clears his throat and grins, "So, when I came back a week later many of the students had turned against me, convinced I was keeping them from accessing the many powers I displayed or have access to. I eventually got them all straightened out and found out Richard was behind it. Richard's excuse was that he was trying to weed out those who loved me as a teacher and those who were only there for the power."

Matthew laughs, "Nice. Hooked you up, like a little favor."

Eric chuckles and nods his head. "Exactly, he was doing it for me. But like, he's also set up other 'ambushes'. Once, he gathered a small following of students of his own to teach when he lived in Orange County. Then he arranged for me to come down and speak on a specific topic, which he had studied in advance without telling me what it was going to be. Richard read and memorized half a dozen books from other so-called, 'masters' or 'spiritual teachers'." Eric tells us fingering quotes around Richard's sources of knowledge. Eric laughs again. "Richard saw what he believed was a contradiction between what these other teachers were saying and what I teach. Because all these other teachers agreed Richard thought I must be in the wrong... and he was going to prove it in front of all these witnesses."

Eric admits he isn't a big reader and barely reads anything by any other spiritual teachers. He'd never read any of the books Richard was going to use against him and Richard never mentioned they would be talking about a particular topic.

"So, when I walked into the meeting with Richard and all of his students I knew pretty fast what was up. Richard started citing passages, names, books and just went off in this big long presentation of his argument." Eric grins mischievously. "Part of the problem," he confesses, "is that I like challenges. I need stimulation like anyone else and it's hard for me to find something that I really have to work for. Richard isn't the greatest challenge but he keeps me on my toes."

I laugh. I can think of better ways to get stimulation.

Eric shrugs it off, "In this case I just thought okay, I'll give him what he wants, I shifted into a higher state..." he puts his hand near his forehead and moves it towards the ceiling of the car to signal this. It's a gesture I've seen him use before and something about the movement of it triggers some kind of emotion in me. "And then once I shifted up into that higher place I started downloading knowledge and laid it all out. I just tore right into his argument. I dissected each part of the case he presented and even took it beyond where Richard had gotten with all his studies without ever having read the books. Then I took it beyond where even those books had left off and demonstrated where they had all collectively made their errors.

A quick hour or two later, after fumbling through all his researched books, Richard submitted. His students were at a complete loss, they were totally unable to keep up without having read the material and the conversation really, I mean it just went beyond them. Richard really hadn't gotten them very far but the whole point of the meeting anyway was to demonstrate Richard's defeat of me more than teaching them anything. It really didn't matter to him if they learned anything or not. It was all about him." Eric throws back his head and gives us his best maniacal laugh again. "After it was done, Richard had to turn and explain to his students how I was right and that there was no question about it."

I'm surprised someone so bent on disputing Eric would give in like that. "So, he just gave up?"

Eric shrugs and throws a hand up while turning down a street. "Well, here's the thing. Richard desperately wants to be the master. He wants to dominate and be in control. He wants the power. By finding flaws in me he feels he can deny what he knows in his heart that I am. But, where he's screwed is that Richard also knows the truth. He could never be satisfied besting me only on the surface because inside he would know and that would eventually drive him crazy. He has to do it in such a way that he feels fully vindicated, for himself. So he'll be the first to fall down and admit when he's wrong, that's why he's lasted as long as he has. He's done some horrible, horrible shit to me. I mean really, betrayals. But each time he'll see his wrong and come back crying, and moaning about how he screwed up but truly humbled. Not like... pretending, but in his heart really humbled and... how can I turn away someone who comes to me like that? I am very forgiving. Sometimes I think too forgiving. It takes great strength to do that if you think about it."

Many students, Eric tells us, will do a wrong to him. The shame of facing that wrong and their pride keeps them away. If we ever screw up we should remember that. It is stupid to let pride and arrogance come between us and serving or finding our way to the Force. Us and God. God is too great a thing to let something as petty as pride come in our way of awakening.

"In his heart," Eric offers softening his tone, "Richard loves me more than any of my other students. Not even a contest. But he's like Judas to Christ. Not that I'm saying I'm Christ but there's a similarity in their relationship. He would betray me out of that love, thinking it's for my benefit. Judas hoped the people would rise up in rebellion when they took Christ away. He thought that would spark a great revolution and Christ would be king. He never thought it would lead to his crucifixion. The road to hell you know..." he says with a wink.

"Paved with good intentions." Matthew says flashing a smile and laughing. I want to laugh too but don't. It's crazy that Eric would keep someone like this in his life. Someone who's constantly looking to screw you over first chance they get.

Eric nods his head. "So, here's the deal. You're both going to meet him and you're going to like him. Richard is very charming and very charismatic. Just remember, he's been around a long time. He's an old dog. He knows how to manipulate your energy, he knows how to read you, and he knows how to play you. He's a snake and you're both tiny little puppies to him. That's really how he'll look at you. According to Richard none of my students are worthy of me. That said there is a lot to learn from him. He has seen some crazy, crazy, I mean crazy shit! He was around for the peak of my young, dumb flashy days! But, you know, I learned and got better but it's good to hear first hand. That said..." Eric raises his index finger with a serious look on his face, "You shouldn't ever speak to him if I'm not there. If he does approach you then you need to tell me, okay? He's taken students away before, which is really why I'll never teach him again. To take someone away when they find this path is like losing a soul. You just dismantled someone's awakening. I don't think either of you can appreciate the gravity of that. In the end Richard does everything for Richard. He will use you up and never look back. You both get me?"

We agree that we understand.

Eric pulls up next to a house with a tall wooden fence much like his. Something about fortress fences in Tujunga.

We get out of the car and walk up to the wooden fence. Eric thinks he knows where the door is, which blends into the rest of the fence. As he's searching for the gate he bangs on the fence and yells towards the house. He waits two seconds and then reaches over the gate trying to find the latch. He finally gets the gate open as a man's voice rings out a hello from near the house.

"Hey! I thought I felt you out here." The voice shouts.

"Yeah, well, not too welcoming for visitors you know? You gotta get that latch fixed." Eric complains.

Matthew and I follow Eric through the gate into a large yard. A driveway is right by the gate leading up to a small garage. The left opens up into a large sprawling yard with lots of little trees. It has more shrubs and grass than Eric's yard but is still mostly dirt and leaves. The house seems like a small country home with a stretching porch on the front.

The man walks up to greet Eric with a broad, genuine-seeming smile. He beams at Eric and happily shakes his hand. They exchange a few words about fixing up the property and the work he's done.

Eric turns to us and tells us not to stand back trying to hide. I crack a grin which probably looks more like a smirk.

"This is Matthew and Eric." he says pointing to each of us.

Richard smiles and shakes Matthew's hand. "Hi, I'm Richard. Eric's told me about you." Turning to me he looks uncertain and glances over his shoulder toward Eric. "And you, you must be the brother."

He grins at me and I feel instantly at ease. He isn't tall but he's grizzly with broad shoulders. His hair is short and black. The best part is his fat, Tom Selleck style mustache. Normally mustaches are really funny to me. They're an odd style of facial hair that's hard to pull off and not look too 70's but it fits him perfectly. His whole demeanor leaves me feeling comfortable and relaxed.

"Yeah, I'm the brother Eric, nice to meet you." I say.

He gives me a firm but reassuring handshake. "Well, I'm Richard but I'm guessing you guys have already heard about me." He says with a huge, almost child-like grin, looking at Eric.

"Oh yes." Eric says loudly walking towards the porch. "They've been warned. I've told them all about the things you've done trying to tear down the poor teacher."

Richard gives an easy, bellowing laugh.

You're smiling too much. Stop smiling. What am I doing? Eric warned us he's charming and I've gone right for it. I stop smiling and pay more attention to Richard's actions. Whatever quick expectation I had of him from Eric's stories are quickly dashed out the window. There's nothing villainous about Richard at all. He's instantly likable. He beams a peaceful, energetic radiance that's like Jason but intensified. His presence is the complete opposite of threatening or malicious. I'd completely forgotten to mistrust him as soon as he smiled.

Usually cautious and distrustful of strangers I dropped my normally high barriers and felt we could have sat and talked for hours without a thought in the world.

Richard turns his head to look at the ground. "Well..." he says in a softer tone. "What is it they call me? The name I got?"

"Evil Richard." Eric says it as if he's trying out a movie title.

Richard laughs. "Yeah, that's it. Well, I'm afraid it's all true. You name it, I've probably done it. But, Eric's stood up every time."

"God, but the drama and stress I've had to go through to get you there. They don't know the half of it. I only gave them a taste." Eric shrills out in a painful, but joking way, so we understand his suffering.

Richard looks up towards Eric walking on the porch. His smile is different, his lips are closed and he has a look that seems... grateful.

I'm surprised how easily and openly they talk about the subject. I thought it would be taboo. Things that happened in the past but are too painful to bring up. Richard's look makes me think there are things there he'd rather not have us know and he appreciates Eric kept some things from us. It must be hard to have your mistakes so well known.

"I'm definitely not proud of them." Richard confirms. "But, I had to go through them, I think."

"Only you." Eric said not letting him get away with any excuses. "No one else gives me so many hassles."

Eric changes the subject asking about the porch and inside the house. Richard tells us how he tore apart the living room and the remains of it are in a huge pile on the lawn. They're marking a place to dig a septic tank as well. When he describes how much he'd done I get the distinct impression Richard is a hardcore worker. At first I thought he'd done the work with other workers he'd hired then I start to realize he's done almost everything himself.

We go inside his living room. The ceiling is low but it's cozy. He has a couch and a bookshelf with a fireplace. It's furnished simply and modestly. Many of their belongings are still in boxes but they don't have much. It fits with everything I've seen of Eric and his other students. They are all mostly poor but have enough to not worry about their safety or where their next meal is coming from.

Richard shows Matthew and I his bookshelf. He beams with a mix of excitement and pride as he relays the story of when he first met Eric. He's the oldest student Eric ever started teaching. He was 25. Eric was 20 or 21 at the time, they can't decide. When Eric met Richard he could barely read comic books. He was below High School reading level and about as dumb as a brick.

His wife comes out from the kitchen and confirms it. She's as tall as Richard with long, straight black hair. Her face is strong but her eyes look tired. They recently had a baby so she's been exhausted.

"Hi, I'm Joyce." She says to Matthew and I. Richard jumps, apologizing and introduces us.

The three of them start sharing stories, telling us that Richard would drink a case of beer and ride dirt bikes off this ramp that shot him straight into the air 15, 20 feet and then straight down. He was all out guy, like, crush beer cans on your forehead and stuff type of guy.

Joyce complains in a thick New England accent how many bones Richard broke riding those things.

Richard bellows with hearty laugh. Then, Richard tells us, everything about him started to transform when he met Eric. Richard becomes excited and his enthusiasm is contagious. What Eric showed him fed his mind and Eric pushed him to improve himself. Richard took after it with all his energy. "Part of it," Richard says with a grin, "was to figure Eric out. I taught myself to read and within a few years was reading 600 page books and memorizing whole chapters, with page numbers!"

Eric confirms it, shouting back from the porch where he's taken a seat. "No really, he's not joking. He could barely read and then he'd recite any page you'd want from a book he'd read."

Richard's whole face starts lighting up and I want to share his excitement. He grabs a book on his shelf and brings out the Bahavagita.

"I devoured everything, everything!" He said. "And I memorized it too. Page numbers, paragraphs. It's all in my head." He flips the book open and shows us pages marked with little red and blue tapes, underlined, highlighted with notes scrawled on the side. He says a page number and tells me to flip to it then starts reciting a passage. I quickly flip to the page while he's still reciting it and find the passage he's recalling. He follows it word for word.

He puts his finger to his head and taps it. "I'm a motor-head. I was a dumb motor-head and now I've read more than most people who have masters. This whole shelf, I've read every single book."

Matthew and I look at the bookshelf with new wonder. It's stuffed with hundreds of books.

Eric howls in delight at Richard's insanity. "He's not just saying that either. Lot's of people have books on their shelves they've never even opened, like me!" he jokes. "But no, he's serious. Trust me. He's fanatical. He really is. He deserves most of the credit for doing it all too."

Richard avidly shakes his head and smiles at us. "Don't believe that. That's not true. He's more humble and modest than most people would ever guess."

Eric laughs.

"No, really. Listen to me, really. If it weren't for him I'd be a beaten down, useless, gear head and probably would have killed myself in an accident or drank myself to death long ago. I mean, I was going nowhere. I owe it all to him. Seriously."

"Well, some of that is true. I'm surprised you didn't kill yourself even after I met you some of the things you'd do." Eric jokes.

I find myself smiling happily. They both play off each other perfectly. It's like a reunion between two best friends from High School. They act so familiar with each other and each bounce back and forth so well it's like watching a tennis match. It's fun to stand there and listen.

Staring at all the books on Richard's shelf I can't imagine going from comic books to books so thick I would never even attempt to read them and I like to read.

Richard shifts to look at the bookshelf and puts the Bahavagita back. He takes a breath in and looks at Matthew and I. "You know, let me give you guys some advice."

Eric howls in the background that this is gonna be good.

He looks at us and with his calm, happy demeanor and mustache he suddenly seems very father-like. "I've read all these books and they've filled my head with all these ideas, and data and information. But..." he sweeps his hand through the air as if to cast them all away, "all worthless. Worthless. Useless knowledge. All it's given me are more dead-end's. I thought they'd help me figure it out but the more I read the more I realize... none of them know it. All you need, is to listen to him." He turns slightly and points at Eric.

"Really. You're both so young, you know, learn from my mistakes at least some good will come out of them!" he says grinning and bellowing with a big laugh.

"Yeah, that's true. He's got the monopoly there. If someone ever decides they want to do something I'll send them to Richard and he can tell them everything he's already tried." Eric grumbles.

Richard grins, "Yeah, it's true. I've tried it all. I've had detectives following him. I've stolen things from him."

"My journals." Eric says sourly. "I learned after that never to keep a journal. You know how much you guys have lost because of that? Things I might brush off but could be gold for you."

"But you know, someone who's real will stand up and I've never found one thing." Richard holds up a thick, worn finger. It's the finger of someone who knows manual labor yet his mind is so keen you can see the intelligence in his eyes. "Not one thing to suggest he's anything other than what he says he is."

His statement sends me reflecting inward. I'm not sure if Eric has ever said he's anything. I can't tell what Richard means by that but don't feel like now is the time to ask. Enlightened maybe. Not that I'm entirely sure what that means.

"Not that it stops you from trying." Eric scowls. "Now, you gonna offer me something to drink or do I have to leave because I'm going to dehydrate?"

Richard laughs and goes to the kitchen praising how Eric's greatest asset is his honesty and directness.

We go and sit out on Richard's porch at a small kitchen table. It's a pale smooth wood. His wife, Joyce, brings out chips and sits down to join us. I sit with my back to their yard looking at their house. Eric sits on the side of the table with his back to the house looking out facing the front yard. Richard sits on his left and Matthew's on his right. Joyce pulls up a chair slightly behind Richard. They have a baby who's asleep and she occasionally leans back to listen for her.

They talk about the time they spent on the East coast. Joyce and Richard have been with each other since the time Eric first met Richard. Joyce and Eric fought a lot but have come to terms with each other over the years. Even she seems to have a certain respect, almost gratefulness, for him. Since Richard was outed she admits to missing listening in on Eric's classes.

She tells us about the first time she meditated with Richard and Eric on top of a dam. Right into the meditation she felt herself float into the air and looked down on her body. She's never experienced anything like it in her life.

Richard laughs about his time away from Eric and the group. "He's even got a name for it he spends so much time there." Eric says. "Tell them what you call it."

Richard looks down at the table, smiling, "Outside learning."

Matthew and I laugh.

"Yeah, that's right. It's perfect. That's exactly what it is. Outside learning." Eric says sitting back laughing. "You get ex'd and have to do Outside Learning for a few years."

Richard nods more to himself than us. "It's intense too. Let me tell you. You think it's intense inside it's the same but different."

"Well, it's got to be intense or it wouldn't work." Eric shrugs sipping his Diet Coke.

"Yeah, you guys will want to avoid it if you can. Although I think everyone's been on Outside Learning at some point. Is there anyone who hasn't been ex'd?" Richard asks.

Eric furrows his brow. "Actually, lots of people..." then his expression changes, "Okay, well, I wouldn't say lots but most of the ones I have now."

Richard grins, "Yeah. Give it time."

"No, I mean, Frank has never been ex'd... officially. He's spent time away but not because I sent him away. Danny has never been ex'd..."

They start talking about other students and names I've never heard before. I start to get the idea it's hard to stay in the group for very long without getting ex'd. It's short for what Eric jokingly refers to as ex-communicated. I smirk. So much for it being a very good cult. Cults are supposed to try and keep you in the circle not constantly boot you out. After they list off a long trail of names it seems like Eric boots more people out than come in. I'm surprised there are as many students around as there are.

I finally clear my throat and ask, "Why do you go through so many people? Wouldn't it be better to keep them around?"

It seems like having people with experience around is a good thing. I feel more comfortable and confident knowing there are older, more advanced students like Jason and Peter. It makes me feel like if they've gone through it and survived I can too. If I have any questions they could answer them from experience.

Richard leans back and folds his arms. "Can I tell them?" He asks with a knowing glint in his eyes.

Eric looks at Matthew and then me. "Ohhh!" he whispers like Richard stumbled onto a really good secret, "You mean T7? Nah, they wouldn't care anyway. They're both bored."

"No!" I cry realizing Richard is hiding a special secret. "We're not bored at all!"

Eric waves to Matthew, "Please, look at your brother, he's over there half asleep."

Matthew smirks and chuckles. He's stretched out lounging with his head against the chair. He's always in lounge mode and doesn't seem any closer to sleep than usual. "Hey, I'm not falling asleep, I'm just relaxed. You know, just chillin', enjoying some good company."

Eric doesn't look convinced. He waves Richard off. "It's nothing they need to worry about. Now, that's enough."

He might be baiting us to see if we'll push it. His eyes seem stern enough he could also be serious.

Richard, who knows Eric better, changes the subject.

"Yeah, you know, I'm surprised. I've heard a lot about Matthew," he says pointing at Matthew, "but not a lot about Eric."

"But you," he says pointing at me, "you seem like you're getting it. I mean, you're starting to put it together. I can see it in your eyes and I can feel it from you. But you," he says motioning to Matthew, "I just don't feel it."

Eric leans forward onto the table, "Yeah, you can see it in his eyes. The brainwashed, cultie look." He rolls his eyes in the back of his head and sticks out his arms like a zombie groaning, "Yess, masssterrrr."

Everyone laughs. I shake my head grinning. Eric's so dynamic. He can be so serious and intense in one instant and in the next so full of humor. The strange thing is that even when he's being funny it's like part of him doesn't change. He still has this weird intensity.

"One thing you should remember," Eric said switching back to serious, "is that I met Eric first. He's had a lot more time with me. It has been a real struggle to get any time with Matthew because of his work. You remember how much time we spent together when I first found you? The first three to six months are of critical importance. It's momentum. I've had that momentum with Eric but I haven't caught it yet with Matthew and it's going to be a problem soon."

Richard nods. "I see. I didn't know that, I thought you met them both at the same time. That makes sense then."

Eric's statement catches my attention. I'm not sure if Matthew thought much about it but I've started to notice that Eric's just as willing to say important things out loud in a group full of people as he is to pull someone aside and tell them directly. The speech he gave us when he taught us the Sword and Pyramid comes to my mind. Talking about showing interest and pursuing the knowledge. I'm certain now he was talking directly to Matthew.

I make a mental note that Eric never answered the question about why he went through so many people even as I quietly worry about Matthew. I secretly curse how casual and laid back he is about everything. It's such a stark contrast to Richard who's so involved and full of energy. Eric called him fanatical and I can see some of that. More than that he seems like he isn't afraid to push himself and is full of passion. I'd like for something to move me to feel like that.

Eric decides it's time to go. He invites Richard over to his house later and suggests it will be good for him to tell us some of the things he's experienced.

Richard's face brightens, "Oh God, which ones, there's so many! Are they ready to hear them?"

Eric shrugs downing the rest of his pop. "They probably won't believe a word of it and will be completely convinced you're totally insane but... that's part of the fun!" he shouts with pretend glee.

We go back to Eric's house and he makes us dinner. We eat quickly. Eric goes through the house informing everyone that Richard will be over later. We catch Frank on the porch.

He shakes his head. "Eric will never learn. In another three month's Richard will screw Eric over again and it will all start over." He laughs as he walks out the gate to his car.

Matthew and I clean up the dishes. The light slowly fades from the sky and the cool smell of night sweeps through the canyons. The fragrance of the end of summer fills the air. It won't really turn cool in Southern California but the air changes. It's reassuring to have some semblance of seasons.

It isn't long before Richard arrives. He has some hard liquor and cigars. Eric prods Richard joking about what a meathead he still is. Richard makes Eric and Matthew a drink. I decline. The memory of my last experience drinking with Farrah turns me off. It seems so pointless. Though I don't imagine Eric or Richard really getting drunk. Eric gags at the drink and proclaims how much he dislikes alcohol. Richard laughs and tells him it's an acquired taste. They talk for awhile about cigars and Eric's hate for cigarettes and big tobacco companies taking money for killing people.

Pointing at Matthew he says how smoking is a sign of weakness he detests and the only reason he doesn't give Matthew more grief over it is because he recently quit smoking pot.

Richard seems a little surprised. "Yeah, see, I never got that stuff. I may be a meathead but I've never had any interest in pot. I just don't get it."

Eric used to do both until one day he ran out of cigarettes and freaked out. Then he realized how addicted he was and how little control he had. Every cell in his body craved it. He was a slave to the addiction and if there was one thing he's kept consistent through his life it's that he allows nothing mastery over him. He is the master. Nothing will control him. He made a decision to quit and that was it. Cold turkey. It was a fate worse than death and he wouldn't wish it on anyone. For years after he'd dream about smoking and his body still craved it. Only in the past few years has he really felt like he's broken away from it.

Richard looks at me and asks if I smoke. I shake my head. "I've never tried a cigarette in my life. I put one in my mouth once and it freaked me out. It felt disgusting. It's always seemed so stupid, I never understood the point."

Eric and Matthew assure me there isn't a point and that's part of it.

Richard asks if our parents smoke. Nope. Never. He laughs and asks how Matthew ended up being the only smoker.

Matthew gets a little defensive and tells them our older brother also smokes. But he didn't get him started. It was one of our friends who, when Matthew was 14, offered him a cigarette like one of those after school specials. "Heeey kids, wanna cigarette? They're cooool."

Richard and Eric switch topics and chat about how cigars are different. Eric likes the smell but isn't convinced he wants to try one. Richard tells him he'll light one up later on and let him try it if he wants.

Sitting on the porch, Eric and Richard at the small round table kick back like old friends. I sit on the stone wall, my feet dangle near Angus who is asleep beneath me. Matthew sits in a fold out camping chair near the edge of the darkness so he can smoke and blow it toward the garage.

It seems like a perfectly normal evening. A refreshing breeze blows, rustling the vines that envelop the porch. The lamps inside the living room cast out a warm orange glow that mixes with the dim overhead porch light.

"What was the first thing you ever experienced with me?" Eric asks Richard.

I cock my head to the side, interested in what he'll say but not thinking much of it. They could start talking about politics or what life was like in their childhood and I wouldn't think anything of it.

Richard leans back and rubs his hand through his hair. "Oh man." He grins broadly. He even looks like Tom Selleck when it's darker.

"I don't know about the first, there were lot's of things. You were relentless in those days. It was so intense!" Richard laughs and leans forward on one of his knees. "You guys have no idea. He's so much different now. A completely different person. He's much more relaxed now. Things were very different in those days."

"Well, of course, I was 8 or 9 years younger! What was I, like, 20 something! A kid!" Eric yells out.

"Yeah, those were the good days, when you never knew what was next." Richard whispers... shiny glint forming in his eye.

"Yeah, those were my flashy days... I think is what Danny calls them. I was just hitting my big Enlightenment cycles and figuring stuff out." Eric nods in the warm light spilling from the house.

It suddenly strikes me that Eric was not always as he is now. That should be a complete no-brainer, but something about Eric makes me think he's always been the way he is with only slight changes. To think of Eric as just, 'figuring stuff out', is strange. It feels reassuring in a way. Like anything he says I can do I really could because he'd once been unable to do it.

Richard thinks for awhile and then sits up beaming at Eric. "You remember the tape?"

Eric looks at Richard, puzzled. "Tape? What tape are you talking about?"

Richard chuckles and shakes his head. "The tape you brought to play for me but there was nothing on it?"

Eric sits staring at Richard blankly and then smiles. "Well, don't ruin it. Tell them about it."

Richard turns toward us and takes a sip of his drink. "Once, Eric came over to my house. I was living with Joyce at the time. I'd been trying to figure out who this guy was and he'd shown me some stuff, like reading my mind and telling me what I was thinking, you know, enough that I didn't know what the hell to think!" He laughs.

"Anyway, one day Eric just showed up at my door and of course I was home. And Eric said to me, I've got this tape you should listen to. So I let him in and said, 'OK, well, I guess we can listen to it.' We sat in my living room where I had my stereo. He takes out a perfectly normal cassette tape. It was one I could've run down and bought at the store. He puts it in and hits play and boy, was I not prepared for what it played."

Richard's eyes well up slightly. His voice is tinged with emotion as he raises his hands up trying to grasp the impact it had on him. "It played, or said, or talked... I still don't know exactly how it happened, but it told me about my life. It was a song about me. It was a song about everything I was going through and it gave me the key. The key!" Richard emphasizes with striking heart-felt emotion.

Eric mocks him with a grin, "The key! The key! Listen, you're confusing them! You say it like the little guy from that island show. The plane! The plane! Explain it more clearly so they get it. Right now they look lost."

I know I'm lost. I look over at Matthew who doesn't seem to be getting it.

Richard shakes his head. "You know, it's really hard to explain."

Eric throws his hands up. "How do you think I feel?"

Richard laughs. "Yeah, I get how hard that would be. Really, I get it."

Richard leans back in and lowers his voice. "It told me the key to myself. It relayed to me my inner-most thoughts and feelings, everything that I was struggling and fighting with, and it told me how to get out of it. It gave me the key to awakening. I mean, it was so powerful, I'm like a strong guy, especially in those days, trust me, I didn't cry for nothing! Nothing! But this tape was playing and singing to me about... things only I knew. And it was so releasing, so freeing and liberating I just broke down crying right there. And it gave me the key to let it all go." Richard sits back in his chair and sighs taking a sip of his drink. Then he grins at us.

"Then, it stopped playing and hit the end of the tape. Eric got up and just kinda said, okay, see you later. And I asked him, you know, can I keep this! Can I keep the tape? He looked at me and shrugged like it was nothing and said yeah, you can keep it." Richard chuckles and shakes his finger at Eric.

"Then he really got me. As soon as I saw him drive away I ran to find Joyce and I was pulling at her arm, crying, saying you know, you gotta come here! You gotta listen to this tape, and I kinda freaked her out." Richard throws his head back laughing, "I mean, here was her big strong guy that she'd never seen cry in her life even when he really hurt himself and I was bawling so she got all white and thought something was really wrong. I ran her into the living room and got the tape ready... and I'm crying all telling her how it's the most beautiful thing I've ever heard in my life, and it told me everything I needed to hear... and her mouth is hanging open like I've lost my mind... so I hit play and... nothing."

Picking up his drink he swishes it around and makes the ice clink together. "There was nothing on it. It was completely blank. I played the other side and tried every tape player I could get my hands on," Eric sits back in his chair laughing to himself. His face is bright red, "and there was nothing there. So Joyce asked me to explain it and then I finally stopped to think about it and I couldn't. I mean, to this day I don't know if it was a song, or if it was talking or if it was even in

English! All I knew is I understood it perfectly and it sang directly to me about things that were closest to me. And it told me about the key to it all and I forgot it." He turns and looks at Eric and shakes his head. "That was a good one! I'm still working on figuring that one out!"

"What's to figure out?" Eric said with a slight smirk on his face. "The Universe needed you to hear something and you heard it. It doesn't have a language like we speak. It has its own way."

"Well, whatever it was, that one had me thinking for awhile. You know, the wheels were spinning for sure!"

Eric tells Richard his wheels are always spinning in overtime. It's because he met him at such a late age he only had a few good years left to really get Richard to where he needed to be. He had to push him a bit harder.

Richard relays a time he was trying to figure out if Eric was an angel or a demon. "I thought I was losing my mind. I even thought I might run away! So, to clear my head I drove out to the middle of nowhere. I mean, it was so far out there I'm not even sure where I was. It was down so many farm roads and dirt paths. I was gone. Then I got out of my car and ran through this forest where there wasn't a sign of civilization. Once I got way out into the woods I completely lost it and broke down. I was screaming and swearing and pushing at trees. I didn't know which way was up or down because everything I knew was tumbling down. Eric was doing things that weren't supposed to be possible! Nothing made any sense. Finally, I found my way back to my house and there's Eric, waiting for me. Not only did I not tell anyone where I was going, because I didn't know myself, but there wasn't a car in sight the whole way there and back."

Eric looks at Matthew and I and twirls his hand around the side of his head in a circle to suggest Richard is crazy. Richard shoots a broad grin.

"Yeah, you made me that way! I mean, Eric was sitting right on my porch without a care in the world. I come up and he asked me if I'd had a nice time in the woods. Then he starts telling me about everything I'd done. What I screamed and yelled about and how I roamed aimlessly around the woods, everything in perfect detail. I was completely shocked."

The tape story is up in the air for me. It's neither here nor there and I can't understand it. But this one is interesting. I can see the possibility of it. It's like Eric could see Richard in his mind or something and could follow him and that's why he knew everything Richard said and did. The possibility is engrossing and I lean forward. Richard's openness and sincerity is convincing. There's no reason to doubt he believes it's true. The truth of the tales make them all the more exciting. These aren't just stories... this is his life. Could someone do that with their mind? Can Eric do that? Eric was right when he told Richard earlier we wouldn't believe his stories. They're enthralling fantasies but hard to place in reality.

"You should tell them about the park." Eric says quietly.

"Oh man..." Richard says with a huge smile on his face. He wipes his mustache with one hand. "They're never going to believe that one."

"Doesn't matter. It'll give them something to think about." Eric assures him.

"One day," Richard tells us, "Eric decided to take me to a park. It was the perfect summer day. The sky was bright blue without a single cloud. The air had an occasional slight breeze, enough to cool you off. When we got to the park it was a movie scene. People were throwing frisbee's, playing fetch with their dogs, families were out picnicking, others were riding bikes, all enjoying an ideal day."

Eric nods grinning. "It was the perfect day. It had to be."

Richard chuckles and continues, "Eric and I walk into the park, sit down and start talking. I gotta confess guys, to say I was stubborn is a severe understatement. I mean, I know! Eric tells me but I know. I'd already seen Eric do things I couldn't explain. Pick any kind of explanation you can think of, scientific, side show magician tricks or anything else and it didn't make sense. The only explanation is what

Eric kept telling me. Enlightenment is real but nobody knows what it is. Psychic abilities are real and they are the way to reach Enlightenment. When you achieve Enlightenment you're able to change reality and perform miracles, just like every religion says you can. The real mind fuck, pardon my French, is that Eric was an Enlightened master unlike any to walk the planet before and he's here talking to me. Of all people. The meathead!"

Richard laughs as he tells us how stubbornly he refused to accept this. "I just kept thinking there was another answer. I was so sure of it. So sure of it! The problem is I didn't know what the other answer was."

I'm surprised how open he is about being stubborn. I'm cautious, some would say stubborn, but it isn't necessarily something I'm proud of. Eric and Matthew often make fun of how I over-analyze and over-think everything to the point where I get stuck. Richard's brashly laughing about how block-headed he'd been and even still is.

Richard swirls his drink and continues, "This time, in the park, I was really hassling Eric. You know, maybe I'd seen some things but it was hard to tell. Eric tried to explain it with every angle he could but I was not going to listen. No way. Finally Eric stops me. He got real, real serious and he told me enough was enough and he would show me once and for all. And I'm like, great, now I've done it. I've pissed him off what's he going to do to me now?

So, Eric pointed to the sky and asked me if it looked like it would storm. Looking up it was the same, perfect summer day as when we came in. Bright, clear blue... without a single trace of a cloud." Eric starts chuckling. Richard grins as he tells us Eric asked him to pay attention to the wind. "And his face, Eric's face just perfectly serene. So I stopped and did as he asked. I looked around at the trees and paid attention to what I could feel." Richard holds his hand out to feel the wind in the air on the porch. It's quiet and still. "It was still like it is now."

"There was barely any wind at all. Occasionally, the lightest of breezes would blow through. I remember, Eric moved his arm out away from his body and turned his palm so that it was facing the sky.

And he slowly moved his hand up about six inches. I didn't even have time to think about what he was doing because a blasting wind blew through the park about 20 seconds later. I mean it just blasted! Plates of food, napkins, and clothes from people picnicking all blew away. People were chasing after things all through the park!" Richard launches his head back laughing at the memory of the sudden chaos.

"Eric turned his palm so that it was facing the ground and then lowered his hand six inches. Almost immediately, the wind died off completely." Richard loves it. His whole face is lit up with the memory.

I smirk. It's a funny story. It could have been well-timed coincidence.

"So, I wasn't convinced. A little worried maybe but I wouldn't let myself feel that. I told Eric it could have been coincidence. Eric nodded and told me that was fine." I chuckle to myself. It sucks we thought the same thing.

Richard puts his drink on the table to act this part out, "So, Eric, what he did was, turned his palm back up to the sky and raised his hand. Less than half a minute later another blasting wind came through. It tore through the park and sent Frisbee's sailing through the air. Then Eric held his hand in the air and the wind didn't stop.

So, then he looked at me and he was like, you know, tell me when it should stop. But man, I was defiant. You guys don't know. In my mind, I refused, this wasn't proof. Finally, I said stop. So, Eric turned his palm downward and lowered his hand. Seconds later the wind completely died off. I mean nothing!

But still... I still wasn't convinced. It could all be timing, so I thought. That didn't phase Eric at all. He didn't get pissed off or nothing. He nodded again. All he said was fine, then pointed toward the sky.

And I didn't show it then but, I mean, I almost freaked out. I was shocked. Directly above us all these huge black clouds started swirling in the sky. It was like the clouds were all pouring out of a hole forming a huge swirling you know, whirlpool, or vortex over us. Within minutes, it happened so fast, the clouds completely blocked out the sky. People around us were all yelling and pointing at it, up in the sky. Some were packing up and running for their cars. It went from the bright, clear, middle of the afternoon to as dark as night.

Trust me, these weren't puffy, white wispy playful clouds. They were huge, thick storm clouds. Black as night and it extended as far as I could see. They pushed out and swallowed the sky so fast it was like water crashing out from a hose."

Matthew and I are still. Frozen imagining his story. Not even the dogs move.

Quietly, assuredly Richard continues, "Eric moved his hands and wham! The wind blasted in. Then, perfectly calm, Eric looked right into my eyes and told me the rain was coming. And, sure enough, seconds later I sat and watched a sheet of torrential, hurricane like rain moving towards us across the park in a wall. It was just a wall of water. People screamed and all ran for their cars but Eric and I just sat. Who knows what anybody would of thought but we just sat, staring at each other, not going anywhere. At this point, I was scared, but I was so mad that I'm sitting there trying to convince myself it's all nothing.

The rain came down so hard it stung my face and the wind was blasting. I felt like I was in the middle of a hurricane and we never really get Hurricanes in the Northeast and definitely not in the dead of summer.

Eric yelled to speak over the storm, because the rain was coming down so hard." Richard laughs as he tells us. "Then Eric told me, now it's going to stop."

Richard looks away for a moment, as if he can barely recall the memory without still being affected by it, "Seconds later you could see the line where the rain was stopping. It's like it didn't start to sprinkle and then dry up. It was a downpour of huge, biting, drops of water and then it stopped and you could see the line where the final drops went across the sky.

Then it was perfectly still again. No wind, no rain. The storm clouds were still right above us, directly overhead."

Richard starts shaking his head like he still can barely believe it. "I can't really explain why. But I still refused to accept Eric was doing it. I refused to believe a man could have that kind of power. But... he didn't stop. Eric snapped his fingers and almost instantly the wall of rain drove in from the distance. I could see it coming. The wind hit us with a blast and then rain tore through the park.

The people who were left all ran for cover. Branches were flying through the air, with leaves being torn off of trees. Eric and I... we just sat there. Eric kept it right up. He'd say stop and everything would stop. He'd say start and everything would start. He'd have wind with no rain and rain with no wind. Then he told me to say when it should start and stop. Just as I'd say start it would start and when I said stop, click like a switch, it'd stop. I wasn't controlling it but Eric wanted me to be convinced, without a shred of doubt, that he wasn't trying to time it. I waited, purposely, this is how stubborn I was, to find moments where the rain and wind were so hard there was no doubt in my mind they wouldn't stop on their own. But then, as soon as I said stop it would end just like someone shut off a faucet.

We even had it going in 10 second bursts. A sheet of rain would come, I'd say stop, it would stop, I would immediately say start and bam, the rain would come." Richard bellows a deep laugh at the insanity of it. I can't help but laugh with him. To see something like that is beyond crazy. It's unimaginable. But to see it and still defiantly refuse is off the record out of your mind.

Eric points at Richard. "You see! You see what I've had to deal with? Can you imagine seeing that and still refusing? It's beyond stubborn it's psychotic!"

Richard throws his hands up, "Yeah, I agree. It probably is. There was no way to deny it. It was a completely unnatural way for rain and weather to work! Finally, Eric told me I'd seen enough. You know, I was frozen and soaked!" He laughs as he suggests he was partly frozen by how cold the wind had been and also in shock. His whole reality was blown and he felt like smoke should've been coming out of his ears.

"As soon as Eric told me I'd seen enough the sun shot through the dark, black storm clouds. It was like a beam, just cut right through it. By then, we were like, we need to get out of here and walked pretty quickly back to their car. We were sloshing through, I'm not kidding, at least a half a foot of water." Richard puts his hand about four inches below his knee to show us where the water line was. He grins. "When the rain came down it dumped. I even asked to make it sprinkle and Eric did that too.

There were branches, leaves and all kinds of vegetation thrown all over the place. The whole park was wrecked, totally trashed, and there wasn't a person left. By the time we got back to the car, less than 3 minutes, there wasn't a cloud in the sky. It was right back to the perfectly bright summer's day."

Eric starts to laugh in his seat, shaking his head. "I told you he was as dumb as a brick. See, that's why I don't do miracles anymore. They don't do a damn bit of good. Ain't worth nothing."

Eric mimics a whiny, pleading voice, "Oh, if I could just *see* something I'd believe. Yeah, oh, show me what you can do, then I'll follow and devote my life to you. Ha! What a joke. Tell them, after all that, what you did when I dropped you off."

Richard nods his head. "He's right. He's absolutely right. I always said if I'd see something, that'd be enough. I thought it would be too but after that..." he laughs, mostly to himself.

He raises his head to look us in the eye. "Eric took me straight home and dropped me off. Neither of us said much of anything. I was gone. In total shock and denial but I definitely wasn't proclaiming Eric as some kind of divine master. As soon as I got home I ran into the house and turned on a local channel to see if they said anything about the weather.

A local weatherman was talking about a small patch of severe weather that opened up out of nowhere and disappeared almost as fast. And guess where this small patch of severe weather was?"

Richard grins, shaking his head, "Man, you guys don't believe a word of this. The radar was showing it and I looked, it was right over the area where we were. Right there. They had it on the screen and I could see it."

"See?" Eric said motioning to Richard. "Even the weatherman confirmed it and did he believe? Was he convinced? Nope."

Richard shakes his head. "Nope, I wasn't. Even after all that."

"So, do you blame them for not believing you?" Eric asks Richard.

Richard beams a smile at us. "Not at all. I wouldn't believe me. I mean, I think I sound crazy. I freaking saw the thing and I didn't believe it!" he laughs his face turning bright red. "It's the weirdest thing. You'd never think you'd react like that but I'm telling you... your brain, it shuts down or something or blocks it out or doesn't care... I don't know, but I saw it all and it didn't matter."

"Well, that's not completely true. It helped you. Not enough to keep doing it. See, if you guys ever want to blame someone for why I won't show you anything amazing... any amazing miracles... right there... " Eric points at Richard. "You can blame him. He's the reason I don't do miracles. I learned my lesson. Richard and Danny. They burned it all out and ruined it for everyone else. Miracles don't matter."

Richard gets quiet and looks down into his glass swirling his ice. He's still smiling but it seems even though Eric said everything somewhat jokingly, Richard's reaction tells me he's being more serious than he's letting on.

I don't see how they can be serious. Their stories are so much fun! It's an exciting adventure ride, an incredible fantasy come to life! But are they serious about it all being real? If I saw something like that... I mean... God! What a moment! It'd change you forever!

My lips push around slightly, I'm vaguely aware of doing it. It helps me think. It doesn't seem possible. They treat it so casually. We could be sitting here listening to them talk about pranks they pulled back in High School. To me, if someone's talking about changing reality and creating storms it would be more... well, serious.

My lips twitch around again. When did I start doing that? God, I probably always do it I just never noticed. My lips are stuck out too far from my mouth so I pull them back in. I'd never noticed it before but they went out so naturally it's probably a habit.

It almost makes sense that they tell the stories the way they do. Richard's passionate about telling them. The emotion rolls off of him and sucks you in, completely engaging. Once I started to hear them and considered the possibility... I felt such... hope. That's what I feel; hope, happiness, lightness.

Lightness! I smile to myself. Paying attention to how I feel I notice I'm bubbling with cheer. It's like the weight of the world, gravity itself, is suspended for a moment inside of me. It's wonder. What a wonder it would be if it was real. Richard's whole life must have become a mysterious adventure. But it's so unpractical to think things like that can really happen.

Eric's right, I'd love to believe them but it's so hard. They're great stories to hear. It's amazing to consider the possibility. It makes my head hum with joy, my whole heart feels more open but... I don't see how it could be. You'd think the whole world would know about him if it were true. He wouldn't be holed up, hidden away in some small mountain town in a bookstore.

My thoughts start drifting down the road of analyzing everything Richard has said but then I stop. Another part, a quiet little piece of me from when I was younger, doesn't want me to beat reality back into his tales. Not yet. My whole life I've always believed the human mind could do anything if we only knew how. I believed faith could move mountains... literally, not as a fun thing to say. I believed we could fly, like Superman, only we'd forgotten how. That forgotten voice inside of me, in the gentlest way, brushes aside the cynical, skeptical adult and lets me soak in the possibility... what if.

I haven't drank a thing all night... not even water... but I feel like I'm floating.

Richard makes them more drinks. Eric coughs when he tastes it wondering how anyone ever enjoys alcohol. Richard chuckles and smiles. He pulls out his cigars and starts smelling them. They talk for awhile and Richard prepares to smoke.

I don't want to talk or interrupt or drink or anything. It feels perfectly good to sit and watch these two men, who could be crazy, but if crazy feels this good it's not such a bad thing. I sit and watch them. Enjoy their company and laugh and feel a world of infinite possibility.

When they settle in and Richard's puffing on his cigar he bursts out laughing. Eric turns to look at us and reminds us Richard is hopelessly brainwashed and a fanatic. Richard grins and tells us it's true. He smiles at Eric and tells him how good it is to see him again. He tells us we can't know what it's like to be away from him.

Eric waves him away with a whatever. Richard takes a puff and then sits smiling at Eric. It's a simple, genuine grin.

"Now what?" Eric says suspiciously.

"I want to tell them about the entity."

Eric sits unsure. "Which entity? I need more details than that." Eric scowls a little at him.

Richard pulls up to the table chuckling. "Do you remember the group of super smart Asian MIT students I introduced you to?"

Leaning back in his chair Eric keeps staring at Richard, an uncertain look on his face. Then he slips a slight smile and rolls his eyes. "Oh God, that. I don't know if you want to tell them that... well, go ahead, sure!"

With a deep chuckle Richard tells us he was once a caretaker of this huge property. "The place was huge. It had sprawling lawns, tennis courts, pools... a real nice place. Since meeting Eric I was always looking for really smart people I could speak with that might understand where I was coming from or figure out Eric from a scientific perspective. One time I found a group of these really smart guys who were attending MIT or had already graduated. I can't remember exactly but some of them were into engineering, others science and math. When I first met them I talked with them about the universe, and physics and then I told them about Eric and figured they'd give him a run for his money.

I arranged for them to meet Eric at my place on this big property I was running. There were 7 or 8 of them. Anyway, I get them together and Eric starts talking to them and it didn't take long before I realized they weren't going to get it. Instead, they started hounding Eric to show them something. Like if what he was saying was true he should just prove it. Eric kept going round and round with them until I had to go out to check the property.

I'd been gone for awhile and started walking back across the lawn toward the house. To get up to the house there was a long staircase along the side. It goes up about two stories. So, as I'm walking back I watch all 7 or 8 of them fly out the door running down the steps." Richard starts howling and slapping his knee. "I mean, they weren't just running down the steps they were taking dangerous leaps of 5 or 6 steps, falling all over each other, to get down. They hit the ground running and sprint right towards me."

Eric starts laughing. Richard looks at him, "You remember that? Did you see them run out?"

Eric nods his head yes as he tries to stop from laughing. Richard continues, "So I call out to them, like hey guys where you going? They didn't say a word. They flew right past me never even slowing down. They all looked sheet white with terror-stricken faces.

So I ran back to the house as fast as I could to see Eric sitting there, casually, as if nothing had happened at all. Out of breath I asked what happened to all the students. Almost indifferently, Eric mentioned they thought they knew it all and had it all figured out. They got on the topic of entities and ignorantly started proclaiming how impossible it was and started being rowdy and stupid. Finally Eric asked them if they wanted to see an entity. They all said they did, laughing at him like it was a joke. So, Eric opened a portal and summoned one on the spot, right into the room in front of all of them. They freaked out and took off!"

Eric confirms Richard's story. "Yep. They thought they knew it all. No way could something like that happen."

Richard takes a puff of his cigar. "Now, I wasn't sure if I should believe Eric or not."

"As always." Eric cuts in.

"Right, so I eventually tracked one of the guys down and asked him about it. At first he wouldn't talk but I persisted, you know not letting up stubborn like I am, until the guy broke down and confessed about what he'd seen. For me, I was a little floored. I asked him, doesn't that blow your mind? Don't you want to learn and figure out how he did it? You know what he told me. No, he said. He wanted nothing to do with me, or Eric or any of it.

I was amazed. I didn't get it! Rather than be curious or intensify their interest in how it had all taken place none of them wanted to learn from Eric. None of them even wanted to talk about it. Brilliant guys."

Eric points at Richard. "There's another reason. There you go. Miracles don't work. People always whine and whine about seeing is believing, it's a joke. I did eventually learn that if someone's not ready to see somethin', they'll go the opposite direction. Rather than having more belief and being more curious they lose any interest or curiosity they had and it cuts them off the rest of their life. They shut down and you can never approach them again. It went too far outside their world and how they believe it works. It doesn't matter how smart they are, it even makes it worse, because they think they know how it all works."

What a sucky dilemma. You want to see something in order to believe in it but then when you see it you freak out because it breaks all the beliefs you had in the first place which was the reason you didn't believe in it. Classic catch-22.

Richard's antics and animated storytelling makes the episode extremely funny. My side hurts from laughing but I know if I was there, I probably would have been pushing them out of the way to get out of there first. Part of me wishes that wasn't true. It would be such an amazing moment to witness someone summon a being from another place, made of brilliant shining blue energy, right in front of you. What a confirmation of all my hopes and dreams from childhood. It's so easy to hear Richard speak and think I'd be one who didn't run and would stand in amazement but after my entity encounter I know reality is unexpectedly more intense than hearing about it.

That's what throws me off so much. I never expected the entity to be like it was. It should have been like this is. Fun to hear about and think about... a fun story to tell. I never imagined the real intensity and I couldn't even see it. If I had seen something... maybe I would have never talked to Eric again.

Suddenly I remember Eric telling Peter how full of fear I am. He said I had one foot out the door, ready to run. I never pictured myself as fearful. I've taken lots of risks and never let fear hold me back... in fact fear used to piss me off. If there was something I was afraid of I'd immediately attack it. But now... Eric is right. I don't know why but I do feel afraid. It's strange to think he's right about that.

I turn to look at Eric. He and Richard are laughing about other people who'd seen Eric do things and their reactions. Part of me feels free. I know I'm afraid and knowing it I can conquer it. Another part feels more fear. If he's right about me being afraid before I realized it myself, what else could he be right about?

We sit out on the porch long through the night. Richard has endless stories to tell. Eric starts telling stories as well... times and students he's had before Richard. Times when he knew even less than he did when he met Richard and was still figuring things out. Manipulating and changing reality just to see how far he could go and what he could do.

In the few short years Richard has spent with Eric he's lived lifetimes. He has stories nobody in the world would believe but they are his. He's seen them with his own eyes. It's the perfect dream, all the better because it's real and he's come through. There he sits, feet away from me, describing things you'd only see in movies and laughing about them as if they were commonplace. What's more, he's only one of Eric's students.

I wonder what the others have seen.
The morning dew fills the air and they hardly ever stop talking. Even when Eric decides it's late and we should go to bed, they don't stop. The end finally comes, not because there's nothing left to tell. They stop because we can barely stay awake to hear them. They could have gone on for days.

Matthew and I thank Richard and Eric for sharing the stories with us and go into the living room to pass out.

Somewhere in my mind, I separate the Eric I know from the Eric in the stories. Subtly, I make the tales fantasy, so that they're safe to think about without accepting them as real. Even thinking about them makes my pulse quicken and my heart surge with a hopeful lightness. There's a truth to them.

It's a good sleep.

when calling out to the Universe... do not expect your lonely echo to be that which answers...

Eternity Sings

chapter twenty-five

The next day Eric and I wake up and go to the bookstore to pack. Matthew stays and sleeps in. Most of the store is already packed up. The shelves, once filled with books, are now bare except for an occasional plant or trinket. The glass display cases still have some of the larger crystals. Everyone that I know is there. They are all bustling. Eric is animated and light, warning people what's fragile and how to mark the boxes, but he is quieter than normal. I chalk it up to lack of sleep... I feel a little tired too.

Scanning the shelves for any left over items I spy a little brass bowl with a short, thick stick in it. I take it off the shelf and look at it. Intricate carvings are engraved all along the inside with a strip painted on the outside. The wooden stick is like a small mallet. It's short but thick at one end and becomes thin at the other, like a small bat. I start clinking the little stick at the bottom of the bowl. It's like something that might be used to crush herbs. Each time I hit the bottom the bowl makes a bright, ringing, 'ting!' sound. Eric comes from the back and looks at me sitting on the edge of the couch holding it.

He smirks. "You know what that is right?"

I nod my head absently.

"Oh really? What is it?" Eric asks sarcastically.

"It's to crush herbs... for ceremonial potions or something like that."
I push the stick on the bottom to show him the crushing movement I
made up.

He rolls his eyes at me and shakes his head. "No, that's not what it is.
Here, let me teach you yet another thing." He takes the bowl and
sticks his palm firmly out, resting the bowl so that it's flat on his
palm. Taking the little wooden stick he strikes the side of the bowl
and quickly starts running the stick along the outside of the bowl in a
circle. The ringing quickly stops and Eric mutters to himself. He tries
again. This time instead of the ringing dying off when he runs it along
the outside of the bowl it starts to make a new tone, like when you run
your hand along the rim of a wine glass. It quickly dies as a horrible,
dragging clang spits out from the bowl. Eric swears and hands the
bowl back to me.

"Here, I don't want to bother with it now. It's a Tibetan Singing bowl.
You sit and hold it and run the mallet on the outside of the bowl and
it starts to make a clear ringing sound. You hold the ringing sound
and it shifts your mind. It puts you into a special state of
consciousness." He explains.

"So, you meditate with it?" I ask, uncertain about what 'special state
of consciousness' really means.

"Yeah, basically. Go ahead and try it."

Peter comes swooping in from behind me, having watched Eric try,
and takes the bowl. Excitedly he tells us he'll show us how it's done.
He holds it in his hand but doesn't hit it as hard as Eric did. After a
few times around the bowl the same awful dragging clang rings out.
He tries again, this time not starting with a hit at all but he keeps
circling the bowl and doesn't get anywhere. Eric tells him to let me
try it but Peter moves away declaring he's very good at it and just
needs to find the right spot. Three tries later and he's only gotten it
around four or five times until the awful clang happens. It's the best
ring yet but when the mallet sounds like it's dragging it's so disruptive
I can't imagine anyone meditating through it.

Peter gets frustrated. It isn't working so he hands it back. Eric prods, joking and asking Peter what happened. They start bantering back and forth. It all fades into the background. All I can see are the designs inside the bowl. They're so detailed and intricate. I love them. I can hear it ringing inside my head from the few times Peter had it going.

Taking the mallet I run it along the outside ever-so-gently. Smoothly, softly, it starts to ring. I smile to myself. I've got it – BLRAAANG!! It spits the awful sound at me and I jump. Eric's looking at me from the corner of his eye while prodding Peter. He tells me to not hold the mallet slanted and instead hold it straighter so it's pointing up. Holding the mallet to the singing bowl again I see what he's talking about. When I start to swirl the mallet around I keep my hand in the middle above the center of the bowl. The mallet is almost horizontal with the rim of the bowl. I change my hand so that it's straight over the rim. Staring straight into the bottom of the bowl I feel the cool touch of the brass on my hand.

My fingers unconsciously turn the mallet so they can feel the grain of the wood. Something about the way the light catches the brass and shines along the intricate runes makes me feel very peaceful. The business of everyone packing and Eric and Peter joking with each other slips into the background as I start running the mallet along the rim. The first vibrations of the bowl sing through my hand but I can't hear them yet. I feel them vibrate through my palm until it starts to ring softly. I keep running it along and then the ringing gets louder as I feel the vibration get stronger. It hits a good rhythm and I keep going. Smiling I listen to the ringing of the bowl as I feel the vibration run through my arm. I imagine the bowl isn't the only thing ringing but the vibration running through my body is ringing as well. My arm and the bowl are ringing in unison.

It keeps ringing and grows louder and louder. I'm aware that Peter and Eric stop talking and start watching me. Finally the ringing and vibration grow so loud it clangs out and it all abruptly stops. My head tosses back as I burst out laughing. "This is awesome."

Peter nods his head. "Heeey, check him out. Not baaad. You're pretty good for having never seen it before."

I grin. "Beginner's luck."

I catch Eric staring at me. "Or... maybe you remember from a past life." His tone is steady and doesn't seem to have any hint of humor in it. He smiles and walks away. I laugh nervously. How do I take that? Is he joking? Past lives... pffft. I look at the bowl and put it back on the shelf.

We stay for awhile and I pack a few boxes. Some of the guys are hungry so they send me up the street to get everyone lunch. I come back and Eric decides he's had enough and we go back to the house to wake Matthew.

When Matthew's up and ready Eric tells us everyone's moving the sign on top of the store today. I laugh, assuming it's another joke. The sign is huge.

"I don't know why you're laughing. I'm not joking." He informs me. "Don't worry. It'll be easy."

"How did you guys get the sign up there in the first place?" I ask naively.

"The sign company had a giant crane truck set it up there while a crew fastened the bolts."

My mouth drops a little.

We go back to the store and, sure enough, Eric's truck is out front and a few of the students are on the roof. I smile a bit as I spy Richard on the roof with Peter. Eric told us the other students would tie Eric up if they thought he was talking to him. Here he is helping. After spending the previous day with him I can't see why they don't like him. He obviously has great respect for Eric and underwent an amazing transformation learning from him. I find it hard to believe anyone could dislike him.

When I climb up on the roof any shred of hope that the sign can actually be moved vanishes. It's about seven feet tall, nine or ten feet long and three feet thick. I wonder out loud how much it weighs and everyone chimes in they'd already estimated it at around eight or nine hundred pounds. Eric scoffs at them all and says it's mostly plastic. He shouts out that their attitudes and beliefs will only make it heavier. Everyone laughs at the idea that their thinking will actually have that much impact on how heavy it really is.

The bolts keeping it in place are intimidating. They're about as large and round as my wrists. Everyone has moving straps and ropes. The plan is to unbolt it, lift it off the steel post it's sitting on, which means lifting it at least 4 feet into the air, put ropes around it and then lower it to the truck below. It's madness.

Everyone starts to complain about being crushed and how once it's off the pole they'll never be able to move it. Eric quiets them all down and tells them they don't know what they're talking about and are only being pessimistic and negative. Eric's the only one who seems to think we can move it without heavy machinery.

My job is to help lift it off the pole and keep it steady while they rope it once it's off. I'm pretty sure it will topple onto to me and I'll be horribly maimed if not killed outright. Still, I'll try it anyway.

We finally start to lift it. Richard's face is blazing red. The veins in his arms and forehead are alarmingly large. It distracts me and my legs shake. The veins in his face will pop and blood will spew all over me. Plus then the sign will fall and I'll be killed... I play the episode out in my head. Richard's bulging veins pop, spewing incredible amounts of blood all over the place like a burst water pipe... it will all splash in my face as he cries out and falls over... which will cause the sign to groan and start falling over in slow motion toward me. I'll be desperately trying to wipe the gallons of blood off my face as everyone screams for me to run... unable to tell which way to flee I'll be smashed... but because the sign will have a taste for human flesh it won't stop there. It'll skid to the edge of the roof, with me stuck on it like a bug on a windshield, move itself like some kind of giant slug monster, fall off and crush the others waiting below... not to leave more than one survivor... it will slide off of Eric's truck into the side of the bookstore collapsing part of the roof which will make one of the two people, Peter or Frank, on the roof fall into the debris. The weight of the person and the debris will hit the sign on the bottom causing it to flip over and land on top of them. One person will be left alive to tell the tale and the sign will be assured of living on in local legend.

The whole scene makes me start huffing a laugh out of my mouth while trying to breathe to carry the weight. Richard tries to look back to see why I'm laughing. It's a desperate, worried, are you trying to get us both killed look.

Get it together. I force myself to think about something else. Richard has to be carrying the bulk of the weight. Somehow we get it wrapped and roped and lift it down onto the truck where two guys hold it. Nobody says anything when Eric asks them about how it can't be done. Mental note... despite everyone else wanting to give up and certain the task couldn't be done, Eric is proven right. Nobody wants to admit this. Instead claiming it was much harder than it looked, which he wouldn't know since he didn't help lift it. We'd gotten lucky that nothing went wrong.

They drive up to Eric's house with the huge sign wobbling in the back and it starts over again. Lifting it down the roof was one thing but now they have to carry it into Eric's back yard. With only ropes it will be extremely difficult to haul it so far without dropping it. They aren't quite as adamant as taking it down but they protest quite a bit. I keep quiet this time having been proven flatly wrong thinking I'd be killed earlier. Eric rolls his eyes and tells them to keep quiet. He grabs a large piece of cardboard from one of the moving boxes and places it at the base of the truck. He instructs them to lift it onto the cardboard and then with two people holding the sign the others will drag the cardboard with the sign on it into the backyard. It's a straight shot with mostly driveway.

Nobody says a word. They do as he says and slide it straight into the backyard.

I start carrying boxes into the house while some of the others go to get another load of big items. It isn't long before they come back with the glass display cases the crystals were in. Peter leaps into the back of the truck to position himself to carry one. Eric comes over and starts directing him to take out as much glass as he can first and to have several people help. Peter sharply tells him that they moved them into the truck and they can move them out without being told what to do. Eric raises his arms up in the air and tells him to do it his way and walks off.

Less than a minute later I jump when I hear a loud, shattering crash. The display case slipped out of Peter's hands while he was trying to lift it down from the truck. It hit the tailgate and most of the top glass shifted and fell shattering in the bottom of the case. Eric starts yelling at Peter about how if he had listened and asked for help and wasn't out to prove something it could have been avoided. Peter argues back but Eric cuts him off telling him the problem is that he really doesn't care because it's Eric's display case, not his. Peter throws his hands up and screams that it's Eric's fault for saying he needed help and if he wasn't all over their shit they wouldn't be so nervous and mistakes wouldn't happen.

Everyone freezes.

Peter's up in Eric's face, his face is beet red. The way he threw his hands up makes me think he's almost considering pushing Eric and starting something. Eric and Peter lock gazes for a moment and Eric tells him he needs to think about who he's talking to. Peter spins on his heels and walks away.

I look around to gauge everyone's reaction. They look shocked, shaking their heads in disbelief. Eric turns to the others and asks if they think Peter's right or out of line. Frank acknowledges that Peter's in a pissy mood and isn't accepting help and that it was his fault. Looking back over my shoulder I don't see Peter. He'd wandered into the back yard. This is one of Eric's top students? I'd never talk to someone I had any respect for that way, much less someone that I'm supposed to admire. It's taken some time but I'm starting to get that the group is less of a structured school or organization and more like a family. They've long ago skipped the formalities and polite civilities. They all act as they are. It's all out in the open, real and raw.

I make another mental note that Eric was right about the cases and in trying to direct Peter. The whole episode cost a case and more time than if others had been allowed to help. More than that... even when I thought Peter might actually hit Eric I didn't see a single movement on Eric's part that he was going to try to defend himself. Eric is bigger than Peter's pixie frame but a hit to the face is a hit to the face. Maybe Eric knows Peter well enough to know where the line is. There's something else there. His whole reaction to it. He didn't make any physical gestures to intimidate Peter or try to appear threatening like someone else in that situation would. His face didn't get flush from any real anger the way Peter's did. He looked calm. He didn't seem bothered by it at all. I toss it in my mind back and forth. I can't put my finger on it but there's something to that... I just don't know what it is.

Everything returns to normal and everyone starts carrying more boxes into the house. After awhile Peter comes back and doesn't say a word. He starts unloading with everyone else. The house quickly fills up and the living room is stacked with stuff. It starts to get dark and the bookstore still isn't completely empty but it's close. Eric tells Matthew and I that we've done enough and should go home. The others will finish the move tomorrow. He thanks us for helping and we drive home.

When I wake up the next morning I'm wiped out. The day slowly strolls by. I do little more than write in my journal, play on the computer and stare out the window. I wonder about the possibility of past lives and what it would mean to remember them all.

According to Eric not everyone has past lives. The thought seems cold, uncaring. But then, the idea of living more than one life is like a childhood fantasy. Impractical and not logical. What about the illogical part?

Is it illogical? Are you sure?

Hrmm, no I'm not sure. You're right. That doesn't seem true. Eric's explanation has a strange logic to it.

The idea of creating an energy body that can carry over from one life to the next resonates with what I've always felt was true. Even that the world, Gaia, learns when others die and they give their life experiences to the world's consciousness makes a strange kind of sense. It's hard to wrestle with the two emotions.

On one hand feeling like the concept creates an uncaring world, removed from the idea that humans are the top of the ultimate food chain. Like we aren't the main reason for the universe to exist. One the other hand, maybe it does make sense but it makes spirituality too scientific and creates a sense that some people are more important than others.

But doesn't it allow for them to have a choice?

Well, yes, they have a choice.

So, isn't that as it should be?

You mean like, knock and it will be answered and seek and you will find stuff? Well, I guess but... I've gotten lost. I'm trying to make a point clear here. Trying to clarify my two conflicting emotions. I lost my train of thought so I pace in circles in my room, trying to air it out.

Can the two meet? Is there a way to make them both happy? I groan out loud. Frustrating. Taking a deep breath I try again, "One hand it seems cold. Ah yes. On the other hand it feels like an over-reasoned explanation for something that is only a hopeful dream. Of course everyone wants to live forever so let's find some way to explain it to make it seem possible and rational. On the other hand I've always thought it could be possible and Eric's reasoning makes sense. But now that it makes sense... it seems too... sensical." Walking close to my bed I jump up and flop on it. You say you want the truth, you want science... but science is cold... so what's the problem? Sighing, "Damn. I want it both ways."

It makes me want to go to sleep. Throwing my blanket on, I roll over and notice my foot sticking out from the bottom of my blanket. I move it slightly and suddenly catch a halo-like outline in my vision.

The aura. I move my foot slightly back and forth. A bright translucent fog or outline extends about an inch away from my foot. It keeps the same figure as my foot and even bubbles evenly with each toe. As I move my foot one way it follows it perfectly and doesn't trail like a sunspot does.

If you watch it you can see it more clearly.

I watch it against my white wall, moving my foot slightly back and forth. It starts to glow brighter. Is it glowing brighter or am I seeing it more clearly? I think about the things Eric has told me. He said energy is a frequency that I can tune into, like a radio station. I have to tune my consciousness to it. For an hour I lie there in bed studying the aura of my foot and then start to alternate looking at the one on my hand.

"Here it is, test one." I tell myself out loud. "Every morning, as you wake up, you'll study your own aura. If Eric's right I'll get better and start to see energy more clearly." I commit to the project. I have to start doing things I can see for myself and do it by myself so I can track results without feeling pressure from other people who can see them better or tell me I'm crazy for trying at all.

The apartment is quiet so in between playing on the computer I find myself reflecting. Everything he's ever said always fits so perfectly. Nothing ever seems out of order. One idea flows into the next and as far as I think on it I can find no end. I can't see the ceiling of where he's going with it all. Usually I can find a block or a cap, some kind of limit where it all breaks down and flaws or problems start to appear.

Evening comes quickly as I sit in my window ledge pondering the Universe according to Eric Pepin. Matthew and Justin come home and are pretty beat. They wake me out of my thoughts. Looking around my room it suddenly bothers me how messy everything is. At the foot of my bed is a giant stack of dirty clothes falling out of my closet... as always. The round glass table by my window is piled up with mail, books and papers from a script I've been putting off for six months. Feels like I just cleaned this place!

Frantically, I start cleaning my table and computer desk. Justin and Matthew are sprawling out in the living room with the glass door open. I get the feeling they'll be passing out soon so I shut my door and start gathering laundry. Sneaking into the living room I take a peek at what they're doing. Matthew's propped up slightly with a pillow against the wall laying on his bed. Justin's lying on Peggy's single bed and both seem like they're already asleep.

I don't feel comfortable going to sleep with my room so wrecked. It feels good to have it start to look clean. I gather my laundry into a giant stack and stuff it into the laundry basket. I carry it down the stairs into the basement laundry room and then climb back up. Back in the apartment all the lights are off except for my bedroom. My bed is made nice and orderly. It actually looks inviting so I put the laundry basket next to me and lay down facing up at the ceiling. Man, I'm tired. I suddenly realize how exhausted I feel. It feels good to lie down.

The ceiling is white textured with the little speckles of gunk. I wonder why they do that to ceilings? Slowly... starting... to drift off asleep but shake myself back awake as soon as I realize it. I have to stay awake to get my laundry.

Lying, listening to the quiet of the apartment compared to the noise of outside traffic I hear a voice start to softly sing.

It isn't a brash, radio voice with lots of instruments and a band, it's pure song. Voice without any backup. What song is that? Straining my ears I try to make out the words. It's some kind of foreign language. The song grows louder, echoing strangely through the room. Suddenly, it's easy to hear and I can clearly make the song out.

It's unlike any voice I've ever heard. It's hauntingly beautiful. The quality of it is beyond anything I can remember. If a female opera singer sang slowly, alluringly, but was able to sing in unison with · herself and could wrap her notes together, neither overpowering the other but mingle some in the background and have others fall and rise into the foreground but not in the way that's done with electronics or choirs... it might come close at least to the sound of it. A choir has many distinct voices. Electronic looping is clearly one voice over another. The same singer but separate parts of them singing. This voice however, is one, single voice that has a quality where I can tell it's one single voice but it sounds like many words being spoken at once. The chorus of movements within the song are the way it's speaking.

Imagine hearing someone sing a song that makes no sense by itself. Only when 14 other voices sing with it, is the message clear. This is it. This is the song chiming through my room. My mind is still, wrapped in wonder at what dances in the air around me. Where is it coming from? It's so beautiful... I gotta know how they made this thing... it's incredible. The traffic from outside is constant. It doesn't float in through the window. No radio has ever played through the walls of the apartment and it doesn't have a muffled sound. It's so clear and crisp.

In my mind. It's playing in my mind. No... it can't be. It's coming from the ceiling... from up there. I stare at the white speckles on the ceiling. The voice sounds as if it's coming down a pipe in the ceiling from very far away. It's clear, crisp, but distant.

Is it distant? It doesn't sound distant. No... it feels... distant. Suddenly I feel a soft caress of emotion, a wishful yearning. Stirring, deep in my heart. It's not a sexual yearning, or even emotional. It calls to a place deep inside of me. So deep it feels as if it pulls at the root of my soul. Some place so distant... even I was unaware. But... it's calling to me.

The words make no sense. There isn't a language on Earth that comes close to it. Yet, I understand some meaning. Slowly, sweetly... softly... but present. What rapture... To me... it's calling to me. It doesn't make sense how I know that, but I'm as certain as if it were singing English. It wants me to come. This voice, if it can be called that. This angelic serenade... it's beckoning me. The yearning grows stronger... I want to go with it. Yes, I want to answer. How it pulls me... no human voice could ever express so much... deepest love and longing no human heart could know... follow it... and suddenly panic strikes me.

I'm shocked out of wanting to follow it as if someone slashed me with a whip. This isn't normal! Paranormal! The yearning is so strong, and the certainty that it's speaking to me and calling to me so clear, if I listen it will pull my soul away and I'll die! No human could ever sing like that!

The pyramid! Quick! Recalling Eric's lesson I instantly engage the pyramid of psychic defense he showed me. Immediately the voice is gone. I shoot up in bed as if I'd been unable to move as long as it sang to me.

I look around the apartment trying to see or feel something there like the entity before. There's nothing. Matthew and Justin! I run into the living room to see if the other two are caught by it. They're both quiet and fast asleep. My breathing is fast and I concentrate on slowing it down. Listen...

Listening intently I hear nothing. If she was singing to them... she's gone now. Looking in the dim light I make out Justin's body on the bed. Justin's been learning a lot longer than I have. If there was something here he would have felt it and woken up. I pace nervously in my room for a few minutes maintaining my focus on the pyramid.

"The pyramid works. Pyramid works. You're safe... just calm down." I try to assure myself out loud. I grab my laundry basket and finish my laundry. I feel nothing else and the voice doesn't come back. Eventually, I go to bed, ready to call up the pyramid at the first sign of anything strange.

Morning comes and I hear Matthew and Justin talking. I roll out of bed and go to pour myself some cereal.

"So, how did you guys sleep?" I ask wondering if they heard anything.

"Good." Justin says, "I slept like a baby."

"Cool." I say. "How'd you sleep Matthew?"

Matthew doesn't answer right away. Rather than answering he lingers and finally rolls out a question, "Why you didn't sleep good?"

"No, I slept fine." I tell him. "I heard something a little weird last night, that's all."

He grins and laughs to himself. "Ahhh yeaaaah. You heard her too huh?"

His openness catches me off guard. If he heard what I heard he wouldn't sound so jokey. "Heard who?" I ask suspiciously.

"Did you or didn't you hear her? The voice? Did she sing to you?" Matthew asks sounding unsure now.

My jaw drops a little and I stir my spoon in my cereal unconsciously. "You heard the singing too? That's it. That's what it was. Singing." I tell him. I'm surprised. I can't believe he heard it too. Maybe it was a radio.

"Yeah man, I couldn't sleep at all. I figured she'd move on eventually but she sang all night long. I thought it was the radio at first but none of the radios were on." Matthew tells me.

I start to laugh, "You heard her all night long? No way! I only heard it for a few minutes."

Now Matthew seems surprised. "A few minutes? No, she sang all night long. Believe me. It was cool at first but after awhile I was like, come on, let me go to bed."

"Huh." I say trying to put it together in my head. "You know what, I freaked out and put up a pyramid and she stopped right away. I didn't hear her after that."

"The pyramid? I didn't do that. She didn't seem bad it just, like, you know, kept going for a long time." Matthew says sounding confused that I did that.

Suddenly, it makes sense. I put up the pyramid which broke the connection. If the connection was in our minds I blocked it out as soon as I put up my defenses. Matthew was more trusting and so he was able to hear it all night long. Waves of failure and defeat drop on me like wet sandbags. Damn it. My fear. His reaction makes me rethink my own. Why am I so afraid? He thought she was cool but I freaked out. God, Matthew went with it, the whole thing all night long. How can he do that? Why wasn't he afraid...

Not a little kid like you. Scared of everything.

How did I get like this? I never thought I was like this but now... it's all the time. Everything I do. Why couldn't I be like Matthew? Have a little courage... he woke up fine... what did I seriously think was going to happen?

Shame and regret. I feel embarrassed and stupid. Not only is Matthew better at feeling and sensing things, he's braver and more trusting too. I blew it. He could feel that it wasn't a bad thing and look what he got. Staring at the counter the sound of the strange, mysterious voice echoes through my mind. The most amazing, unnatural, inspiring... haunting thing I've ever heard. And I was afraid of it. God, it could have been the Universe itself singing me to sleep and I cut it off. What does that say about me?

Looking at Matthew I can't help but wonder how he does it. Eric says it's the way he is, the way his mind works that makes it easier for him. I say if I could only experience something I'd believe... then I get it and I flip. I'm an idiot.

Justin is strangely quiet and doesn't offer much about what it could have been. I don't tell them but she reminded me of a siren. Right out of a Greek legend. The sea serpents with the upper bodies of women who would sing so beautifully they'd put a spell on any sailor who heard them and they would be enchanted and turn their ship toward the sirens only to crash on the rocks. But she wasn't like that all. Why do I have to assume everything is out to get me? Why meet life with so much fear? I have never heard anything so strange and hauntingly beautiful in my life, when will I ever get a chance like that again? And the way it called to me... the yearning it created like it was pulling me. It was calling to me and I hung up on it.

Next time I won't be afraid. Next time I'll listen.   If only I knew what to expect. What's going to call next?

forget what you think you know, you don't know it well enough.
no amount of intellect, power, practice, or influence can
prepare you for...

The Discovery of God

chapter twenty-six

Frustrated and disappointed with myself for being so afraid all the time I focus on reality and try to get a steady job. I go through several attempts to schedule an interview with the web company but it keeps getting canceled. Finally we set a solid date for next week. Mentally, this relieves me of any obligation to think about work. I've got a plan, the plan is in motion. Now... what the hell do I do with my time? I'm happy to have this problem.

Eric is also clear of any obligations. The bookstore's gone and he seems to either want his mind off of it or is happy to be relieved of it. I'm not sure which. This leaves us both with nothing else to do but wander L.A.

We spend our time looking for new places and frequenting coffee shops. Traveling around Melrose and Los Feliz up through La Crescenta and Pasadena. Our conversations flip from casual to delving deeper into things he feels I don't understand or simply likes to repeat. I can't tell which. He talks to me about the Earth as a living organism and the consciousness of the planet. Or, moving farther out, the Universe as a living organism and the body of God. Then there's the Force. Which is the living consciousness that moves through the Universe, and is also God. As if that isn't confusing enough he also uses God for... God. God is also the Universe but not the physical universe and it is also the Force, but not strictly the energy moving through everything.

It's strange how he picks and chooses the names for it, seemingly at random. Most of the time I'm able to understand what he means. Most of the time. Sometimes I get confused. It is most difficult to know if he's talking about the universe or the Universe. He makes a distinction.

The universe is the whole big, fat space of stuff in a flat way. Oh look, there are some planets, spinning rocks, and there are some galaxies, gases, and so on until it becomes such a large scale I feel my brain strain. The brain strain is enjoyable, challenging, but also eye-poppingly frustrating. Like trying to play four-square with a tennis ball.

The Universe is the universe but in the context that it is the physical body of a gia-normous being infused with consciousness. God. One's flat. One's full. The way I think about it changes the meaning of what he says. It's an interesting twist.

Then there are topics that we've covered many, many times but he constantly goes over again and again. Red Cells, White Cells and how everything is energy. Energy, energy, energy... it's all about energy. If I understand energy I'm on my way he tells me. When I over-complicate everything I have to go back to the basics. Energy. I nod my head and say things like, "Right, right, uh-huh, uh-huh," so he knows I remember.

Instead of prompting him to skip over the topic, it actually cues him to delve into greater detail, to expand on concepts that we've already covered.

Slowly stirring my coffee I try to think of reasons he might do this as I begin to fill in what he's about to say. We're sitting at a 24 hour coffee shop off the Sunset strip. It's the middle of the day so it's slow.

"You probably think you know this stuff by now don't you?" He stops talking and stares at me. I sit still and don't say anything. Crap. I've been repeating, 'uh-huh', for the past five minutes. I was actually listening. I always do. What if I've overdone it and rather than letting him know I'm following the conversation he's insulted?

Well, you were saying it a little sarcastically.

Dude, who's side are you on?

"Huh? Come on, you think you know everything I'm talking about don't you?" His eyes, while not glaring in any way, hold a definite laser-like quality that makes my brain freak out and go into panic mode. He's sitting abnormally still. Feels like I'm under the microscope.

"Um, well, I mean, it's not that I know it because of me but..." I'm confused and my brain searches for a way to not fan the flames. I've insulted him. I can feel him like waves of heat rolling through me. "I mean, I know it only because you've talked to me about it before."

He nods. "Yeah, that doesn't mean you know it. You know what the problem is with most people?" His voice is steady, light. It sounds nice and normal. Only it feels heavy with an underlying seriousness.

I shake my head no.

"Lazy. People are fucking lazy. They don't want to think. People have to hear things three times, three times before it sticks. The first time you hear somethin' you might remember, oh, twenty percent and I think that's generous. Okay, no offense but you're no rocket scientist. You know what I mean by that. You seem intelligent enough, don't get me wrong, it's just the way the brain works unless you've really trained it otherwise and I don't think you really have. That means the first time you hear something you get twenty percent, the next time you hear it maybe you get thirty or forty percent and then the next time you might get sixty or seventy and that's pretty good. You're skimming the surface. Okay? You sitting there nodding your head means you might be able to follow the general flow but you don't have the details and even when you do finally get the details it doesn't mean you really 'get it', it hasn't 'clicked'." His voice has a distinct no-nonsense tone. It demands examination of what he's trying to communicate.

Eric's very adamant. He drills the point for some time. Even though I'm certain I understand what he's talking about he tells me I have no idea. I'm being naïve, young and dumb. He doesn't pull any punches and levels it at me the way it is.

I weigh what he tells me and then I slide in my come back response. "It's not that I disagree with the idea that someone has to hear things three times before they've absorbed the entirety of any content I just think we've talked about these things a lot and I've got it. I know I'm no genius but my memory is pretty good." I laugh because the honesty of saying I'm not a genius seems funny. Eric doesn't seem to get it so I quickly move on. "Even if you want to argue about whether or not I can remember... I mean, we have talked about this stuff at least three times if not more. So, I think I'm at seventy percent and I get it."

He nods and slightly rolls his eyes. "You're not listening but okay. Believe what you want. Even if that's true there's another reason I continually repeat myself."

Of course, I have to ask why that is. "Why is that?"

"Forced reflection." He says flatly. "This knowledge, what I teach, what I talk about, it's a living thing. It's alive... alive! Do you get it? Of course you don't get it! The second you think you get it before you actually do you cut yourself off. Arrogantly, in your mind, you stop reflecting and listening because you think you already know it all. Just like the planet is a living organism with a living consciousness so is the knowledge I pass on creating something inside of you that's alive. When you reflect on the knowledge I teach you, in a way, you feed it. When you teach others, which you will do someday, you feed it. The way this knowledge dies is stagnation. Reflect, think and ponder, it grows, it flowers." He stops and looks at my face.

I can't hide it... I don't get it. How can he say his ideas and theories are living things?

He shakes his head. "Nope. You don't get it." He sighs. "Listen..." he pauses and rubs his forehead, "how do I explain this? Okay, forget about what I just said. There are levels to this knowledge. There are degrees of understanding. You can get what I'm saying on one level and you can say, yeah, okay, I get it. Then two months later you'll suddenly have this amazing realization and be like, wow, holy crap, amazing! And what you thought you understood you'll suddenly see in a whole new light. It's like you'll make all these connections to other things you never saw or understood before and you've just moved up to this next level. You've gained higher ground and you can see so much more of it. It's become more real. Part of it is intellectual. Another part, you could say, is energy."

I turn my head to the side to signal I'm not sure how it could be energy. He gets it.

He rolls right along, "By energy I mean, that your energy consciousness has risen to a level that you can access or download the information from a different place, a dimensional place. Some of this knowledge you simply cannot understand or really know with your brain! You have to understand it with your dimensional consciousness. If you don't have the energy you can't get there. Just by thinking about this kind of knowledge you are changing your tonal. You're raising your frequency. When you listen to me talk about the knowledge your frequency shifts by the act of attempting to absorb it. The more frequently you shift to that higher tonal the more often you're there. So I sit here and bombard you with this stuff over and over again because it's changing you. It's forcing you to think about it and reflect on it. Even if you think you know 90 percent of this stuff I might throw little bits you've never heard before and that causes you to reflect."

Eric sighs and leans back in his chair, "If you would go home and actually think, reflect, on what I say, my job would be like, 200 times easier. But people don't reflect. Life is too busy, there's too much stimulation. As soon as you walk away from me you're immediately bombarded and absorbed back into the DOE. By reflecting you keep the DOE at bay and you give yourself more time in that place absorbing that energy. But it's too hard. Most people want to think about it once and then arrogantly, or ignorantly I guess, believe that they get it! It's ridiculous! Laziness! I don't know what else to call it! But part of it is the DOE itself. The DOE pushes against you and moves you back into a lower tonal which makes it harder to even think to remember to reflect on the knowledge I've given you. That's why it's so important in the beginning to have a teacher. It's important to have someone who's out of the DOE who can pull you out of the DOE with them for awhile and teach you how to swim until you get strong enough to pull yourself out of it. If I removed myself from your life right now you'd be absorbed back into the DOE in a matter of days. It would happen that fast. And you would forget everything you know and have experienced. You would forget everything you've learned. You can nod your head now but it would all vanish. It would be like a distant dream."

His face is getting red and his forehead has traces of sweat. He wipes it off and looks at his hand. "Psychic sweat, you know? It's like when I get into that psychic zone and start to shift I start to break out. It's cold, it's a cold sweat. Gotten em' ever since I was young."

We sit for a moment in silence. I think about what he's said. Everything makes a kind of sense. I can understand how someone can learn something and then find there are degrees of understanding. I learned arithmetic but don't know everything there is to know about math. But I can't see how, unless he tells me something new, that he can say the same is true for his knowledge. It seems more like biology. Once you know there are types of cells in your body that perform a specific function, that's it. That's what you learn and you know what they do and there's nothing else to learn except what other cells do. There isn't another level to understanding how cells perform unless there's a new discovery.

It also doesn't make sense what he says about the knowledge being alive. It's an idea all his own because I can't think of anything to compare it to that helps me figure out what he really means. That's the thing, figuring out what he really means. Some things he says definitely are more than the words he speaks. I can't take it literally or straight in the way I normally would. It's always more metaphorical even when it doesn't seem to be. It's verbal imagery and the words have no value except as brush strokes in the broader picture.

That makes me think a bit harder. An artist could describe their work as 'alive' or some kind of beautiful 'living' thing even though it's only a bunch of paint on a canvas. Maybe he means it like that.

We wander around the rest of the day and he goes back to telling me things I already know. I listen all the same trying to remove my assumption that I understand. I put aside his strange idea that the knowledge is somehow alive. Even tossing out the whole suggestion that I have to repeat it to understand it. I do know there's something I'm not getting. I'm missing something.

I don't understand. I listen more closely trying to think of it in different ways.

It gets late so he drops me off at the apartment. Matthew and the others are nowhere to be seen. I thank Eric for his time and he drives off.

The apartment's quiet. My head feels like it's full and buzzing with electricity. I relax for awhile going over the day in my head until I start to fall asleep. I linger sitting in my window watching the city lights a little longer. The smell of the city air is so different compared to the mountains above in Tujunga. The smog and chemicals are so strong I'm surprised I never really noticed them before.

I stretch and let out a big yawn. "Go to bed, go to bed, go to bed." I move over to my bed and crawl across it stretching out like a giant cat.

The bed feels good and I turn around in circles and put my head on my pillow smiling. Slowly, I drift off to sleep...

I wake up with a deep inhale. It feels like I'm catching my breath. *Something is wrong. I know something is wrong.*

Was I dreaming? What was I dreaming about? I rub my face and it's wet. A brief moment of panic and sadness washes through me as I sit up and swing my feet to the floor.

I hold my head in my hands and wipe the tears off my cheeks.

Crying. God, I was crying in my sleep. What was I dreaming about?

I struggle to remember what woke me. I can't really remember. Immediately, my mind drifts searching for memories of my grandmother. She's the only reason I ever wake up crying.

"It's been so long. Why now?" I ask myself out loud. I haven't dreamt of her since college. She died of cancer when I was young. Too young to understand. Too young to tell her everything I wish I had. I knew enough to know she was sick and in pain and I didn't want her to be. I knew enough then to know all the adults wouldn't say much around us. I'd spent hours, hours each night when everyone thought I'd gone to bed praying for her to get better. Please God, if you make her better, I'll do whatever you want. I'll give my life for her. I'll walk the world for you, please make her well. I was so certain she would recover. There wasn't a doubt in my mind that God had heard me and would take me up on the offer. I wasn't scared. God loved me. We knew each other well. It didn't seem to me then that God would want me to do anything, all I needed to do was ask, but I insisted night after night that I be allowed to repay the kindness.

Then, I was told, she'd made a miraculous recovery. Suddenly she'd gotten better and the cancer went into remission. The doctors were amazed. I was forever grateful and told God so in my prayers. Only problem was that I stopped praying for her. I only prayed my thankfulness and asked God to allow me to repay what he'd done for me. Soon after, she took a turn for the worse, the cancer came back and she died.

After a few years I grew up some and cleared my conscious of the idea that it was my fault. It took time to feel as if my failure of faith or to remain vigilant for her recovery hadn't caused the sudden turn of events. But even when I no longer felt guilt, the strange sadness remained.

There were many times I would wake up, my face wet with tears, and I could recall the brief flickers of a dream with her in it. Sometimes I would wake up and it would feel as if she were there, in the room, with me. Those were the most hurtful. When she felt so near but I knew she was not.

Not here.

My head shakes as tears start to flow. I shut my eyes hard and take a deep breath in.

"I'm too old for this. I'm not going to do this anymore. What are you crying about?" I ask myself in the darkness.

Then, the most subtle feeling whispers through my mind. With my eyes shut tight I picture myself when I was young, curled up in my bed clutching my covers to my chest praying to God. Praying to God. My mind goes blank, silent, as this subtle feeling suddenly comes to my conscious attention.

I don't feel sad. I'm not sad at all.

The darkness with my eyes closed doesn't look like it normally does. It doesn't *feel* like it normally does. When I close my eyes I can feel my eyes closed, I can feel my head around me and I can see black with some shapes or vague dark colors. It basically makes sense that I'm looking at the back of my eyelids.

Now, with my eyes closed, it looks like distance. It looks like I'm not looking at the back of my eyes but looking out into the darkness of space. There's this feeling of extreme depth. While I can also feel the boundary of my head, this overwhelming sensation of space pushes out beyond it, but I know it's still contained within it. It feels like if I opened my head, rather than seeing the small little space for my brain to sit, it would open up to an entire football stadium. Sitting there, with my eyes closed, on the side of my bed with cold tears drying on my face I feel my head, my body and this strange, inconceivable opening space, inside me. It's like an enormous ocean, a void, no... not a void... it doesn't feel empty.

The space, unfolding inside of me, isn't cold and empty. It's warm.
It's... present. Immediately it comes to my mind, like an unraveling
idea coming to the surface of my thoughts without trying to think
about it, that I'm seeing the Universe. I was dreaming about galaxies,
and solar systems, with the Force running through it all.

Yes. That's it! My breath suddenly stops. Flickers of recall from the
dream. Huge, brilliant rotating galaxies. Shining, beautiful stars and
planets and... a presence behind it all. The Force. A surge of tingling,
crackling electrical warmth shoots through me the moment I think of
the Force. Clarity, perfect, absolute clarity... like baseball stadium
lights suddenly rising to life awakens in my mind. A sudden
realization dawns on me as if seeing the sun for the first time.

"God. Oh my God. Oh my God!" I whisper to myself out loud.

I bend over and grab my knees.

How could I not have seen it? How could I not have known!

"It was there... it's been there the whole time... why didn't I see it?" I
start to rock back and forth every-so-slightly trying to comfort myself.
I start to cry again but I'm not sure what emotion I'm feeling.

The warm feeling of space unfolds in my mind, farther and farther it
stretches, like giant waves rolling out across unfathomable distances.
I don't think about measuring distance. I feel it. Like standing before
the ocean and being humbled by feeling its breadth and depth. No
need to think because there it lies before you. Real. Tangible. My
eyes are open looking around my dimly lit bedroom while at the same
time I can see and sense space unfolding inside of me. Staring ahead
at my floor, the image of what I'm feeling starts to merge into my
sight with my eyes open. I see stars, solar systems, infinite distance.
Translucent but visible.

A vision before me, like someone playing a film by projecting it
against a wall and being able to walk in front of it, to see it's not
there... but there. Only this is like a 3-D surround hologram. It's
overlapping what I see with my eyes. My room, desk, clothes and

stars, crystal rings of unknown planets. Both are there. I see them both, at once. It feels like I'm somehow in both places. Two places at once and I'm seeing them both. I'm experiencing them both. My room, familiar, here. Then, the strange space..: I feel its breadth. Its depth makes me shudder. No boundaries. No limit. I feel its living, conscious warmth. Conscious warmth. It's aware!

The feeling and thought makes me close my eyes. I raise my head to the ceiling. My body shakes as the full realization of the moment causes tears to run down my cheeks.

"I'm so sorry! I didn't know! How could I have missed it! Why didn't I see it sooner?" I croak out to the thing I have not spoken to in five years.

God. It's all about God. It is God. Everything Eric has been talking about is God.

"It's everything." I say choking up to harshly whisper out loud. "It's what we've been talking about this whole time. He's been pointing at it the whole way."

I bend over again and start laughing. I arch my back and throw my head back and laugh out loud. It doesn't even occur to me to worry if someone hears me or not. I'm half in the room, half in the ever-expanding universe opening up inside of me... but not inside of me.

"He even called it God! He even told me it was about you!" I laugh again. It's a laughter of startled, unexpected joy.

The whole time I've known Eric he's been talking about it. All of our conversations center around it. He even said God, the Universe, the Force.

"We've been talking about God! I never knew! I never thought he meant it!"
I stop and look at my hands in the light that comes in through my window. I can see the lines running through my palms and feel the warm stretch of space inside of them. The two images overlap... the simple, soft pink hands of my humanness, the boundary of my body.

The familiar, comforting expanse of the universe flowing over them... through them.

It seems like he meant it only as a theory. I thought we've just been philosophizing. We were discussing ideas, numbers, science, what-ifs. I didn't know he really meant it! It didn't seem like he'd meant it as if it were real. Real! Present! Oh my God... alive.

Somehow I missed it. I thought we've been discussing things intellectually. Pure information. Something to analyze and hypothesize about separate from reality. Like talking about literature or philosophy.

Only now it's all so clear. It's real. He isn't throwing out ideas only to have something to talk about he's trying to show me reality as it is. God is real. It's all real. Everything we've been talking about is with me, in reality, and I dismissed it all! Somehow I kept it all separate as funny theories and interesting facts to spin through my brain.

It never occurred to me that he meant it all!

I feel like a fool. The happiest fool ever!

The warmth surges through me. Everywhere. Immediately, I feel a profound sense of comfort. Like finding an old friend after losing them for many years. The best of friends. Even better it's finally seeing them as they are. All pretenses put aside. No fences... borders... masks. Open... embracing.

My emotions shift and dance. They're hard to place. A strange mix of sadness and guilt for having left for so long but such blissful wonder and excitement to be with them again and know them for the first time. I walked away from God so long ago. I never dreamed it could be real, so real...

The stretch of space within me keeps expanding. I see it even as I look at the floor, clutching my knees. I can't stop grinning as I pay attention to the feeling of having a universe expand inside my head and the feeling of comfort and warmth it gives me.

The Universe and the Earth have a consciousness. He means the world is really alive too! I laugh to myself again.

"My god, how could I have not understood that? He means it really is an organism." I stop and look at my hand.

Alive and conscious, just like me.

It's a profound realization. Suddenly I don't think about God having the universe as a body with the Force as its consciousness moving through it all... *I know it is.* It's startling! It's as real as the bed I'm sitting on.

"It's like talking about my bed only I think it's just a theory!" I laugh at myself. "I can be so stupid." I can't get the huge smile off my face. Stupid or not it's amazing to recognize. The feeling of it is incredible.

I sit, grinning, laughing and talking to myself into the night. A blind fool who finally gets they've been walking around with their eyes closed and nothing else. It's so liberating. There's so much comfort and brilliance, unrestrained happiness in feeling the expanse and knowing the certainty of it.

God is real. The Force is real. Everything Eric told me he meant as truth. Now, strangest of all, it seems he's right. Only now, I finally 'got it'. Now it 'clicked' and I see with great clarity that I haven't understood what he's said to me. There are levels of understanding and now, even more, I understand what he means when he said his knowledge is alive.

In the dimly lit darkness of my room, sitting on my bed clutching my knees grinning like a fool, I feel something inside of me expanding and growing without boundaries but contained within me. It's warm and alive. It goes hand-in-hand with my sudden realization of God and the Force. The reality of them are as clear to me as this strange space inside my head. It's the knowledge, alive, growing and connected.

every decision requires information. when do you finally stop searching and realize you have...

Enough to Know

chapter twenty-seven

Awake the next morning I clearly remember the night. I stayed up for a long time not wanting to face the day. Not wanting to lose the experience, the reality. The feeling and vision of the growing universe inside me is gone. I close my eyes and my vision seems normal. Thinking for a moment about God I find what remains...

So clear. Real. I understand it beyond words. I try to picture what God is, what the Force is, and it comes to life with details, a richness beyond what I can describe in words. It's still there. Alive, awake.

Smiling I roll back over to try and sleep for a few more hours. There's a knock at the door. It's Matthew. "Hey. Kathy's on the phone."

I groan and moan and yell out incoherently on purpose. There's silence and I grin to myself wondering what kind of reaction I'll get.

Matthew's voice comes through the door, "Yeah, so, what does that mean? You don't want to talk to her?"

I laugh. "No, I'll talk to her." Kathy wants me to go down to Orange County this weekend because her parents are out of town.

It's a quick conversation. She has time to come pick me up and take me down there. I can stay all Saturday. We agree to meet early in the evening to beat traffic and have time to do something tonight.

Without even trying to pass time, the day flies by. Kathy shows up and I finish packing at the last minute. We planned to leave at 6 and it's 20 til. Now that's amazing.

"Finally going to work out huh?" I joke with her. We aren't only on time we're early. I walk around turning off all the lights. The phone rings. She looks at me a bit nervously.

"Don't worry about it." I assure her. "I never answer it normally and I'm definitely not going to answer it now." The answering machine kicks in as I pick up my backpack to leave when I hear Eric's voice. I turn to look at Kathy who frowns and rolls her eyes. "Oh boy, here we go. You better get it!" She says throwing a hand helplessly in the air.

Picking it up Eric starts talking about Matthew. The story is scrambled and I can't follow what he's telling me so I ask him to start over. He hasn't seen Matthew in awhile. They made plans but those plans keep falling through. I look over at Kathy. I know how that goes.

Finally, he tells me, they made plans for tonight but Matthew called and cancelled.

Eric pauses for a moment and sounds reluctant, "I don't know how to tell you this any other way. Matthew is going his own way and seems to have made up his mind. Now, I'm not one to give up on anyone so I need to talk to him before he really makes the decision."

I look over at Kathy. She stares at me and tries to figure out what we're talking about. "Can't he talk to you tomorrow?" I ask Eric. Kathy quickly turns her head like I've caught her spying.

Eric sighs. "I hate saying it like this Eric but I've told you before and here it is; it's a two package deal. I can't teach you and have you turn around and share what you know with your brother. You're too close to each other and I can't expect you to keep the knowledge I give you to yourself. If he goes, you go."

That seems a little extreme but he's always brutally honest so I know he'll do what he says. Most people would think about doing it but not bother telling you.

"Timing is everything and right now your brother is running out of time. It's something I feel, internally. It's a knowing, that's all." Eric admits openly.

Matthew's really freaking easy-going and never wants to put anyone out. I confirm with Eric that he only needs 30 minutes and then assure him I'll get Matthew to go over there. I hang up and look at Kathy.

"Don't worry, it's a little misunderstanding. I just have to call Matthew and ask him to go talk to Eric." Kathy shrugs her shoulders and brushes back her blonde hair, trying to act indifferent.

I call Matthew on his cell phone. "Hey, what's up?" I ask.

"Nothing, nothing. What's going on? What's up with you?" He asks.

"Ah nothing, I'm getting ready to go down to Kathy's." I say casually.

"Ah, right, right. That's cool, that's cool. I forgot about that. Is she there now?" Matthew asks in his normal tone.

"Yeah, she's all ready to roll." I say looking over at her.

"That's cool. Hey Kathy." He says. I chuckle to myself. We could banter back and forth for hours.

"So listen," I tell him, "I got a call from Eric."

"Oh yeah?" He says nonchalantly.

"Yeah, and he said he wants to sit down and talk with you for a bit tonight because he hasn't seen you in a long time. He said you guys had plans or something but you had to cancel."

"Yeah." Matthew says as if it's just one of those things.

"Well, you think you could just stop by there and talk to him for a bit? He said it won't take long." I ask sounding unsure but hopeful.

"Uh, yah, sure, I could do that." Matthew tells me in his normal it's-all-good vibe.

I thank him and hang up. Easy as pie. Matthew's always laid back and flexible so that should be that.

"Now we can go." I tell Kathy. I pick up my backpack again and we head for the door when the phone rings. I look at her and she groans. Not even looking at me she walks over to the couch and sits down.

I answer the phone. It's Eric. Matthew called him. Smiling I tell him I talked to him and he'd be on his way over.

"No," Eric tells me, "he won't be."

I'm confused. "I just talked to him and he said he would."

Eric tells me Matthew just called him to say he'd come over tomorrow, not tonight. Eric told him it needed to be tonight, even for a short time. Matthew made it clear tonight wasn't going to work and he would try tomorrow. Eric starts to tell me that Matthew won't come over tomorrow either and it's the beginning of the end. I cut him off and tell him there's a misunderstanding. I'll call Matthew back to clear it up.

I hang up and call Matthew again. After our routine of aimless banter back and forth I ask him if he called Eric.

"Yeah," he says, "I called and told him I'd meet him tomorrow."

I'm baffled. "What if it's important to talk to him tonight? Couldn't you at least stop by for a little bit?" I ask.

Matthew pauses and after awhile tells me he can try. I explain that trying is too vague and he needs to make a definite plan to drop by. I look at the clock. It's almost 6. I tell him what time it is and how early it still is. He has all the time in the world.

He finally gives in and says he'll definitely stop by.

"Cool, thank you." I tell him and hang up. Looking over at Kathy sitting on the couch I apologize.

"Don't worry," she says dryly, "I'm used to it."

I look up at the clock, "We're still on time." I say with a smile.

I quickly call Eric back and relay the message. He's happy that I've gotten a commitment but he's doubtful Matthew will follow through.

Shaking my head, I assure him Matthew just told me, his brother, he'd do it. Twice. It would be too much trouble for him to back out now. Matthew wouldn't do that. Eric's unconvinced but if I think so he'll wait. I ask Eric why he thinks that.

"It happens with everyone who learns from me. There are certain windows, you could say, that I have to either make a connection to them or lose them. If I don't have enough time to give them a breakthrough and create that bond something else comes along and lures them away. I've had the time to put into you. We've created that bond and you've had the breakthroughs you need. Your brother has always been shaky which is why I've always tried to include him more by making sure people know him and recognize him. He's an actor you know, like or not he needs the attention, you don't. If someone doesn't put in the time in the beginning that they need to, rest assured I have seen it time and time and time again, something always comes along and pulls them away." Eric's tone is blunt. There's not much doubt in his mind... if any.

My forehead scrunches as I try to read between the lines of what he's telling me. Other than finally realizing why everyone knew about

Matthew but not me I know I'm missing something. He's trying to say something but isn't saying it.

I don't air my concerns that he's suggesting something I don't get. Instead, I repeat Matthew told me he'd show so he'll show. I have total confidence that Eric doesn't need to worry. As soon as I hang up I call Matthew back. Eric's doubt has me nervous. Skipping all of our banter I bluntly ask him if he's stopping by to see Eric. He pauses for a long time.

"No, I wasn't going to." He tells me. My eyes pop open a little wider than normal as a shock of surprise makes me jump. Damnit, Eric was right again.

"Dude, what? Were you going to tell me?" I ask astonished.

He pauses again and then admits to me he wasn't. I can't believe it. Who am I talking to? He told me he was going and then, minutes later, decided to blow it off. He's always so easy going and laid back. I can't believe he's capable of acting like this. It's so out of character I can't figure out where it's coming from.

He explains that he doesn't understand the big deal and will stop by tomorrow. He wasn't going to worry about telling anyone about not stopping by tonight because he doesn't want the 'drama'. Everything will be fine and tomorrow is just as good as tonight.

My jaw clenches. I don't argue whether or not tomorrow is as good as tonight. I calmly explain how surprised I am that he would tell me one thing and then turn around and do something completely different. When I got off the phone with him, I tell him, I called Eric and told him that he'd be coming over.

Matthew sounds surprised I called Eric and told him that.

My mind burns. "Dude! Do you think he is going to sit around all night wondering if you will or won't stop by? Now, you told me you were going. Don't lie to me like that. You told me you were, I told Eric you'd made a commitment. Now don't make a liar out of me.

Stop by to see him. Rather than going through all of this you could have gone over there and you'd be on your way by now. The only person who is making 'drama' is you!" I exclaim raising my voice slightly.

After a moment of silence he agrees to go over since he told me he would.

"Good!" I say. "Finally. How hard was that? Christ." He laughs and apologizes for being difficult.

Looking at the clock I notice it's 30 minutes after six. Now we're late. Kathy sits patiently waiting on the couch. Only now... her arms are folded. That's an increase in the irritation factor. I scratch my head and apologize explaining that Matthew is never like this. Which he isn't! I can't figure out why he's being so weird.

We make another attempt to leave when the phone rings. I yell out. Now, this is getting really ridiculous.

It's Eric again. He spoke to Matthew. I sigh in relief.

"Good, finally." I tell him.

"Not quite," he says matter-of-factly, "he's not coming over."

"What?!" I'm dumbfounded.

"He's with Justin. They're going to some kind of party being thrown by Justin's agency so he's not going to stop by." Eric explains.

My mind spins. He told me twice... no, three times, he would! He told me he wouldn't make a liar out of me! I'd asked him directly, over and over, if he was going and he said he would.

"What is going on?" I think out loud.

"Well, he's being influenced. You need to keep up to speed. Justin wants to go to this Dragon party. Now it's about them as actors and ego. Justin needs Matthew as backup and to take him there and now it's a matter of influence. It's you against Justin and, no offense, Justin has been with me longer and knows how to manipulate and pull strings better than you do. It's a battle of wits and control and he's going to win but in the process Matthew will lose because his window of time will be over and your time will end with it. I wish I could tell you tomorrow would work and things would be different but I used to make my career looking into the future and I already know that he won't come tomorrow and each time will get more and more difficult and he'll already be pulled away." His tone is low with a sharpness.

It doesn't make any sense. Justin's a student. Shouldn't he be on my side? I decide to ask Eric about it.

"Well, trust me, I'll deal with Justin. He has his own issues and he's making decisions and has decided to make choices for Matthew as well. Before you guys met me he thought of himself as the most interesting person in your lives. He was the smartest, most knowledgeable and had all the time he wanted. Then you guys met me and now he feels like he's not on top. What's more he feels like you guys get more time and attention from me than he does and he feels like you guys give me more time than him. So it's jealousy and envy and a few other things thrown in. What he forgets is that in the beginning he got just as much time."

It's a stretch to think that Justin believes he was the most interesting person in our lives before Eric. I never thought about it much but it's obviously more about Matthew than me.

"Now, this is his way of showing me that he's more important than I am and he's wrestling for power and control. There are some other issues but really, when you boil it down, it's Darkside. I hate to make everything sound so dramatic but that's what it is. When I find a student with potential and they start learning from me things in their lives suddenly start appearing and not all of them are bad. They might suddenly get this great new job or position but to take it they have to move away. They might meet the girl of their dreams but she needs more time or to live somewhere else. I've seen all kinds of things you wouldn't believe. The Darkside is just as present as the Force and it doesn't always show itself as bad, evil things. It can appear as very good things but the end result is to remove and distract the student from the path of learning. Right now Matthew is being influenced by Justin with the dream and hope of going to this party and suddenly they're going to hit it big by meeting this person or that person and it's all temptation. It's all about luring him away from the path. Do you get it?" Eric's agitated but his message is clear.

He can't see it but I nod my head to the phone. Two days ago I may have doubted everything he's saying. But not today. Today is a new day. Today that connection is real. God is real. If God is real so is the Darkside. Interwoven through it all. Matthew's actions are so bizarre it makes sense. But Justin? Why am I working against Justin?

"Yeah, I think I get it." I say, unsure what to do next.

"So, I don't know what else to tell you but once they move on it's usually done."

My mind spins through possibilities. Can the Darkside influence something like this? Is that something I'm willing to consider?

I can't decide. Even with my realization last night I can't reach a firm place where I believe it. I have to go on what I know. Matthew is not acting like himself. He's never done anything close to this and his reasoning and resistance is alarming bordering on psycho. Justin must be working him over as soon as he's off the phone.

"Uh, listen, don't worry about it, I'll take care of it. I'll get him over there." I assure Eric.

Eric sighs then offers, almost casually, "Listen Eric, no offense, but you're not the take charge kind of person. Justin is working your brother over even as we speak and he's being tempted with fame, fortune and all the stuff that goes with it. That's what he's selling him on and you know your brother, that's where he's going to go. If that's his choice, so be it. But you do understand why I won't be able to teach you after this right?"

I do understand. When Matthew and I promised not to share what he taught us we did it together. It would be difficult for me to learn things like that knowing I couldn't share them with Matthew if I thought they would help him. I might be able to do it but his decision is the right thing to do. "Yeah. I do understand." I admit with a hard swallow.

I hang up the phone and look over at Kathy. Her arms and legs are crossed. I can't help it. This is beyond our planned night together. There's no use in apologizing. I have to see this through.

Dialing up Matthew again his tone changes when he answers. We're past casual banter. His tone is guarded and has a 'now what' air to it.

I cut to the chase and tell him I talked to Eric and he told me about the party. "These parties go long into the night. Why don't you explain to me why you can't take 30 minutes out of your way to go see Eric?" I cut at him.

His answer shoots out in a flash. I get the impression it's been fed to him. "Because it won't take 30 minutes." He tells me coolly. "You know how Eric talks and it will drag out long into the night."

"Not so!" I snap back. "Eric's aware of your schedule and it's up to you to set that time limit. Eric keeps his word, unlike what you're doing..." I jab at him, "and if he says 30 minutes that's what it'll be. Plus, if you bring Justin along then Eric will know you are both waiting to go."

Matthew seems ready for that one as well. Rather than his long, delayed answers he slaps it right back at me. "Exactly. That's another reason." He shares. "I have Justin with me and if it does take longer then he'll miss the party too."

I pause a moment. It doesn't make sense why he's drawing the line at this one party. I bring that to his attention. "Dude, this is Hollywood. There are lots of parties all the time. Why are you making such an issue about this one?"

He stutters a bit. Aha, I'm in new territory. He explains how someone important is supposed to be there or someone Justin knows. Someone speaks to him in the background.

Justin...

Matthew repeats what Justin said and tells me Justin said it's a key contact and if they get in good with this person it will be a big boost for them.

Now I'm getting somewhere. Justin's game is finally coming out. "Is it a key contact for you or for Justin? Who is it really going to help?" I snap.

He starts to answer and I cut in. "What's more, you know as well as I do a career isn't made from a party. You've met lots of people at parties and nothing ever came of any of them. More Hollywood pointless talk and it sounds like Justin is looking out for Justin."

Matthew is quiet for a moment. He admits it might be better for Justin but, so what. If he's Justin's friend he should be willing to help. But he wants into Dragon so meeting them might help.

I start to get mad. Matthew's known Justin for almost a year. Justin's had every opportunity to push to get Matthew into Dragon. If he hasn't done it by now a single party isn't going to make a damn bit of difference.

Trying to calm my voice down I tell him what I think. We go back and forth for awhile. He keeps going back to the same key points; he has Justin with him, Eric isn't going to take 30 minutes, it's key to their careers to go to the party.

Each time I try slightly different approaches to make him see how bizarre his view is. He has total control of when he goes to and leaves Eric's. Had he gone when he said he would he'd be done with it by now. This isn't the first party he's gone to and won't be the last so there's nothing all that special about it. Justin has more to gain from it and is asking Matthew to make that the priority rather than

Matthew's life. He isn't looking out for Matthew he's looking out for himself.

Time quickly rolls by and I don't feel like I'm getting anywhere. He isn't budging. Stubbornly, I start to wear him down. Finally, he caves and gives in.

Angrily, he tells me, "Fine. I'll go already."

Maybe I wore him down, maybe not. I don't buy it. "Promise me, swear that you'll go right now as soon as we get off the phone."

Matthew won't promise. He's got to know I'm pissed so I throw my hands around and beat the phone on the counter swearing. I yell at him that he's lying to me. He starts to try and get out of promising but I work on cornering him. I pull out the last trick I've got left; our mother's guilt. Soft, subtle, but deadly. "Matthew. You're my brother. I don't feel like I'm asking much. If I didn't think it mattered I'd let you go but... I feel like it does. Now, I've got Kathy sitting over here. Sitting for hours now. We've been trying to hang out for weeks. And I'm here, stuck on the phone... for you. All I'm asking for is 30 minutes."

He sighs defiantly. "Fine. I promise to go."

Afraid he'll find some kind of loophole I pull out a backup, "And promise you'll call Eric right now to let him know you're coming over."

Reluctantly, he promises.

Relieved, I let out a sigh. God, I've never had to fight with him so much to do something so small. I thank him and hang up. Finally! The power of guilt...

It's pushing eight and I'm not in a hurry anymore. I flop on the couch. "That was exhausting." I blurt out. I go into the bathroom to splash water on my face.

The phone starts ringing. Oh crap. Which way is it going to go now? It could be Eric calling to tell me it's done. I can't imagine Matthew backing out of a promise like that.

Unsure, I answer the phone. Eric tells me it's time to give up. Matthew called and pleaded with him to come tomorrow. He promised he'd come tomorrow. He thinks Eric is being unreasonable.

I'm stunned. Eric doesn't need to say anything. Far from Eric being unreasonable is Matthew's complete and total reversal each time I get off the phone. It doesn't even seem like Justin could get him to break a promise but there it is.

"He's coming over." I tell Eric. "I'll call you back."

This is it. It's gone too far. He's going over if I have to drag him. Picking up the phone I call his cell again. He doesn't answer. I swear out loud. "He's not going to answer now! I can't believe this!"

I call again and he still doesn't pick up. I'm never going to stop. Do everyone a favor and pick up. I call a few more times and finally he picks up sounding annoyed.

"What is wrong with you?!" I yell.

"What is the big deal!" He shouts back.

I go off the hook. "First you tell me you're going, then you back out! Then you tell me you really are, then you aren't and won't tell anyone. Then you swear! You promise me, your brother, and then you back out! I can't believe you! I can't believe how you're acting! You've never, ever, ever lied to me or anyone so blatantly! Do you see what you're doing? Do you even know why you're acting this way?!"

He tries to convince me it wasn't a lie and Eric told him it's okay if he stops by tomorrow.

I'm furious. Now it's a matter of principal. He promised! "Too late for that now! That isn't good enough for me. You promised.

Promised me tonight!" I recount every part of our conversation for the last few hours. Every time he agreed, every time he changed his mind, every inch of movement only to have him pull away.

Then I take a deep breath. It's bigger than Justin. This is beyond Justin. He's never acted like this his whole life. Nobody could make him be like this. Then it hits me.

I believe.

I know God is real. I experienced it. I feel so connected to it beyond a mental understanding. Beyond words, beyond thoughts, I can feel the realness of it. Now is the test. I refuse to be blinded by logic. It's illogical to accept some other force is influencing him. That is how it gets you. It uses my rational mind as a cover. If I cannot refuse God... I cannot refuse its counterpart.

There's only one thing I've got left. No amount of logic and reason is reaching him. I have to do the hardest thing in the world for me; I have to lay out how I feel. I slow down. I lower my voice and calm my mind. "Matthew," I tell him. "You are my brother and I love you. Okay? I love you. I want the best for you. I may do everything I can to not make decisions for you because I want you to lead your own life but I do want the best for you."

He's quiet on the other end. His voice comes through softer as well. "Yeah, I know that, you know? I love you too."

My body starts to feel fuzzy. Everything swims and becomes disoriented like I'm on laughing gas. I feel floaty and physically expanded somehow. I struggle to concentrate.

It's real... God is real.

The expansiveness of the universe inside of me, the feeling of space, starts to fill me. "Now, it may seem strange that I try so hard on one hand to not tell you what to do and now I'm doing it but there's something I don't think you're seeing. And, I feel like it's really important you try to. I mean, think about how you're acting and being. You're going so far out of your way. You're making promises to me you know you're not going to keep. I mean, do you see how crazy you're being? It's weird. And, I gotta tell you, I don't know what to think of what Eric says about the Darkside or anything like that but if it's true... and I'm starting to think it is... I do know it seems like every reason you can come up with you're doing to avoid talking to him. And he's telling me too it's not a big deal and you can come over tomorrow but he's also telling me he doesn't think you'll come and I gotta admit, how you're acting now, I don't think you will."

I hear him take a deep breath, "Yeah, I wasn't planning on going over there."

His voice sends a pulse through me. It feels like truth. Now we're there, on some other level, in this strange bubble. Memories of times when I pushed away God... walked away from any belief in anything... and Matthew, standing by me, telling me how crazy it is. Trying to convince me there has to be something. He was there for me... now I have to be there for him.

"I gotta tell you, there's something to this. I mean, you were always the one who believed more than I did, you know? I mean, remember that time in the apartment I'd had that crazy experience where I felt like something was sitting on my chest and the intense vision about God and you couldn't believe even then I refused to believe in God? You remember that?"

He says he remembers.

"Well, I know you feel like there's something here. And I've felt it too but now I'm really starting to get it. There is something here. I don't know how or why but it is and it's God. Every part of me is telling me it's God and I know it. And... I don't want to see you lose that. I mean, he won't teach me if he's not teaching you so I don't want to lose it either!" I laugh. Might as well put it all out there. I'm not even thinking about what I say before I say it. I open my mouth and the words come stumbling out. There's barely a thought in my head. Instead there's this strange feeling all over me and the emotion and connection I felt last night is welling up inside of me. All I can do is focus on what I feel and try to find words to express it.

"I know if I say you should do it for yourself there will be all these reasons why you won't. So, even if you think this is unfair I want you to do something for me. Trust me, just this once. For me, your brother, who loves you and is trying his best to look out for you, go over there. Don't throw it away before you figure out what it is. Now, I don't have all the answers and that makes me scared too. What I do know is that I don't know what this is and you don't find that every day. We've experienced things other people we know never have. That's saying something. There's something here but if you don't go over there tonight we will never know what it is. I gotta tell you, I think it would be the biggest mistake of your life. I really do. So if you can't do it for yourself, do it for me. And I'm sorry for playing that card but that's what I have to do because in my heart that's what I feel."

He's quiet for a long time. I don't know what he'll do. I poured my heart out and don't know how he's taking it. My whole body feels tingly and light. Shifted. I feel serene, content. Whichever way he goes this is the end. I tried my best. I spoke my truth.

"Okay," he said quietly. "I'll go. This time I'll go. Fuck it, what the hell, right? You're right. I'll see what it's about." He's voice is choked with emotion.

I nod my head. I believe him. He feels me. "Okay man. I believe you. No promises this time." I say quietly.

"No, trust me, what you're saying makes sense. Justin will go over there with me." Matthew confides quietly, assuring.

We sit quietly for a moment then I thank him. We say our good-byes and I tell Kathy it's okay to go. Before we leave I call Eric to tell him Matthew is coming over. He tells me he's already called and said they were on their way. I smile. Everything feels good, it's right. Whatever anxiety or frustration was overwhelming me during the last few hours is replaced by a feeling of lightness.

Now pushing nine Kathy and I leave for Orange County.

There isn't much to do when we finally arrive. She shows me around the area and then we go back to her house.

Her parents are devout Catholics and I wonder how she finds the freedom to pursue her own beliefs living with them. She admits it's difficult and the process has its ups and downs. It makes me think about people I know from Missouri and how they'd deal with some of the things I've experienced the last few months. I have this feeling like I can never tell them. They wouldn't believe me. I wouldn't believe me!

We get ready for bed and change into more comfortable clothes. Kathy's room has its own entrance to the back yard. She has a small greenhouse in the back where she grows her own plants. Opening the door and peeking inside I can't believe she's never mentioned it. I'm overwhelmed by the range and number of plants.

"All you?" I ask breathing in the thick humidity of the little jungle.

Kathy smiles bashfully and turns her head slightly away from me. Grinning I realize I was staring at her with a look of mystified disbelief. She's not good with all the attention on her. She runs her hand along one of the leaves. "Yeah. All me."

"Umm, obsessive, childhood hobby gone horribly out of control?" I joke.

Quickly turning her head she tries to glare at me but I catch her smile. "Whatever asshole." She laughs. "It's what I want to do. I'm studying it in school but I love plants."

No way. I'm shocked. Kathy's skin is so porcelain white I always pegged her as a library dweller. Never would have thought she liked digging in the dirt. "You like the dirt huh? I never would have thought that. You always seem so..."

Even in the dim light when she spins her head I can make out one sharply raised eyebrow. "Always seem what?" She snips.

Chuckling, "Clean and proper."

"Well," she says softly, "I guess you don't know as much about me as you thought. I used to be a big hippie chick."

My mouth hangs open. "No way! You?" I try and picture Kathy. Perfect posture. Clean, straight blonde hair. Quiet, reserved Kathy the hippie chick? "I can't see that at all."

Throwing back her head she let's go and laughs. She must love my surprise. "Oh yes." She tells me quickly regaining composure. "When I first met Eric I had my little VW Van and everything."

"Damn, who knew?" I say smirking.

We leave the greenhouse. Kathy locks the door as I wander into the courtyard. There's a large round potter with some big elephant ears in it. She brushes past me and sits on top of it looking up at the sky.

The moment we stop talking I'm suddenly filled, or finally notice, I'm buzzing and giddy. My whole body feels like it's floating and expanding, like a helium balloon. I'm tingly, almost like I've been drinking wine even though I haven't. Not right. Not like drinking. It's far different from a buzz. It's so peaceful and happy. It's like the first time I meditated with the whole group. Every part of me starts to crave the feeling. I want to disappear into it. Kathy finally speaks. Her voice is changed. It's musical. Every tone, every uttered syllable is an instrument in a great orchestra. There are so many layers of sound in her voice! I laugh out loud. She becomes uncomfortable. She thinks I'm laughing at her.

She seems very different to me. My emotions pull as I feel hers change... the line between our emotions blur. I know they're her emotions... but they feel like mine. It's so noticeable. I can't understand. She's strong, willful, when she's by herself, or discussing spiritual matters. In the presence of a man that she likes, she becomes fragile, exposed, insecure... but also precious.

I'm overcome with this great compassion for Kathy. I want her to be okay and safe. I want to protect her but not in a sexual way. In fact, at this moment, there's nothing sexual at all. I've debated whether I will allow myself to feel that way about her. Finally it's settled. Somewhere, inside of me, my hearts made its decision. I feel certainty. I can't jeopardize the experiences I've had and this strange pull I feel. For even the chance to know God, to explore a real mystery, and understand what Eric has to teach I'm willing to sacrifice sex and a relationship with Kathy.

I walk closer to her. Looking up at me she flashes a mischievous smirk. I've never seen Kathy give that look before. "You know, I've never shaved my legs."

Both my eyebrows raise with my best, 'you've got to be kidding' look. "You weren't kidding about being a hippie chick huh?" Memories of my time spent at Evergreen College flash through my head. Half the women going to that school had hairier legs than I did. Not something I ever really liked.

Kathy moves to pull up her pajama leg. Trying not to grimace when I see the expected thick rug of blonde hair I'm suddenly surprised. Sliding her pajama up to her thigh it looks like it's just been shaved.

"Whaaat?" I ask unsure of why she told me she's never shaved. "You mean you do something else other than shave? Some plant sap wax or something?"

She shakes her head at me like I'm an idiot. I find her doing that a lot with me. Running her hand along her leg she motions for me to do the same. "No, there's hair there. Feel it."

I run my hand along her leg and it feels incredibly smooth. Rather than feeling turned on, which seems logical as I run my hand up her leg, I'm caught by this strange joy. I laugh again and marvel at the perfection of the moment. I can smell moisture in the air from all of her plants. The night is still and warm. All above me are shining stars. Her voice rings in my ears as if I were hearing speech for the first time. And as I run my hand along her leg it's as if I can feel the electricity of my touch that she's feeling.

"That's impossible!" I exclaim. "How can your leg feel like this and not be shaved?" Paying closer attention I notice there are very small blonde hairs on her leg. Small and soft enough to barely be noticeable. An electric giddiness flushes through me as I feel what Kathy feels as I touch her leg. I want to scream but instead I toss my head back and laugh. There's no separation! It's like we're two parts of the same body. Left arm and right arm. The words to tell her what I'm experiencing can't come out. She keeps asking me why I'm smiling so much but I can't describe it! Everything is so amazing! The things I smell, feel, and hear are all so new! It's like I'm young again and summer vacation has just started and all I want to do is lay down in my backyard early in the morning when the dew is still fresh on the grass and place my face near the ground and sit, watch and marvel at the complexity of the thing I walk across every day. There's so much joy and simplicity in it. The thought of feeling anything sexual doesn't cross my mind. It isn't even something I have to push away. It never occurs to me.

Taking the hem of her pajama leg I pull it back down. She slides off the stone plant potter and walks toward the open doorway to her room. I follow her. Her bed is a small single. Big enough for her thin frame but not both of us. We put two sleeping bags out on the floor of her room. We're starting to go to sleep, laying there talking when she reaches out her hand and places her palm open near me. I take two of my fingers, the ones I use to help me meditate, and place them in her open palm. Then I try to send little jolts of energy through my arms out of my fingers and into her.

To my surprise I feel little pulses surge through me into her palm. Even more surprising I feel them move through her. It's as if they're something I can see, or some electricity I can track. I follow them running through her arms, move into her torso, spread out and then run down her legs. I track each pulse from me, through me and into her. We lay there quietly. I smile in the darkness at how much I can physically feel. After a minute she breaks the quiet.

"What are you doing?" She asks.

I grin and laugh. It's incredible to be able to feel it but I don't know what she can feel or even what I'm doing, other than being absorbed in feeling it.

"I don't know." I say, not sure what she can feel or not. I'm suddenly afraid it's all in my head and she can't sense anything except my fingers on her palm. My cheeks heat up in embarrassment at the thought.

"I can feel that you know." She whispers. The moment she speaks I connect to what she feels. It's as if I'm suddenly aware of her awareness and without any way of speaking I know that she feels the little pulses moving through her body.

"I know." I laugh quietly even though there's nobody around to hear us.

"It's funny, how many things there are to experience. Things, small things you never thought you could experience. Like little energy surges." She whispers.

Smiling I nod my head. It is a small thing. Two people, laying in the darkness, sending pulses of energy to one another. To share such a thing and have both people aware of it... is small, simple and yet profound. Who would care if they could feel something like this or not? Who would bother with it? But it's the most amazing thing to me, to do it, to feel it and share it. We say good-night and I roll over in awe of the dream I'm living.

This is the last time I would see Kathy for a few months. When she would see me next, she'd marvel and tell me how amazed she was at how much I changed. Like a completely different person.

It was no accident that we stopped seeing each other. It was the end of August and Kathy began school soon after. More than that my understanding of God combined with an event the next day led me to realize something...

This is Kathy's final and greatest gift to me.

You see, through Kathy I began to understand something about choice. When I spoke to Kathy, Richard and some of the older students I started to see that much of their focus was centered on Eric. What can Eric do? How does Eric do these things? Why did Eric find me? Why is he teaching me? What does he want? On and on.

In my mind this kept them facing Eric, like a sparring partner. Always intent on his every movement.

Despite the fact that Kathy had been learning from Eric for four years I became certain that internally, she'd never made a choice. She never sat down, with herself, humbled before the Force and committed.

She went through all the motions of learning, having experiences and doing everything externally as if she were engaged in the pursuit of awakening. Part of her always held back.

I used to think this was unique to Eric's direct students perhaps created by the difference between finding Eric and being found. When Eric finds you it seems right to question, focus on him, watch and wonder why. Those who seek Eric out know what they want. They come to him so their decision must already be made.
After Higher Balance opened to the public I started to see this wasn't true. Someone can be practicing spirituality for many years, on the surface, and never have made a firm choice, a commitment. Maybe they float from practice to practice, never sticking with one. Or they try doing several at once, looking for that perfect combination. Still more... they only practice one system, are doing all the motions, but in their heart they have not decided.

Kathy made me question what Eric really wanted. Was it all about Eric? That night, when I saw the Universe in my mind, felt it within me, I knew it was not about Eric. He was the signpost, pointing the way. Everything he said and did was trying to get us to realize the Force.

As soon as my focus turned from it being all about Eric to being all about the Force, everything about Eric changed. When I look at him directly, I see the sparring partner. He throws a punch, I learn to dodge it. When I shift my eyes to gaze upon what he's pointing at I find his arms beside mine, showing me how to move. He makes a step and I shadow it. All the while, he's been trying to guide us, show us how to move, how to walk. Only to do so requires you to let your guard down, surrender, a leap of faith.

With that I would be confronted with the choice. The difference between doing and becoming. Students have learned from Eric for years but in their heart I have felt they have never made the choice. Kathy made that clear to me. There are levels of choices. In my time with Eric I have made more than one. Each as surprising as the last. With every decision I marvel at how distinct the other side is.

In her I saw the moment... when I would be confronted with my first choice. Because of her, I chose to take it...

how many paths will you walk? exhaust yourself, stumble, rise
and begin again? to what end? can you accept that the
greatest mystery is real? are you truly willing to take...

The Step Beyond

chapter twenty-eight

Kathy and I return to my apartment the next day. As she drops me off
neither of us mention trying to get together again. It doesn't seem
uncomfortable or tense. More like both of us have other things on
our minds. Or we both recognize something has changed. She drives
away and I don't know if I'll see her again.

When I get up to the apartment Matthew is sleeping. Strangely, no
one else is home.

I retreat to my room to hamster away on my computer and wait for
Matthew to wake up.

It's almost evening when he does. I want to know if he went to Eric's
so I don't waste much time before I ask him.

He pulls himself out of bed and leans against the wall. Staring off
toward the glass patio doors he says quietly, "Yeah. I did but... it
didn't take thirty minutes. We were there for awhile and never made
it to the party..."

Rather than being resentful about it he seems settled. He thanks me
for pushing him like I did and leaves it at that. I have no insight into
how he feels or what happened.

"We talked..." He says and shrugs his shoulders. He doesn't say
more.

Not long after that Eric calls and asks us to come up. Matthew doesn't struggle or fight like the night before, instead he gets ready to go and we leave.

When we reach Tujunga everything in the house has a strange calm. Like the morning after a storm. I put that together with Matthew and realize that's probably how he feels. Battered but peaceful.

Matthew goes to use the restroom and I take the chance to ask Eric what happened.

Eric's quiet for a moment, his eyes wandering somewhere else, then he turns and looks straight at me. "You know, let's just say that I had to peel back the layers and show him a bit of the being he was dealing with underneath."

An image flashes through my head of Eric becoming translucent and glowing with a bright white light. His skin slowly fading to reveal organs, veins underneath followed by a steadily rising glow from within. It's too strange of a thought. Where did that come from? The image feels intense and it's uncomfortable, scary even.

Eric falls silent and then continues, "I don't like doing it but with your brother I felt like something else had stepped in and intervened so I had to intervene myself... although it wasn't me myself, like the person standing here. I used to do it a lot when I was young but don't ever really do it anymore. In this case, I felt like I didn't have any other options. Make sense?"

I nod my head. I'm afraid to ask more. He's intense enough as the person standing in front of me. To see him peel back the layers and reveal the being beyond may be way too much. I'm reminded of the stories Richard told us. The image of Eric replaced by a glowing white energy being flashes through my head again. It freaks me out a little to think of him like that. I'm only now starting to accept that I'm more than the flesh of my body. As I've recently learned thinking about something and knowing it are vastly different things. I don't feel comfortable with 'knowing' the truth of it yet.

When Matthew comes out of the bathroom Eric asks him to knock on Frank's door and tell him we're leaving. I look up and ask him where Justin is.

"Justin has decided to go his own way." Eric says.

I raise my eyebrows a little surprised. "Really?"

Eric nods. "It's probably for the best. But he did it the right way. He didn't burn any bridges and did it respectfully. He came and told me about his decision and said he respects me and everything I've taught him and he's grateful for everything he's learned and experienced. He just feels he needs to be on his own for awhile and that's that. He was respectful and was very thankful. So when he wants to come back it means the door is open, you know, he didn't do it like Richard normally does or anything where I had to boot him."

I sit, a little stunned. Justin introduced us to Eric. He's been a student long before we came around and now he's gone. A large part of my initial comfort with Eric was drawn from my comfort with Justin. Thinking about it a little longer I realize Eric's proven to be trustworthy and true to everything he's said. I'm sorry to hear Justin is leaving but see no reason for it to affect my relationship with Eric. Considering the night before and the way he was influencing Matthew it's easier to accept him leaving. He made a strange choice that I don't completely understand.

Eric asks us if we're ready to go. I look up and see Frank and Matthew. It doesn't really matter where we're going so I don't ask.

We get in Eric's car and start driving. The sun is slipping below the mountains everything is cast in rosy red. Feels like a transition. One orb descends, another rises. Justin exits Matthew enters. I've only been around the summer but there are already so many strange things. Justin's been around for years. Justin and I never spoke of him being a student. Of what he'd seen or experienced. How could someone choose a normal life over this? If Justin knew this was real, why would he ever leave? Is it real? Are the things I've seen real?

I've only seen them. I suddenly remember the singing voice. Well, and heard them. But were they only in my mind?

Everyone is silent. I drift off watching the scenery. We end up in downtown Pasadena. I've never been here before but have heard it's nice.

It feels like an outdoor mall, common in Los Angeles. The shops are all bright, new and clean. People are all over the place walking along the sidewalks and sitting in outdoor cafes. It's the end of August and nights have the scent of fall.

We walk along the sidewalk weaving through crowds of people. I glance down the occasional alleyway. Even the alleyways have people walking through them and hidden coffee shops. It has a mysterious, magical feel. A veil of ivy covers the brick buildings.

I'm walking beside Eric. Matthew and Frank are right behind us. Nobody says anything. I wonder if I'm the only one who doesn't know why we're here.

Eric moves closer. "Do you remember what I taught you before, Scanning? It's the way of feeling, or touching, with your mind or like your psychic sensory?"

It's hard to forget. Soon after he taught me that the entity came. I nod in confirmation.

"Good. Now pay attention."

Crap. He's going to point out something and I'll miss it. I try and calm myself down. Paying attention to my body and the sound of the crowd I focus on meditating to shift my consciousness. Need to be aware.

"As I taught you, you can use Scanning to do things like pull information from buildings, or places but also people. Anything really, once you adapt to it. What we did before was more for your awareness. Now I'm going to show you how to use it for people. Are you with me?"

When he asks the last part his voice seems to slow down. Glancing over at him something's changed. He's walking different, or posture... shifted. He shifted. That's what he means by, 'are you with me?' He's asking if I'm shifting. I nod my head remembering all the details from the lesson he'd given me by our apartment walking up and down the stairs.

As we walk he begins to explain to me how Scanning works again. I look over my shoulder at Matthew and Frank and realize he must have already taught Matthew. Frank and Matthew both look similar. They're already doing what Eric's explaining to me.

There are several stages to Scanning. Eric explains how I have to build to reach higher levels. He uses an analogy of a plane taking off. First it has to gather momentum going down the runway. Only when it has enough speed on the runway can it attempt to pull into the sky and attain flight. He describes how in the beginning I will be limited to my brain. I have to use my intellect but once I have momentum I can pull off and use my dimensional mind or psychic senses. They will allow me to tap information that I could never know intellectually.

"Look at that man." He motions to a man walking toward us. "Think about where he lives, who he loves, what he does for work. Think about what his parents look like. Does he have any hobbies? What kind of car does he drive?"

Looking at the man I try to scan him for the specific information. Where does he live? What does he do for work? What kind of car does he drive?

Eric moves in closer to me. "Don't think the questions in your head. Ask them here..." He points to his heart. "Feel them. You can feel a question without thinking it."

I smirk. Thinking the questions in my head is exactly what I was doing.

He motions to a woman, "Look at that woman. What's her name? Where was she born? Is she single, married, divorced? Start general then get more specific."

We walk down the street weaving through people. I struggle trying to follow his instructions. He feels my frustration as I try to force it to happen. Each time he pulls me back.

He looks over his shoulder and motions to Matthew. "Your brother has an easier time. See, you need to be more fluid, more balanced. You're too structured. You're too solid and masculine. A woman has a higher degree of empathy and is more flexible. Your brother is very feminine in that way but because he's a guy he's also masculine so he's really pretty balanced. You need to stop trying to be a man and force your way in. Think more like how you think your brother works. Try and be more fluid. Feel it, don't force it."

His direction makes me struggle more. I don't understand what he means by 'fluid'. I can act feminine but I don't see how that makes a difference. The idea of one person being more internally fluid than another is beyond me. There's no sense to it. I have to put aside the idea that one person can be more fluid than another and concentrate on the technique. In fact, I have to throw out the whole 'fluidity' thing completely. I can't get the meaning. He must mean I need to be more relaxed and that I'm trying too hard.

We look at people and I begin. Trying to relax I look at different people walking by us and feel what it is to wonder about them without thinking in my head. Once my attention is focused on the center of my chest it gets easier. It's like coaxing it out of them rather than reaching in and yanking it out with my brain. Eric sporadically tells me what he picks up from people as we walk. I compare what he says to what I get. It's strange. Even though I try to 'ask' the questions from my heart I still see the images flash through my head. It's like the two are working together.

Some of the details are ridiculous. A richly dressed man with a thick black beard and dark tan skin walks by us. I feel the question asking myself what his wife looks like. An image of him standing in front of a mirror with a wedding dress on flashes through my head. This sucks. Eric motions to a couple who appear around a corner walking towards us.

"The woman, what does she do?" Eric asks me.

Looking at the woman I analyze her first. She's tall, over six foot. Thin body. Nice legs. Long blonde hair that moves perfectly. I catch sparkling jewelry around her neck and on her wrist. Red with some white? Diamonds maybe. She's got money and looks like a model. This is L.A. she could do anything. Everyone looks like that. Long flowing black skirt. Conservative except for when she steps it exposes one of her legs. Not conservative fashionable. Taking a deep breath in I feel the question about what she does. I try to take the whole of her, how she feels, and pull her into me. Absorb her frequency. Flashes of heat, sweat, arms flailing and loads of food being shoved in my mouth. A big cutting board.

"Well?" Eric asks impatiently as she's close to passing us.

Shaking my head in defeat I confess. "I don't get anything." Stuffing her face definitely isn't her. Not an ounce of fat on her. Stupid brain.

"She's a chef."

"Really?" I ask surprised. Maybe I was getting something! It was scrambled but I had the right idea. Only I gave up too early.

"She was good because it was so active. You could practically smell all the food and taste it in your mouth just from looking at her."

"Huh." She looked too refined to be a chef. Analyzing her definitely didn't help. Still, happy I got something. It works! I don't tell Eric I saw the flashing images. I don't want him to shoot me down or expect me to do as well. Better to just compare for myself. After awhile I improve but he gets more detail. Soon, I become more relaxed and begin to match more of what he says. It's strange the information that matches.

We work our way to the end of the main street and cross it to work our way back. It's difficult trying to Scan for information, seeking specific information, but trying not to think about it. Doing what Eric tells me I try to stay relaxed and not push it. Feel what comes.

The amount of people should be overwhelming, the sidewalks are packed, but as we work our way back it seems everyone is walking casually as if they have all the time in the world. Things are less frantic and I start to realize it's like everything has slowed down a notch.

We aren't walking slower it's everything around us. The crowds become easier to navigate and a cushion opens up and we have the whole sidewalk to ourselves.

Turning to Scan a couple shopping in a window I snap my head back down the sidewalk like someone screamed at me. What the hell! Suddenly, every hair on my body stands straight up and my whole level of attention shoots through me with a crash of adrenaline.

Danger! Something's wrong! You're going to be killed!

Something inside of me screams out like I've been walking through a peaceful field and suddenly hear the shake of a rattlesnake. My pulse races with the electricity of unexpected fear. My awareness shrieks out forcing me to look frantically ahead.

About four stores down a large crowd of people are packing into a small space filling the sidewalk. Red ropes stretch out to the curb and flashes strobe from a mass of cameras. Several limos sit parked in front of the crowd. It looks like a red carpet event for a movie.

Somewhere, in the crowd, is the thing that caught my attention. Every sense is pushing into high gear and full alert. Danger! Something's wrong! Look out! I half expect to hear a gun shot ring out from the crowd. If I don't find could the person it's coming from, someone is going to die. An undeniable certainty pushes through my veins. My gut twists with fear.

Find the source. Find it before it's too late!

Using the Scanning technique Eric's been teaching I squint my eyes and push my awareness forward into the crowd. I can only use it on what I see. I can't feel without my eyes. I try to move from person to person as quickly as I can. My fear and adrenaline pumps higher and higher. My heart is pounding in my chest. I push harder into the crowd to locate the exact place and person that it's emanating from. Him? No. Her? No. Him? Him? No. Find them damn it! Push it! I grit my teeth and mentally shove my energy harder into the mass of people.

Immediately after, a force wave shoots out from the direction of the crowd and slams into me. Force hammers my chest! Breath is knocked from me!

My legs stumble, tripping from the attack. I catch myself from falling backwards. Did someone just kick me? It's like I've just walked out into the ocean and a wave crashed into me! Only I can't see the wave! It hit my body with so much force it knocked the wind out of me! A moment of panic grips me. Physical. My chest throbs from the blow. It physically hit me. How can someone's mind be powerful enough to push me down?

Eric's right behind me. I stop thinking about fear or running. Eric is behind me with Matthew and Frank. The knowledge of who my backup is gives me courage. Shaking off the surprise and shock I get pissed and throw my awareness forward trying to push back. I regain my footing and take a step forward.

I'm frozen! My legs aren't moving! Cold spikes of panic grab me for a split second until, with great effort, my leg takes a step. It's then I feel the invisible pressure being thrown against me.

I can't believe it! However it's happening I'm being psychically pushed. The force is so strong that I struggle as if I am literally walking through four feet of snow. My whole body drags like I have weights attached to every muscle. Thoughts spin out of control. I don't believe it, there's nothing but air in front of me! I'm fighting for every step!

Moving my arms forward is like pushing through hard, dense sand! Like forcing two opposing magnets together! I can feel the waves of energy pulsing against me. I don't know what to do but push harder with my mind against the force I can feel holding my entire body from moving forward.

It would be easier to walk with 100 pound weights strapped to my arms and legs!

As I fight to take even a few steps I catch a movement out of the corner of my eye and look to my left. Matthew and Frank are coming up from behind me. Both of their heads are cocked and eyebrows knotted as they scan into the crowd. Their expressions are a mix of uncertainty, curiosity and fear.

But they're walking normally!

They must have been able to push it away!

Determined to not be overcome so easily I grunt and try to refocus my mind to find the source.

Suddenly, all of the pressure against me releases and I trip forward almost falling on my face! I glance up just in time to see a limo pull away from the curb. He's inside the limo. He got inside and now are driving away.

It was like I'd been walking through a giant snowdrift that suddenly vanished. Every muscle in my body was pushing forward with nothing to push against. I look over at Frank and Matthew to see if they saw me fall forward but they're watching the limo too.

Eric comes up from behind me and stands on my right. He's staring ahead, not even watching the limo. Doesn't seem like he's actually seeing what he's looking at either. He's somewhere else.

Trying to catch my breath I ask, "What was that? I couldn't move."

Frank and Matthew hear my question and move closer. After a

minute of silence Eric turns to us with a slight smile on his face. It seems sad but comforting.

"Well, let's just say that this world is filled with many kinds of beings. All of us have a choice to make." He turns to look at us. My brain spins to understand what he's talking about.

"That choice is... which side will you serve?" His words send a chill down my spine and my whole body tingles. His eyes hold a defiant certainty.

"That person recently chose the other side. Now that he has felt us and knows the presence of the Force, you could say he is considering he made the wrong choice."

He says nothing more. There's more I want to ask... more I want to know! For some reason, I feel that the topic is over. I experienced it and now I have to put the pieces of the mystery together.

Bits and pieces of conversations I've had with Eric swim through my mind. The story he told me about psychically battling the group in the restaurant, the concept that the Darkside always mimics the Force and that the two are battling through reality on several levels.

This was a glimpse of another level. If we are being trained for the Force, are others being trained for the Darkside? What kind of choice did they make? What knowledge did he have making it?

Then suddenly I realize; Eric said he can scan whole buildings, blocks of cities...

No, he can do more, it's limitless how much you can plug into... he can scan whole cities. It's energy. It has no limit. Eric knew where to find this person. It's no coincidence we happened to be here, walking this street, at this time... learning the exact skill that would allow me to sense them among the crowd.
Eric led us here. From all the way in Tujunga he could feel him, found him and brought us within a few feet of him. If he can do that...

and that person could push me back by the sheer will of his mind...
what is possible? What can Eric really do?

Richard's tales come to my mind with the realization Richard didn't
tell us everything he knew. There were things Eric didn't think we
were ready to hear... that he left out. What could be more incredible
than what he already told us?

It's strange to think it landed on me, how I came to live this. Perhaps
he found me, as he found this person. Scanned, searched and pulled.
I was found. That's how Kathy felt... why me? Why am I going
through this and not someone else? Surely Eric is looking for others
to train, or they're looking for him. How will they find him? In the
way that I came to him?

Then I feel something I quickly try and push away. It makes no sense
to feel it. Fear. How is such power possible? How can a human have
that kind of ability? My chest still aches from the psychic blow that
knocked me back. I'm afraid to think about what Eric can do. Is that
why Justin left? To know it as a reality is to fear it more? Or perhaps
that's why after four years Kathy still doesn't trust him. She's afraid
of the possibilities.

Except that Eric is showing us how to do it too. He's saying it's
possible. If they want it, he's telling them how. What's more, behind
everything Eric says is God. If these abilities help you find God, how
can that be bad?

How often have I heard Justin or Kathy talk about God? I think
trying to remember. Never.

Looking down the sidewalk we walked up I can hardly believe it. Fifty
feet ago I was living in a different world. Ten minutes ago I was a
different person. What do I do? I can't believe this. Now I know
these abilities exist outside my mind. This wasn't flashing lights. It
wasn't invisible things turning on water or singing to me. It hit me
with real, physical force. Incredible force. From the mind.
If a mind can do that... what else can it do?

It can find God.

Yes it can. Eric said the other person made a choice... they chose the Darkside.

All my life, I called out to God... the Universe. Maybe it just took 10 years to answer. But now that it's here, have I made a choice, or is it something I have yet to do?

Staring down at my feet on the concrete I start to realize I do have a choice. I can run, get away from all of this, back the way I came. Forget Eric, forget entities in your home, forget people who can do unbelievable things with their minds. Things that shouldn't be possible. I've only scratched the surface. It doesn't feel safe. It's dangerous. It will only get worse.

I can forget all of this.

Can you forget God?

A lump catches in my throat. The sound of cars moving by creates a hum in my head. No. You're right. I can't do that. Not now. I've caught a piece of it. I take a deep breath and sigh. It's worth the risk.

Looking over at Eric, his face is still, eyes distant. His mind is elsewhere. For the first time I think that could be literal. He's not lost in thought, he's in another place. The way he feels... reminds me of the first time I met him. Far different from the psychic I thought I would meet or anything else I ever expected.

My eyes drift over the crowds of people walking across the street. Shopping, laughing, talking. Totally unaware that anything unusual has taken place. Asleep. Like I was asleep. Probably still am. Yes, still asleep but now it's time. Time to take the step away from all this Eric's brought me this far. I'll see where he goes. I'll follow him farther. Into the unknown.

Into the mystery of God.

Unlike the experiences before where I fought myself quickly trying to push the memory away, I embraced this one. It was the moment I stopped questioning if Eric's teachings were real. I knew they were. Now, having lived the moment, I needed to know where it went.

Later, I learned the reason I was affected so much by the psychic attack was because of my energy. My thinking was so structured and masculine it made me more solidified. My internal structure gave them a form to push against. Matthew was more fluidic. His natural balance of feminine grace, empathy and masculine strength made his energy more like water. Try to push against it and you move through it. Frank through his greater balance and experience with Eric was also untouched.

My aching body was an important lesson for me. When Eric tries to teach me a concept it's more than philosophical fun. I'd blown off all his talk of 'fluidity' as confusing wordplay. It took a psychic kick in the chest to make me reconsider.

Does this sound impossible to you? To think, in the world outside, the real world beyond this book, there are people and beings with extraordinary abilities. Operating on another level of reality that exists within this one. Right now they are living amongst you, walking beside you, but they are not like you. Or are they?
You are capable of extraordinary abilities.

Perhaps it sounds too fantastic. More like a comic book or movie than real life. I told you at the beginning of this book you would doubt that it is all true. It is all true. This is my life, exactly as it happened. You should also trust me when I say you are capable. I know what you can do. I've done it myself. Remember, this is only my first four months of knowing Eric Pepin. I have known him seven years. In those seven years the mystery has only deepened and experiences have accelerated.

Don't think I'm all that unusual either. I'm not alone. Others have, through his teachings, stepped far beyond the boundaries of ordinary reality.

The boundaries of ordinary reality. This is what Eric showed to me over the summer. He took my old, outdated, lifeless perceptions of God and reality and he forged new life into them. It's not that he changed and shaped God into something else. It was the box I'd placed God into that he unlocked. Bending God so that it could be free. So I could see it as it truly is.

When you begin to see God as it truly is all else fades away. I said before you are capable of extraordinary abilities. Put aside, for a moment, any thoughts you may have of great and mysterious psychic abilities. Since learning them from Eric I have always held little interest in them except for one reason. This reason is the greatest thing you are capable of.

You can experience God.

As it truly is. Far beyond what I have written here. We are surrounded in a living mystery. This mystery is conscious, aware, and it is waiting. It is waiting for you to step beyond the veil. Beyond this moment, this time. To see where no eyes can peer. No hands can reach. No ears can pierce the silence.

Will you go? The choice is always yours but, if you have made it this far, I suspect I know the answer. In pursuit of it I wish you well.

About the Author

Now a student of Eric Pepin's for over seven years, ERIC ROBISON, continues his journey and learning. True to what Eric Pepin requested of him many years ago he contributes the work of passing on the knowledge given to him through his work at Higher Balance Institute.

For current information follow Eric on his blog at: www.bendinggod.com/blog.

You will also find special reader-only material that expands on the lessons from Bending God.

Continue Your Journey

If you would like to continue your experience, we suggest reading The Handbook of the Navigator by Eric Pepin.

Visit www.navigatorhandbook.com to begin.

Higher Balance Institute

The knowledge and techniques discussed in the book, and many more, are shared through the work of Higher Balance Institute.

Discover how to apply the techniques and knowledge from this book to experience awakening for yourself and learn the Multi-Dimensional Meditation technique taught to Eric.

Visit us at www.higherbalance.com.

Realizing the need for the knowledge to spread beyond Eric Pepin's ability to teach one person at a time is a founding reason for Higher Balance's purpose.

Higher Balance's programs are designed with the purpose of stimulating and activating the dormant sixth sense, the missing link to spiritual awakening. Discover how people all over the world, like Eric Robison, have been transformed by accessing mystical states lost by modern spiritual teachers.

Higher Balance Institute
515 NW Saltzman Road #726
PORTLAND, OR 97229
www.higherbalance.com